Webster's

Vest Pocket

Dictionary

New Webster's Vest Pocket Dictionary

Copyright © 1976
by Commonwealth Books, Inc.

Library of Congress Catalog Card
Number 75-39798

New

Webster's

Vest Pocket

Dictionary

This pronunciation guide explains the diacritical marks used throughout this dictionary. Unusual pronunciation not covered by diacritical marks is shown in parentheses following the word.

PRONUNCIATION

a	as in	at		o	as in	rod
ā	as in	bāy		ō	as in	ōld
à	as in	àkín		ö	as in	wön
â	as in	fâre		ô	as in	fôr
ä	as in	cär		ōō	as in	tōō
ă	as in	ăll		oo	as in	good
				ou	as in	out
e	as in	end		oi	as in	oil
ē	as in	hē		ow	as in	owl
é	as in	défy				
ê	as in	hêr				
				u	as in	pup
				ū	as in	ūnit
i	as in	ill		û	as in	ûrn
ī	as in	ice				
î	as in	sîr		qu	as in	quit

The following endings are always pronounced as shown, except where noted in text.

-cial	(shil)	-sion	(shin)	-tion	(shin)
-cian	(shin)	-sure	(zher)	-tious	(shis)
-cient	(shint)	-tial	(shil)	-ture	(cher)
-cious	(shos)	-tian	(shin)	-tūre	(chur)
-lous	(lus)	-tient	(shint)	-ble	(bil)

The following is a guide to the phonetic pronunciation found throughout the text.

(ah)	as	ä	(eh)	as	ê	(oo)	as	ōō
(ay)	as	ā	(ew)	as	ū	(y)	as	i
(ee)	as	ē	(oh)	as	ō	(ý)	as	ī

A hyphen (-) denotes the syllable breaks within a word. An accent (´) denotes the syllable to be accented. The difference in spelling between a word and its derivative is indicated by bold face type at the end of the definition. If a hyphen precedes this ending, it is added to the base word. If there is no hyphen, then the ending replaces the last syllable or syllables.

ABBREVIATIONS

a.	adjective	*etc.*	and so on
adv.	adverb	*inter.*	interjection
art.	article	*n.*	noun
coll.	colloquial	*prep.*	preposition
conj.	conjunction	*pro.*	pronoun
cont.	contraction	*v.*	verb

A

äard'värk, *n.,* ant eater
à-back', *adv.,* toward back, by surprise
ab'á-cus, *n.,* counting board
à-baft', *adv.,* at the stern
à-ban'dön, *v.,* forsake, **-ed, -ment**
à-bāse', *v.,* degrade, **-ment**
à-bash', *v.,* embarrass, shame
à-bāte', *v.,* lessen, **-ment**
ab'á-tis, *n.,* barricade
a-bát-toir' (twär), *n.,* slaughterhouse
abb, *n.,* yarn for the woof
ab'be, *n.,* priest
ab'bess, *n.,* governess of nuns
ab'bēy, *n.,* convent
ab'böt, *n.,* abbey chief
áb-brē'vi-āte, *v.,* make shorter
ab'di-cāte, *v.,* resign office
ab'dö-mèn, *n.,* belly, **-minal**
ab-dūce', *v.,* draw from
ab-duct', *v.,* kidnap, **-or**
à-beam', *adv.,* at right angle to keel of ship
à-bed', *adv.,* in bed
ab'ẽr-rāte, *v.,* go astray
ab-ẽr-rā'tion, *n.,* deviation, **-al**
à-bet', *v.,* encourage

wrong-doing, **-tor**
à-bey'ánce (bay), *n.,* suspension
ab-hôr, *v.,* detest, **-rence**
à-bīde', *v.,* live, last, **-biding**
à-bil'i-ty, *n.,* talent, skill
ab'ject, *a.,* mean, base, **-ion**
ab-jūre', *v.,* deny upon oath
ab'lá-tive, *n.,* Latin case of nouns
à-blaze', *adv., adj.,* on fire
ā'ble, *a.,* capable, **bly**
ab-lū'tion, *n.,* washing, cleansing
ab'nè-gāte, *v.,* deny to self, **gation**
ab-nôr'mál, *a.,* irregular, **-ly**
à-bōard', *adv.,* on ship, etc.
à-bōde', *n.,* home
à-bol'ish, *v.,* end completely, **ition**
à-bom'i-nà-ble, *a.,* loathesome, **nate**
ab-ö-rig'i-nē, *n.,* earliest inhabitant, **nal**
à-bôrt', *v.,* miscarry, fail, **-ion**
a-bor'tion, *n.,* expulsion of fetus
à-bôr'tive, *a.,* unsuccessful
à-bound', *v.,* be plentiful
à-bout', *adv.,* somewhere around
à-bout'-fāce, *n.,* reversal

---

at bāy àkin fâre cär àll end hē defy hêr ill īce sîr

à·böve′, *adv.*, over, greater

à·bräde′, *v.*, scrape off, **brading**

à·brä′sion, *n.*, rubbed off place, **sive**

à·breast′, *adv.*, side by side

à·bridge′, *v.*, shorten

à·bridg′mént, *n.*, shortened form

à·bröad′, *adv.*, out of own country

ab′rö·gāte, *v.*, repeal, abolish

à·brupt′, *a.*, sudden, **-ly**

ab′scess, *n.*, pus-filled swelling

ab·scond′, *v.*, go off secretly, **-er**

ab′sence, *n.*, being away, lack

ab′sént, *a.*, not present

ab·sén·tēē′, *n.*, absent person, **-ism**

ab′sinth, *n.*, wormwood liquor

ab′sö·lūte, *a.*, unconditional, **-ly**

ab·sö·lū′tion, *n.*, pardon

ab·solve′, *v.*, free from blame

ab·sörb′, *v.*, swallow up, **-ent**

ab·stāin′, *v.*, refrain from

ab·stē′mi·ous, *a.*, moderate

ab·sti′nénce, *n.*, refraining from

ab′stract, *a.*, not concrete, **-ion**, **-ed**

ab′stract, *n.*, summary

ab·strūse′, *a.*, obscure

à·bun′dánce, *n.*, plenty, **dant**

à·būse′, *v.*, mistreat, misuse, **busive**

à·būse′, *n.*, unjust treatment

à·but′, *v.*, be adjacent to

à·but′mént, *n.*, bridge support

à·bys′mál, *a.*, bottomless

à·byss′, *n.*, bottomless pit

à·cā′cia, *n.*, tropical tree

ac·à·dem′ic, *a.*, of schools, scholarly

à·cad′e·my, *n.*, advanced school, cultural society

à·can′thus, *n.*, prickly plant

ä cáp·pel′lä, *adj.*, without accompaniment

ac·cēde′, *v.*, agree, **-nce**

ac·cel′ér·āte, *v.*, speed up, action

ac′cent, *n.*, dialect, stress

ac·cent′, *v.*, emphasize, **-uate**

ac·cept′, *v.*, receive, **-able**

ac·cept′ánce, *n.*, approval

ac′cess, *n.*, admittance

ac·ces′si·ble, *a.*, approachable

ac·ces′sion, *n.*, attainment of office

ac·ces′sö·ry, *n.*, accomplice, added ornament

ac′ci·dént, *n.*, unexpected happening, **-al**

ac·claim′, *v.*, hail, approve of, **-ed**

ac·clà·mā′tion, *n.*, applause, cheers

ac·cli′máte, *v.*, become accustomed, **matize**

ac·cliv′i·ty, *n.*, steep ascent

ac·cö·lāde′, *n.*, honor, praise

ac·com′mö·dāte, *v.*, oblige, **-dation**

ac·com′pà·ni·mént, *n.*, music played along with, **-nist**

ac·com′pà·ny, *v.*, go with

ac·com′plice, *n.*, partner in crime

ac·com′plish, *v.*, achieve, **-ment**

ac·côrd′, *n.*, agreement, **-ance**

ac·côr′di·ön, *n.*, musical instrument

ac·cost′, *v.*, approach, speak to

ac·count′, *n.*, computation, explanation, worth, report, **-able**

ac·count′ánt, *n.*, examiner of accounts

ac·coū′têr, *v.*, equip

ac·cred′it, *v.*, give credit for

ac·crē′tion, *n.*, increase in size, growth

ac·crūe′, *v.*, add toward, grow, **-ment**

ac·cū′mū·lāte, *v.*, collect, amass, **-lation**

ac′cū·rate, *a.*, exact, correct, **-racy**

ac·cûrse′, *v.*, curse, **-d**

ac·cū·sā′tion, *n.*, charge

ac·cūse′, *v.*, blame

ac·cus′töm, *v.*, make familiar, **-ed**

āce′, *n.*, expert, playing card

à·cêr′bi·ty, *n.*, sour, bitterness

ac′e·tāte, *n.*, salt or ester of acetic acid

à·cē′tic, *a.*, like vinegar **-tify**

à·cet′y·lēne, *n.*, gas to weld metals

āche, *n.*, pain

à·chiēve′, *v.*, accomplish,

-ment

ach·rö·mat'ic, *a.*, without color

ac'id, *a.*, chemical compound, **-ic**

ac·i·do'sis, *n.*, poisoning by excessive acids

á·cid'ū·lāte, *v.*, make sour, lous

á·cid'ū·lous, *adj.*, sharp or sour

ack'ack, *n.*, anti-aircraft fire

ac·knowl'édge, *v.*, admit, recognize, -ment

ac'mē, *n.*, highest point

ac'nē, *n.*, skin disease, pimples

ac'ö·lyte, *n.*, altar boy

ac'ö·nīte, *n.*, poisonous plant

ā'côrn, *n.*, fruit (nut) of oak

á·coūs'tic, *a.*, relating to sound, hearing, **-al**

á·coūs'tics, *n.*, science of sound

ác·quaint', *v.*, become familiar

ác·quaint'ance, *n.*, person who is known

ac·qui·esce', *v.*, agree

ác·quīre', *v.*, obtain **-ment**

ác·qui·si'tion, *n.*, something acquired

ác·quis'i·tive, *a.*, possessive

ác·quit', *v.*, discharge, set free, **-tal**

ā'cre, *n.*, 43,560 sq. ft.

ac'rid, *a.*, sharp, bitter

ac·ri·mō'ni·ous, *adj.*, bitter, mony

ac'rö·bat, *n.*, tumbler, **-ic**

ac'rö·nȳm, *n.*, word formed from first letters of other words

á·crôss', *prep.*, over, beyond

act, *n.*, deed, part of program, law

ACTH, *n.*, hormone

act'ing, *a.*, performing

ac'tin·ism, *n.*, action of radiant energy in causing chemical changes

ac'tion, *n.*, movement

ac'ti·vāte, *v.*, make active

ac'tive, *a.*, moving, busy, **tivity**

act of God, flood, storm, etc.

ac'tör, *n.*, dramatic performer, **tress**

ac'tū·al, *a.*, real, **-ity**

ac'tū·âr·y, *n.*, one who figures insurance rates

ac'tū·āte, *v.*, put into action

á·cū'i·ty, *n.*, sharpness

á·cū'men, *n.*, keen insight

á·cūte', *a.*, sharp

ad'áge, *n.*, old saying

á·dā'gĭö, *adv.*, slowly

ad'á·mànt, *a.*, firm, unyielding, **-ine**

á·dapt', *v.*, adjust, **-able**

add, *v.*, join together

ád·den'dum, *n.*, thing added

ad'dêr, *n.*, poisonous snake

ad'dict, *v.*, slave to habit, **-ion, -ed**

ád·di'tion, *n.*, something added, **-al**

ad'dle, *v.*, confuse

ád·dress', *n.*, *v.*, speech, speak or write to

ád·dūce', *v.*, conclude

ad'duct, *v.*, bring together

ad'ē·noids, *n.*, growth at back of nose

ád·ept', *a.*, skilled, expert

ad'ē·quate, *a.*, suitable, **-ly**

ad·hēre', *v.*, stick firmly

ad·hēr'ence, *n.*, attachment to

ad·hē'sion, *n.*, sticking together

ad·i·á·bat'ic, *a.*, without gain or loss of heat

á·dieū', *inter.*, good-by

ád·jā'cênt, *a.*, adjoining

ad'jéc·tive, *n.*, word qualifying noun or pronoun

ád·join', *v.*, be next to

ád·joûrn', *v.*, postpone, suspend, **-ment**

ád·jū'di·cāte, *v.*, judge

ad'jūre', *v.*, swear under oath

ád·just', *v.*, regulate, settle, **-ment**

ad'ju·tànt, *n.*, military assistant

ad·lib', *v.*, speak without script

ád·min·is·têr', *v.*, manage

ad·min·is·trā'tion, *n.*, management, **tor**

ád·mi·ra·ble, *a.*, worthy of admiring, **bly**

ád·mi·rál, *n.*, high ranking naval officer, **-ty**

ád·mīre', *v.*, regard highly, **miration**

ad·mit', *v.*, acknowledge, let in, **mission, -tance**

ad·mix', *v.*, add in mixing, **-ture**

ad·mon'ish, *v.*, warn, **ition**

á·dō'bē, *n.*, sun dried brick

ad·ö·les'cênce, *n.*, period

a·dopt′, v., take for one's own, -ion, -ed

a·dôr′a·ble, a., worthy of being adored

a·dôre′, v., love greatly, worship, doration

a·dôrn′ment, n., decoration

ad·ren′al·in, n., extract of adrenal gland

a·drift′, adv., drifting

a·droit′, a., skillful

ad′u·late, v., falsely flatter

a·dult′, a., mature, grown up

a·dul′ter·ate, v., make impure

a·dul′ter·y, n., sex relations outside marriage, er

ad·um′brate, v., overshadow

ad·vance′, v., improve, go forward, -ment

ad·van′tage, n., superior position, -ous

ad′vent, n., coming

ad·ven·ti′tious, a., coming from without, -ly

ad·ven′ture, n., exciting happening, -r

ad·ven′tur·ous, a., daring, exciting

ad′verb, n., word qualifying verb

ad′ver·sâr·y, n., opponent

ad·verse′, a., opposite, versity

ad·vert′ent, a., attentive

ad′ver·tise, v., call attention to, -ment

ad·vice′, n., offered opinion

ad·vis′a·ble, a., sensible, desirable

ad·vise′, v., counsel, -ment, -r, visory

ad′vo·cate, v., support

adz, n., ax-like tool

âer′ate, v., expose to air

âer′i·al, n., a., antenna, pertaining to air, -ist

âer·ō·dy·nam′ics, n., study of air in motion

âer′o·naut, n., pilot

âer·ō·nàu′tics, n., science of aircraft flight

âer·ō·stat′ics, n., study of equilibrium of air

aes·thet′ic, a., appreciating art and beauty

a·fär′, adv., far away

af′fa·ble, a., easy to talk with

af·fâir′, n., business, love interest

af·fect′, v., influence, act on

af·fec·tā′tion, n., pretense

af·fec′tion, n., love, fondness, -ate

af·fi′ance, v., pledge troth to

af·fi·dā′vit, n., sworn written statement

af·fil′i·ate, v., join with, ation

af·fin′i·ty, n., attraction

af·firm′, v., assert as true, -ation, -ative

af·fix′, v., attach

af·flā′tus, n., inspiration

af·flict′, v., cause pain, distress, -ion

af′flu·ence, n., wealth, ent

af·förd′, v., be able to pay

af·frāy′, n., battle in public

af·frönt′, n., insult

a·field′, adv., away

a·fire′, adv., on fire

a·flâme′, adv., flaming

a·flôat′, adv., floating

a·fôot′, adv., on foot

a·foul′, adv., entangled with

a·frâid′, a., fearful

a·fresh′, adj., again

Af′rō, adj., African style

aft, adv., toward stern

af′têr, prep., following, later

af′têr bûrn·er, n., auxiliary fuel injecting burner

af′têr deck, n., ship's stern deck

af′têr ef·fect′, n., result that follows

af′têr·math, n., occurrence afterwards

af′têr·nōōn′, n., hours between noon and evening

af′têr·ward, adv., later

a·gain′ (gen), adv., once more

a·gainst′ (genst), prep., in opposition, toward

a·gāpe′, adv., amazed, wondering

āge, n., length of life, count of time

a′gèd, a., old

āge′less, a., without age

a′gen·cy, n., bureau performing action, office

a·gen′dà, n., list of items for discussion

ā′gènt, n., person acting for another, cause

ag·glom′êr·ate, v., collect together in mass, ation

ag·glū′ti·nate, v., join together

ag·gran′dize, v., make more powerful, increase in rank,

rod ōld wön fôr tōō good out oil owl pup ūnit ûrn

-ment

ag'gra̅-vāte, v., make worse, upset, **vation**

ag'gre̅-gāte, n., total, gathering, **gation**

ag-gres'sion, n., attack, invasion, **sive, sor**

ag-grieve', v., offend, injure

a̅-ghast', adv., filled with horror

ag'ile, a., moving easily and quickly, **ility**

ag'i-tāte, v., disturb, excite, **tation**

ag-nos'tic, n., one who believes God unknown, **-ism**

a̅-go̅', adv., past

a̅-gog', a., excited

ag'o̅-nīze, v., suffer pain

ag'o̅-ny, n., intense pain

a̅-grâr'i-an, a., concerned with land

a̅-grēe', v., hold same opinion, **-able**

a̅-grēe'ment, n., consent, contract

ag'ri-cul-ture, n., science of farming

a̅-gron'o̅-my, n., crop production

a̅-ground', adv., on the ground

ā'gue, n., tropical fever

äh, inter., exclamation

a̅-head', adv., in front, forward

a̅-hoy', inter., call used by sailors

āil', v., be sick, **-ment**

āim, v., point at, direct, objective

āim'less, a., purposeless

āin't (coll.), cont., am not

âir, n., nitrogen-oxygen mixture in atmosphere

âir'bôrne, a., transported through air

âir'co̅ach, n., low cost air travel

âir' co̅n-di'tion, v., control air temperature indoors

âir'craft car'ri-êr, n., ship carrying airplanes

âir'fôrce, n., military branch using airplanes

âir'līne, n., company providing air travel

âir'māil, n., mail carried by airplanes

âir'man, n., aviator

âir'plāne, n., machine for air

travel

âir'pôrt, n., airplane landing base

âir' pres'sûre, n., pressure of atmosphere

âir' rāid', n., attack by planes

âir'ship, n., craft lighter than air

âir'y, a., breezy

āisle, n., passageway

a̅-jär', a., adv., partially open

a̅-kin', a., related by blood

ä là cärte', adv., price per dish

a̅-lac'ri-ty, n., liveliness

ä là mo̅de', adv., in style

a̅-lärm', n., warning, fear of danger, **-ing**

a̅-lärm' clock, n., clock which awakens with sound

a̅-lärm'ist, n., one quickly alarmed

a̅-las', int., cry denoting sadness

ăl-bē'it, conj., although

al-bī'no̅, n., person pale skinned, pink eyes, light hair

al'bum, n., blank page book for photographs, stamps

al-bū'men, n., egg white

al'chē-my, n., medieval chemistry

al'co̅-ho̅l, n., liquid product of fermentation, **-ic**

al'co̅ve, n., recessed space

ăl'dêr-man, n., member of local council

āle, n., type of beer

a̅-lêrt', a., attentive

al'gē-brà, n., branch of math

al'i-bī, n., excuse

āl'ien, n., a foreigner, foreign

āl'ien-āte, v., make hostile

āl'ien-ist, n., psychiatrist

a̅-līght', v., get down

a̅-līgn', v., place in line

a̅-līke', adv., similar

al-i-men'tà-ry, a., relating to food

al'i-mo̅-ny, n., maintenance money paid in divorce

a̅-līve', a., living

al'kà-lī, n., acid neutralizer, **-ze**

ăll, a., n., adv., whole, entire

al'lay', v., soothe

ăll' clēar', n., signal ending air raid

al-lege', v., assert without proof, **legation**

ál-lē´gi-ance, *n.*, loyalty

al´lē-gō-ry, *n.*, story using symbols

ál-le´grō, *a.*, lively

ál-lêr-gy, *n.*, special sensitivity substance, **gic**

ál´lē´vi-āte, *v.*, lighten

ál´ley, *n.*, narrow street

al-lī´ance, *n.*, union by agreement

ál´līed, *a.*, united by consent

al´li-gā-tōr, *n.*, reptile

al-lit´êr-āte, *v.*, start with same letter, **ation**

ál´lō-cāte, *v.*, distribute

ál-lot´, *v.*, apportion, **-ment**

al-low´, *v.*, permit, **-able**

al-low´ance, *n.*, concession, money distributed

al-low´ed-ly, *adv.*, admittedly

al´loy, *n.*, mixture of metals

ȧll right´, *a.*, satisfactory

ȧll round, *a.*, surrounding, capable

ȧll´ stȧr, *a.*, outstanding player

ál-lūde´, *v.*, refer to

al-lūre´, *v.*, attract by charm, luring

al-lū´sion, *n.*, passing mention, **sive**

al-lū´vi-um, *n.*, earth deposit by rivers

al-lý´, *v.*, unite by agreement, bind by treaty

al´má mä´têr, *n.*, school attended

ál´má-nac, *n.*, calendar with special facts

ál-mīght´y, *a.*, all powerful

ál´mŏnd, *n.*, nut

ál´mōst, *adv.*, nearly

ȧlms, *n.*, money for poor, charity

á-lŏft´, *adv.*, up high

á-lōne´, *a.*, by oneself, apart

á-lŏng´, *prep.*, by side of, together

á-lōŏf´, *adv.*, detached

á-loud´, *adv.*, with sound

al-pac´á, *n.*, Peruvian sheep

al´phá-bĕt, *n.*, the letters in order, **-ical**

al-read´y, *adv.*, by now

al´sō, *adv.*, in addition

al´tar, *n.*, holy table

al´têr, *v.*, change, **-ation**

al´têr-cāte, *v.*, argue, **cation**

al´têr-nāte, *v.*, do in turns, substitute, **nation**

al´têr´ná-tive, *a.*, allowing a choice

ăl-thōugh´, *conj.*, despite, even though

al-tim´ė-têr, *n.*, instrument measuring altitudes

ál´ti-tūde, *n.*, height

al´tō, *n.*, low female singing voice

al-tö-geth´êr, *adv.*, wholly

al´trū-ism, *n.*, concern for others, **istic**

al´um, *n.*, astringent substance

á-lū´mi-num, *n.*, light metal

á-lum´nī, *n.*, graduates of a school

al-vē´ō-lus, *n.*, small cavity

ȧl´ways, *adv.*, forever

am, *v.*, to be (1st per. sing.)

á-mal´gám, *n.*, mercury alloy, mix

a-mal´gam-āte, *v.*, combine

á-mal-gá-mā´tion, *n.*, union, mixture of

á-man-ū-en´sis, *n.*, stenographer

am´a-ranth, *n.*, plant with showy flowers

á-mass´, *v.*, gather, collect

am´á-teůr, *n.*, participant without payment, **-ish**

am´á-tō-ry, *a.*, relating to love

á-māze´, *v.*, greatly surprise, **-ment**

am-bas´sá-dōr, *n.*, highest ranking diplomat

am´bêr, *n.*, yellowish-brown resin

am´bêr-gris (grē), *n.*, spermwhale secretion

am-bi-dex´trous, *a.*, both hands used as well

am´bi-ênt, *a.*, surrounding

am-bi-gū´i-ty, *n.*, vague meaning

am-big´ū-ous, *a.*, vague, confusing

am-bi´tion, *n.*, earnest desire, **tious**

am-biv´á-lence, *n.*, indecisive feelings, **lent**

am´ble, *v.*, walk slowly

am-brō´sia, *n.*, food of the gods

am´bū-lance, *n.*, vehicle for transporting sick

am´bū-lāte, *v.*, walk, **latory**

am-bush´, *n.*, surprise attack, concealed attack, **-ed**

á-mēl´iō-rāte, *v.*, improve, **ration**

ä-men´, *inter.*, so be it

à-mē'ná-ble, a., submissive

à-mend', v., change

à-mend'ment, n., addition or change

à-men'i-ty, n., pleasant behavior

à-mêrce', v., punish by fine

A-mer'i-cá, n., Western Hemisphere, -n

A-mer'i-can-ism, n., devotion to the United States

am'é-thÿst, n., purple precious stone

ā'mi-à-ble, a., good-natured

am'i-cà-ble, a., friendly

à-mid', prep., among, midst

à-miss', a., faulty

am'i-ty, n., good relations, friendship

am-mo, n., slang, ammunition

àm-mō'ni-à, n., pungent gas

am-mū-ni'tion, n., shells for guns

am-nē'si-à, n., loss of memory

am'nes-ty, n., general pardon

à-moē'bà, n., one-celled animal

a-mok', adv., amuck

à-mŏng', prep., mixed with

ā-mor'al, a., neither moral nor immoral, unconcerned with morals

am'ôr-ous, a., inclined to love

à-môr'phous, a., without shape

am'ôr-tīze, v., pay off debt

à-mount', n., sum, quantity

à-môur', n., love affair

am'pēre, n., unit of electric current

àm-phet'-a-mine, n., stimulant drug

am-phib'i-àn, a., n., adapted to land and water, ous

am'phi-thē-a'ter, n., stadium-like theater

am'ple, a., sufficient, ply

am'pli-fy, v., make louder, clearer, fication

am'poŭle, n., sealed glass tube

am'pū-tāte, v., cut off, tation, tee

à-muck', adv., in wild frenzy

am'ū-lĕt, n., magic charm

à-mūse', v., humorously entertain, -ment

an, a., one

à-nach'rō-nism, n., out of keeping with the time

an-à-con'dà, n., large snake

an'à-gram, n., new word formed from old

a'nal, adj., pertaining to anus

an-ál-gē'si-à, n., insensitivity to pain

an'à-lŏg computer, n., computer utilizing physical analogs

à-nal'ō-gous, a., similar, gy

à-nal'ý-sis, n., examination

an'à-lÿst, n., examiner, lyze, lytic

an-à-môr'phö-sis, n., distorted image

an'àr-chism, n., advocating violent overthrow of government, chy

à-nath'é-mà, n., religious curse

à-nat'ö-my, n., study of the parts of the body, mic

an'ces-tor, n., person from whom descended

an'chŏr, n., iron piece to hold ship in place, -age

an'chō-ret, n., hermit, ess

an-chō'vy, n., herring-like fish

ān'cient, a., very old, -ly

and, conj., in addition

ăn-dän'te (tay), a., moderately, tino

and'ī-rŏn, n., fireplace support for wood

an'éc-dōte, n., short entertaining tale

à-nē'mi-à, n., red corpuscle deficiency

à-nem'o-ne, n., wild flower

an-êr'oid, adj., without fluid

an-ès-thet'ic, n., drug causing loss of feeling, thesia

an-es'thē-tist, n., one giving anesthetic, tize

à-new', adv., again

ăn'gĕl (jil), n., God's messenger, -ic

an'gêr, n., wrath, gry

an-gī'na pec'to-ris, n., pain caused by coronary disease

an'gle, n., corner, -gular

an'gle (gul), v., fish

an-glō-mā'ni-à, n., imitation of English behavior

An-gō'rà, n., a silky wool

an'guish, n., much pain, -ed

an'īle, a., old womanish, ility

an-i-mad-vêr'sion, n., adverse criticism

an'i-mál, n., a living creature,

-ism, -istic
an'i·mal·ist, n., sensualist
an'i·māte, v., make alive
an'i·mism, n., belief in souls
an·i·mos'i·ty, n., hatred
an'i·mus, n., hostility
ankh', n., Egyptian symbol of
enduring life
an'kle, n., joint connecting
foot with leg
an'klĕt, n., band around foot,
sock
an'nāls, n., yearly records
an·nēal', v., temper by
heating, cooling
an·nex', v., add, -ation
an·ni'hi·la·ble, adj.,
susceptible of annihilation
an·ni'hi·lāte, v., fully destroy,
utterly ruin, lation
an·ni·vér'sà·ry, n., yearly
recurring date of past event
an'nō·tāte, v., make notes,
tation
an·nounce', v., make known
publicly, -ment
an·nounc'ĕr, n., one who
announces, introduces
programs
an·noy', v., bother, disturb,
-ance
an'nū·al, a., yearly, -ly
an·nū'i·ty, n., money paid
yearly
an·nul', v., make void, -ment
an·nun'ci·āte, v., announce,
ation
an'ōde, n., positive electrode
an'ō·dyne, n., pain reliever
à·noint', v., consecrate with
oil
à·nom'à·lous, a., abnormal,
-ly
à·non'y·mous, a., nameless,
unknown, -ness
àn·oth'êr, pro., different one
An'schluss, n., political
union
an'sêr·īne, a., gooselike
an'swêr, n., reply, -able
ant, n., tiny insect
an·tag·o·nist, n., opponent
an·tag'o·nīze, v., arouse
opposition, nism
an·tal'gic, n., pain reliever
Ant·ärc'tic, a., South Pole
area
an·tē, n., poker bet
an·tē-, prefix, before
an·tē-bel'lum, a., before Civil
War
an·tē·cēde', v., go before,

precede, -nce
an·tē·dāte', v., prior date
an·tē·di·lū'vi·àn, a., before
the Flood
an'tē-hall, n., waiting room,
entrance
an'tē·lōpe, n., type of deer
an·ten'nà, n., aerial
an·tē'ri·ŏr, a., toward front
an'tē-rōōm, n., waiting room
an'them, n., hymn of praise
an·the'ma, n., skin eruption
an'thêr, n., part of stamen
ant'hill, n., ant habitat
an·thog'rà·phy, n., flower
description
an·thol'ō·gy, n., literary
collection, book of selected
writings
an'thrà·cīte, n., hard coal
an'thrō·pō-, prefix, relating
to man
an'thrō·poid, a., man-like
an·thrō·pol'ō·gy, n., study of
mankind
an·thrō·pō·mŏr'phic, a., God
in human form, ascription
of human form
an·thrō·pŏph'à·gī, n.,
cannibals, man-eaters
an'tī-, prefix, against
an·ti·āir'craft, n., air defense
weapon
an·ti·bī·ŏt'ic, n., germ killer
an'ti·bod·y, n., substance in
blood to combat antigen
an'tic, n., funny act, playful
trick
an·tic'i·pāte, v., expect
beforehand, -pation
an·ti·clēr'i·càl, a., opposed to
clergy
an·ti·clī'max, n., ludicrous
descent from climax
an'ti·dōte, n., remedy to
counteract poison
an'ti·frēeze, n., freezing
preventive for engines
an·ti·his'tà·mine (meen), n.,
medicine for allergies, etc.
an·ti·knock', n., noise
deadener added to fuel
an'ti·mō'ny, n., metallic
element
àn·ti·pàs'tō, n., appetizers,
hors d'oeuvres
an'ti·pá·thy, n., serious
dislike
an·tip'ŏ·dàl, a., opposite sides of
earth, des
an·ti·pov'er·ty, adj.,
legislation to relieve

poverty

an'ti-quat-ed, *a.*, old-fashioned

an-tique' (ēek), *n.*, something aged

an-tiq'ui-ty, *n.*, ancient times

an'ti-Sem'i-tism, *n.*, hate of Jews

an'ti-sep'sis, *n.*, infection safeguard, **tic**

an'ti-so'cial, *a.*, unfriendly

an-tith'e-sis, *n.*, contrast

an'ti-tox'in, *n.*, disease preventive

an'ti-trust', *n.*, against illegal business centralization

ant'lêr, *n.*, deer's horn

an'tō-nym, *n.*, opposite word meaning

ā'nus, *n.*, lower bowel opening

an'vil, *n.*, block for metal hammering

anx-ī'e-ty, *n.*, concern, uneasiness

anx'ious, *a.*, worried, wishing

an'y (enee) *a.*, one of several, whatever

an'y-bod-y, *pro.*, any person

an'y-thing, *pro.*, any one thing

ā-ôr'ta, *n.*, artery of heart

à-pāce', *adv.*, quickly

à-pärt', *adv.*, away from, alone

a-part'heid, *n.*, racial discrimination in S. Africa

à-pärt'ment, *n.*, living quarters

ap'à-thy, *n.*, absence of feeling

āpe, *n.*, large tailless monkey

ap'êr-ture, *n.*, an opening

ā'pex, *n.*, highest point of

aph'ō-rism, *n.*, short proverb embodying general truth

aph-rō-dis'i-ác, *n.*, sexually stimulating drug

ā'pi-ār-y, *n.*, bee keeping place

ā'pi-cul-ture, *n.*, bee keeping

à-piēce', *adv.*, for each one

ā-pi-ol'ō-gy, *n.*, study of bees

à-plomb', self-assurance

à-poc'à-lýpse, *n.*, divine revelation

à-poc'rý-phá, *n.*, doubtful religious writings

ap'ō-gēe, *n.*, furthest point of celestial

á-pol-ō-get'ic, *a.*, admitting fault

à-pol'ō-gīze, *v.*, express regret, **gy**

ap'ō-plex-y, *n.*, brain illness, **plectic**

à-pos'ta-sy, *n.*, desertion of religion

à-pos'tle, *n.*, missionary

à-pos'trō-phē, *n.*, a mark of punctuation, **-phize**

à-poth'e-cá-ry, *n.*, pharmacy

ap'ō-thegm, *n.*, short saying

à-poth-e-ō-sis, *n.*, elevation to rank of god, ideal

ap-pâll', *v.*, fill with terror, **-ing**

ap-pà-rā'tus, *n.*, necessary equipment

àp-par'el, *n.*, clothing, garment

àp-par'ént, *a.*, plain to see, **-ly**

àp-pà-ri'tion, *n.*, ghostly appearance

àp-pēal', *v.*, make earnest request, attraction

àp-pēar', *v.*, seem, show **-ance**

àp-pēase', *v.*, calm, give in

àp-pel-lā'tion, *n.*, name

àp-pend', *v.*, attach to

àp-pen-dec'tō-my, *n.*, removal of appendix

àp-pen-di-ci'tis, *n.*, inflammation of appendix

àp-pen'dix, *n.*, something added, projection

àp-per-cēive', *v.*, recognize, understand, **ception**

àp-per-tāin', *v.*, relate to

ap'pè-tīte, *n.*, craving for food

ap'pè-tīz-êr, *n.*, appetite arouser

àp-plause', *n.*, approval by handclapping

ap'ple, *n.*, fruit

ap'pli-cà-ble, *a.*, applies to, **cant**

àp-pli-cā'tion, *n.*, use

àp-plīed', *a.*, put to practical use

àp-plī-qué', *adj.*, *n.*, *v.*, ornamentation with small pieces of material

àp-ply', *v.*, place in operation

àp-point', *v.*, name to position

àp-point'ment, *n.*, selection, engagement

àp-pôr'tion, *v.*, distribute, **-ment**

ap'pō-site, *a.*, suitable, **sition**

àp-prāise', *v.*, determine value, **praisal**

àp-prē'ci-à-te, *v.*, estimate

justly, **able, ably**

ap-pre-hend', v., arrest, understand

ap-pre-hen'sion, n., arrest, afraid, **sive**

ap-pren'tice, n., learner of trade

ap-prise', v., inform

ap-proach', v., draw near

ap-pro-ba'tion, n., approval

ap-pro'pri-ate (it), a., suitable

ap-pro'pri-ate, v., take for self, **ation**

ap-prov'al (proov), n., consent

ap-prove', v., regard favorably

ap-prox'i-mate, a., nearly correct, **-ly, mation**

ap-pûr'te-nance, n., something additional, **nant**

a'pri-cot, n., a fruit

a'pron, n., protective garment

ap-ro-pos', a., relevant

apt, a., suitable, quick to learn, **-ly**

ap'ti-tûde, n., fitness

aq'ua-naut, n., skin-diver

aq'ua-plāne, n., board towed by boat for rider

a-quâr'i-um, n., bowl, tank for fish

a-quät'ic, a., pertaining to water

aq'ue-duct, n., water channel

a'que-ous, a., containing water

aq'ui-līne, a., eagle-like

Ar'ab, n., Semitic race member, **-ian**

ar'a-ble, a., plowable

Ar-a-mā'ic, n., Semitic language

är'bi-têr, n., referee

är'bi-trâr-y, a., despotic

är'bi-trāte, v., settle arguments

är'bôr, n., shaded place, **-eal**

ärc, n., part of a curved line

är-cāde', n., arched passageway

ärch, n., curved structure

ärch, a., chief, cunning

är-chae-ol'o-gy (kee), n., study of ancient civilizations

är-chā'ic (a), old-fashioned, **ism**

ärch'ān-gĕl (k), n., chief angel

ärch-bish'ŏp, n., highest bishop

ärch'dēa'cŏn, n., chief deacon

ärch-dī'ō-cese (sis), n., bishop's district

arch-du'cal, adj., pertaining to archduke

ärch-duch'ĕss, n., arch-duke's wife

ärch'dūke, n., ranking duke

ärch-en'ė-my, n., chief enemy

är'chêr, n., bowman, **-y**

är'chė-type (kih), n., original pattern

är'chi-tect (k), n., building designer, **-onic, -ure, -ural**

är'chīve (kyv), n., public records

ärch-prīest', n., highest priest

ärc'tic, a., North Pole area

är'dent, a., passionate, **-ly**

är'dôr, n., enthusiasm

är'dū-ous, a., difficult

āre, v., to be (pres. indic. pl.)

âr'ė-â, n., surface

âr'ė-â côde, n., number identifying telephone service area

âr'ė-â-way, n., sunken area leading to basement

â-rē'nà, n., place of contests

är'gūe, v., disagree vocally

är'gu-fy, v., argue or wrangle

är'gū-ment, n., discussion, **-ation**

à-rīght', adv., correctly

à-rīse', v., get up

ar-is-toc'ra-cy, n., upper class

à-ris'tō-crat, n., nobleman

à-rith'mĕ-tic, n., science of numbers, **-ian**

ärk, n., ship

ärm, n., upper limb of body

ärm, v., equip with weapons

är-mā'dà, n., battle fleet of ships

är'mà-ment, n., war equipment

är'mà-ture, n., part of motor

ärm'chāir, n., chair with arms

ärm'ful, n., all arms can hold

ärm'hōle, n., opening in garments for arms

är'mi-stice, n., truce

ärm'lĕss, a., without arms

ar-moire', v., large wardrobe or cover

är'mŏr, n., protective covering

är'mŏr-y, n., storage place for weapons

är'my, n., group organized for fighting

a-rō'ma, n. odor, -tic

a-round', prep., on all sides

a-rouse', v., awaken, stir to action

är-rāign', v., accuse, -ment

är-rānge', v., place in order, -ment

är'rant, a., downright

är'räs, n., tapestry

är-rāy', v., set in order

är-rēar', n., overdue, -s

är-rest', v., stop, apprehend

är-rī'val, n., one who arrives

är-rīve', v., reach destination

ar-ri-viste', n., one who has recently acquired wealth

är'rŏ-gănce, n., false superiority, gant

är'row, n., projectile for bow

är'sē-nāl, n., place for storing, making weapons

är'sē-nic, n., poisonous compound

är'sŏn, n., illegal setting on fire

ärt, n., skill

ärts, n., subjects of skill

är-tē'ri-ăl, a., like arteries

är'tēr-y, n., blood vessel

ärt'ful, a., clever, deceitful

är-thrī'tis, n., inflammation of body joint

är'ti-chōke, n., leafy vegetable

är'ti-cle, n., short written piece, thing

är-tic'ū-lāte, v., utter distinctly, lation

är-tic'ū-lāte, a., distinct

är'ti-fice, n., crafty trick, -r

är-ti-fī'cial, a., not real, ly

är-til'lēr-y, n., large guns

är'ti-sän, n., craftsman

ärt'ist, n., creator of fine arts, -ic

ärt'less, a., crude

as, adv., like

as-bes'tŏs, n., fireproof mineral

ås-cend', v., move upward, -ant

ås-cent', n., rising

ås-cêr-tāin', v., determine, -able

ås-cet'ic, a., rigidly abstinent, -ism

ås-crībe', v., credit

a-sep'sis, n., absence of germs, tic

ā-sex'ū-ăl, a., without sex

ash, n., residue from burning, -es

å-shāmed', a., feeling shamed

å-shôre', adv., on shore

å-sīde', adv., to one side, apart

as'i-nīne, a., silly

ask, v., inquire of

å-skance', adv., sideways

å-skew', adv., to one side

å-slēep', a., in a state of sleep

ås-pär'å-gus, n., stalk vegetable

as'pect, n., appearance to the eye

as'phălt, n., tar-like substance

as-phyx'i-āte, v., suffocate

as'pic, n., gelatine mold

as-pi-rā'tion, n., goal

as'pi-rā-tŏr, n., suction machine

ås-pīre', v., seek

as'pi-rin, n., headache pill

ås-sāil', v., attack violently, -ant

ås-sas'sin, n., killer, -ate

ås-sault', v., attack

ås-say', v., test metal for purity

ås-sem'ble, v., collect, gather, bly

ås-sent', n., agree

ås-sêrt', v., state strongly, -ion

ås-sess', v., determine and set tax, -ment

ås-sev'êr-āte, v., declare seriously, ation

ā-si-dū'i-ty, n., diligence, duous

ås-sīgn', v., allocate or give

as-sig-nā'tion, n., appointment

ås-sīgn'ment, n., given duty, something assigned

ås-sim'i-lāte, v., be like, lation

ås-sist', v., help, -ance

ås-sō'ci-āte, v., connected with, ation

ås-sôrt', v., arrange by kind, -ment

ås-suāge', v., relieve, soften

ås-sūme', v., suppose

ås-sump'tion, n., supposition

ås-sūre', v., make sure,

surance

as'têr, *n.*, flower

as'têr-isk, *n.*, star-shaped mark used in writing

à-stêrn', *adv.*, toward stern

as'têr-oid, *n.*, small planet

asth'ma, *n.*, breathing disease, **-tic**

às-ton'ish, *v.*, astound, **-ment**

ás-tound', *v.*, amaze

à-stráy', *a.*, lost

à-stríde', *a.*, legs apart

às-trin'gent, *a.*, contracting

às-tri-on'ics, *n.*, application of electronics to astronautics

ás-tro-bi-ol'o-gy, *n.*, study of extraterrestrial organisms

ás-tro-dôme, *n.*, dome housing navigational instruments

ás-trol'o-gy, *n.*, study of stars

ás'trö-nâut, *n.*, space traveler

ás-tron'ö-mêr, *n.*, one studying stars, **my**

as-trō-phys'ics, *n.*, study of physical aspect of stars

às-tūte', *a.*, crafty, clever

à-sun'der', *a.*, into pieces

à-sy'lum, *n.*, refuge, mental hospital

at, *prep.*, near to, toward

at'à-vism, *n.*, resemblance to one's ancestor, **istic**

ā'thē-ism, *n.*, denial of God's existence, **ist**

ath-lēte', *n.*, sport participant, **letics**

at-hōme', *n.*, home reception

à-thwärt', *adv.*, crosswise

At-lan'tic, *n.*, pertaining to Atlantic ocean

at'làs, *n.*, collection of maps

at'mö-sphêre, *n.*, air surrounding earth, **-spheric**

at'öm, *n.*, small particle, **ic**

à-tom'ic bomb, *n.*, bomb made by splitting atoms

at'öm-īze, *v.*, vaporize

a-ton'al, *adj.*, music having no key

à-tône', *v.*, make amends

à-top', *adv.*, on top of

a-trem'ble, *adv.*, in trembling state

à-trö'cious, *a.*, viciously cruel, **city**

at'rö-phy, *v.*, wasting away, **phic**

àt-tach', *v.*, fasten, seize,

-ment

at-tá-che' (shay), *n.*, embassy official

àt-tack', *v.*, set upon aggressively, **-er**

àt-tāin', *v.*, reach, achieve, **-ment**

àt-tāin'dêr, *n.*, loss of civil rights due to conviction

at'tár, *n.*, perfume from flowers

àt-tempt', *v.*, try

àt-tend', *v.*, be present at, **-ance, -ant**

àt-ten'tion, *n.*, giving heed, **tive**

àt-ten'ū-āte, *v.*, weaken, **ation**

àt-test', *v.*, bear witness

àt-tīre', *v.*, dress, **-ment**

at'ti-tūde, *n.*, manner

at-ti-tu-di-nar'i-an, *n.*, person who assumes attitudes for effect

àt-tôr'nêy (terr-nēe), *n.*, lawyer

àt-tract', *v.*, draw by allure, **-ive**

at'trib-ūte, *n.*, character trait, **ution**

àt-trib'ūte, *v.*, regard as cause of

àt-tūne', *v.*, tune

ā-typ'i-cál, *a.*, untypical

àu'bûrn, *a.*, reddish brown

àuc'tion, *n.*, sale to highest bidder, **-eer**

àu-dā'cious, *a.*, extremely bold, **-ness**

àu'di-ble, *a.*, capable of being heard

àu'di-ence, *n.*, gathering of listeners or spectators

àu-di-om'è-têr, *n.*, machine to record hearing power

àu'dit, *n.*, examination of accounts, **-or**

àu-di'tion, *n.*, tryout

àu'gêr, *n.*, wood boring tool

àught, *adv.*, at all

àught, *n.*, zero

àug-ment', *v.*, add to, **-ation**

àu'gur, *v.*, predict

àu-gust', *a.*, majestic, **-ly**

Au-gust', *n.*, 8th month

aunt, *n.*, a relative

àu-rē-ōle, *n.*, halo, radiance

àu'ri-cle, *n.*, heart chamber, outside ear

àu-ric'ū-làr, *a.*, pertaining to ear

àu-rif'êr-ous, *a.*, yielding or

containing gold

ăus·pi'cious, *a.*, good omen

ăus·tēre', *a.*, severe, plain
terity

ău'tär·chy, *n.*, absolute
government

ău·thĕn'tĭc, *a.*, genuine, **-ity**

ău'thŏr, *n.*, originator, **-ess**

ău·thŏr·ĭ·târ'ĭ·ăn, *a.*, favoring
strict authority

ău·thŏr'ĭ·ty, *n.*, legal right,
intellectual weight, **tative**

ău'thŏr·īze, *v.*, give
permission, **-d**

ău'tō, *n.*, automobile

ău·tō·bī·ŏg'rȧ·phy, *n.*, story
by and about one's self

ău'tō cŏurt, *n.*, motel

ău·tŏc'rȧ·cy, *n.*, absolute rule
by one person

ău'tō·crăt, *n.*, absolute ruler

ău·tō·gī'rō, *n.*, airplane with
horizontal propeller

ău'tō·graph, *n.*, person's
signature

ău'tō·mat, *n.*, food machine
restaurant

ău·tō·măt'ĭc, *a.*, self working,
self moving

ău·tō·mā'tion, *n.*, electronics
control in manufacturing

ău·tom'ȧ·ton, *n.*, thing acting
of itself, robot

ău'tō·mō·bīle (bēel), *n.*, car

ău·ton'ō·mous, *a.*,
self-governing, **my**

ău'tŏp·sy, *n.*, examination
and dissection of dead body

ău'tō·trāin, *n.*, train carrying
automobiles and
passengers

ău'tumn, *n.*, third season, fall
of year

ăux·ĭl'ĭȧ·ry, *a.*, supplemental

ȧ·vāil', *v.*, be of assistance,

-able

ăv'ȧ·lanche, *n.*, snow slide

ăv'ȧ·rice, *n.*, greed

ȧ·vast', *inter.*, stop

ȧ·venge', *v.*, take revenge, **-r**

ăv'ė·nūe, *n.*, street

ăv'êr·āge, *n.*, mean quantity

ȧ·vêrse', *a.*, opposed

ȧ·vêr'sion, *n.*, dislike

ȧ·vêrt', *v.*, avoid

ā'vĭ·ȧ·ry, *n.*, bird house

ā·vĭ·ā'tion, *n.*, science of
airplanes

ā'vĭ·ȧ·tŏr, *n.*, airplane pilot,
trix

ăv'ĭd, *a.*, eager

av·ō·cä'dō, *n.*, fruit

av·ō·cā'tion, *n.*, hobby,
diversion

ȧ·void', *v.*, keep away from

ȧ·vouch', *v.*, guarantee

ȧ·vow', *v.*, declare, **-al**

ȧ·wāit', *v.*, wait for

ā·wārd', *n.*, prize

ȧ·wāre', *a.*, conscious of

ȧ·way', *adv.*, from a place

ȧwe, *n.*, reverence

ȧ·weigh'(way), *a.*, raised
anchor

ăwe'struck, *a.*, filled with
wonder

ȧw'ful, *a.*, terrible, **-ly**

ȧ·whīle', *adv.*, for a time

ăwk'wȧrd, *a.*, ungraceful, **-ly**,
-ness

ăwl, *n.*, hole-making tool

ax, *n.*, chopping tool

ăx'ĭ·ŏm, *n.*, evident truth

ăx'ĭs, *n.*, line around which
something revolves, **ial**

ăx'le, *n.*, shaft on which
wheel turns

aye, (ī) *adv.*, yes

ȧ·zāl'ėȧ, (ya) *n.*, a flower

az'ūre, *a.*, sky blue

B

bab'ble, *v.*, utter childish
sounds, **-r**

bābe, *n.*, baby

ba·bōōn', *n.*, type of monkey

bā'by, *n.*, infant, **-ish**

bā'by, *v.*, coddle

bā'by sĭt, *v.*, take care of
children, **-ter**

băc·cȧ·lâur'ē·āte, *n.*, college
bachelor degree

bac'chȧ·nál, *a.*, follower of

Bacchus, drunken orgy,
-ian

băch'ė·lŏr (lér), *n.*,
unmarried man, **-hood**

bȧ·cil'lus, *n.*, rod-shaped
bacteria

back, *n.*, *a.*, rear of something
as body, chair, etc.

back, *adv.*, toward rear

back, *v.*, support

back'bŏne, *n.*, spine,

character

back'ẽr, n., one who gives support

back'field, n., four back football players

back'fire, v., auto engine explosion, reverse action

back'gam-mŏn, n., board game

back'ground, n., past events, back part of picture

back'hand-ĕd, a., not sincere, performed with back of hand

back'ing, n., support

back'lŏg, n., reserve or accumulation

back' num-bẽr, n., not in fashion, out-of-date issue of publication

back'sīde, n., rear side

back'slīde, v., fail, fall back into error or sin

back'stāge, adv., toward rear stage, theatre dressing rooms

back'stop, n., screen to stop ball in game

back'strōke, n., backward swimming stroke

back'tȧlk, n., impudent responses

back'tract, v., return over same path

back'wȧrd, adv., toward back

back'wȧrd, a., ignorant, out-of-date

back-woods', n., unsettled wooded regions

bā'cŏn, n., salted hog meat

bac-tē'ri-ä, n., single-celled microscopic animals, **-l**

bac-tē-ri-ŏl'ŏ-gy, n., study of bacteria, **-gist**

bad, a., not good, dangerous

badge', n., symbol worn to show occupation, position, etc.

badg'ẽr, v., bother, tease

bad-i-nȧge', n., banter, joking

bad'mĭn-tŏn, n., game, like tennis

Bae'de-kẽr, n., guidebook for travelers

baf'fle, v., confuse, puzzle, **-ment**

bag, n., paper container, baseball base

bag, v., catch

bag-ȧ-telle', n., trifle, game, musical composition

bag'gȧge, n., suitcases, trunks, etc., for traveling

bag'gy, a., hanging loosely

bag'pīpe, n., Scotch musical instrument

ba-guette' (get), n., rectangular cut for gems

bāil, n., security to guarantee prisoner's return

bāil, v., dip water from boat

bāil'iff, n., sheriff's assistant

bāil'i-wick, n., district where bailiff has authority, individual scope of work, knowledge, etc.

bāit, n., food to attract fish or animals

bāke, v., cook in oven

bāk'ẽr, n., maker of baked goods

bāk'ẽr-y, n., store for selling baked goods

bāk'ing, n., cooking in oven

bal-ȧ-laī'kȧ, n., Russian musical instrument

bal'ȧnce, n., scale for weighing, amount remaining

bal'ȧnce sheet, n., tabular sttement of accounts

bal'cō-ny, n., projecting platform

bȧld, a., lacking hair, **-ly**

bȧl'dẽr-dash, n., nonsense

bāle, n., large bundle

bāle'ful, a., evil, disastrous, **-ly**

bȧlk, v., refuse, stop, **-y**

bȧll, n., round object, sphere used in games, dance

bal'lȧd, n., song

bal'lȧst, n., heavy material to steady ships

bal-le-rī'nȧ (ree), n., female ballet dancer

bal-let' (lay), n., artistic dance

bȧl-lis'tics, n., science of bullet motion

bal-lōōn', n., inflated bag of thin material capable of floating

bal'lŏt, n., vote by paper or machine

bȧll'rōōm, n., dance hall

bȧll-point pen, n., self-inking ball-tipped pen

bal'ly-hōō, n., noise, clamor, blatant advertising

bȧlm, n., healing ointment

bȧlm'y, a., soothing, (coll.) crazy

bá·ló'ny (coll.), *n.*, nonsense, not so

bál'sá, *n.*, light wood

bal·us·tēr, *n.*, railing support

bal·us·trāde', *n.*, railing on balusters

bam·bōō', *n.*, tree with hollow stems

bam·bōō'zle (zil), *v.*, fool, trick

ban, *v.*, prohibit, church curse

bā'nál, *a.*, trite, common, **-ity**

bá·nan'á, *n.*, yellow skinned fruit

band, *n.*, group of persons, musical company

band, *v.*, join together

band'āge, *n.*, gauze strip for binding wound

ban·dan'ná, *n.*, large handkerchief

ban·deau' (dō), *n.*, head band, brassiere

ban'dé·róle, *n.*, small flag

ban'dit, *n.*, thief, outlaw, **-ry**

band'mas·tēr, *n.*, leader of band

band'sāw, *n.*, mechanical saw

band'stand, *n.*, concert stage or platform for band

band'wag·ŏn, *n.*, (coll.) wagon for carrying band in parades, winning or popular side

ban'dy, *v.*, throw from side to side, one to another

bāne, *n.*, that which brings ruin, **-ful**

bang, *n.*, sudden loud noise, fringe of hair, (coll.) excitement

ban'gle, *n.*, ring shaped bracelet without clasp

bang'tail, *n.*, race horse

ban'ish, *v.*, force to leave, **-ment**

ban'is·tēr, *n.*, stairway balustrade

ban'jō, *n.*, instrument like a guitar

bank, *n.*, raised earth, river edge, money lending-receiving institution

bank' book, *n.*, bank depositor's book

bank·êr, *n.*, bank manager

bank'rupt, *n.*, unable to pay bills, **-cy**

ban'nêr, *n.*, flag or ensign, leader

ban'quĕt (kwit), *n.*, feast, lavish dinner

ban'shēē, *n.*, wailing woman who appears as sign of approaching death

ban'tám, *n.*, small fowl

ban'tám weight, *n.*, boxer lighter than 118 lbs.

ban'tēr, *n.*, joke, **-ing**

ban'yan, *n.*, East Indian tree

bap'tism, *n.*, holy water immersion, **tize**

bär, *n.*, thick or long solid, musical measure, counter serving drinks, relating to law

bär, *v.*, obstruct, block off

bärb, *n.*, fishhook point, unkind remark

bär·bár'i·án (ee-un), *n.*, uncivilized person, **-ism**

bär·bá·rism, *n.*, uncivilized condition

bär·bä·rous (rus), *a.*, cruel, savage, **rity**

bär·bé·cūe, *n.*, meat cooked over fire coals

bärbed, *a.*, sharply pointed

bär·bēr, *n.*, one who cuts hair

bär'bēr·ry, *n.*, a shrub

bär·bi'tū·rāte, *n.*, a medicinal chemical, **ric**

bär'cá·róle, *n.*, boating song

bärd, *n.*, poet

bāre, *a.*, naked, **-ness**

bāre'back, *a.*, ride without saddle on horse

bāre'fāced, *a.*, shameless, face uncovered

bāre'legged, *a.*, without stockings

bāre'ly, *adv.*, nakedly, almost

bär'gain (gin), *v.*, discuss terms of agreement

bär'gain, *n.*, something bought cheaply, **-er**

bärge, *n.*, flat-bottomed boat

bar'i·tōne, *n.*, voice between tenor and bass

bar'i·um, *n.*, chemical element

bärk, *n.*, tree covering, ship, dog noise

bär'kēep·êr, *n.*, drink server at bar

bärk'êr, *n.*, attention getter

bär'ley, *n.*, cereal plant

bär'māid, *n.*, woman who serves drinks

bärn, *n.*, farm building

bär'ná·cle, *n.*, clinging sea

animal

bärn'stôrm, v., campaign in the country, **-er**

bärn'yärd, n., yard next to barn

bär'ö·graph, n., instrument measuring air pressure, **-ic**

bä·rom'e·têr, n., instrument indicating weather change, **tric**

bar'ön, n., English nobleman, **-ess**

bar'ön·et, n., English nobleman below baron, **-cy**

ba'rö·ny, n., baron's estate

bä·rôque' (rōhk), a., extravagantly ornamented

bar'ö·scöpe, n., instrument indicating air pressure changes

bä·roûche' (roosh), n., four-wheeled carriage

bar'räcks, n., soldiers' sleeping place

bar·rä·cū'dä, n., large predatory fish

bär'räge' (räzh), n., artillery fire

bar'rå·tör, n., dishonest ship's officer, **try**

bärred, a., having bars

bar'rēl, n., round wooden container made of staves, tube of gun

bar'rên, a., not productive, **-ness**

bär·rette', n., girl's hair clasp

bar·ri·cäde', n., defensive barrier

bar'ri·êr (rēe), n., something that separates

bär'ring, prep., except for

bar'ris·têr, n., British lawyer

bär'rōōm, n., place selling drinks

bar'rōw, n., one-wheeled cart, hill

bär'tend·êr, n., drink server at bar

bär'têr, v., trade

bär'ti·zän, n., overhanging turret

bä'sad, a., toward base

bäs'al, a., fundamental

bä·sält', n., type of rock

bäse, n., bottom, principle, starting place, baseball touch point

bäse, v., found upon

bäse, a., low, dishonest, immoral

bäse'ball, n., game using

bäse'bôard, n., board near floor

bäse'born, a., of low birth, illegitimate

bäse'less, a., without cause, groundless

bäse'män, n., baseball player

bäse'ment, n., underground room

bash (coll.), v., hit

bash'ful, a., shy

bäs'ic, a., relating to base, **-ally**

ba·sil'i·cà, n., ancient Roman building

bäs'i·lisk, n., mythical reptile, lizard

bä'sin, n., round bowl

bä'sis, n., foundation, reason for

bask, v., rest in warmth

bas'kêt, n., type of container, wooden, etc., **-ry**

bas'kêt·ball, n., game using basket

bas rē·lief', n., type of sculpture

bäss, a., lowest singing voice

bass, n., a fish

bas'sêt, n., a dog

bas·si·net', n., baby basket

bäs·sōōn', n., wind instrument

bass'wood, n., a tree

bas'tärd, n., child of unmarried parents

bäste, v., moisten meat while cooking with fat, sew, beat, scold

bäst'ings, n., temporary stitches

bas'tion, n., fortification

bat, n., club, winged mammal

bat, v., use bat in baseball

batch, n., baked bread, things taken together

bà·teau' (tōh), n., flat-bottomed boat

bath, n., cleaning body with water, water for washing

bäthe, v., wash body

bà·thom'e·têr, n., instrument measuring water depth

bä'thos, n., artificial or emotional speech or writing, **thetic**

bath'rōbe, n., lounging garment

bath'rōōm, n., room with toilet, bath-tub, wash-basin

bath'tub, n., tub for washing

body

bath'y̆-sphēre, *n.*, globe for under-sea descent

bá-tik' (teek), *n.*, method of fabric dyeing

bá-tiste' (tēest), *n.*, thin cotton fabric

ba-ton', *n.*, wand for beating time, symbol of authority

bát-tal'ion, *n.*, two or more companies of regiment

bat'tĕn, *n.*, strip of wood used in building

bat'tĕn, *v.*, fasten down

bat'tĕr, *v.*, beat severely, repeatedly

bat'tĕr, *n.*, flour mixture, baseball player at bat

bat'tĕr-y, *n.*, series of galvanic cells generating electricity, baseball pitcher and catcher

bat'ting, *n.*, cotton-wool sheets used as filling for quilts

bat'tle, *n.*, fight between sides, war

bat'tle fá-tigue' (tēeg), *a.*, emotional disturbance due to war

bat'tle-field, *n.*, fighting place

bat'tle-mĕnt, *n.*, wall openings for shooting, parapet

bat'tle-ship, *n.*, heavily armored ship

bat'ty (coll.), *a.*, crazy

bău'ble (bàw), *n.*, a trinket

bäux'īte (bàwx), *n.*, a mineral

bawd, *n.*, prostitute

bāwd'y, *a.*, obscene

bāwl, *v.*, cry

bāwl' out (coll), *v.*, criticize

bay, *n.*, sea extension into land, dog's bark, type of horse

bay'ber-ry, *n.*, type of shrub

bay'ö-net, *n.*, blade attached to gun

bay'oū (by-ōō), *n.*, river extension inland

bay-win'dōw, *n.*, projecting window

bá-zäar' (zär), *n.*, oriental shops, charity sale

bá-zōō'ká, *n.*, rocket gun

bē, *v.*, am (pres. ind.), exist, take place

bē-, *prefix*, about, all around

bēach, *n.*, sandy shore line, **-less**

bēach'cōmb-êr, *n.*, tramp living on beaches

bēached, *a.*, stranded on shore

bēach'head, *n.*, invasion landing spot

bēa'cŏn (kin), *n.*, warning or guiding signal

bēad, *n.*, small round glass or metal ornament, **-ed**, **-ing**

bēa'dle, *n.*, church official

bēads'man, *n.*, one who prays for others

bēa'gle, *n.*, hunting dog

bēak, *n.*, bird's bill, **-ed**

bēak'êr, *n.*, large cup

bēam, *n.*, wooden plank, happy smile, radio signal, ship right angle to keel, **-ed**

bēam'ing, *adj.*, radiant, **-ly**

bēan, *n.*, seed eaten as vegetable

bēan (coll.), *v.*, hit on head

bēar, *n.*, an animal, **-ish**

bēar, *v.*, support, carry, endure, reproduce, push, behave, **-able**

bēard, *n.*, growth of hair on man's face, whiskers, **-ed**

bēar'êr, *n.*, carrier

bēar'ing, *n.*, way of conducting self, relationship, posture, machine part

bēast, *n.*, animal

bēast'ly, *a.*, crude, cruel

bēat, *v.*, strike, (coll.) win, tired, mix, **-en**

bēat, *n.*, stroke, path

bēat'nik, *n.*, unconventional person

bē-à-tif'ic, *a.*, blessed, **-ally**

bē-at'i-fy̆, *v.*, declare as blessed, **fication**

bē-at'i-tūde, *n.*, blissfulness

beau (bōh), *n.*, boy friend

beaū'ti-ful (bū), *a.*, delightful to eye, **-ly**

beaū'ti-fy̆, *v.*, make more attractive

beaū'ty, *n.*, pleasing excellence, good looks

beaū'ty shop, *n.*, women's hair dressing establishment

beaū'ty spot, *n.*, mole

bēa'vêr, *n.*, amphibious rodent

bē'bop (coll.), *n.*, type of popular music

bé-cāuse' (càws), *conj.*, for reason that

beck, v., nod to call, **-on**

be-come', v., come to be, coming

bed, n., furniture to sleep on

be-dab'ble, v., make dirty

be-daz'zle, v., overwhelm with brightness

bed'bug, n., insect

bed'ding, n., bed materials

be-deck', v., decorate, adorn

be-dev'il, v., bother, upset, torment

bed'fel-low, n., one who shares bed

be-di'zen, v., decorate showily

bed'lam, n., confusion, uproar

bed'pan, n., bed toilet

be-drag'gle, v., make dirty

bed'rid-den, a., confined to bed

bed'rock, n., unbroken hard rock layer

bed'room, n., sleeping room

bed'time, n., time for sleep

bee, n., insect that makes honey

beech'nut, n., a tree

beef, n., cow or bull meat

beef'y, a., muscular, thick set

bee'hive, n., shelter for bee colony

bee'line, n., direct line

beer, n., malt alcoholic drink, **-y**

beet, n., root vegetable

bee'tle, n., insect, wooden hammer

be-fall', v., happen to

be-fog', v., confuse, **-aged**

be'fool, v., deceive

be-fore', prep., ahead of, in front of, **-hand**

be-friend' (frend), v., give friendship

be-fud'dle, v., confuse

beg, v., request charity

be-get', v., bring forth, give birth to

beg'gar, n., one who begs alms, **-ly**

beg'gary, a., poverty

be-gin', v., start, **-ning**

be-go'ni-a, n., waxy flowering plant

be-grudge', v., be jealous of

be-guile', (gyl), v., cheat, charm

be-half', n., the interest of

be-have', v., act in certain way

be-hav'ior, n., activities

be-head', v., cut off head

be-hest', n., order

be-hind', prep., in rear of, past, slow

be-hold', v., see, look at

be-hold'en, a., indebted

be-hoove', v., proper or necessary for

beige (bayj), n., very light brown

be'ing, n., anything living, person, existence

be-la'bor, v., criticize, beat

be-lat'ed, a., late

be-lay', v., fasten rope

belch, v., expel gas through mouth, **-er**

bel'dam, n., ugly old woman

be-lea'guer (ger), v., lay siege to

be-lie', v., misrepresent

be-lief', n., accepted opinion

be-lieve', v., accept as true

be-lit'tle, v., make feel inferior

bell, n., hollow instrument which rings

bel-la-don'na, n., poisonous plant, drug

bell'bottoms, n., widely flared trousers

bell'boy, n., hotel porter

bell'buoy, n., water warning marker

belle, n., young girl, beauty

belles-let'tres (bel-letr), n., good literature

bel'li-cose, a., desirous of fighting

bel-lig'er-ent, a., desiring battle, **ence**

bel'low, v., roar out, animal cry

bel'lows, n., air producing mechanism

bell'weth-er, n., sheep flock leader

bel'ly, n., stomach, underside

be-long', v., be in possession of, **-ing**

be-lov'ed, a., greatly loved

be-low', adv., under, lower than

belt, n., leather band worn around waist area

belt, v., hit

be-mire', a., smear with mire

be-moan', v., mourn over, lament

be-muse', v., confuse

bench, n., long seat

bend, v., curve, **-er**

bĕ-nēath', adv., under

bĕn'ē-dict, n., newly married bachelor

bĕn-ė-dic'tion, n., blessing

bĕn-ė-fac'tion, n., good deed, **tor**

bė-nef'i-cĕnce, n., kindness, goodness, **cent**

bĕn-ė-fi'cial, a., favorable, helpful **-ly**

bĕn-ė-fi'ci-ȧr-y, n., receiver of benefits

bĕn'ė-fit, n., help received, charity entertainment

bė-nev'ō-lĕnce, n., kindly action, **lent**

bė-nīgn', a., kindly, **-ant**

bĕn'i-sŏn, n., blessing

bent, a., curved

bė-numb', v., remove sensation from

bĕn'zēne, n., inflammable chemical

bĕn-zō'in, n., resin

bė-quēath', v., will belongings, **-al**

bė-quest', n., property left by will

bė-rāte', v., scold, insult

ber-ceuse', n., a cradle song

bė-rēave', v., thoughtlessly remove, rob **-ment**

bė-rēt' (ray), n., soft cap

bĕr'ga-mŏt, n., a pear

bĕr'i-bĕr'i, n., disease from vitamin deficiency

bĕr'ry, n., a fruit

bėr-sĕrk', a., frenzied job

bĕrth, n., bed, ship station, job

bĕr'thȧ, n., style of woman's collar

bĕr'yl, n., a mineral

bė-rȳl'li-um, n., a metallic element

bė-sēech', v., earnestly request, **-ingly**

bė-sēem', v., be suited

bė-set', v., surround, attack

bė-set'ting, a., constantly afflicting

bė-sīde', prep., by side of, in addition

bė-sīdes', adv., furthermore

bė-siēge', v., attack persistently, **-r**

bė-smirch', v., make dirty, insult, **-er**

bė'sŏm, n., broom of twigs

bė-sŏt', v., make drunk, **-ted**

bė-span'gle, v., decorate with spangles, **-d**

bė-spat'tėr, v., spatter with dirt, defame

best, a., most desirable, highest quality

bes'tial (tyil), a., beastlike

bė-stir', v., stir to action

bė-stōw', v., present

bė-tāke', v., go

bĕ'tĕl (til), n., pepper plant, **-nut**

bête noire' (bayt nwär), n., something frightening, dreaded

bė-tīde', v., happen to

bė-tīmes', adv., early

bė-tō'kĕn, v., indicate, show

bė-trāy', v., reveal wanted information to enemy, deceive, **-er**

bė-trōth', v., promise in marriage, **-al**

bet'tėr, a., more desirable, larger

bet'tėr-ment, n., improvement

bė-twēen', prep., in relation to two things, separation, connecting, interval

bev'ėl (il), n., angle

bev'ėr-age, n., drink

bev'y, n., group

bė-wāre', v., be careful of, watch, guard

bė-wil'dėr, v., confuse, **-ment**

bė-witch', v., cast a spell, **-er**

bey (bay), n., Turkish governor

bė-yŏnd', prep., farther away

bė-zique' (zēēk), n., card game

bi-a'ly, n., small onion flavored roll

bī-an'nū-ȧl, a., twice yearly

bī'ȧs, n., diagonal line, prejudice, and

bib, n., under-chin napkin

bi'be-lŏt (bib-lōh), n., small rare object

Bī'ble, n., Old and New Testament

bib'li-cȧl, a., pertaining to Bible

bib-li-og'rȧ-phy, n., book or article listing, **-pher**

bib'li-ō-phile, n., book lover

bib'li-ō-phōbe, n., one who hates books

bib'li-ō-pōle, n., rare book dealer

bib'ū-lous, a., absorbent,

desires drinking

bī-cam'ër-ál, *a.,* having two legislative bodies

bī-cen'tē-nâr'y, *n.,* two hundred years

bī-cen-ten'ni-ál, *a.,* two hundredth

bī'ceps, *n.,* arm muscle

bī-chlō'rīde, *n.,* chemical

bick'ër, *v.,* argue in petty manner

bī-cus'pid, *n.,* two-pointed tooth

bī'cy̆-cle, *n.,* two-wheeled pedaledvehicle, **clist**

bid, *v.,* ask for, tell, declare, suggest price, command, **-ding**

bīde, *v.,* wait, stay

bi-det' (day), *n.,* bathroom fixture for bathing private parts

bī-en'ni-ál, *a.,* every two years, **-ly**

biēr, *n.,* coffin holder

bī-fā'ri-ous, *a.,* in twos

bi-fō'cál, *a.,* near-far sighted eyeglasses

bi-func'tion-ál, *a.,* having two functions

bī'fûr-cāte, *a.,* forked, divided in two, **cation**

big, *a.,* large, important

big'a-mist, *n.,* person who commits bigamy

big'á-my, *n.,* having two mates at same time

bīght, *n.,* bend, curve

big'it, *n.,* binary digit

big'ŏt, *n.,* intolerant person, **-ed**

big'ŏt-ry, *n.,* intolerance

big'top, *n.,* main circus tent

big'wig, *n.,* important person

bī'joū (be´zhōō), *n.,* jewel

bīke, *n.,* a bicycle

bi-ki'ni, *n.,* brief two-piece swimsuit

bī-lat'ĕr-ál, *a.,* two-sided

bil'bō, *n.,* iron bar to confine prisoners

bīle, *n.,* liver fluid

bilge, *n.,* ship hull section, stagnant water

bī-lin'gual, *a.,* using or fluent in two languages

bil'ious, *a.,* bad-tempered, relating to bile

bilk, *v.,* escape paying, cheat

bill, *n.,* money owed, bird's beak, paper money, intended law

bill, *v.,* attempt to collect money

bill' bōard, *n.,* advertising sign board

bil'lĕt (it), *v.,* order to house soldiers

bil-let-doux' (dōo), *n.,* love letter

bill'fōld, *n.,* wallet

bill'head, *n.,* printed business name and address

bil'liards (yĕrds), *n.,* table game using cue and balls

bil'lings-gāte, *n.,* vile language

bil'liŏn, *n.,* one thousand millions, **-aire**

bill of fâre', *n.,* menu

bill of lād'ing, *n.,* transportation receipt

bil'lōw, *n.,* large wave or mass, **-y**

bil'ly, *n.,* policeman's club

bil'ly gōat, *n.,* male goat

bī-mŏnth'ly, *a.,* every two months

bin, *n.,* box or enclosure for coal, etc.

bī'nà-ry, *a.,* having two parts

bī'nà-ry com-pūt'er, *n.,* computer utilizing power of 2

bī'nāte, *a.,* in pairs

bīnd, *v.,* tie together, unite, wrap, obligate, (coll.) predicament

bīnd'ĕr, *n.,* that which binds, harvester part that ties grain

bīnd'ĕr-y, *n.,* book binding place

bīnd'ing, *n.,* book cover

bīnd'ing, *a.,* requiring enforcement

bin'gō, *n.,* game using cards and numbers, form of lotto

bīn-oc'ū-lär, *n.,* glasses for seeing at a distance

bī-nō'mi-ál, *a.,* using two terms

bī-ō-chem'is-try, *n.,* chemistry of living matter

bio-de-grād-able, *adj.,* breaks down into harmless components

bī-og'rà-phy, *n.,* story of person's life, **pher**

bī-ö-log'i-cál, *a.,* relating to living matter

bī-ol'ö-gy, *n.,* science of life

bī-om'ė-try, *n.,* measurement of life span

bi·os'co·py, *n.,* examination to determine whether body is alive

bī·pär'ti·sàn, *a.,* representing two groups or parties

bī·pär'tīte, *a.,* having two parts

bi'ped, *n.,* two-footed animal, having two feet

birch, *n.,* smooth bark tree

bird, *n.,* flying, feathered animal

bird'ie, *n.,* less than par (golf)

bird's'·eye, *a.,* seen from above or afar, type cloth

bi·ret'ta, *n.,* priest's cap

birth, *n.,* being born, beginning, **-day**

birth'·rāte, *n.,* number of children born in population

bis'cuit (kit), *n.,* type of bread

bī·sect', *v.,* divide into two parts, **-ion**

bish'ŏp, *n.,* church official, **-ric**

bis'muth (mith), *n.,* metallic element

bī'sŏn, *n.,* buffalo

bis·sex'tile, *n.,* leap year

bi·sex'u·al, *a.,* having both sexes

bit, *n.,* tool, bridle part, little amount

bitch, *n.,* female dog, nasty woman, swear-word, *(slang) v.,* complain

bīte, *v.,* tear with teeth

bīte, *n.,* tooth wound, sting, hold, snack

bīt'ing, *a.,* sharp, sneering

bit'tèr, *a.,* sharp, sorrowful, **-ness**

bit'tèrn, *n.,* marsh bird

bit'tèrs, *n.,* herb liquid

bit'tèr·swēet', *n.,* a poisonous plant with red orange capsules

bī·tū'mèn, *n.,* mineral affected by heat, **minous**

bī'valve, *n.,* two-shelled mollusk, oyster, clam, mussel, etc., **valvular**

biv·où·ac (ōō-ak), *n.,* soldiers camping out

bī·wēek'ly, *a.,* every two weeks

bī·yēar'ly, *a.,* twice a year

bi·zärre', *a.,* strange, unusual

blab, *v.,* chatter, gossip

blab'bèr, *v.,* talk foolishly, babble

black, *n.,* opposite of white,

absence of color or light

black'bäll, *v.,* vote against, keep out

black'bèr·ry, *n.,* fruit

black'bŏard, *n.,* slate for writing on with chalk

black'ĕn, *v.,* make black

black'guärd (blagèrd), *n.,* cheat

black'head, *n.,* dirt in pore, comedo

black'jack, *n.,* steel-loaded club, card game

black'list, *n.,* list of undesirables

black'mäil, *v.,* obtain money by threat of exposure

Black Mà·rī'à, *n.,* police wagon

black mär'kèt, *n.,* selling of goods illegally **-eer**

black'out, *n.,* all lights out, loss of consciousness

black'smith, *n.,* iron worker, one who shoes horses

black wid'ōw, *n.,* poisonous spider

blad'dèr, *n.,* part of body storing urine, air bag in ball

blāde, *n.,* edge that cuts on knife

blāme, *v.,* find fault with, **-fully**

blanch, *v.,* turn white, dip in boiling water

bland, *a.,* smooth, easy-going, mild, **-ly**

blan'dish, *v.,* coax, flatter

blank, *n.,* empty space, omission

blan'kĕt, *n.,* bed covering

blan'kĕt, *v.,* cover evenly

blâre, *v.,* raucous loud sound

blär'nèy, *n.,* insincere flattery

blä·sē' (zay), *a.,* bored, uninspired

blas·phēme', *v.,* speak irreverently, **-phemy**

blast, *n.,* strong gust, explosion, loud noise

blast'off, *n.,* launching of rocket or missile

blat, *n.,* sheep cry

blā'tànt, *a.,* harshly noisy, showy

blāze, *n.,* fire, brightness, spot or mark

blā'zŏn, *v.,* decorate colorfully, **-ry**

blēach, *n.,* chemical used to

whiten, make white

bleach'er, n., cheap stadium seats, one who bleaches

bleak, a., empty and dismal

blear'y-eyed (coll.), a., very tired

bleat, n., animal cry, **-ing**

bleed, v., lose blood, **-er**

blem'ish, n., scar, defect

blench, v., turn pale

blend'er, n., mixing machine

blend, v., mix, harmonize

bless, v., consecrate, **-ed**

bless'ing, n., God's favor, prayer

blight, n., plant disease, destruction

blind, a., unable to see, prejudiced, **-ing**

blind'fold, v., cover the eyes

blink, v., open and shut eyes, flash on and off

blink'er, n., flap to shut off side view

blintz, n., thin filled pancake

bliss, n., happiness, joy, **-ful**

blis'ter, n., skin swelling

blithe, a., happy, **-ly**

blitz'krieg, n., swift military attack

bliz'zard, n., severe snowstorm

blob, n., small mass, globule

bloc, n., group acting together

block, n., solid mass, platform, mold, obstacle, city square

block-ade', n., shutting off of a place to prevent entrance

block'bus-ter, n., extremely destructive large bomb

block'head, n., dunce, ignoramus

blond, a., light haired

blood (bluhd), n., fluid in veins and arteries, **-less**

blood' pres-sure, n., pressure of blood against blood vessels

blood'shed, n., spilling of blood, killing

blood'shot, a., red and inflamed

blood'stained, a., stained with blood

blood'thirst'y, a., eager to kill or do harm

blood trans-fus'ion, n., blood of one given to another

blood' ves-sel, n., vein, artery, or capillary

bloom, n., plant's flower, healthy glow

bloom'ers, n., type of female pants gathered at the knee

blos'som, n., flower, **-ing**

blot, n., spot, absorb, destroy, **-ted**

blotch, n., irregular spot or blot

blot'ter, n., paper that absorbs

blouse, n., shirt

blow, n., stroke, shock

blow, v., direct a movement of air, sound, **-n**

blow'out, n., sudden explosion of tire, (coll.) wild party

blow'torch, n., torch giving hot flame used in metalworking

blow'up, n., explosion, expression of anger

blow'zy, a., coarse looking, disheveled

blub'ber, v., weep noisily, **-y,** **-ing**

blub'ber, n., whale fat

bludg'eon (jin), v., heavy short club

blue, a., color of the sky, **-ish,** **-ness**

blue'bell, n., flower

blue'ber-ry, n., edible berry

blue'bird, n., blue songbird

blue' blood, a., upper-class society, aristocrat

blue' book, n., book naming upper class society

blue'grass, n., Kentucky grass

blue'jay, n., bird

blue' laws, n., puritanical laws regulating moral behavior

blue'nose, n., a snob

blue-pen'cil, v., edit

blue'print, n., exact print of plans

blue rib'bon, n., first prize

blues, n., sad type of song

blue-streak', n., flash

bluff, n., cliff

bluff, v., fool, deceive

blu'ing, n., laundry whitener

blun'der, v., make a mistake, **-ing**

blun'der-buss, n., old-type gun, bungler

blunt, a., dull, direct, honest, **-ness**

blur, v., make dim or

indistinct, **-red**

blurb, n., praising declaration

blurt, v., say suddenly

blush, n., reddening

blus′ter, v., storm violently, talk loudly

bō′á, n., type of snake

bōar, n., male pig

bōard, n., flat piece of wood, group of directors

bōard, v., get on (train, etc.), get meals

bōard′walk, n., beach promenade made of boards

bōast, v., brag, **-ful**

bōat, n., small ship, **-ing**

bōat′swain (bōh-sin), n., ship officer

bob, v., n., move up and down, hair cut

bob′bin, n., thread holder

bob′by pin, n., hairpin

bob′by socks, n., girl's short socks

bob′cat, n., American wildcat

bob′sled, n., large sled with steering wheel

bob′tāil, n., short tail, animal with short or docked tail

bob′ white, n., quail bird

bock, n., dark beer brewed in spring

bod′ice, n., upper part of dress

bod′i-ly, a., pertaining to body

bod′y, n., physical part of man or animal, mass of things

bod′y cav′i-ty, n., opening of body

bod′y-guärd, n., one who protects a person

bog, n., wet, swampy ground, marsh

bog, v., become stuck, sink

bog′gle, v., become frightened, hesitate, astound

bō′gus, a., counterfeit

bō′gy, n., fearful sight, goblin

boil, v., bubble, seethe at high temperature

boil, n., red, swollen sore

boil′ēr, n., tank for heating water

bois′tēr-ous, a., loud, rough, noisy, **-ly**

bōld, a., courageous, daring, rude, **-ly**

bōld′fāce, n., heavy printing type face

bō-le′rō (lay-rōh), n., Spanish dance, short jacket

bōll′wēe-vil, n., insect

bō′lō, n., Philippine knife

bō-lō′gnä, n., meat sausage

bōl′stēr, v., support

bōlt, n., metal fastener with nut, roll of cloth, sudden withdrawal

bomb (bom), n., shell that explodes

böm-bärd′, v., attack incessantly, **-ment**

bom-bär-diēr′ (dēer), n., airplane bombing director

bom′bast, n., pompous talk, bragging, **-tic**

bomb′ēr, n., airplane that drops bombs, one who bombs

bomb′prōōf, a., safe from bomb effects

bomb′shell, n., bomb, highly active person (coll.)

bō′nà fīde′, a., sincere, honest

bō-nan′zà, n., sudden wealth

bond, n., something that ties, document for borrowing money, agreement

bond′āge, n., slavery, involuntary servitude

bond′ēd, a., put under bond, in warehouse

bond′hōld-ēr, n., bond owner

bōne, n., hard tissue of skeleton

bōne, v., remove bones, (slang) study hard

bōn′ēr, n., silly error

bon′fīre, n., outdoor fire

bon-hö-miē′ (êh-mēe), n., pleasing manner

bon′nēt, n., woman's or child's hat

bō′nus, n., extra reward or payment

bōn′y, a., of or resembling bone

bonze, n., Buddhist priest

bōō, inter., cry of dislike, cry to startle

bōō′by, n., dull-witted person

bōō′by trap, n., hidden exploding device

bōō′dle, n., the lot, pack, bribe, large sum of money

boog′ie woog′ie, n., jazz music

bōō′ hōō, n., sound of noisy crying

book, n., bound, printed or

written work

book'bind'êr, n., one who binds books, **-y**

book' case, n., shelves for books

book' club, n., group selling books to members at reduced rates

book' end, n., support to hold books up

book'ish, a., studious, reading constantly

book'keep'êr, n., business account record keeper, **-ing**

book'mak'êr, n., gambler who accepts bets

book'mark, n., marker to keep place in book

book'plate, n., label showing book ownership

book'sell'êr, n., one who sells books

book'wôrm (wûrm), n., avid reader

bōōm, n., ship spar, financial prosperity, deep sound

bōōm'êr-ang, n., v., Australian weapon, return, go contrary

bōōn, n., a., blessing

bōōn'dŏg'gle, v., waste time at work

boor, n., crude, ill-mannered person, **-ish**

bōōst, v., lift, help

bōōt, n., high top shoe, navy trainee

bōōt, v., kick

bōōt'black, n., one who shines shoes

bōōth, n., stall, shed for selling goods compartment in restaurant

bōōt'lĕg, v., make or sell whiskey illegally, **-ger**

bōōt'less, a., useless

bōō'ty, n., captured goods, prize

bōōze, n., alcoholic drinks, **-d**

bō'rax, n., cleaning chemical

bôr'dêr, n., edge, boundary, **-land**

bôre, v., make weary with dullness, make hole, **-dom**

bô'ric ac'id, n., chemical

bôrn, a., brought into being, by birth

bôrne, v., carried

bŏr'ōugh (bûr-oh), n., self-governing area

bŏr'rōw, v., obtain on loan

bôrscht, n., beet soup

bos'cage, n., forest

bosh, inter., foolishness

bos'ŏm (bŏoz'm), n., breast, midst

bôss, n., v., supervisor, **-y**

bot'a-ny, n., study of plant life, **nical**

botch, v., spoil, do poor work

bōth, a., each together

bŏth'êr, n., trouble, annoyance, **-some**

bot'tle, n., glass

bot'tle-neck, n., block to progress, narrow entrance

bot'tŏm, n., underneath, lowest part

bot'ū-lism (botch-ōō-lism), n., type of food poisoning

boū-cle' (bōō-clay), n., cloth with looped surface

bou'doir (bōō-dwär), n., lady's private room

bough, n., tree branch

bouil'lon (bool'-yon), n., clear broth

bŏul'dêr, n., large rock

bou'le-värd (bool), n., wide street

bounce, v., spring back, throw out,(col.) **-r**

bound, v., a., jump, limited, determined, **-less**

bound'a-ry, n., limit, border

boun'te-ous, a., generous

boun'ti-ful, a., plentiful

boun'ty, n., gift, generosity

boū-quet' (bōō-kay), n., bunch of flowers, aroma

bour'geois (boor-zhwä), a., middle class, not refined

bout, n., contest, fight

boū-tŏn-niēre' (bōō-tun-ēer), n., buttonhole flower

bō'vīne, a., resembling a cow, dull

bow, n., bending forward, front of ship

bōw, n., violin part, weapon for shooting arrow

bowd'lêr-īze, v., prudishly censor

bow'ĕls, n., intestines, inner part

bow'êr, n., tree-lined shelter, arbor

bōwl, n., round dish

bōw'leg, n., outward curved legs

bōwl'ing, n., game with balls and pins

bōwl'ing al'ley, *n.*, enclosure for bowling, containing wooden lanes

bōw'sprit, *n.*, ship pole

box, *n.*, container, enclosed group of seats, special section

box, *v.*, put into box, fight, **-er**, **-ing**

box'cär, *n.*, freight car

box' of'fice, *n.*, office for ticket selling

box'wood, *n.*, shrub

boy, *n.*, male child, **-hood**

boy'cott, *v.*, refuse to buy, sell or use

boy'ish, *a.*, like a boy

brāce, *n.*, clamp, support, pair

brāce'let (lit), *n.*, wrist jewelry

brāc'ěr, *n.*, alcoholic stimulant

brāc'ing, *a.*, healthful, refreshing

brack'ěn, *n.*, fern

brack'ět, *n.*, wall support, punctuation

brack'ish, *a.*, salty, distasteful

brad, *n.*, small nail

brag, *v.*, boast, **-gart**

brāid, *n.*, plaited hair, tape, band

brāin, *n.*, nerve tissue in head, **-less**

brāin'wäsh, *v.*, change past beliefs by drugs, torture

brāin'y, *a.*, intelligent

brāise, *v.*, to brown meat, sauté

brāke, *n.*, device for stopping auto, machine, etc.

brāke, *v.*, stop, slow down

brāke'man, *n.*, train brake controller

brāke'shoe (shoō), *n.*, brake on wheel

bran, *n.*, outer covering of oats, wheat, etc.

branch, *n.*, offshoot from part, part of

brand, *n.*, stamp of identification or disgrace, label

bran'dish, *v.*, wave or shake threateningly

bran'dy, *n.*, alcoholic liquor

brash, *a.*, acting impetuously, **-ly**

brass, *n.*, copper-zinc alloy, **-y**

bras'särd, *n.*, armor

brás-sière' (zēer), *n.*, female breast supporter

brat, *n.*, naughty child

brāve, *a.*, bold, courageous, **-ly**

brāv'ěr-y, *n.*, courage, boldness

brä'vō, *inter.*, well done!

brawn, *n.*, strength, powerful muscles, **-y**

brawl, *n.*, fight

bray, *n.*, donkey sound

brā'zěn, *a.*, made of brass, shameless

brā'ziěr (shēr), *n.*, pot for burning charcoal

brēach, *n.*, a break or opening

bread (bred), *n.*, baked food product made of flour and yeast

bread'līne, *n.*, people in line for charity gift of food

breadth, *n.*, degree of wideness

bread'win-nêr, *n.*, income earner of family

brēak, *v.*, shatter into pieces violently

brēak'down, *n.*, failure to work, collapse

brēak'fást (brek), *n.*, morning meal

brēak'up, *n.*, ending

breast (brest), *n.*, front part of chest

breast'strōke, *n.*, swimming stroke

breath (breth), *n.*, exhaled or inhaled air

brēathe, *v.*, draw air into and expel air from lungs, **-able**

brēath'ěr, *n.*, pause, rest

brēath'ing, *n.*, air movement from lungs

breath'less, *a.*, short of breath

breath'tāk-ing, *a.*, exciting, thrilling

brēech, *n.*, lower part

brēech'ěs, *n.*, trousers

brēech'ěs buŏy, *n.*, type of buoy

brēed, *v.*, produce, hatch

brēed'ing, *n.*, upbringing, manners

brēeze, *n.*, light air movement

brēeze, *v.*, move quickly and lightly

breth'rěn, *n.*, spiritual brothers

brē'vi-ār'y, n., Catholic prayer book

brev'i-ty, n., shortness

brew, v., boil, make beer, **-ing**

brew'êr-y, n., place where beer is made

brew'mas-ter, n., supervisor in brewery

bribe, v., corrupt with money, buy favor, **-ry**

brick, n., hardened clay building material

brick'bat, n., insult, broken piece of brick

brick'lāy-êr, n., one who builds with bricks, **ing**

brick'yärd, n., place where bricks are made

brīd'ál, a., relating to wedding

brīde, n., woman getting married

brīde'grōōm, n., man getting married

brīdes'māid, n., attendant to bride at wedding

bridge, n., structure over water, ship platform, card game

bridge'head, n., position established by attacking troops in enemy's territory

bridge'wörk (wûrk), n., false tooth mounting

brī'dle, n., head harness for horses

brī'dle path, n., horseback riding trail

brief'', a., short, **-ly**

brief, n., legal summary

brief'cāse, n., carrying case for papers, etc.

brief'ing, n., instruction

brī'êr, n., thorny shrub

brig, n., two-masted ship, navy jail

bri-gāde', n., Army unit

brig-à-dîer' (deer), n., general-grade officer

brig'ánd, n., robber

bright, a., giving light, cheerful, clever, smart

Bright's dis-ēase', n., kidney disease

bril'liánt (bril-yint), a., brightly shining, very intelligent, **liancy**

brim, n., top edge, projecting edge, **-ful**

brīne, n., salt water

bring, v., take with, lead, cause, carry

brink, n., edge, verge

bri'ōche, n., sweet roll or bun

brisk, a., active, alert, lively, **-ly**

bris'ket, n., meat of animal breast

bris'tle, n., stiff animal hair

bris'tle, v., cause to stand up, make bristly

brit'tle, a., easily broken

brōach, v., suggest

brōad, a., wide across, clear, general, **-en**

brōad'cast, v., announce by radio or television

brōad'clōth, n., finely woven cotton or woolen cloth

brōad'mīnd-ēd, a., fair, not prejudiced

brōad'sīde, n., attack

brō-cāde', n., cloth with woven pattern

broc'cō-li, n., vegetable

brō-chette', n., small skewer

brō-chūre', n., pamphlet

brōgue, n., Irish accent, coarse shoe

broil, v., n., cook, quarrel

broil'êr, n., young chicken, cooking device

brō'ken, a., separated into pieces, ruined

brō'kêr, n., agent

brō'mīde, n., sedative, platitude

bron-chī'tis, n., bronchial disease

bron-tō-său'rus (ris), n., prehistoric dinosaur

bronze, n., copper-tin alloy

brōōch, n., breastpin

brōōd, n., v., family, group of birds, meditate, worry

brook, n., small stream

brōōm, n., sweeper with handle, shrub

brōth, n., thin soup

brōth'êr, n., male with same parents

brōth'êr-hood, n., being brothers, association

brow, n., forehead, eyebrow

brow'bēat, v., threaten, bully

brown, n., dark reddish or yellowish color

browse, v., look through book, etc. leisurely

brūc'ine (sēen), n., poisonous alkaloid

brūise (brōōz), v., wound without breaking skin

brūis'êr, n., enormous person,

bully

brū-nette′, *n.*, dark-haired person

brunt, *n.*, main shock

brush, *n.*, bristled utensil for cleaning, painting, etc., thicket

brush, *v.*, rub, paint, push lightly

brusque (brusk), *a.*, coarse, unmannerly

brū′tál, *a.*, cruel, **-ity**

brûte, *n.*, cruel person, animal

bub (coll.) *n.*, fellow, friend

bub′ble, *n.*, round air-filled water film, gurgle, belch

buc-cá-nēer′, *n.*, pirate

buck, *n.*, dollar bill, male deer

buck, *v.*, oppose, **-ing**

buck′bōard, *n.*, four-wheeled carriage

buck′et, *n.*, wood or metal container, **-ful**

buck′le, *n.*, *v.*, clasp for fastening two ends together, bulge, bend

buck′rám, *n.*, stiff cloth

buck′shot, *n.*, large leaden shot

buck′tōōth, *n.*, protruding tooth

bū-col′ic, *a.*, rural

bud, *n.*, beginning of flower, child

bud, *v.*, produce buds, grow

bud′dy (coll.) *n.*, friend, fellow

budge, *v.*, move slightly

budg′et, *n.*, breakdown of spending, plan, **-ed**

buff, *v.*, polish, **-er**

buf′fá-lō, *n.*, type of oxen, bison

buf′fet (fit), *v.*, strike, hit

buf-fet′ (fay), *n.*, dining-room cabinet

buf-fōōn′, *n.*, clown

bug, *n.*, insect

bug′á-bōō, *n.*, something frightening, bogy

bug′gy, *n.*, four-wheeled cart

bū′gle, *n.*, small trumpet, type of bead

build, *n.*, form

build (bild), *v.*, erect, create, put materials together, **-er**

build′ing, *n.*, structure, something built

build′up, *n.*, planned concentration, promotion

bulb, *n.*, plant bud, electric light apparatus, **-ous**

bulge, *v.*, stick out, rounded projection

bulk, *n.*, large amount or size, structure, **-y**

bull (bool), *n.*, male of cattle, elephant, whale, etc., Pope's announcement, prosperous stock market

bull′dōze, *v.*, intimidate, clear land

bull′dōz-ēr, *n.*, earth mover

bul′let, *n.*, projectile fired from gun

bul′le-tin, *n.*, announcement

bull′fīght, *n.*, contest between man and bull

bull′head-ĕd, *a.*, stubborn

bul′liŏn, *n.*, gold bars, heavy fringe

bull's-eye (i), *n.*, exact target, direct hit

bul′ly, *n.*, rough person hurting weaker ones

bul′rush, *n.*, swamp plant

bum, *n.*, loafing, useless person, **-ming**

bum, *v.*, beg, in disrepair

bum′ble, *v.*, blunder

bum′ble-bēe, *n.*, large bee

bump, *v.*, knock against, push, demote

bump′êr, *n.*, metal auto guard, crib guard

bump′kin, *n.*, yokel

bump′tious, *a.*, outspokenly arrogant, pushing

bun, *n.*, sweet cake or roll

bunch, *n.*, group, collection

bun′dle, *n.*, things tied together, package

bun′dle, *v.*, tie together, wrap

bun′dling, *n.*, pre-marital courting custom among the Pa. Dutch

bung, *n.*, barrel stopper

bun′gà-lōw, *n.*, one-story house, cottage

bun′gle, *v.*, do clumsily

bun′iŏn, *n.*, swelling on foot

bunk, *n.*, shelf-like bed, camp sleeping quarters, **-ing**

bun′kō, *n.*, swindle

bun′ny (coll.) *n.*, rabbit

bunt, *v.*, push

bunt′ing, *n.*, colorful cloth for decoration

buŏy, *n.*, floating anchored warning

buŏy′ánt (boi), *a.*, capable of floating, cheerful

bûr, *n.*, prickly flower part

bûr'dĕn, *n.*, load, heavy weight, **-some**

bū'reau (rōh) *n.*, chest of drawers, government division

bū-reauc'ra-cy (rok), *n.*, strong administrative organization

bûrg, *n.*, small town

bûr'glâr, *n.*, thief, **-ize**

bur'i-âl, *n.*, interment

bûr'lap, *n.*, rough fabric

bûr-lesque' (lesk), *n.*, cheap imitation, sexy entertainment

bûr'ly, *a.*, large, rough

bûrn, *v.*, be on fire, shine, anger, **-ing**

bûr'nish, *v.*, polish by friction

burn'out, *n.*, stoppage of fuel to jet engine

burp', *n.*, a belch

bûrp' gun, *n.*, type of machine gun

bûrr, *n.*, Scotch manner of speech, rough edge

bûr'rōw, *v.*, dig hole in ground

bûr'sär, *n.*, college treasurer

bûr-sī'tis, *n.*, sac inflammation

bûrst, *v.*, explode, fly apart

bury (berry), *v.*, put in the ground, hide

bus, *n.*, large passenger vehicle

bush (boosh), *n.*, shrub, **-y**

bush'ĕl, *n.*, four pecks

bush'ĕl, *v.*, alter suits

bus'i-ly (biz), *adv.*, continuously occupied

busi'nĕss (biz), *n.*, work activity, concern, trade, policy, occupation

bust, *n.*, from the chest up, woman's breast, failure, (coll.) break

bus'tle, *v.*, hurry busily

bus'y (biz), *a.*, continuously active

bus'y bod'y, *n.*, person

concerned with affairs of others

but, *conj.*, except that, were it not, yet

butch'ĕr, *n.*, meat seller, one who kills animals, cruel killer

butch'ĕr-y (booch), *n.*, violent killing

but'lĕr, *n.*, chief male servant

butt, *v.*, *n.*, push, thick part, stub, target, (coll.) buttocks

būtte, *n.*, solitary hill

but'tĕr, *n.*, churned cream fat, **-y**

but'tĕr-cup, *n.*, yellow flower

but'tĕr-fat, *n.*, milk fat

but'tĕr-fin-gĕrs, *n.*, clumsy person

but'tĕr-fly, *n.*, colorful insect

but'tĕr-milk, *n.*, sour liquid from churned cream

but'tĕr-scotch, *n.*, candy

but'tŏcks, *n.*, back of hips, rump

but'tŏn, *n.*, round object for fastening

but'tŏn-hole, *n.*, slit in garment for button

but'trĕss, *n.*, wall support

bux'ŏm, *a.*, plump

buy (bī), *v.*, obtain with money

buy'ĕr, *n.*, one who buys

buzz, *n.*, low humming sound

buz'zârd, *n.*, bird of prey

by, *prep.*, near, on the side of

bye (bī), *n.*, position of odd person in game

by'gŏne, *a.*, that which is past

by'lâw, *n.*, secondary law

by'līne, *n.*, writer's name above news article

by'pass, *v.*, pass around

by'prod-uct, *n.*, secondary product

by'rōad, *n.*, side road

by'stand-ĕr, *n.*, spectator standing near, spectator

by'wŏrd (wûrd), *n.*, saying, object of contempt

--- C ---

cab, *n.*, taxi, locomotive room

cá-bal', *n.*, group plot

cáb-ä'lá, *n.*, secret belief, listic

ca-bál-le'rō (yàr-o), *n.*, S.

Am. horseman

cá-bä'ná (nyä), *n.*, beach cabin, bathhouse

cab-à-ret' (ray), *n.*, restaurant having

entertainment, small table

cab'bage, n., leafy vegetable

cab'in, n., roughly built cottage, ship or plane passenger section

cab'i-net, n., kitchen furniture, government council

cab'i-nèt māk'êr, n., skilled furniture maker

cā'ble, n., thick wire or rope, bundle of wires

cā'ble, v., send message overseas, all of it, **-gram**

cà-bōō'dle (slang), n., gang, everyone, all of it

cà-bōōse', n., last car on freight train

cab-ri-ō-let' (lay), n., light two-wheeled carriage

cache (cash), n., hiding place

ca-chet' (shay), n., official seal

cach'in-nāte, v., laugh loudly

cack'le, v., shrill sound

cà-coph'ö-nous, a., harsh discordant sound, **-ny**

cac'tus, n., spiky desert plant

cà-dav'êr, n., dead body, **-ous**

cad'die, n., person who carries golf bag, also **cad'dy**

cā'dénce, n., rhythm

cà-den'zà, n., unaccompanied musical section

cà-det', n., student in military school

cadge', v., borrow without repaying

cad'mi-um, n., metallic element

cad'rē, n., basic military group

cà-dū'cē-us, n., medical symbol, staff of Mercury

cà-dū'ci-ty, n., old age weakness

ca-fe' (fay), n., restaurant

caf-è-tē-ri-à, n., self-service restaurant

caf'feine (feen), n., chemical in coffee

cāge, n., a barred enclosure

cāge'y, a., cautious, cunning

cà-hōōts' (dial.), n., together, as partners

cáirn (cärn), n., round pile of stones

cāis'sön, n., ammunition wagon

cāi'tiff, n., base individual

cà-jōle', v., attempt to persuade, **-ry**

cāke, n., baked delicacy, piece of soap

cāke, v., form a mass

cāke' wâlk, n., a dance

cal'-à-bōōse, n., jail (coll.)

cal'-à-mīne, n., a mineral

cà-lam'i-ty, n., tragic happening, **-tous**

cà-lash', n., open horse carriage

cal'cic, a., relating to lime

cal'ci-fy, v., become like bone, **-fication**

cal'ci-um, n., metallic element

cal'cū-lāte, v., use arithmetic, reason, **lation**

cal'cū-lus, n., higher algebra

cál'drön, n., pot, kettle

cal'én-dár, n., listing of days and months

calf, n., young animal

cal'i-bêr, n., diameter, quality

cal'i-brāte, v., measure, check scale, **-bration**

cal'i-cō, n., cotton cloth

cal'i-pêr, n., instrument for measuring

cā'liph, n., Moslem head of state

cal-is-then'ics, n., physical exercises

câlk (cáwk), v., fill seam openings

câll, v., cry out, announce, summon, telephone, visit, **-er**

câll'ing, n., job, vocation

cál-lī'ö-pē, n., steam pipe organ

cal'lous, a., hardened, insensitive

cal'lōw, a., youthful, immature

cal'lus, n., hardened skin

calm, a., still, motionless, not excited, **-ly**

cal'ö-riē, n., unit of food value, **ric**

cal'ū-met, n., N. Am. Indian tobacco pipe

cal'um-ny, n., malicious, false statements, **niate**

calve, v., give birth to calf

cà-lyp'sō, n., West Indian Negro music

cā'lyx, n., flower part

cam, n., wheel extension that changes motion

cam'bêr, n., arching piece of

wood or metal

cam'bric, *n.*, linen or cotton cloth, usually white

cam'el, *n.*, one or two humped large ruminant animal

cá-mē'li-á (ya), *n.*, shrub, flower

cá-mel'ö-pärd, *n.*, giraffe

cam'é-ō, *n.*, carved stone

cam'er-á, *n.*, device for taking pictures

cam'i-sōle, *n.*, garment worn under sheer top, woman's dressing gown

cam'ou-flåge (i-fläzh), *v.*, disguise to deceive enemy

camp, *n.*, place of campers

camp, *v.*, live outdoors

cam-påign' (payn), *n.*, military action, political competition

cam'phör (fẽr), *n.*, chemical for protecting clothing against moths, **-ate**

cam'pus, *n.*, school grounds

campy, *adj.*, in amusingly bad taste

can, *v.*, be able to, know how, place food in cans

can, *n.*, tin or metal container

cá-nal', artificial waterway **-ize**

can'á-pé (pay), *n.*, small party sandwich

cá-närd', *n.*, false rumor

cá-när'y, *n.*, yellow song bird

cá-nas'tä, *n.*, card game

can'-can, *n.*, kicking French high-dance

can'cěl, *v.*, wipe out, make void, **-lation**

can'cẽr, *n.*, diseased malignant tumor growth, **-ous**

can-dē'lá (cd), *n.*, unit of luminous intensity

can-dē-lä'brá, *n.*, candlesticks

can-des'cěnt, *a.*, glowing

can'did, *a.*, honest, outspoken, **-ly**

can'di-dāte, *n.*, office seeker, **dacy**

can'diěd, *a.*, sugar covered

can'dle, *n.*, wax lighting device with wick, **-r**

can'dle, *v.*, check eggs

can'dle-līght, *n.*, light by candle

can'dle-stick, *n.*, candle holder

can'dör, *n.*, honesty, sincerity

can'dy, *n.*, sugar confection

cāne, *n.*, walking stick

cā'nīne, *n.*, pertaining to dogs

can'is-tẽr, *n.*, small metal container

can'kẽr, *n.*, ulcerous sore, any decay

canned, *a.*, sealed in can

can'nēr-y, *n.*, place for canning food

can'ni-bál, *n.*, person who eats human flesh, **-ism**

can'ning, *n.*, preserving of food in cans

can'nŏn, *n.*, large gun firing heavy shells, **-eer**

can-nŏn-āde', *n.*, continuous firing

can'nŏn-båll, *n.*, steel ball for cannon

can'ny, *a.*, careful, shrewd

cá-noe' (new), *n.*, light boat, **-ist**

can'ŏn, *n.*, law of church

can'ŏn, *n.*, clergyman attached to cathedral, **-ical**

can'ö-py, *n.*, overhead covering

cant, *n.*, insincere talk

can't, *cont.*, can not

can-tä'bi-le (lay), *a.*, flowing, song-like style

can'tá-lŏupe, *n.*, melon

can-tan'kẽr-ous, *a.*, argumentative, **-ly**

cän-tä'tä (kän-täh-ta), *n.*, story in song for chorus

can-tēēn', *n.*, metal water container, military store

can'tẽr, *n.*, slight gallop

can'ti-cle, *n.*, religious chant

can'ti-lē-vẽr', *n.*, projecting beam in architecture

can'til-lāte, *v.*, chant, **ation**

can'tō, *n.*, long poem

can-ton'ment, *n.*, military camping place

can'tör, *n.*, traditional singer in synagogue

can'vás, *n.*, heavy woven cloth

can'vás-back, *n.*, type of duck

can'vass, *v.*, examine, seek for, solicit, **-er**

can'yŏn, *n.*, deep narrow valley

cap, *n.*, cloth head covering

cā'pá-ble, *a.*, having ability,

able, **-bility**

cá·pā'cious, *a.*, holding much, **-ly**

ca·pac'i·ty, *n.*, power content, volume

cap-a-pie' (pē), *adv.*, from head to foot

cá·par'i·sòn, *n.*, horse covering

cāpe, *n.*, sleeveless garment covering shoulders

cā'pẽr, *v.*, frolic about

cap'il·lār·y, *n.*, slender tube, **ity**

cap'i·tál, *n.*, place where government is located

cap'i·tál·ism, *n.*, private ownership, **ist**

cap'i·tál·īze, *v.*, take advantage of

cap'i·tál·ly, *adv.*, excellently

cap'i·tā'tion, *n.*, tax on each individual, head tax

Cap'i·tŏl, *n.*, U. S. Congress meeting place

cà·pit'ū·lāte, *v.*, surrender, **lation**

cā'pon, *n.*, castrated rooster

cà·pric'ci·ō (prēe-chi-ō), *n.*, irregular form

cà·prīce' (prēes), *n.*, unpredictable change of mind, whim, **pricious**

cap·sīze', *v.*, overturn

cap'sule (sil), *n.*, small gelatin container

cap'tain (tên), *n.*, chief, military rank

cap'tion, *n.*, page or picture title

cap'tious, *a.*, fault-finding

cap'ti·vāte, *v.*, charm, attract by beauty

cap'tive, *n.*, person caught and held, **tivity**

cap'ture, *v.*, seize, take by force

cap'ū·chin, *n.*, monkey of C. and S. America

cá·put' (coll.), *a.*, dead, finished

cär, *n.*, automobile

car'á·cul, *n.*, flat-type fur of Asian sheep

car'a·mel, *n.*, chewy candy

car'at, *n.*, unit of weight of precious stones, ⅕ ounce

car'a·van, *n.*, group traveling together

car·a·van'sá·ry, *n.*, Oriental hotel or inn

cär'bīne, *n.*, short rifle

cär-bō-hy'drāte, *n.*, organic compounds: starch, sugar, etc.

cär·bol'ic, *a.*, obtained from coal

cär'bòn, *n.*, non-metallic element: diamond, coal, etc. **-ic**

cär'bŏn mŏn-ox'īde, *n.*, poisonous gas

cär'bòn pā'pẽr, *n.*, prepared paper for making extra typed copies

cär-bō-run'dum, *n.*, an abrasive

cär'bun-cle, *n.*, inflammation of skin tissue, boil

cär'bu-re-tôr (bi-ray), *n.*, engine fuel mixer

cär'cáss, *n.*, dead body of animal

cär-ci-nō'má, *n.*, cancer

cärd, *n.*, stiff piece of paper, show-off

car'da-mom, *n.*, aromatic seed

cärd'bôard, *n.*, thick gauge paper

cär'di-ac, *a.*, relating to heart

cär'di-gan, *n.*, knitted woolen jacket

cär'di-nál, *a.*, *n.*, of chief importance, bird, Catholic Church official

cärd'shärp, *n.*, professional cheater at cards

câre, *n.*, concern, anxiety

câre, *v.*, be concerned about, have regard for

cà·rēen', *v.*, lean to one side, clean ship on side, lurch

cà·rēen', *n.*, ship lying on side, **-er**

cà·rēer', *n.*, occupation in life

câre'frēe, *a.*, without worry

câre'ful, *a.*, performed with caution, **-ly**

câre'less, *a.*, unconcerned, performed thoughtlessly

cà·ress', *v.*, kiss, touch lovingly

car'ét, *n.*, mark to show an insertion in printing

câre'tāk-ẽr, *n.*, person who looks after a building or estate

câre'wôrn, *a.*, worried, troubled

cär'fāre, *n.*, money charged for transportation

cär'hop, *n.*, waitress serving patrons in cars

car'i-bou (boo), n., reindeer

car'i-ca-ture (chewr), n., exaggerated portrait, cartoon

cãr'ies, n., tooth decay, **ious**

car'il-lon, n., bells which play tunes

cari'-ole, n., horse carriage

cãr'line, n., witch, hag

cãr'nage, n., killing of many people

cãr'nal, a., of the flesh, sexual, **ity**

cãr-nā'tion, n., many-petalled flower

cãr'ne-ous, a., flesh-like

cãr'ni-val, n., traveling circus-like show

cãr'ni-vore, n., flesh-eating animal, **vorous**

car'ol, n., joyful song, **-er**

car'om, n., shot made in billiards

cã-rouse' (rowz), v., drink, entertain noisily

cãrp, v., criticize, complain

cãrp, n., fish

cãr'pel, n., flower part

cãr'pen-ter, n., worker with lumber, **try**

cãr'pet, n., floor covering, rug, **-ing**

cãr'pôrt, n., roofed wall-less shelter for auto

car'riage (rij), n., wheeled horse drawn transport for people, way of walking

car'ri-êr (ree), n., one who carries

car'ri-ôn, n., decaying flesh

cãr'rot, n., yellow vegetable

car-rõu-sel' (i-sel), n., merry-go-round

car'ry, v., take something from place to place, transport

car'ry õ'vêr, n., something which remains, postponement

cãr'sick, a., made sick by motion

cãrt, n., vehicle for carrying goods, **-age**

cãrte blanche' (blonsh), n., complete power

cãr'tel', n., international monopoly

cãr'ti-lãge, n., bone-like tissue, gristle, **laginous**

cãr-tog'ra-phy, n., drawing of maps, **pher**

cãr'tõn, n., cardboard box

cãr-tõõn', n., sarcastic or amusing drawing, **-ist**

cãr'tridge, n., tube-like container

cãrve, v., cut

cãrv'ing, n., carved work

car-y-at'id, n., female carved figure

cas-cãde', n., waterfall

cas-car'á, n., laxative

cãse (coll.), v., inspect

cãse, n., container, box, holder

cãse'ment, n., window opening

cã'sē-ous, a., resembling cheese

cash, n., money

ca-shew', n., nut

cash-iêr', n., person in charge of money

cash'mere, n., woolen cloth

cash' reg'is-têr, n., machine holding money, and showing amounts, making change

cãs'ing, n., covering

cá-si'nõ (sēe), n., building for amusement purpose

cask, n., barrel

cas'ket, n., coffin

cas-sā'tion, n., annulment

cas'se-rōle, n., baking dish

cas-sette', n., case holding tape recorder reels

cás-si'nõ (sēe), n., card game

cas'sock, n., garment worn by ministers

cast, v., throw, throw off

cas-ta-net', n., shells used as musical instruments

cast'a-way, n., person shipwrecked

caste, n., social group

caste'mark, n., mark on forehead denoting social class

cast'êr, n., small wheel under furniture

cas'ti-gãte, v., severely criticize, **-gation**

cast'ing, n., selection of persons to act in a show

cast'i-ron (êrn), n., alloy of iron

cas'tle, n., stately walled residence

cas'tle, n., chess move, chess piece, **-d**

cast'-ôff, a., thrown aside

cas'tôr oil (ter), n., laxative

cas'trāte, v., remove

testicles, **-tration**

cas'ū·ál, *a.,* occurring by accident, chance

cas'ū·ál·ty (kazh), *n.,* accident, person injured

cas'ū·ist·ry (n), *n.,* ethical principles applied to conduct, misleading reasoning

cat, *n.,* domestic feline animal

cá·tab'ō·lism, *n.,* breaking down of tissue

cat'á·clysm, *n.,* upheaval, violent physical change, **-ic**

cat'á·cōmb, *n.,* underground burial place

cat'a·falque (falk), *n.,* coffin raised on stand

cat'á·lep·sy, *n.,* state of rigidity, loss of contact

cat'á·lóg, *n.,* list of books, articles arranged along a specific line

cat'á·lyst, *n.,* something causing a chemical reaction but remaining unchanged, **-lytic**

cat·á·má·ran', *n.,* boat with two hulls

cat'á·pult, *v.,* hurl with force

cat'á·ract, *n.,* waterfall, eye disease

cá·tärrh', *n.,* nose and throat disease

cá·tas'trō·phē, *n.,* sudden disaster, **-phic**

cat'cáll, *n.,* cat-like noise expressing disapproval

catch, *n.,* something caught, **-er**

catch, *v.,* capture, seize

catch'-all, *n.,* bag or basket for odds and ends

catch'ing, *a.,* attractive, infecting

catch'up (also ketchup, catsup), *n.,* tomato sauce

catch'y, *a.,* easily caught (as a tune)

cat'ē·chism (kism), *n.,* training in religious doctrine, **-chize**

cat·ē·gōr'i·cál, *a.,* direct, unqualified

cat'ē·gō·ry, *n.,* grouping, classification

cā'tēr, *v.,* provide food for, serve, **-er**

cat'er·cor·nered, *a.,* diagonal

cat'ēr·pil·lár, *n.,* butterfly larva, type of tractor

cat'ēr·wäul, *v.,* imitate cat sounds

cat'gut, *n.,* musical instrument string of animal intestines

cá·thär'sis, *n.,* purge or release, cleanse, **-tic**

cath'ōde, *n.,* negative electrode

cath'ō·lic, *a.,* universal, **-ity**

Cath'ō·lic, *a.,* pertaining to universal church

cat'nap, *n.,* short sleep

cat'nip, *n.,* mint attractive to cats

cat-ō'·nīne'-tāils, *n.,* type of whip

cat'sup, *n.,* same as catchup, ketchup

cat'tle, *n.,* bovine animals

cat'ty, *a.,* gossipy

CATV, *n.,* community antenna television

cat'wälk, *n.,* narrow bridge high above area

cäu'cus (cäw), *n.,* political party meeting

cäu'dāte, *a.,* possessing tail

cäu'li·flow·ēr, *n.,* vegetable

cäus'ál, *a.,* relating to a cause, **-ity**

cäuse, *n.,* something that brings about a happening

cäu·se·riē', *n.,* informal chat

cäuse'way, *n.,* raised pathway or road

cäus'tic, *a.,* substance that burns, critical, **-ally**

cäu'tēr·īze, *v.,* burn with hot iron, **-ization**

cäu'tion, *n.,* alert, careful behavior, **-tious**

cav·ál·cāde', *n.,* procession, parade

cav·á·liēr', *n.,* horseman, gentleman, **-ly**

cav'ál·ry, *n.,* soldiers on horseback

cāve, *n.,* a hollow inside earth

cāve'man, *n.,* prehistoric man

cav'ērn, *n.,* large cave, **-ous**

cav'i·är, *n.,* delicacy made of sturgeon eggs

cav'il, *v.,* find fault with

cav'i·ty, *n.,* hollow place, hole

cá·vōrt', *v.,* prance around

cay·enne', *n.,* hot red pepper

cay·use', *n.,* Indian pony

cēase, *v.,* stop, **-less**

cēase' fīre, *n.,* halt to

fighting

ce′dar, n., evergreen tree

cēde, v., yield to someone else

ceil′ing, n., top of a room

cel′e·brate, v., observe by ceremony, **-bration**

ce·ler′i·ty, n., speed

cel′er·y, n., a long stalked vegetable

ce·les′tă, n., musical instrument

ce·les′tial, a., relating to heavens

cel′i·bàte, n., unmarried person, **-bacy**

cell, n., tiny room, smallest bit of living matter, unit of organization

cel′lar, n., underground room

cel′lō (chel), n., stringed musical instrument, **-list**

cel′lō·phāne, n., a transparent paper material

cel′lū·loid (cel-yoer), n., product of cellulose

cel′lū·lōse, n., substance from plant cell walls

cè·ment′, n., construction material

cem′e·ter·y, n., graveyard

cen′ō·bite, n., convent dweller, **-bitic**

cen′ō·taph, n., sepulchral, monument

cense′, v., burn incense

cen′sŏr, n., official examiner of movies, books, etc., **-ship**

cen′sure, n., strong expression of disapproval

cen′sus, n., official counting of inhabitants

cent, n., 1/100th of a dollar

cen′taur, n., mythical man-horse

cen·te·nar′ian, adj., having age of 100 years

cen′te·nâr·y, a., relating to 100 years, **-ian**

cen·ten′ni·ăl, n., 100th anniversary

cen′têr, n., middle point

cen′têr·piēce, n., flowers for middle of table

cen′ti·grāde, a., divided into 100 degrees

cen′ti·mē·têr, n., 100th of a meter

cen′ti·pēde, n., many legged insect

cen′tral, a., middle, main center, **-ize**

cen·trif′u·găl (i-găl), a., directed away from center, **-ly**

cen·trip′è·tăl, a., directed toward the center

cen′tu·ry, n., one hundred years

cè·phal′ic, a., relating to the head, **-ous**

cè·phal′ic in′dex, n., measurement of head

cè·ram′ic, a., pottery

cē′rate, n., drug ointment

cer′á·toid, a., hornlike

cē′rē·ăl, n., edible grain

cer·è·bel′lum, n., lower brain part

cer′è·brum, n., upper brain part, **-bral**

cer′è·mō·ny, n., formal act for some occasion, **-monial**

ce·rise′, a., red

cē·rog′rà·phy, n., writing in wax

cêr′tain (tèn), a., for sure

cêr′tain·ly, adv., without question

cêr·tif′i·cäte, n., document stating facts to be true, **-cation**

cêr′ti·fy, v., declare as truthful

cêr′vix, n., neck-like opening, **-vical**

ces·sā′tion, n., stoppage

cess′pōōl, n., drainage pit

cè·tol′ŏ·gy, n., study of whales

chāfe, v., rub against, irritate

chāf′ing dish, n., pan to keep food warm

chà·grin′, n., disappointment

chāin, n., connected links

chāin′man, n., surveyor helper

chāin rè·ac′tion, n., continued atomic explosion

chāin′stōre, n., number of retail stores belonging to same company

chāir, n., a seat with back

châir′man, n., presiding officer, **woman**

chāise (shayz), n., two-wheeled carriage

chāise longue′ (long), n., couch-like chair

chal′ice, n., wine cup

chälk, n., limestone used for writing

chal′lenge, n., summons to complete, **-r**

chăm'bĕr, n., room, hall

chām'bĕr-lain (lĕn) n., household manager

chām'bĕr-māid, n., female domestic

chăm'bĕr mū'sic, n., string music played by small group

chá-mē'lē-ŏn (ki-mēe-li-in), n., lizard which changes skin color

cham'ois (sham-y) n., cloth from sheep skin

champ (coll.), n., champion

cham-pāgne' (payn), n., sparkling wine

cham'pāign (payn), n., open country

chăm'pi-ŏn, n., best in its field, **-ship**

chance, n., accident, opportunity

chance, v., risk

chan'cĕl, n., space near church altar

chan'cĕl-lŏr, n., judge, university official

chan'cre (kĕr), n., sore of syphilis

chan'cy, a., risky

chan-dē-liĕr' (di-lēr), n., light fixture from ceiling

chan'dlĕr, n., supplier of ship goods

change, v., alter, exchange, substitute, **-able**

change, n., something different, coins

change'lĕss, a., never changing

change'ling, n., one child substituted for another

chan'nĕl, n., stream bed, groove, television frequency band

chan'nĕl, v., form groove, direct something, body of water

chan-sŏn-nette', n., song

chant, n., form of song, intonation, **-er**

chant'ey, n., sailor's song

chā'os, n., confusion, **-otic**

chap, v., roughen

chap, n., boy or man (coll.)

cha-peau' (sha-pō), n., hat

chap'ĕl, n., place of prayer

chap'e-rŏn, n., female accompanier

chap'lain (len), n., religious minister, **-cy**

chap'tĕr, n., division of book,

branch of organization

chär, v., burn

char'ác-tĕr (k), n., combination of qualities

char-ác-tĕr-is'tic (k), n., distinguishing quality, **-ally**

char-ác-tĕr-i-zā'tion, n., description

chá-rāde (shi-rayd), n., game involving acting out

chär'cōal, n., carbon left after burning wood

chärge, v., give order, send electricity through battery, create debt, **-able**

chärge, n., duty, responsibility, attack by soldiers

chärge' ác-count, n., account for credit purchases

chär-ge-d'áf-fāires' (shär-zhay d'fayr), n., diplomat

chärge'plāte, n., identification plate for credit buying

char'i-ŏt, n., ancient two-wheeled vehicle, **-eer**

char'i-ty, n., assistance given to the needy, **-table**

chär'lâ-tán, n., quack, fake, **-ism**

chär'ley hôrse, n., painfully contracted muscle

chär'lŏtte, n., fruit dessert

chärm, n., fascination, **-ing**

chärm'ĕr (coll.), n., attractive person

chärt, n., summation of figures, maps, graph

chär'tĕr, n., certificate giving rights and privileges

chär'tĕr mem-bĕr, n., original member

chär-treūse' (shär-trōoz), n., yellowish-green color

chär'wom-án, n., cleaning woman

chär'y, a., careful

chāse, v., pursue

chāse, n., hunt

chās'ĕr, n., water, etc., taken after alcohol

chasm (kazim), n., gap in the earth

chas'sis (ēē), n., framework for auto

chāste, a., pure, virtuous

chās'tĕn, v., discipline

chas'tīse (tyz), v., punish, esp. corporal **-ment**

chas'ti-ty, *n.*, virtue, virginity

chat, *v.*, talk informally

châ-teau' (to) (n.), house

chat'tel, *n.*, moveable property

chat'ter, *v.*, talk rapidly

chat'ter box, *n.*, person who talks excessively

chauf'feur (shō-fēr), *n.*, one who drives for someone else

chau'vin-ism (shō), *n.*, false patriotism

cheap, *a.*, low cost, low grade, **-ly**

cheap'en, *v.*, make inferior, lower

cheat, *v.*, deceive, be dishonest

cheat, *n.*, dishonest person

check, *n.*, order for bank to pay money, restraining action

check, *v.*, stop, restrain, examine

check'ered, *a.*, having variety, squared

check'ers, *n.*, game played on board with squares

check'mate, *v.*, winning chess move, **-d**

check-off, *n.*, collection of union dues

check'up, *n.*, examination, verification

cheek, *n.*, face below the eye and above jaw, impudence

cheep, *n.*, bird sound, peep

cheer, *v.*, acclaim with loud shout, **-ful**

cheer'y, *a.*, happy, bright

cheese, *n.*, milk curd

cheese'bûrg-er, *n.*, hamburger cooked with cheese

cheese' cake, *n.*, cake made of cheese, (coll.) leg art

cheese' cloth, *n.*, loosely woven cotton cloth

chees'y, *a.*, resembling cheese, (coll.) cheap-looking

chef, *n.*, male cook, head cook

ché-mise' (she-mēez), *n.*, female undergarment

chem'ist (kem), *n.*, scientist who studies substances and elements, **-ry**

chem-ō-ther'a-py, (k) *n.*, chemical treatment of disease

cher'ish, *v.*, to consider fondly

chê-rōōt' (shi) (n.), cigar

cher'ry, *n.*, bright red fruit

cher'ub, *n.*, little angel, sweet child, **-ic**

chess, *n.*, game played on board marked with squares

chess'board, *n.*, board with 64 squares

chess'men, *n.*, 32 pieces used in chess game

chest, *n.*, body immediately below neck, furniture for storage

chest'nut, *n.*, tree, edible nut, (coll.) often-repeated joke

chest'y, *a.*, large-chested, large bosomed

chev'rŏn, *n.*, stripes designating military rank

chew, *v.*, crush between teeth

chi-ä-rō-scū'rŏ (k), *n.*, placement of light and shade in a picture

chic, (eek) *a.*, stylish

chi-cān'ér-y (shi), *n.*, trickery

chick, *n.*, baby chicken

chick'en, *n.*, domesticated fowl

chick'en-heärt'éd, *a.*, timid

chick'en pox, *n.*, disease

chic'ō-ry, *n.*, plant, used in preparing salad or coffee

chide, *v.*, scold

chief, *n.*, main leader of group

chief'ly, *adv.*, most important, main

chif-fon' (shi), *n.*, sheer fabric

chif-fö-nier', *n.*, chest of drawers

chig'gér, *n.*, insect

chi-huä'huä (shi-wä-wä), *n.*, tiny dog

child, *n.*, baby or infant, **-ish**

child'birth, *n.*, giving birth

child'hood, *n.*, period of infancy to puberty

chil'i (ee), *n.*, highly spiced seasoning

chil'i cŏn cär'nē, *n.*, Mexican dish of meat and beans

chill, *v.*, make cold, **-y**

chime, *n.*, musical sound

chi-mē'ra (ki), *n.*, legendary monster, imaginative monster, **-rical**

chim'ney, *n.*, structure for carrying off smoke

chim-pan'zēe, *n.*, ape

chin, *n.*, jaw front

chin, *v.*, pull self up and down by hands

chī'na, n., crockery, **-ware**

chin-chil'lä, n., Peruvian fur-bearing rodent

chink, n., crack

chintz, n., shiny cotton cloth

chip, n., small broken off piece

chip'pêr, a., spirited, cheerful

chi-rog'ra-phy (ki), n., handwriting

chi-rop'ö-dist (ki), n., doctor who treats feet

chī'rö-prac-tör (k), n., treater of diseases by massage, **-tic**

chirp, n., bird or insect sound

chis'él, n., cutting tool

chis'él-êr (coll.), n., one who borrows without repaying

chit'-chat, n., informal talk

chiv'ál-ry, n., gallantry, **-rous**

chīve, n., type of onion plant

chlô'rine (klōrēen), n., chemical element, **-ride**

chlô'rö-fôrm (k), n., type of anesthetic

chlô-rö-my-cē'tin (k), n., antibiotic drug

chlô'rö-phyll (k) (fil), n., green substance in plants

choc'ö-läte, n., flavor from cacao beans

choice, n., that which is chosen

choir (kwyr), n., group of singers

chōke, v., be unable to breathe, strangle

chōk'êr, n., short necklace

chol'êr-á, n., stomach

chōöse, v., select

chop, v., cut up into small parts

chop, n., meat slice, sharp blow

chop'py, a., rough

chop'sticks, n., Chinese eating utensils

chop sü'ey, n., Japanese vegetable and meat dish with rice

chō'rál (k), a., pertaining to chorus

chôrd (kôrd), n., musical notes combined

chôre, n., small task

chō-rē'á (k), n., muscle disease, St. Vitus's dance

chō-rē-og'ra-phêr (k), n., designer of a ballet, **-phy**

chôr'is-têr (k), n., one who sings in choir

chôr'tle, v., chuckle

chô'rus (k), n., group of singers or dancers

chō'sèn (zén), a., selected

chow, n., dog food, breed of dog

chow'dêr, n., fish soup

chow mein' (mayn), n., Chinese vegetables served with noodles

chres-tom'á-thy, n., collected passages

chris'tèn, v., baptize into Christian church

chrō-mat'ic, a., relating to color, half-tone musical steps

chrō'mi-um, n., metallic element

chrō'mö-sōme, n., human matter affecting heredity

chron'ic, a., continuous, long-term

chron'i-cle, n., account of happenings

chrō-nol'ö-gy, n., arrangement of events according to time, **-logical**

chrō-nom'e-têr, n., very accurate watch or clock

chry-san'thê-mum, n., showy flowering plant

chub'by, a., plump

chuck, n., v., beef cut, (coll.) get rid of

chuck'le, n., laugh to oneself

chug, n., short, sudden sound, as engine

chum, n., friend, **-my**

chump (coll.), n., fool

chunk, n., thick piece, **-y**

chûrch, n., place of Christian worship, **-ly**

chûrl, n., crude person, **-ish**

chûrn, v., agitate, make butter

chūte, n., long tube

ci-cā'dä (si-kay), n., chirping insect

cī'dêr (sy), n., drink made of apples

ci-gär', n., tobacco leaves rolled together

cig-á-rette', n., shredded tobacco rolled in paper

cil'i-âr-y, a., hairlike

cinch (coll.), n., something easy or certain

cinc'ture, n., belt

cin'dêr, n., piece of burned wood or coal

cin'e-mä, n., moving picture

Cin'e-mä-scōpe, n., moving

picture on wide, curved screen

cin′nà-mön, n., spice

cī′phêr, n., zero

cîr′cá (sir), adv., approximate date

cîr′cle, n., closed curve in which all points are equidistant from center

cîr′cuit (kit), n., movement in a specified course, electric current path

cîr-cū′i-tous, a., round-about

cîr′cū-làr, a., form of circle, -ize

cîr-cū-lā′tion, n., blood flow through body, sending something from place to place, -te

cîr-cum-am′bi-ènt, a., surrounding

cîr′cum-cīse, v., remove foreskin, -cision

cîr-cum′fêr-ence, n., boundary of circular area

cîr-cum-flū′ènt, a., flowing around

cîr′cum-scrībe′, v., set limits to, encircle, -scription

cîr′cum-spect, a., cautious

cîr′cum-stance, n., happening, -stan′tial

cîr-cum-vent′, v., go around, outwit

cîr′cus, n., traveling show with clowns, animals, etc.

cîr′rus, n., fleecy type cloud

cis-lū′nar, adj., space between earth and moon

cis′têrn, n., tank for water storage

cit′à-dĕl, n., guarded fortress

cī-tā′tion, n., mention of, official praise

cīte, v., quote an authoritative source

cit′i-fied, a., influenced by ways of city

cit′i-zĕn, n., person belonging to a community, -ship

cit′ric ac′id, n., acid from citrus fruits

cit-rön-el′lá, n., aromatic liquid to keep mosquitoes away

cit′rous, a., relating to citrus fruit, grapefruit, oranges, etc.

cit′y, n., large incorporated community

civ′ic, a., relating to citizenship or community

civ′ics, n., study of citizenship

civ′il, a., relating to civilians, polite

ci-vil′ian, n., non-military person

ci-vil′i-ty, n., politeness

civ-i-li-zā′tion, n., society at an advanced level in culture

civ′i-līze, v., refine, educate away from barbarous living, -d

civ′il lib′êr-ty, n., personal freedom

civ′il wâr, n., war between citizens of same country

civ′viês, n., non-military clothes worn by soldiers, sailors off duty

clack, v., produce sharp sound

clāim, v., make demand for, -ant

clāim, n., demand, right to something

clâir-vōy′ance, n., ability to predict future, -ant

clam, n., oyster-like bi-valve

clam, v., say nothing, (coll.)

clam′bāke, n., picnic

clam′my, a., cold and damp

clam′ör, n., loud noise, -ous

clamp, n., device for holding something

clan, n., families living together, relatives

clang, n., loud metallic sound

clan′nish, a., closely allied, disliking outsiders

clap, n., applaud

clap′bōard, n., wood covering for house

clap′trap, n., foolish talk

claque (clak), n., professionally hired applauder

clar′ĕt, n., dark red wine

clar′i-fy, v., make clear, -fication

clar′i-net′, n., musical woodwind instrument, -ist

clar′i-ön, a., clear, sharp

clar′i-ty, n., clearness

clash, n., disagreement, noise of a collision

clasp, n., device which fastens

clasp, v., embrace, hold firmly

class, n., group of people, type

class, v., group by category

clas'sic, a., of best taste, relating to Greece or Rome, **-al**

clas'si·fy, v., arrange in orderly groups, **-fication**

clas'si·fied, a., secret, arrange in sequence

class'māte, n., friend in same class

class'rŏŏm, n., teaching room in school

class'y (coll.) a., fancy

clat'tĕr, n., banging sound

clău·di·ca'tion, n., a limp

clause, n., part of a sentence

clău·strŏ·phō'bi·å, n., fear of being enclosed

cla'vĕr, n., idle talk

clav'i·cle, n., collarbone

clā'vi·êr, n., musical instrument

clăw, n., toenail on animal foot

clay, n., earth substance

clēan, a., free from dirt, pure, **-ly**

clēan, v., get rid of dirt

clēan'-cut, a., neat

clēan'êr, n., chemical or person that cleans

cleanse (klenz), v., make clean

clēan' up (coll.), v., make huge profits

clēar, a., bright, easy to see, calm

clēar, v., prove innocence, remove blemish, **-ly**

clēar'ance, n., sale of goods reduced price

clēar'-cut, a., understandable

clēar'head'ĕd, a., intelligent, not intoxicated

clēar'ing, n., open space in forest

clēar'ing house, n., establishment for bank check clearance

clēat, n., shoe spike for sports

clēav'age, n., division

clēave, v., split, separate

clēav'êr, n., large butcher knife

clef, n., musical symbol

cleft, n., split

clench, v., grip firmly

clêr'gy, n., religious ministers, **-man**

cler'ic, n., clergy member, **-al**

clêrk, n., office or store worker

clev'êr, a., smart, intelligent, **-ness**

clew, n., thread, yarn

cli·ché (shay), n., trite, worn out expression

click, n., sharp sound

clī'ént, n., one who receives services, **-ele**

cliff, n., steep rocky surface

clī·măc'tĕr·ic, n., crucial time

clī·măc'tic, a., forming a climax

clī'māte, n., weather

clī·mà·tŏl'ŏ·gy, n., science of weather conditions

clī'max, n., peak, culmination

clīmb, v., move upward

clinch, v., fasten together, (coll.) win

clinch'êr (coll.), n., decisive happening

cling, v., stick, hold tightly

clin'ic, n., out-patient treatment center, **-cál**

clink, n., jingling sound

clip, v., cut

clip, n., metal piece for holding objects together

clip'pêr, n., old-time sailing vessel

clip'ping, n., article cut from newspaper or book

clique (klik), n., exclusive group of people

clit'ŏ·ris, n., sensitive female sex part

clō·ā'cá (ka), n., toilet, sewer

clōak, n., loose hanging outer garment

clŏche (klosh), n., woman's hat

clock, n., device for telling time

clock, v., measure time or speed

clock'wīse, a., circling to the right

clod, n., clump of earth

clog, v., obstruct

clog, n., shoe, type of dance

clois'tĕr, n., quiet place, religious retreat

clōse (klōz), v., bring together, end, shut, obstruct

clōse, a., near, without fresh air, stingy, united

clōse'cáll, n., narrow escape

clōsed shŏp', n., hiring only union members

clōse′ fist-ĕd, *a.*, stingy

clōse′ mouthed, *a.*, not talking, reserved

clos′ĕt, *n.*, small area for storing clothes, toilet

clōse′up, *n.*, picture at close range

clot, *n.*, clump, **-ted**

clŏth, *n.*, fabric

clōthe, *v.*, put on clothes

clōthes′hōrse, *n.*, frame for drying clothes on, (coll.) stylish person

clŏth′ing, *n.*, apparel

clō′ture (chĕr), *n.*, stopping debate

cloud, *n.*, water mass in sky, **-y**

cloud′bûrst, *n.*, sudden rainstorm

cloud′-capped, *a.*, surrounded by clouds

clout, *v.*, *n.*, strike, blow

clōve, *n.*, spice

clō′vêr, *n.*, plant

clown, *n.*, circus funny man, **-ish**

club, *n.*, heavy stick, persons organized together

club′cel-lár, *n.*, cellar entertainment room

club′foot, *n.*, deformed foot, **-ed**

club′ sand-wich, *n.*, three-tiered sandwich

cluck, *n.*, sound of hen

clūe (klōō), *n.*, guide to solution of mystery

clump, *n.*, mass, cluster

clum′sy, *a.*, awkward

clus′têr, *n.*, things bunched together

clutch, *v.*, hold tightly

clut′têr, *n.*, disorderly mess

cōach, *n.*, auto with two doors, instructor of athletes

cōach, *v.*, instruct in athletics, or other subjects, **-ing**

cō-ag′ū-lāte, *v.*, dry into a mass, as blood, **-lation**

cōal, *n.*, carbon mineral

cō-à-lĕsce, *v.*, grow together

cō-à-li′tion, *n.*, union

cōarse, *a.*, rough, crude

cōast, *n.*, shore-line, **-al**

cōat, *n.*, heavy outer garment

cōat′ing, *n.*, surface covering

cōat ŏf arms, *n.*, family crest

cō-au′thôr, *v.*, join with another in writing

cōax (kōhx), *v.*, attempt to

persuade

cō-ax′i-ăl (ĕē), *a.*, type of insulated cable used in television

cob, *n.*, inside of ear of corn, horse

cō′bălt, *n.*, metallic element, shade of blue

cob′blêr, *n.*, shoe repairman

cob′ble stōne, *n.*, type of paving stone

cō′brà, *n.*, poisonous snake

cob′web, *n.*, spider web

cō-cāine′, *n.*, narcotic

coc′cus, *n.*, single-celled organism, (pl.) **ci**

cock, *n.*, rooster

cock, *v.*, turn head to one side

cock′á-tōō, *n.*, parrot

cock′êr, *n.*, breed of dog

cock′eyed, *a.*, off center, wrong

cock′pit, *n.*, pilot room

cock′rōach, *n.*, insect

cock′tāil, *n.*, mixed alcoholic drink

cock′y, *a.*, conceited, sure

cō′cōa, *n.*, ground cacao seeds, beverage

cō′cō-nut, *n.*, hard-shelled edible seed

cō-cōōn′, *n.*, insect's silky covering

cod, *n.*, fish

cō′dà, *n.*, added musical passage at end of composition

cod′dle, *v.*, treat gently

cōde, *n.*, secret message, set of rules

codg′êr, *n.*, queer old person

cōd′i-fy, *v.*, arrange in code, **-fication**

cō′ed′, *n.*, female student at college

cō-ed-ū-cā′tion, *n.*, classes with both male and female, **-al**

cō-ĕf-fi′cient, *n.*, that which combines

cō-êrce′, *v.*, force, **-ercion**

cō-ē′vál, *a.*, similar in age

cō-ĕx-ist′, *v.*, exist together

cŏf′fēe, *n.*, beverage from coffee beans

cŏf′fin, *n.*, casket for burying corpse

cog, *n.*, tooth fitted in gear wheel

cō′gĕnt, *a.*, powerful

cog′i-tāte, *v.*, think seriously

cō′gnac, (nyak), *n.*, brandy

cog'nāte, a., related by birth

cog'ni·zánce, n., knowledge

cog·nō'mén, n., nick-name

cō·hab'it, v., live as husband and wife

cō·hēre', v., stick

cō·hēr'ént, a., clear

cō·hē'sion, n., sticking together

cō'hôrt, n., associate or partner

coif·fūre' (kwäf), n., hair arrangement

coil, v., arrange in rings

coin, n., metal money

cō·in·cīde', v., happen exactly, agree

cō·in'ci·dénce, n., happening accidentally, occurring at same time as another, -dent

col'án·dér, n., strainer

cōld, a., low temperature

cōld, n., disease marked by nasal congestion and sneezing

cōld'blŏŏd'éd, a., cruel, having low blood temperature

cōld' crēam, n., cleansing facial salve

cōld' shŏŭl·dér, v., shun

cōld' wär, n., intense political rivalry between nations

cōle'slåw, n., salad of cabbage

col'ic, n., abdominal pains

col·i·sē'um, n., large building for public events

cō·lī'tis, n., colon inflammation

cōl·lab'ō·rāte, v., work together, assist enemy, -ration

cŏl·läge', n., form of modern art

cŏl·lapse', v., crumble

col'lär, n., article worn around neck

col·lāte', v., arrange pages, -lation

cŏl·lat'ér·ál, a., side by side

cŏl·lat'ér·ál, n., security for loan

col'lēague (leeg), n., associate

cŏl·lect', v., receive payment, gather together, -ion

cŏl·lec'tive, a., taken together, -ly

cŏl·lec'tiv·ism, n., government control of production and

consumption

cŏl·lec'tôr, n., person who collects items or bills

col'lēge, n., school of higher learning

cŏl·līde', v., come forcibly into contact with

col'lie, n., breed of dog

col'liér·y (yér-ēe), n., coal mine

cŏl'li·māte, v., make parallel

cŏl·lī'qui·ál, a., informal, slang, -ism, -ly

col'lō·quy, n., discussion

cŏl·lūde', v., conspire

cŏl·lū'sion, n., secret agreement

cō·lōgne' (lone), n., perfume

cō'lon, n., punctuation mark, part of intestine

colo·nél' (kér), n., army officer

cŏl·ō'ni·ál, a., relating to colonies

col'ō·ny, n., group who settle in another country

cŏl'ôr, n., yellow, blue, green, etc., -ful, -less

cŏl'ôr blīnd, a., unable to distinguish colors

cŏl'ôr līne, n., social distinction between white and black persons

cō·los·sál, a., huge, -sus

cōlt, n., young horse

col'um·bīne, n., plant

col'umn, n., pillar, row of figures

col'um·nist, n., newspaper article writer

cō'må, n., unconsciousness

com'á·tōse, a., slow moving, unconscious

cōmb (kōm), n., device to groom hair

cŏm'bat, n., fight, -ant

cŏm·bat', v., fight

cŏm'bat fá·tigue (tēeg), n., nervous condition due to battle

com·bi·nā'tion, n., union of individuals, lock, mechanism

cŏm·bīne', v., put together

com'bīne', n., harvesting and threshing machine, association

cŏm·bus'tion, n., process of burning

cōme, v., move toward

come′back, n., success after failure

cö-mē′di-àn, n., humorous actor, **-enne**

com′e-dy, n., humorous entertainment

come′ly, a., pleasing to the eye

com′ét, n., long-tailed celestial body moving around sun

com′fŏrt, v., sympathize with, **-ing**

com′fŏrt-à-ble (kumf-tèr-ble), a., giving ease, pleasant feeling **-ly**

com′fŏrt-êr (fèrt-èr), n., quilted bed cover

com′ic, a., humorous

com′i-ty, n., courtesy

com′mà, n., punctuation mark

com-mand′, v., give order, **-ing**

com-man-dànt, n., officer in charge

com-man-deēr′, v., seize property for military use

com-mand′êr, n., person who is in charge

com-man′dŏ, n., military group for organized raids

com-mem′o-rāte, v., honor the memory of, **-ration**

com-mence′, v., start

com-mence′mént, n., graduation, beginning

com-mend′, v., praise **-ation**

com-men′su-rāte (shi-rit), a., equal to

com′ment, n., remark

com′mén-tär-y, n., explanatory presentation

com′mén-tā-tŏr, n., person who discusses events

com′mêrce, n., trade

com-mêr′cial, a., pertaining to commerce, radio or TV sales talk, **-ize**

com-min′gle, v., mingle together

com-mi-nūte, v., break into small pieces, **-ion**

com-mis′êr-āte, v., sympathize with, **-ation**

com′mis-sär, n., political chief in Russia

com′mis-sär-y, n., store in army camp

com-mis′sion, n., authority to act, payment for selling

com-mis′sion-êr, n.,

government official

com-mit′, v., perpetrate act, give into keeping, **-ment**

com-mit′tēe, n., persons working together

com-mit′tēe-mán, n., member of a committee

com-mōde′, n., bureau

cö-mō′di-ous, a., large, roomy

com-mŏd′ity, n., article of commerce

com′mo-dŏre, n., naval officer

com′mon, a., ordinary, public, **-ly**

com′mon car′ri-êr, n., vehicle for hire

com′mon dē-nom′i-nā-tŏr, n., least divisible number

com′mon-êr, n., person not of royal blood

com′mon-plāce, a., ordinary

com′mons, n., college dining hall

com′mon-sense, a., sensible

com′mon-wealth, n., independent nation

cöm-mō′tion, n., uproar

com′mū-nàl, a., relating to community, public, **-ism**

com-mūne′, v., exchange thoughts

com-mū′ni-cànt, n., one who receives communion

com-mū′ni-cāte, v., give or receive information, **-cation**

com-mūn′ion, n., sharing together, religious rite

com-mū-ni-qué (kay), n., message, announcement

com′mu-nism, n., government which directs all production and consumption, **-nist**

com-mū′ni-ty, n., people living together

com-mū′ni-ty chest, n., organizations sharing in charity contributions

com′mū-tāte, v., reverse, alter direction, **-tation**

com-mūte′, v., change, travel regularly to a place, **-r**

com′pact, n., agreement, face powder container

com-pact′, a., placed tightly together, neat

com-pan′ion, n., friend, **-ship**

com′pá-ny, n., business organization, guests

com'pa-ra-ble, *a.*, can be compared with, **-bly**

cŏm-par'a-tive, *a.*, demonstrating comparison

cŏm-pāre', *v.*, determine similarity and differences, **-parison**

cŏm-pärt'ment, *n.*, room, enclosed area

cŏm'păss, *n.*, device for direction finding

cŏm-păs'sion, *n.*, sympathy, **-ate**

cŏm-păt'i-ble, *a.*, getting along together, **-bly, -bility**

cŏm-pā'tri-ŏt, *n.*, fellow citizen, **-ism**

cŏm-pel', *v.*, force

cŏm-pen'di-um, *n.*, summary

com'pen-sāte, *v.*, pay for, make up for, **-sation**

cŏm-pēte', *v.*, contest against

com'pe-tent, *a.*, skillful, capable, **-tence**

com-pe-ti'tion, *n.*, rivalry

cŏm-pīle', *v.*, collect and put together

com-pi-lā'tion, *n.*, collection

cŏm-plā'cĕnt, *a.*, self-satisfied, **-cency**

cŏm-plāin', *v.*, find fault with, **-ant**

cŏm-plāint', *n.*, objection

cŏm-plāi'sănt, *a.*, cooperative

com'ple-ment, *v.*, complete, **-ary**

cŏm-plēte', *v.*, fulfill, finish

cŏm-plēte', *a.*, whole, **-pletion**

cŏm-plēte'ly, *adv.*, wholly

com'plex, *n.*, obsession

cŏm-plex', *a.*, difficult, **-ity**

cŏm-plex'ion, *n.*, facial coloring

cŏm-plī'ance, *n.*, yielding, agreement, **-able**

com'plī-cāte, *v.*, make difficult, **-cation**

cŏm-plic'i-ty, *n.*, dishonest act with another against someone

com'pli-ment, *v.*, praise **-ary**

cŏm-ply', *v.*, act in agreement with

cŏm-pō'nent, *n.*, part

cŏm-pōrt', *v.*, behave properly, **-ment**

cŏm-pōse', *v.*, create something original

cŏm-pōsed', *a.*, calm

cŏm-pōs'ĕr, *n.*, writer of music

cŏm-pos'ite, *a.*, made of different parts

com-pō-si'tion, *n.*, creation, make-up, **-tor**

com'pōst, *n.*, decayed refuse

cŏm-pō'sure, *n.*, self-control

cŏm-pound', *v.*, mix together

com'pound, *n.*, mixture of 2 or more parts

com-prē-hend', *v.*, understand

com-prē-hen'sion, *n.*, understanding

com-prē-hen'sive, *a.*, all-inclusive

cŏm-press', *v.*, press together

cŏm-pres'sion, *n.*, pressure produced in engine

cŏm-prīse' (īz), *v.*, include, contain, consist of

com'prō-mīse (īz), *v.*, agree by yielding certain points

comp-trŏl'lĕr, *n.*, director of finances

cŏm-pul'sion, *n.*, force

cŏm-pul'sŏ-ry, *a.*, absolutely required

cŏm-punc'tion, *n.*, regret

cŏm-pūte', *v.*, figure, calculate, **-putation**

com-pūt'er-ize, *v.*, control by computer

com'rade, *n.*, friend

con, *adv.*, against

con (coll.), *v.*, cheat

con-cat-ē-nā'tion, *n.*, joined together

con-cāve', *a.*, curved inward, **-cavity**

cŏn-cēal', *v.*, hide

cŏn-cēde', *v.*, yield, agree to

cŏn-cēit', *n.*, self-importance, **-ed**

cŏn-cēive', *v.*, originate, imagine

con'cen-trāte, *v.*, think hard, bring together, **-tration**

con-cen-trā'tion camp, *n.*, prison camp

cŏn-cen'tric, *a.*, with a like center

con'cept, *n.*, thought, idea, **-ual**

cŏn-cep-tion, *n.*, originating idea

cŏn-cĕrn', *v.*, worry, care about, **-ing**

cŏn-cĕrn', *n.*, business organization, affair

con'cĕrt, *n.*, musical presentation

cŏn-cĕrt'ĕd, *a.*, united

cön·cer'tō (cher), n., solo orchestral composition

cön·ces'sion, n., yielding, right to conduct business

cön·cil'i·āte, v., please, reach an agreement, **-ation**

cön·cīse', a., short and to the point

con'clāve, n., private meeting

cön·clūde', v., reach decision, end, **clusion**

cön·coct', v., make, **-ion**

cön·com'i·tänt, n., following, something which goes with

cön·côrd', n., harmony, agreement, peace, **-ance**

con'côurse, n., avenue, flowing together

con'crēte, a., real, actual

con'crēte, n., cement

cön·cū·bīne, n., secondary wife

cön·cûr', v., agree, **-rence**

cön·cûr'rent, a., happening at same time

cön·cus'sion, n., shock, brain injury

cön·demn', v., disapprove, sentence to death, **-ation**

con·den·sā'tion, n., product caused by condensing

cön·dense', v., change from vapor to liquid, make concise

cön·dens' êr, n., device which stores electricity

con·dē·scend', v., graciously yield, lower oneself

con'di·ment, n., spice

cön·di'tion, n., state of being, term of agreement

cön·di'tion·ál, a., dependent upon

cön·dō'lence, n., sympathy for bereavement

cön·dōne', v., forgive

cön·dū'cive, a., inclining toward

con'duct, n., behavior

cön·duct', v., lead, direct, transmit, behave

cön·duc'tion, n., transmission of heat, electricity, etc.

cön·duc'tôr, n., one who leads orchestra, train or bus official

con'duit (dwit), n., underground pipe or tube

cōne, n., geometrical figure, cake in which ice cream is placed

Con'êl·rad, n., emergency radio system

cön·fec'tion, n., candy, etc.

cön·fec'tion·êr·y, n., store that sells sweets

cön·fed'êr·à·cy, n., joined states, **-tion**

cön·fêr', v., discuss, present, **-ence**

cön·fess', v., admit, **-ion**

cön·fet'ti, n., colored bits of paper

cön·fi·dánt', n., person who may be trusted

cön·fīde', v., impart valuable information

con'fi·dence, n., faith

con'fi·dence gāme, n., robbery by fraud

con'fi·dent, a., sure, certain

con·fi·den'tial, a., secret

cön·fig·ū·rā'tion, n., shape, outline, image

cön·fīne', v., keep in one place, lock up

cön·fîrm', v., show to be true, **-ation**

cön·fîrmed', a., habitual

con'fis·cāte, v., take possession of, **-cation**

con·flá·grā'tion, n., large fire

con'flict, n., fight, battle

con·flū'ence, n., flowing together

cön·fôrm', v., behave by accepted standards, **-ity**

cön·found', v., confuse

cön·frônt', v., accuse directly to someone, oppose

cön·fūse', v., mix up, **-fusion**

cön·fūte', v., prove to be mistaken

con'gà, n., Cuban dance

cön·gēal', v., harden

cön·gēn'ial, a., friendly, **-ity**

cön·gen'i·tál, a., born with

cön·gest', v., fill to excess

cön·glom·êr·ā'tion, n., mixture

cön·grat'u·lāte, v., offer good wishes, **-lation**

con'grē·gāte, v., gather together, **-gation**

con'grèss, n., meeting, conference, **-ional**

con·grū·ent, a., in agreement, **-ity**, **-ous**

cön·jec'ture, n., uncertain opinion, **-tural**

con'jū·gál, a., pertaining to marriage

con'jü·gāte, *v.*, present verb forms, unite, **-gation**

cŏn·junc'tion, *n.*, part of speech

con·junc·tī'và, *n.*, part of eyelid

cŏn·junc'tive, *n.*, part of speech

cŏn·junc·ti·vī'tis, *n.*, inflammation of eyelid

con'jure (jêr) *v.*, raise by magic

cŏn·nect' (nekt) *v.*, join, **-ion**

conn'ing tow·êr', *n.*, observation tower

cŏn·nīve', *v.*, plot secretly, **-nivance**

con·nois·seur' (ni·sêr), *n.*, collector of rare items, judge of art, music, etc.

cŏn·nōte', *v.*, suggest, imply

cŏn·nū'bi·ăl, *a.*, relating to marriage

con'quêr (kêr) *v.*, defeat, **-or**

con'quest (kwest), *n.*, victory

con·san'guine (gwin), *a.*, related by blood

con'science (shintz), *n.*, inner moral self

con·sci·en'tious, *a.*, careful, dictated by conscience

con·sci·en'tious ŏb·jec'·tor, *n.*, one opposed to bearing arms in war

con'scious (shus), *a.*, alert, aware, awake, purposeful, **-ness**

cŏn·scrip'tion, *n.*, compulsory military service

con'sè·crāte, *v.*, ordain as sacred, **-crātion**

con·sec'ū·tive, *a.*, following uninterruptedly

cŏn·sen'sus, *n.*, shared opinion

cŏn·sent', *v.*, agree

con'se·quence, *n.*, result, happening, **-quent**

con·sè·quen'tial, *a.*, following as a result

con'sè·quent·ly, *adv.*, therefore

con·sêr·vā'tion, *n.*, preservation of natural resources

cŏn·sêrv'à·tive, *a.*, opposing fast change

cŏn·sêrv'à·tō·ry, *n.*, school of music

cŏn·sêrve', *v.*, protect, save

cŏn·sid'êr, *v.*, give thought to, regard, **-ation**

cŏn·sid'êr·à·ble, *a.*, a great deal

cŏn·sid'êr·āte, *a.*, thoughtful, kind

cŏn·sid'êr·ing, *prep.*, taking into account

cŏn·sīgn', *v.*, intend for receiver, send, **-ment**

cŏn·sist', *v.*, made up of, contain

cŏn·sist'èn·cy, *n.*, firmness

cŏn·sist'ènt, *a.*, steady, firm

cŏn·sō·lā'tion, *n.*, sympathy

cŏn·sōle', *n.*, comfort

con'sōle, *n.*, cabinet

cŏn·sol'i·dāte, *v.*, combine, **-dation**

con·söm·mé' (si·may), *n.*, clear soup

con'sö·nánce, *n.*, agreement

con'sö·nànt, *n.*, hard speech sound

con'sôrt, *n.*, husband or wife

cŏn·spic'ū·ous, *a.*, easily noticed, outstanding

cŏn·spīr'à·cy, *n.*, plot

cŏn·spīre', *v.*, plan together

con'stà·ble, *n.*, policeman, sheriff

con'stànt, *a.*, never changing, loyal, **-stancy**

con·stèl·lā'tion, *n.*, star group

con·stêr·nā'tion, *n.*, dismay

con·sti·pā'tion, *n.*, inability to empty bowels, **-te**

con'sti·tūte, *v.*, make up

con·sti·tū'tion, *n.*, document giving principles of function and organization of government, etc., makeup, **-al**

cŏn·strāin', *v.*, force, repress

cŏn·strāint', *n.*, force, confinement

cŏn·strict', *v.*, shrink, tighten, **-ion**

cŏn·struct', *v.*, build, **-ion**

cŏn·struct'ive, *a.*, positive, useful

cŏn·strūe', *v.*, explain, infer

con'suè·tūde (swi), *n.*, established custom

con'sul, *n.*, government representative in foreign country, **-ate**

cŏn·sult', *v.*, discuss with, **-ant**

con·sul·tā'tion, *n.*, discussion

cŏn·sūme', *v.*, destroy, waste, use up, eat

cŏn·sūm'êr, *n.*, person who uses something, buyer

con'sum-māte, v., complete, conclude, -mation

cön-sump'tion, n., lung disease, using up

con'tact, n., touch

cön-tā'gious, a., spread by contact, -gion

cön-tāin', v., have within, include

cön-tāin'êr, n., that which holds something

cön-tam'i-nāte, v., pollute, -nation

cön-tém-plāte, v., think deeply, ponder, -plation

cön-tem'pö-rä-ry, a., belonging to same period, living today

cön-tempt', n., hate, disrespect, -uous

cön-tend', v., struggle, assert as true

con'tent, n., what appears within

cön-tent', a., satisfied, -ed

cön-ten'tion, n., argument, strife, -tious

con'test, n., struggle, rivalry, argument, -ant

cön-test', v., rival, question

con'text, n., parts that influence meaning, -ual

cön-tig'ū-ous, a., touching, near, -ity

con'ti-nênce, n., restraint of one's physical desires

con'ti-nênt, n., land mass, -al

cön-tin'gênt, a., dependent upon

cön-tin'ū-âl, a., without interruption, -ly

cön-tin'ūe, v., go on, carry over, -uous

con-ti-nū'i-ty, n., keeping on, being unbroken

cön-tôrt', v., bend, twist out of shape

cön-tôr'tion-ist, n., one who bends body

con'tour (tōōr), n., shape, figure

con'trä-band, n., illegal goods

con-trä-cep'tion, n., prevention of conception, -tive

con'tract, n., agreement, -ed

cön-tract', v., agree, accept task, shrink

cön-trac'tion, n., shortened form

con'trac-tör, n., one who

performs work by contract

con-trä-dict', v., oppose, deny, -ion

cön-tral'tō, n., lowest female singing voice

cön-trap'tion, n., device, gadget

con'trä-ry, a., against, opposed to

cön-trast', v., show differences

con-trä-vēne', v., oppose, break law

cön-trib'ūte, v., donate to, donate, -ution

cön-trīte, a., sorry for, humble, -trition

cön-trīve', v., bring about, plot

cön-trōl', v., have authority over, direct

con'trö-vêr'sy, n., argument, disagreement, -sial

con-tū-mā'cious, a., opposing authority, lawbreaking, -cy

con'tū-mé-ly, n., scorn, disregard for law

cön-tū'sion, n., bruise

cö-nun'drum, n., riddle

con-vá-lesce', v., recover after severe illness, -nce

cön-vec'tion, n., transmission

cön-vēne', v., meet, assemble

cön-vēn'ience, n., suitable, personal comfort, -ient

con'vent, n., nun's place of residence

cön-ven'tion, n., periodic meeting of an organization, custom

cön-ven'tion-âl, a., traditional

cön-vêrge', v., meet together at one place

cön-vêr'sánt, a., familiar with

con-vêr-sā'tion, n., informal talking, -al

cön-vêrse', v., discuss, talk informally

con'vêrse, a., opposite

cön-vêrt', v., change, turn, kick point after touchdown

cön-vêrt'i-ble, n., car with canvas top

con'vex, a., curving outward

cön-vey' (vay), v., carry, send message

cön-vict', v., prove guilty of crime, -ion

cön-vince', v., persuade,

-vincing

cŏn·viv'i·ǎl, *a.*, friendly, **-ity**

con·vō·cā'tion, *n.*, religious meeting, assembly

con'vōy, *n.*, escort

cŏn·vulse', *v.*, go into spasm, **-vulsion**

cōō, *n.*, soft bird sound, loving murmur

cook', *v.*, prepare food for eating

cook'y, *n.*, small cake

cōōl, *a.*, slightly cold, calm

cōōl'ẽr, *n.*, cooling device, jail (coll.)

cōōl'ie, *n.*, Chinese laborer

cōōp, *n., v.*, chicken cage

cō-ŏp', *n.*, short for cooperative

cōōp'ẽr, *n.*, barrel maker, **-age**

cō-ŏp'ẽr·āte, *v.*, work for or together, **-ation**

cō-ŏp'ẽr·ā·tive, *n.*, store owned and run by members

cō-ôr'di·nāte, *v.*, properly adjust, put together, **-nation**

cop, *n.*, policeman

cōpe, *v.*, handle, meet challenge

cō'pī·lŏt, *n.*, second airplane pilot

cŏp'ing sǎw, *n.*, saw for cutting curves

cō'pī·ous, *a.*, many, tremendous, **-ly**

cop'pẽr, *n.*, metallic element

cop'pẽr·head, *n.*, venomous snake

cop'y, *v.*, imitate, manuscript ready for printing

cop'y·rīght (rīt), *v.*, protect written articles from plagiarism

cor'ǎl, *n.*, underwater skeletal material

côrd, *n.*, string, rope, wood measurement

côr'dial (jil), *n., a.*, alcoholic drink, pleasant, **-ity**

côrd'īte, *n.*, gunpowder

côre, *n.*, center

Côr'fam, *n.*, synthetic leather

côrk, *n.*, light bark, stopper

côrk' screw, *n.*, device for removing corks

côrn, *n.*, vegetable

côr'nē·ȧ, *n.*, eyeball covering

côr'nẽr, *n.*, outside of an angle

côr'nẽr, *v.*, trap

côr'net, *n.*, brass musical instrument

côr'nice, *n.*, decorative molding

côr·nu·cō'pi·ȧ, *n.*, horn of plenty

côrn'y (coll.) *a.*, dull, over-used

cor'ŏl·lâr·y, *n.*, understood proposition

cō·rō'nȧ, *n.*, ring of light around moon or sun

cor'ō·nâr·y, *a.*, pertaining to the heart

cor'ō·nẽr, *n.*, official who investigates death causes

cor·ō·net', *n.*, crown

côr'pō·rǎl, *n.*, non-commissioned army officer

côr·pō·rā'tion, *n.*, business organization chartered to act as a unit, **-te**

côrps (kôr), *n.*, military unit

côrpse, *n.*, dead body

côr'pū·lĕnt, *a.*, fat, **-lence**

côr'pus·cle, *n.*, blood cell

côr'rǎl, *n.*, fenced-in place for animals

côr·rect', *a.*, without error, **-ion**

côr·rect', *v.*, rectify mistakes

cor·rē·lā'tion, *n.*, relationship between

cor·rē·spond', *v.*, be in agreement, write letters, **-ence**

cor·rē·spond'ent, *n.*, writer

côr'ri·dôr, *n.*, hall

côr·rob'ō·rāte, *v.*, prove

côr·rō'sion, *n.*, effect of being eaten away, **-de**

cor'ru·gāt·ĕd, *a.*, ridged

côr·rupt', *a.*, wicked, dishonest, **-ion**

côr'sȧge, *n.*, bouquet worn by women

côr'sĕt, *n.*, garment to hold shape in

côr·tege' (tezh), *n.*, funeral procession

côr'ti·sōne, *n.*, drug used to relieve arthritis

côr·us·cā'tion, *n.*, reflection of brilliance

cos·met'ics (koz), *n.*, powder, cream, etc. to beautify

cos'mic, *a.*, relating to universe

cos'mic rays, *n.*, rays from space

cos·mol'ō·gy, *n.*, study of the

universe

cos'mö-nàut, *n.*, space traveler

cos-mö-pol'i-tàn, *a.*, sophisticated, wordly

cos'mös, *n.*, universe

cos'mö-tron, *n.*, machine producing energy

cóst, *n.*, amount needed for payment, price

cóst, *v.*, require expenditure, -ly

cos'tüme, *n.*, type of dress, clothing, -r

cot, *n.*, small portable bed

cö'tê-rïe, *n.*, friends, group meeting together

cö-til'lion, *n.*, type of dance, debutante party

cott'àge chëese, *n.*, lumpy, soft white cheese

cott'on, *n.*, plant, fabric

cott'on täil, *n.*, rabbit

couch, *n.*, bed or sofa

couch, *v.*, express

coü'gàr (köö-gêr), *n.*, large wildcat

cough (kâwf), *n.*, spastic sound air expelled from lungs

coü'lee (köö), *n.*, valley

coun'cil, *n.*, meeting of delegates

coun'cil-màn, *n.*, elected delegate

coun'sel, *v.*, guide, advise, -or

count, *v.*, figure, compute, rely

count, *n.*, title of nobility, total, criminal charge, -ess

count'down, *n.*, backward count to zero in time units before firing rocket

coun'tè-nance, *n.*, face, look

coun'tè-nance, *v.*, agree, permit

coun'tér, *adv.*, against, opposed to

count'êr, *n.*, flat display surface in store

coun-tèr-act', *v.*, revoke, change action, oppose

coun'tèr-àt-tack, *v.*, attack to neutralize an attack

coun-tèr-bal'ànce, *v.*, be of equal action or weight

coun'tèr-feit (fit), *n.*, money dishonestly manufactured, false

coun'tèr-mand, *v.*, change previous order

coun'tèr-point, *n.*, accompanying melody

coun'tèr-sïgn, *v.*, add another signature

count'less, *a.*, too many to count

coun'try (kun), *n.*, rural area, a nation

coun'ty, *n.*, division of a state

cou-pe' (köö-pay), *n.*, car with two doors

cou'ple (kup-il), *n.*, two together, husband and wife

cou'ple, *v.*, join two together

coü'pon (köö), *n.*, detachable portion of page, certificate

coür'àge (kûr-ij), *n.*, bravery, -ous

coür'i-êr (kûr), *n.*, messenger

côurse, *n.*, path or direction

coür'tè-ous (kûr), *a.*, polite, -ly

coür'tè-sàn (ti-sin), *n.*, court lady

coür'tè-sy, *n.*, politeness

côurt'mär'tial, *n.*, military trial

côurt'ship, *n.*, wooing of a mate

cous'in (kuz), *n.*, child of aunt or uncle

cöve, *n.*, protected bay, sheltered small place

cöv'é-nánt (kuv), *n.*, agreement

cöv'êr (kuv), *v.*, place something over

cöv'êr chärge, *n.*, charge for service

cöv'êrt, *a.*, hidden, secret

cöv'ét (kuv), *v.*, desire what belongs to another

cow, *n.*, female of various animals

cow, *v.*, frighten, subdue

cow'àrd, *n.*, person without courage, -ly

cow'bóy, *n.*, cattle herder

cow'êr, *v.*, crouch in fear, shame, etc.

cow-hêrd, *n.*, keeper of cows

cow'lick, *n.*, unruly lock of hair

cowl'ing, *n.*, engine covering

cow'pox, *n.*, cattle disease

cox'cõmb, *n.*, vain, foolish man

cox'swäin (kox-in), *n.*, director of racing shell

coy, *a.*, seemingly shy

coy′ōte (ki ′ōt), n., prairie wolf

cō′zy, a., comfortable, snug, **-zily**

crab, n., shellfish, angry person, louse

crab′by, a., grouchy

crack, v., break, split

cracked, a., split, broken, (coll.) insane

crack′er, n., thin biscuit

crack′up, n., crash, mental breakdown

crā′dle, n., infant's bed on rockers

craft, n., skilled trade, boat

craft′y, a., clever

crag, n., projecting rock

cram, v., stuff, fill, study for exam (coll.)

cramp, n., spasmodic pain

cran′ber·ry, n., tart red berry

crāne, n., machine for moving heavy articles, bird

crank, n., machine arm for turning, mean person (coll.)

crank, v., rotate machine arm

crank′cāse, n., automobile casing

crank′y, a., angry, mean, **-ily**

craps, n., dice game

crash, n., v., loud impact of collision, business failure, join a party without invitation (coll.)

crash′ dīve, n., sudden emergency dive by submarine

crass, a., ignorant, unpolished, **-itude**

crāte, v., pack in box or crate

crā′tēr, n., volcano opening

crá·vat′, n., necktie

crāve, v., desire

crā′ven, a., contemptibly cowardly

crawl, v., move on hands and knees

crāy′on, n., colored wax for drawing

crāze, n., temporary fashion

crā′zy, n., insane, **-zily**

crēak, v., make harsh squeaking sound, **-ily**

crēam, n., milk fat, cosmetic paste

crēam′ chēese, n., cheese made from milk

crēase, n., fold

crē·āte′, v., originate, make

crē·ā′tion, n., universe, something made

crē·ā′tive, a., having skill to create

crēa′ture, n., living thing

crē′dence, n., truthfulness, belief

crē·den′tial, n., statement of introduction

cred′i·ble, a., worthy of belief, **-bly**

cred′it, n., trust, praise, ability to pay, college unit of work

cred′it·à·ble, a., worthy of praise, **-ably**

cred′ū·lous, a., naïve, not critical, accepting slight evidence, **-ly**

crēed, n., belief, way of life

crēek, n., small stream

crēep, v., crawl close to ground

crēep′y, a., scary, fearful

crē·mā′tion, n., burning of corpse

crepe (krayp), n., crinkled paper or cloth, mourning cloth

crē·pus′cū·lár, a., pertaining to twilight

crē·scen′dō (shen), n., increase in volume

cres′cent, n., moon in first quarter

crest, n., coat of arms, ridge, head tuft of bird

crē′tin, n., deformed, idiotic person, **-ism**

crē·vasse′, n., crack in ice glacier

crev′ice, n., crack, split

crew (krōō), n., group of working people

crib, n., infant's bed

crib, v., copy school work, cheat at test

crick′et, n., insect, English game

crīme, n., breaking of law

crim′i·nál, n., one who breaks law

crimp, v., create wavy look

crimp, n., hindrance

crim′sŏn (zin), n., red

cringe, v., draw away in fear

crip′ple, n., lame person

crī′sis, n., turning point, decisive time or event

crisp, a., fresh, sharp **-ply**

crī·tē′ri·ŏn, n., standard, rule

crit′ic, n., one who criticizes, **-al**

crit·i·cism, n., judgment,

opinion, **-cize**

croak, n., hoarse frog cry

croak, v., make throaty sound, (coll.) die

cro-chet' (shay), v., knit with hooked needle

croc'o-dīle, n., alligator-like reptile

cro'cus, n., flower

cro'ny, n., friend

crook, n., dishonest person, (coll.) bend, **-ed**

crōōn, v., sing softly

crop, n., food plants, riding whip

crop, v., pluck, cut off

cro-quet' (kay), n., game with mallet and ball

cross, n., one line across another, symbol of Christianity

cross, v., oppose

cross'-eyed, a., eyes turning inward

cross'ing, n., place to move across

cross'question, v., question severely

cross'word puz'zle, n., word game

crotch, n., point between legs at body

crouch, v., kneel forward, stoop over

croup, n., throat disease

crow, n., large black bird

crow, v., cackle, boast, brag

crowd, n., large group of people

crown, n., top of anything, king's headdress, **-ing**

cru'cial, a., decisive, meaningful

cru'ci-fix, n., figure of Christ on cross, plural

cru'ci-fy, v., kill by nailing to cross, torture

crūde, a., rough, unrefined

crū'el (krōōl), a., causing another suffering, **-ty**

cruise, n., boat trip

cruis'er, n., battleship

crul'ler, n., doughnut

crumb, n., tiny piece of bread, (coll.) bad person

crum'ble, v., fall to pieces

crunch, v., grind between teeth

crū-sade', n., religious journey, campaign

crush, v., press together violently

crust, n., hard covering

crus-tā'cē-an (shin), n., hard shelled marine animal

crutch, n., support for lameness

crux, n., important point or time

cry, n., sorrowful sobbing, loud call

cry, v., make sorrowful noise, express loud sound, **-ing**

crypt, n., underground burial place

cryp'tic, a., secret, mysterious

cryp'to-gram, n., code writing

crys'tal, n., mineral, watch face, glass

cub, n., baby animal, young Boy Scout

cūbe, n., figure with six equal square sides

cūb'ism, n., type of abstract art

cuck'ōō (kōō-kōō), n., bird

cū'cum-bêr, n., long round green vegetable

cud, n., returned food repeatedly chewed by cattle

cud'dle, v., hold snugly in arms

cudg'el, n., heavy club

cūe, n., signal, billiard stick

cuff, n., band at sleeve or pants end

cuff, v., hit with open hand

cui-sine' (kwi-zēen), n., food, type of cooking

cū'li-nâr-y, a., pertaining to cooking

cull, v., select from

cul'mi-nāte, v., reach peak, **-nation**

cu-lottes', n., women's short trousers

cul'pá-ble, a., deserving blame

cul'prit, n., villain, evil doer

cult, n., unusual religious group

cul'ti-vāte, v., raise crops, develop, make refined, **-vation**

cul'ture, n., way of life, breeding, **-tured**

cum'bêr-sŏme, a., clumsy

cū'mu-lā-tive, a., increasing, becoming larger

cū'mu-lus, n., round cloud

cun'ning, a., clever, sly

cup, n., drinking bowl

cup'board (ĕrd), n., furniture for storing

cup'cake, n., round, small cake

cū·pid'i·ty, n., excessive desire for

cū·rā'tor, n., manager of museum, zoo, etc.

cûrb, v., control

cūre, v., make well

cūre'all, n., that which cures everything

cûr'few, n., signal, specified time at night

cū'ri·ous, a., anxious to discover or learn, **-osity**

cûrl, v., twist into circle

cûrl, n., rounded piece of hair, **-er**

cûr·rèn·cy, n., money, daily happening

cûr'rènt, n.,a., electricity, happening at present

cûr·ric'ū·lum, n., program of studies

cûrse, v., swear at, make evil wish

cûr'sö·ry, a., hastily done, superficial

cûrt, a., abrupt, impatient

cûr·tāil', v., lessen, cut off

cûr'tain (tin), n., covering, drape

cûr'tain căll, n., appearance for audience applause

cûr'vá·tūre, n., curved part

cûrve, n., rounded bend

cush'ion, v., pillow, ease shock

cus'pi·dôr, n., spittoon

cuss, n., curse, swear (coll.)

cus'tärd, n., milk and egg dessert

cus·tō'di·án, n., caretaker

cus'tō·dy, n., in charge of, locked up

cus'tōm, n., established practice

cus'tōm·ā·ry, a., usual

cus'tōm house, n., place for paying taxes

cus'tōm māde, a., made to order

cut, v., reduce, separate

cūte, a., attractive

cū'ti·cle, n., fingernail skin

cut'lèr·y, n., eating utensils

cut'lèt, n., small piece of meat

cut'tèr, n., one who cuts, boat

cut'throat, n., murderer

cut'ting, n.,a., plant part

cut'up, n., playful person

cy·bêr·net'ics, n., study of brain

cy'cle, n., time repeating itself

cy'clōne, n., wind storm

cy'clō·tron, n., atom smasher

cyg'nèt (sig), n., young swan

cyl'in·dêr, n., geometrical round figure, motor part, **-drical**

cym'bál, n., brass musical instrument

cyn'ic, n., critic, sarcastic person, **-ism**

cy'nö·sūre, n., center of attraction

cy'prèss, n., evergreen tree

cyst, n., tumor

czär (zhär), n., former Russian emperor

D

dab, v., touch lightly

dab'ble, v., splash, perform superficially

dächs'hund (ăk), n., small long-bodied dog

dā'cron, n., synthetic yarn

dad, n., father

dad'dy long'legs, n., spider-like insect

daf'fō·dil, n., yellow flower

daf'fy (coll.), a., crazy, silly

dag'gêr, n., pointed knife

dā·guerre'ö·type, (gâr) n., early kind of photograph

dahl'ia, n., flower

dāi'ly, a., each day

dāin'ty, a., delicate

dā'is, n., raised platform

dāi'sy, n., flower

dal'ly, v., be playful amorously, waste time

dam, v., block, hold back water

dam, n., female dog, wall to stop water

dam'áge, n., injury, harm

dam'á·scène, n., ornament

dam'ásk, n., material of silk or linen

dāme, n., woman (coll.)

---

damn, v., curse, condemn; **-ation**

damp, a., slightly moist

damp′en, v., make wet, depress

damp′er, n., draft regulator, discouragement

dam′sel (zil), n., girl

dance, n., rhythmic movement to music

dan′de-lī-ŏn, n., yellow weed

dan′der, n., temper, anger

dan′druff, n., scales on scalp

dan′dy, n., fop

dan′ger, n., exposure to harm, **-ous**

dan′gle, v., hang loosely

dank, a., damp

dap′per, a., stylish in appearance

dâre, v., risk doing, have courage for, challenge

dâre′dev-il, n., recklessly brave person

dâr′ing, n., boldness, courage

dârk, a., absence of light, gloomy, unhappy, **-en**

dârk′hôrse, n., unexpected winner

dârk′rŏŏm, n., film developing room

dâr′ling, n., term of love

därn, v., mend; (coll.) expletive

därt, n., v., pointed weapon, dodge, dash

dash, v., strike, break violently, rush

dash′bôard, n., auto instrument panel

dash′ing, a., attractive, lively

das′tàrd, n., sneaking coward

dā′ta, n., collection of facts

dāte, n., period in time, partner, social engagement, fruit

dāte, v., set a time, have a social engagement

dāt′ed, a., out of style, not modern

dāte′less, a., without a date

dāte′line, n., date of newspaper

dā′tive, a., grammatical case

dāub, v., cover with paint

dàugh′tèr (dàw), n., female child

dàugh′tèr-in-làw′, n., son's wife

dàunt, v., discourage, **-less**

dav′en-pôrt, n., sofa

dâw′dle, v., waste time, **-r**

dàwn, n., first daylight

dāy, n., 24 hours, hours of light

dāy′break, n., start of daylight

dāy′drēam, n., dreams while awake

dāy′light, n., light of day

dāy′light sāv′ing tīme, n., one hour faster than standard time

dāy′side, n., daylight side of planet

dāze, v., stun, confuse

daz′zle, v., overcome with brilliance, **zling**

dē′a′cŏn, n., church official, **-ess**

dead (ded), a., without life

dead′ beat, n., person who avoids paying bills

dead′en, v., make less active, soften

dead end′, n., street with no exit

dead′head (hed), n., user of complimentary ticket

dead′line, n., set time limit

dead′lock, n., inability to agree, standstill

dead′ly, a., pertaining to death, fatal

dead′pan, a., without facial expression

deaf (def), a., unable to hear, **-en**

deaf-mūte′, n., person who cannot hear or speak

dēal, v., do business with, distribute cards

dēal, n., business venture, agreement

dēan, n., college department head, oldest member

dēar, a., beloved

dêarth, n., shortage

death (deth), n., end of life, **-ly**

death′house, n., prison section for those condemned to death

dē-bà′cle, n., violent ending, sudden breakup

dē-bär′, v., prevent from joining

dē-bärk′, v., leave ship

dē-bāse′, v., lower, insult dignity of, **-ment**

dē-bāte′, n., public argument on a topic

dē-bāuch′ (bàwsh), v., corrupt, dissipate, **-ery**

dė-bil'i-tāte, v., weaken

deb'it, n., record of debt, debt

deb-ō-nâir', a., courteous, pleasant

dė-bris' (brē), n., scattered remains

debt, n., owed, -or

dė-bunk', v., doubt sentimental occurrences

dė-būt, n., first public appearance, introduction to society

deb'ū-tänte, n., girl introduced to society

dec'āde (dek), n., ten years

dė-cā-dence, n., falling into decay, -dent

dé-cal-cō-mā'ni-ā, n., transfer designs

dé-camp', v., break up camp

dé-cant'ēr, n., wine bottle

dé-cap'i-tāte, v., cut off head

dé-cath'lon, n., athletic contest having ten events

dé-cāy', v., rot, become weaker

dė-cēase', n., die, -d

dė-cēit', n., dishonesty, lying, -ful

dė-cēive', v., mislead, fool

dē'cênt, a., in good taste, fair, tolerant, -cency

dē-cen'trál-ize, v., remove from central place, -ization

dė-cep'tion, n., lying, cheating, misleading, -tive

dė-cīde', v., make decision, -ciding

dė-cīd'ed, a., settled

dec'i-mál, a., relating to tens or tenths

dec'i-māte, v., destroy, -mation

dė-cī'phêr (fer), v., solve

dė-cī'sion, n., answer, judgment

dė-cī'sive, a., conclusive

deck, n., floor of ship

deck, v., trim

dė-clāim', v., speak formally in public

dec-là-mā'tion, n., formal public speech

dec-là-rā'tion, n., announcement, formal statement

dė-clāre', v., announce

dė-clas'si-fy, v., make public what was secret

dė-clen'sion, n., noun endings, bend

dė-clīne', v., refuse, grow

weaker

dė-cōde', v., translate into regular language

de-cŏlle-te' (day-kul-tay), a., low cut neckline

dė-cŏm-pōse', v., rot, -position

dė-cŏn-tam'i-nāte, v., remove harmful substances, -nation

dė-cŏn-trŏl', v., remove from control

dec'ō-rāte, v., adorn, confer honor upon, -ration

dec'ō-rous, a., prim

dė-cōrum, n., polite behavior

dē'coy, v., lure

dė-crēase', v., make less

dė-crēe', n., order

dė-crep'it, a., broken down

dė-cry', v., condemn

ded'i-cāte, v., devote to a serious purpose, -cation

dė-dūce', v., draw conclusions

dė-duct', v., subtract -ion

dēed, n., act, title of ownership

dēem, v., consider

dēep, a., far down, -ly

dēep'ên, v., make deeper

dēep'-frēeze, n., frozen storage device

dēep'-sēat'ėd, a., fixed strongly within

dēer, n., antlered animal

dė-fāce', v., mar

dē fac'tō, adv., in reality

dė-fál'cāte, v., steal money held in trust

dė-fāme', v., harm person's reputation

dė-fáult' (fawlt), v., n., fail to act or participate

dė-fēat', v., beat, -ism

dė-fēat', n., loss of contest

def'e-cāte, v., empty bowels

dė-fect', n., blemish, -ive

dė-fec'tion, n., failing in duty

dė-fend', v., protect, -ant

dė-fense', n., protection

dė-fense'less, a., not protected

dė-fen'sive, a., on guard, protecting

defêr-ence, n., submission, respect, -ential

dė-fī'ánce, n., strong resistance, -ant

dė-fī'cien-cy (shin-see), n., lack, -t

def'i-cit, *n.*, money shortage

dè-file', *v.*, make unclean

dè-fine', *v.*, explain

def'i-nite, *a.*, exact, having set bounds, **-ly**

def-i-ni'tion, *n.*, explanation of meaning

dè-fin'i-tive, *a.*, final, conclusive

dè-flāte', *v.*, let air out, reduce importance, **-flation**

dè-flect', *v.*, turn aside

dè-fôrm', *v.*, disfigure, **-ed**

dè-fraud' (frôwd), *v.*, cheat

dè-fray', *v.*, pay expenses

dè-frôst', *v.*, remove ice

deft'ly, *adv.*, skillfully, lightly

dè-funct', *a.*, not existing, out of date

dè-fy', *v.*, challenge authority

dè-gen'ėr-āte, *v.*, rot, decline

dè-gen'ėr-āte (it), *a.*, depraved

dè-grāde', *v.*, lower in rank

dè-grēe', *n.*, amount, status, scholastic title

dè-hy'drāte, *v.*, remove water from

dē'i-fy, *v.*, make into god

deign (dayn) *v.*, condescend

dē'i-ty, *n.*, god

dè-ject'ėd, *a.*, sad, down-hearted, **-tion**

dè-lay', *v.*, put off for period of time

dè-lec'ta-ble, *a.*, filled with pleasure

del'ė-gāte, *n.*, representative, **-gation**

del'ė-gāte, *v.*, entrust authority

dè-lēte', *v.*, remove, erase

del-e-tē'ri-ous, *a.*, harmful, dangerous

dè-lib'ėr-āte, *v.*, carefully think about, review, **-ation**

del'i-cá-cy, *n.*, luxury food, refinement

del'i-cáte, *a.*, dainty, fragile, soft

del-i-cá-tes'sėn, *n.*, cold meats, pickles etc., store

dè-li'cious (shis), *a.*, highly pleasing, **-ly**

dè-līght', *n.*, pleasure, satisfaction, **-ful**

dè-lim'it, *v.*, set limits for

dè-lin'ē-āte, *v.*, outline, describe

dè-lin'quėn-cy (leenkwin), *n.*, misdeed, neglect of duty

dè-lir'ious (lēer), *a.*, out of mind, raving, **-um**

dè-lir'i-um trē'mėns, *n.*, violent trembling from use of alcohol

dè-liv'ėr, *v.*, bring, give birth to

dè-liv'ėr-ánce, *n.*, rescue, freedom, expressed judgment

dè-liv'ėr-y, *n.*, transfer, way of speaking, child-birth

dell, *n.*, valley

dē-louse', *v.*, remove lice

del'tà, *n.*, Greek letter, river mouth

dè-lūde', *v.*, mislead, deceive, **-lusion**

del'ūge, *n.*, flood

dè-lū'sion, *n.*, false belief, **-ive**

dè-luxe', *a.*, specially elegant

delve, *v.*, seek out, search into

dem'à-gogue (gog), *n.*, political leader or orator who arouses emotions, **-ry**

dè-mand', *v.*, require, **-ing**

dē-mär-cā'tion, *n.*, boundary line

dè-mēan'ôr, *n.*, behavior

dè-ment'ėd, *a.*, crazy

dè-mer'it, *n.*, fault, mark against

dem'i-, *prefix*, half

dem'i-john, *n.*, glass bottle

dē-mil'i-tá-rīze, *v.*, remove military control

dè-mīse', *n.*, death

dem'i-tásse, *n.*, small cup of coffee

dē-mō'bi-līze, *v.*, disband military units

dè-moc'rá-cy, *n.*, government of, by, and for the people, **-tic**

Dem'ō-crat, *n.*, member of U.S. political party

dè-mol'ish, *v.*, ruin, destroy, **-ition**

dē'mön, *n.*, devil, evil spirit

dè-mō'ni-ac, *a.*, like a devil, wicked

dem'ön-strāte, *v.*, show, prove, **-strable**

dem-ön-strā'tion, *n.*, proof, display

dè-mor'ál-īze, *v.*, corrupt, take away courage, spirit

dè-mōte', *v.*, lower in rank, **-motion**

dè-mûr', *v.*, object to

dē-mûr'rǎge, *n.*, fee for delaying unloading

den, *n.*, animal abode, informal room

dē-na'tion-ǎl-īze, *v.*, end as a nation

dēnī'ǎl, *n.*, refusal

den'im, *n.*, heavy cotton fabric

den'i-zěn, *n.*, inhabitant

dē-nom-i-nā'tion, *n.*, group, sect, type coin, **-al**

dē-nom'i-nā-tŏr, *n.*, bottom part of fraction

dē-nōte', *v.*, tell, stand for

dē-noue-ment' (day-nōō-mäwn'), *n.*, ending, solution

dē-nounce', *v.*, speak against, condemn, **-ment**

dense, *a.*, packed closely together

den'si-ty, *n.*, stupidity, compactness

dent, *n.*, hollow mark

den'tǎl, *a.*, pertaining to teeth

den'ti-frice, *n.*, tooth cleaning solution

den'tist, *n.*, dental doctor, **-ry**

den-ti'tion, *n.*, teething

dē-nūde', *v.*, strip

dē-nun'ci-āte, *v.*, criticize, condemn, **-ation**

dē-ny' (nī), *v.*, state to be false

dē-ō'dŏr-ǎnt, *n.*, odor destroying chemical, **-ize**

dē-pärt', *v.*, leave, go, **-ure**

dē-pärt'měnt, *n.*, division of organization

dē-pärt'měnt stōre, *n.*, large store selling many things

dē-pend', *v.*, rely upon, trust, **-able**

dē-pend'ĕnce, *n.*, reliance upon, trust, **-ency**

dēpend'ĕnt, *a.*, relying upon, ant

dē-pict', *v.*, show, describe, **-ing**

dē-pil'à-tŏ-ry, *n.*, chemical for hair removing

dē-plēte', *v.*, use up, empty

dē-plōre', *v.*, be deeply sorry about, **-plorable**

dē-ploy', *v.*, spread out

dē-pop'ū-lāte, *v.*, remove inhabitants

dē-pôrt', *v.*, behave, banish, **-ation**

dē-pôrt'měnt, *n.*, conduct

dē-pōse', *v.*, remove from

office, testify under oath

dē-pos'it, *v.*, put, store, leave, **-or**

dep-o-si'tion, *n.*, written, sworn testimony

dē'pôt (po), *n.*, warehouse, railway station

dē-prāve', *v.*, make bad, corrupt

dep're-cāte, *v.*, disapprove, be against, **-catory**

dē-prē'ci-āte (shi), *v.*, deplete value of, **-ation**

dep-re-dā'tion, *n.*, robbery, laying waste, plundering

dē-press', *v.*, push down, make sad, **-ing**

dē-pres'sion, *n.*, sadness, decline in economy

dē-pri-vā'tion, *n.*, loss, prevention from doing or having

dē-prīve', *v.*, keep from, take from

depth, *n.*, distance down, deepness

dē-pūte', *v.*, assign representative

dep'ū-ty, *n.*, one appointed to act for another, **-tize**

dē-rāil', *v.*, forced from tracks

dē-rānged', *a.*, insane, confused

der'é-lict, *a.*, deserted, neglectful, **-ion**

dē-rīde', *v.*, ridicule, make fun of

dē-ri'sion, *n.*, contempt, mockery

der-i-vā'tion, *n.*, source of origin

dē-rīve', *v.*, originate, deduce

dēr'mä, *n.*, skin

dē-rog'à-tō-ry, *a.*, insulting, contemptuous

der'rick, *n.*, lifting machine

des'cǎnt, *n.*, melodic accompaniment

dē-scend', *v.*, move lower

dē-scend'ǎnt, *n.*, offspring

dē-scrībe', *v.*, tell about

dē-scrip'tion, *n.*, telling of, **-tive**

dē-scry' (ī), *v.*, see, observe

des'é-crāte, *v.*, profane, **-cration**

dē-sêrt', *v.*, abandon

des'êrt, *n.*, dry, barren area

dē-sêr'tion, *n.*, abandoning

dē-sêrve', *v.*, be worthy of

des'ic-cāte, *v.*, dry completely, **-cation**

dé·sīgn′, *n.,* pattern, plan, intention

des·ig·nāte′, *v.,* appoint, name, **-nation**

dé·sīgn′êr, *n.,* creator, plotter

dé·sīgn′ing, *a.,* creative, scheming

dé·sīr′a·ble, *a.,* wanted

dé·sīre′, *n.,* wish, appetite for

dé·sīr′ous, *a.,* wishing

dé·sist′, *v.,* stop

desk, *n.,* writing table

des′ō·lāte (lit), *a.,* ruined, laid waste, **-ation**

dé·spâir′, *v.,* give up hope

des·pêr·ä′dō, *n.,* dangerous criminal

des·pêr·ate (it), *a.,* dangerous, serious, hopeless, reckless, **-ation**

des′pi·cá·ble, *a.,* hateful, low

dé·spīse′, *v.,* hate

dé·spīte′-, *prep.,* even though

dé·spond′ent, *a.,* not hopeful

des′pŏt, *n.,* cruel ruler, **-ic**

dé·sêrt′, *n.,* end of meal, sweet course

des·ti·nā′tion, *n.,* goal, end of trip

des′tin·y, *n.,* events that will occur, fate

des′ti·tūte, *a.,* poor

dé·strōy′, *v.,* do away with, ruin

dé·strōy′êr, *n.,* warship

dé·struc′tive, *a.,* causing ruin **-tible, -tion**

des′uè·tūde (wi), *n.,* disuse

des′ul·tô·ry, *a.,* disconnected

dé·tach′, *v.,* remove from, **-ed**

dé·tach′ment, *n.,* separation, special group

dē·tāil′, *n.,* particular part, special task

dē·tāin′, *v.,* hold back

dē·tāin′êr, *n.,* legal writ for holding one in custody

dé·tect′, *v.,* discover, **-ion**

dē·tec′tive, *n.,* crime investigator

dē·tec′tôr, *n.,* indicator

dē·ten′tion, *n.,* holding in custody

dé·têr′, *v.,* hold back

dē·têr′gent, *n.,* chemical cleaner

dē·tē′ri·ō·rāte, *v.,* rot, become worse, **-ration**

dē·têr·mi·nā′tion, *n.,* decision, firmness, **-mined**

dē·têr′mine, *v.,* decide

dē·têr′rent, *a.,* that which stops

dē·test′, *v.,* hate, **-able**

dē·thrōne′, *v.,* remove from throne, **-ment**

det′ō·nāte, *v.,* explode, **-nation**

dē′tour (toor) *n.,* substitute road

dé·tract′, *v.,* remove from, take away, **-ion**

det′ri·ment, *n.,* disadvantage, **-al,** harm

deūce, *inter.,* devil

deūce, *n.,* 2 spot playing card, tennis score

dē·val′ūe, *v.,* lessen value, **-uate**

dev′ás·tāte, *v.,* ruin, make ugly, **-tation**

dē·vel′ŏp, *v.,* grow, expand, improve, **-er**

dē·vel′ŏp·ment, *n.,* improvement, growth, event, **-al**

dē′vi·āte, *v.,* stray from

dev′il, *n.,* spirit of evil, **-ish**

dev′iled, *a.,* highly seasoned

dev·il·ment, *n.,* mischief, trouble

dē′vi·ous, *a.,* round about

dē·vīse′, *v.,* plan

dē·void′, *a.,* lacking

dē·volve′, *v.,* pass on to

dē·vōte′, *v.,* give time to

dē·vōt′ed, *a.,* loyal

dev′ō·tēe, *n.,* one deeply attached to

dē·vō′tion, *n.,* loyalty, religious service

dē·vour′, *v.,* eat, **-ing**

dē·vout′, *a.,* holy, religious

dew, *n.,* condensed moisture, **-y**

dex·ter′i·ty, *n.,* skill

dex′trōse, *n.,* sugar

di·â·bē′tēs, *n.,* disease from excess sugar

di·â·bol′ic, *a.,* devilish

dī′â·dem, *n.,* crown

dī·àg·nōse′, *v.,* determine cause, **-nosis**

dī′â·gram, *n.,* drawing, combination of figures

dī′âl, *n.,* graduated face of instrument

dī′â·lect, *n.,* sectional language usage, **-ic**

dī′â·lōgue, *n.,* conversation between two′e·têr, *n.,*

diam′ē·têr, *n.,* width of a

circle

dīa'mönd, n., jewel, pure carbon

dī-a-nō-et'ic, n., physical cure by mental treatment

dī-a-pā'sŏn, n., stops of organ

dī'a-pêr (dy-pêr), n., infant's pants

dī'a-pha-nous, a., transparent

dī'a-phragm, n., muscles between chest and abdomen

dī-ar-rhē'á, n., looseness of bowels

dī'a-ry, n., daily personal journal

dī-as'tŏ-lē, n., expansion of heart

dī'a-ther-my, n., heat treatment

dī'a-tribe, n., argument, criticism, discussion

dīce, n., cubes used in game

dī-chot'ō-my, n., division, split

dick'ens, inter., devil

dick'êr, v., bargain

dick'ey, n., false shirt front

dic'tāte, v., order, recite something to be written by another, -tation

dic'tā-tŏr, n., autonomous ruler, -ial

dic'tion, n., clarity in speaking

dic'tion-âr-y, n., word definition book

dic'tum, n., definite opinion

dī-dac'tic, a., instructive, boring

dīe, v., stop living

dīe'hârd, n., stubborn person

dī'ĕt, n., food eaten, selection of foods, -etic

dī-ē-tī'tian, n., diet planner

dif'fêr, v., disagree

dif'fêr-ence, n., disagreement, ent

dif-fêr-en'tial, a., having different effects

dif-fêr-en'ti-āte, v., show distinction between

dif'fi-cult, a., not easy, -y

dif'fi-dĕnt, a., meek, -dence

dif'fract', v., split into parts, -ion

dif-fūse', a., spread out, wordy, -fusion

dig, v., excavate

dī-gest', v., summarize, condense, -ible

di-ges'tion, n., dissolving

food in the stomach

dig'it, n., finger or toe, numbers 0 to 9

dig'ni-fied, a., stately, -ty

dig'ni-târ-y, n., important person

di-gress', v., turn aside, -ion

dīke, n., flood wall

di-lap'i-dāt-ĕd, a., fallen apart, ruined

di-lāte', v., spread, -lation

dil'a-tō-ry, a., late

di-lem'mā, n., perplexing situation

dil'ĕt-tan-te, n., dabbler, follower of arts

dil'i-gĕnt, a., hard working, conscientious, -gence

dill, n., herb

dī-lūte', v., weaken strength of, -lution

dim, a., somewhat dark, pessimistic

dīme, n., ten cents

dīme nov'ĕl, n., cheap novel

di-men'sion, n., measurement

di-min'ish, v., lessen

dim-i-nū'tion, n., lessening

di-min'ū-tive, a., tiny

dim'i-ty, n., thin cotton cloth

dim'ple, n., round hollow

din, n., loud noise

dīne, v., eat

dīn-ette', n., small dining room

din'ghy, n., small boat

din'gy (jēe), a., shabby, dirty

din'nêr, n., chief meal of day

dī'nŏ-sâur (sôr), n., prehistoric reptile

dī'ŏ-cēse (sis), n., religious district, -cesan

dī-ō-ra'mā, n., three-dimensional picture

dip, v., lower and raise again, take a swim

diph-thē'ri-á, n., disease

di-plō'mā, n., document recognizing school completion

dip'lō-mat, n., government representative, -macy

dip'pêr, n., long handled cup

dīre, a., fearful, dreadful, -ful

di-rect', a., to the point, in a straight line

di-rect', v., guide, give orders

di-rec'tion, n., ordering, aiming, -al

di-rect'ly, adv., immediately, straight

di-rec'tör, n., one who guides

di-rec'to-ry, n., book listing names, addresses, etc.

dirge, n., funeral song

dir'i-gi-ble, n., motor-driven balloon

dirk, n., dagger

dirn'dl (dĭl), n., gathered wide skirt

dirt, n., earth, (coll.) gossip

dirt'-y, a., not clean

dis-ad-van'tage, n., unfavorable condition, -ous

dis-a-grēe', v., have different opinion, -ment

dis-al-low', v., refuse to allow

dis-ap-pēar', v., vanish

dis-ap-point', v., not meet person's hopes, wishes, -ment

dis-ap-prove' (prŏŏv), v., condemn, -proval

dis-ärm', v., take away weapons

dis-är'ma-ment, n., weapon reduction

dis-är-ray', n., disorder

dis-as-sem'ble, v., take apart

dis-as'ter, n., tragedy, -trous

dis-à-vow', v., refuse knowledge or responsibility of

dis-band', v., break up

dis-bär', v., expel from law practice, -ment

dis-bè-lièf', n., not to believe

dis-bè-lieve', v., not believe

dis-bûrse', v., pay out money

dis-cärd', v., throw away, reject

dis-cêrn' (zêrn), v., understand, -ment

dis-chärge', v., shoot, unload, fulfill, remove from job

dis'chärge, n., shot, dismissal, release from prison or hospital

dis-ci'ple, n., follower

dis-ci-pli-nâr'i-an, n., strict enforcer

dis'ci-pline, v., train

dis-clâim', v., refuse ownership

dis-clōse', v., show, reveal

dis-clō'sûre, n., telling, revealing

dis-cöm'fi-tûre, n., frustration, defeat

dis-cön-cêrt', v., confuse, -ed

dis-cön-nect', v., break connection, -ed

dis-con-sö-late, a., unhappy

dis-cön-tent', a., not satisfied; -ed

dis-cön-tin'ūe, v., put an end to

dis'cörd, n., disagreement, confusion, -ant

dis'co-theque' (tĕk), n., nightclub, cabaret, etc. where there is dancing to recorded music

dis'count, n., reduction from total

dis-coûr'age (kêr), v., lessen enthusiasm for, -aging

dis'coûrse (kŏrs), n., speech, discussion, conversation

dis-coûr'te-ous (kêr), a., rude, -sy

dis-cöv'êr, v., find, learn about, -y

dis-cred'it, v., disbelieve

dis-crēet', a., careful

dis-crep'an-cy, n., inconsistency, mistake

dis-crête', a., separate

dis-cre'tion, n., judgment, -ary

dis-crim'i-nāte, v., choose between, -nation

dis-cuss', v., talk about, -ion

dis-dâin', v., ignore, scorn, -ful

dis-ēase' (di-zēez), n., illness, sickness

dis-ėm-bärk', v., unload, leave a vehicle

dis-ėn-chant', v., free from enchantment, -ment

dis-ėn-gāge', v., free

dis-ėn-tan'gle, v., free from involvement

dis-fā-vör, n., not like

dis-fig'ûre, v., mar appearance

dis-fran'chise, v., remove rights

dis-grāce', v., shame, insult, -ful

dis-grun'tle, v., make discontented

dis-guîse', v., change appearance

dis-gust', n., strong aversion, -ed

dish, n., plate for food, recipe

dish, v., serve

dis-här'mö-ny, n., absence of harmony

dis-heärt-ėn, v., reduce courage, lose interest

dis-shev'eled, (ĕld) a., not

neat

dis-hon'ŏr, v., shame, insult

dis-il-lū'sion, v., discourage, free from certain impressions

dis-in-fect', v., kill germs, **-ant**

dis-in-gen'û-ous, a., not sincere

dis-in-her'it, v., remove from inheritance

dis-in'tè-grāte, v., break up

dis-in-têr', v., dig up corpse

dis-in'têr-est, n., absence of interest

dis-joint'ed, a., disconnected

disk, n., flat plate, phonograph record

disk' jock'ėy, n., record-playing broadcaster

dis-līke', v., not fond of

dis'lō-cāte, v., put out of place

dis-lodge', v., move from

dis-loy'ál, a., not true to, **-ity**

dis'mal (diz), a., gloomy

dis-man'tle, v., take apart

dis-may', n., unhappiness

dis-mem'bêr, v., cut into pieces

dis-miss', v., remove, put aside, **-al**

dis-mount', v., get down

dis-ō-bē'di-ênt, a., not obeying, **-ence**

dis-ō-bey' (bay), v., not follow orders

dis-ôr'dêr, n., confusion, **-ly**

dis-ôr'dėr-ly house, n., house of prostitution

dis-ōwn', v., refuse to accept as one's own

dis-par'áge, v., lessen importance of, **-ment**

dis'pà-rāte (rit), a., unequal, **-rity**

dis-pas'sion-āte, a., without feeling or pity

dis-patch', v., send

dis-pel', v., scatter

dis-pen'sà-ble, a., not needed

dis-pen'sà-ry, n., free medical treatment place

dis-pense', v., give, distribute

dis-pêrse', v., scatter, **-persion**

dis-plāce', v., remove from, **-ment**

dis-play', v., show

dis-plēase', v., cause dissatisfaction

dis-pleas'ûre, n., lack of satisfaction

dis-pōs'ál, n., getting rid of, settlement

dis-pōs'áll, n., garbage grinder in kitchen sink

dis-pōse', v., settle, arrange

dis-pō-si'tion, n., temper, personality, settlement

dis-pŏs-sess', v., deprive of

dis-prōōf', n., lack of evidence to prove

dis-prō-pôr'tion-āte, a., not in relation with

dis-prove' (prōōv), v., show as false

dis-pūte', n., argument

dis-quál'i-fy (kwál), v., make ineligible, **-fication**

dis-rè-gärd', v., ignore, be unconcerned

dis-rè-pair', n., not in working order

dis-rep'ú-tà-ble, a., of bad reputation

dis-rè-spect', n., lack of politeness, **-ful**

dis-rōbe', v., undress

dis-rupt', v., break up, **-ion**

dis-sat'is-fīed, a., not pleased, **-faction**

dis-sect', v., cut apart, **-ion**

dis-sem'ble, v., conceal, pretend

dis-sem'i-nāte, v., spread, scatter

dis-sen'sion, n., disagreement

dis-sent', v., disagree, **-er**

dis-si-dént, a., not in agreement, **-dence**

dis-sim'i-lár, a., unlike, **-ity**

dis-sim'ū-lāte, v., hide, disguise, **-lation**

dis'si-pāte, v., scatter, waste, **-pation**

dis-sō'ci-āte, v., separate, **-ation**

dis'sō-lūte, a., wicked, immoral

dis'sō-lū'tion, n., breaking into parts

dis-solve', v., cause to melt, fade away, end, **-nt**

dis'sō-nánce, n., confused sound, **-nant**

dis-suāde' (swayd), v., persuade not to do, **-suasion**

dis'taff, n., female side

dis'tánce, n., space between points, **-tant**

dis-tāste', *n.*, dislike, -ful

dis-tem'pêr, *n.*, animal disease

dis-tend', *v.*, stretch

dis-till', *v.*, vaporize, then condense, -ed

dis-till'êr-y, *n.*, place for making liquor

dis-tinct', *a.*, separate, individual, -ion, -ive

dis-tinct'ly, *adv.*, clearly

dis-tin'guish, *v.*, observe difference

dis-tin'guished, *a.*, honored

dis-tôrt', *v.*, pull out of shape, -ion

dis-tract', *v.*, remove attention from, -ion

dis-trāught', *a.*, extremely upset

dis-tress', *n.*, sorrow, anxiety, -ed

dis-trib'ūte, *v.*, give out, -ution

dis'trict, *n.*, geographical area

dis-trust', *v.*, lack faith in, have no trust, -ful

dis-tûrb', *v.*, bother, interrupt, -ance

dis-ūse', *v.*, discontinue using

ditch, *n.*, trench in ground

ditch (coll.), *v.*, get rid of

dith'êr, *n.*, state of trembling

dit'tō, *n.*, same as above or before

dit'ty, *n.*, song

di-ûr'nal, *a.*, every day

di'va (dēe), *n.*, famous woman singer

di'van, *n.*, sofa

dīve, *v.*, plunge head first, -r

di-vêrge', *v.*, separate, -nce

di-vêrse', *a.*, different

di-vêr'si-fīed, *a.*, having variety

di-vêr'sion, *n.*, turning aside, amusement

di-vêrt', *v.*, turn aside

di-vêr-tisse-ment' (mahn), *n.*, entertainment

di-vest', *v.*, remove from

di-vīde', *v.*, separate, -d

div'i-dend, *n.*, payment to stockholders of company

div-i-nā'tion, *n.*, predicting the future

di-vīne', *a.*, relating to God

di-vin'i-ty, *n.*, God, holy

di-vi'sion, *n.*, separation into parts, arithmetic process, -sible

di-vôrce', *n.*, ending of marriage

di-vulge', *v.*, show, reveal, -vulgence

diz'zy, *a.*, sense of whirling

do (dōo), *v.*, perform, accomplish, act

doc'ile, *a.*, easy to handle, tame

dock, *n.*, wharf

dock'êt, *n.*, list of court cases

doc'tôr, *n.*, physician

doc'trine, *n.*, cause, belief

doc'ū-ment, *n.*, official paper, -ation

doc-ū-men'tà-ry, *a.*, factual

dodge, *v.*, evade, -r

doff, *v.*, take off

dôg, *n.*, domestic canine

dôg'dāys, *n.*, humid summer days

dôg'ged, *a.*, determined

dôg'gêr-èl, *a.*, light verse

dôg-mat'ic, *a.*, dictatorially positive, -tism

dôg'tag, *n.*, identification plate

dôg'wood, *n.*, flowering tree

doi'ly, *n.*, small table mat

dōl'drum, *n.*, dull atmosphere

dōle, *v.*, give out, -ful

doll, *n.*, child's toy

dol'lár, *n.*, U. S. monetary unit

dol'ly, *n.*, two-wheeled cart

dōl'ôr-ous, *a.*, sorrowful, sad

dōlt, *n.*, stupid person

dō-māin', *n.*, area of control

dōme, *n.*, round-shaped roof

dö-mes'tic, *a.*, relating to household, -ate

dom'i-nànt, *a.*, ruling, prevailing

dom'i-nāte, *v.*, control

dom-i-nêer', *v.*, control arrogantly, -ing

dö-min'ion, *n.*, territory under control

dom'i-nō, *n.*, mask, game

dō'nāte, *v.*, give as gift, -nation

döne, *a.*, completed

don'kêy, *n.*, mule-like animal

dō'nôr, *n.*, one who gives

dōn't, *v.*, cont. of do not

dōo'dle, *v.*, unconsciously draw or scribble

dōōm, *n.*, destiny, final end

dôor, *n.*, hinged entrance

dôpe, *n.*, narcotic, lacquer

dōpe, *v.*, give drugs

dōpe'fiênd, *n.*, drug addict

dôr'mant, *a.*, asleep, inactive

dôr'mi-tô-ry, *n.*, building to sleep many

dōse, *n.*, amount of medicine to take

dos'si-er (dos-i-ay), *n.*, data on subject or person

dōt'age, *n.*, silly behavior of old age

dou'ble (dub-bil), *a.*, twice, two of

dou'ble crôss, *v.*, betray

doubt (dowt), *v.*, be unsure of

doubt'ful, *a.*, uncertain

doubt'less, *adv.*, without question

douche (dōosh), *n.*, water flow applied within body

dough (dōh), *n.*, flour mixed in water, (coll.) money

dough'nut, *n.*, round cake with hole

dour, *a.*, gloomy

douse, , *v.*, wet, put out

dōve, *n.*, bird

dōve'tāil, *v.*, fit together

dow'a-gêr, *n.*, widow owning husband's property

down, *adv.*, higher to lower

down, *n.*, football term

down'cast, *a.*, unhappy

down'fäll, *n.*, ruin

down'grāde, *n.*, descent

down'heärt-ĕd, *a.*, discouraged

down'pôur, *n.*, heavy rain

down'rĭght, *a.*, absolute

down'stāge, *adv.*, toward audience

down'tōwn, *n.*, city business district

dow'ry, *n.*, money given by bride to husband

dowse, *v.*, search for water for well

dox-ol'ö-gy, *n.*, hymn

dŏz'ĕn, *n.*, twelve

drab, *a.*, unexciting

draft, *n.*, drawing, air current, **-y**

draft, *v.*, call into service, **-ee**

drafts'măn, *n.*, person who draws plans

drag, *v.*, pull, search with net

drag (coll.) *n.*, social partner, puff on cigarette

drag'net, *n.*, intensive search

drag'ŏn, *n.*, mythical monster

drāin, *v.*, remove slowly, make tired, **-age**

dram, *n.*, ounce

drä'må, *n.*, stage play, **-tic**

Dram'á-mine (mēen), *n.*, motion sickness drug

dram'á-tīze, *v.*, give dramatic quality

drāpe, *v.*, cover with folds of fabric

drā'pêr-y, *n.*, curtains

dras'tic, *a.*, desperate, violent, **-ally**

draught (draft), *n.*, portion of beer

drăw, *v.*, pull, sketch, conclude

drăw'back, *n.*, hindrance

drăw'bridge, *n.*, bridge that raises

drăw'êr (drôhr), *n.*, sliding container in furniture

drăw'ing, *n.*, picture, selection by lottery

drăwl, *v.*, talk slowly

dray, *n.*, cart

dread (dred), *v.*, fear

dread'ful, *a.*, fearful

dread'nŏught, *n.*, battleship

drēam, *n.*, vision during sleep, **-y**

drēam'wôrld, *n.*, unreal outlook

drēar'y, *a.*, gloomy, dull

dredge, *v.*, scoop up river bottom

drench, *v.*, wet thoroughly

dress, *n.*, clothing, woman's outer garment

dress, *v.*, put on clothing

dress'cîr-cle, *n.*, boxseats at opera

dress'êr, *n.*, clothes chest, one who dresses

dress'ing dōwn', *n.*, outspoken criticism

dress' shield, *n.*, underarm dress protector

dress'y, *a.*, showy, fashionable

drib'ble, *n.*, small portion, drip

drift, *v.*, move along slowly

drift, *n.*, direction of movement

drift'wood, *n.*, wood washed ashore

drill, *n.*, exercise, tool for making holes

drill, *v.*, make hole by boring, practice, train intensively

drill'press, *n.*, machine for boring holes

drink, *n.*, liquid, alcoholic beverage, **-er**

drink, v., swallow liquid
drip, n., small liquid drop
drip, v., fall in small drops
drip′ö-lā-tör′, n., drip coffee pot
drive, v., operate a vehicle, aim, push, work hard
drive, n., campaign
drive-in, n., restaurant, movie, for motorists served in cars
driv′el, n., foolish talk
driv′êr, n., vehicle operator, golf club, one who pushes
driz′zle, n., slight rainfall
dröll, a., amusingly unusual, -ery
drom′e-dâr′y, n., one-humped camel
dröne, n., male bee
drööp, v., sag, sink
drop, n., fall
drop, n., small liquid mass
drop′sy, n., excessive accumulation of water in body
drought (drowt), n., prolonged dry weather
drown, v., die by water
drowse, v., sleep lightly
drow′sy, a., sleepy
drug, n., medicinal compound, -gist
drug′ stôre, n., store selling drugs, etc.
drum, n., percussion musical instrument
drunk, a., intoxicated, -en
drunk′ârd, n., continuous drinker
drunk-om′e-ter, n., device to measure alcohol on breath to determine amount of alcohol in blood
dry, a., not wet, -ly
dry′-clēan′, v., clean with waterless solvent, -er
dry′ dock, n., repair dock for ship
dry′ goods, n., clothing, materials, etc.
dry′ ice, n., solidified carbon dioxide
dū′al, a., double, -ism
dū′bi-ous, a., doubtful, -ly -table
duch′ess, n., duke's wife
duck, n., water fowl, type of cloth
duck, v., dip, avoid, -ling
duct, n., tube, -less
duc′tile, a., capable of being shaped and stretched

dūde, n., dandy
duds, n., clothing (coll.)
dūe, a., owing at set time, payable
dū′el, n., fight between two persons, -ist
dūes, n., club fees
dū-et′, n., musical rendition by two
dug′out, n., ball player's shelter
dūke, n., nobleman
dūke′döm, n., duke's area of rule
dul′cet, a., sweet, soothing
dull, a., not exciting, boring, unintelligent, not sharp
dumb (dum), a., unable to speak, unintelligent (coll.)
dumb′-wāit-êr, n., hand elevator
dum′my, n., inanimate model, imitation, stupid one (coll.)
dump, n., place for garbage, (coll.), untidy place
dump, v., unload
dump′y, a., short and fat
dunce, n., dull person
dun-gā-rēes′, n., jeans
dun′gèon (jin), n., underground prison
dunk, v., dip
dun′nage, n., protection for cargo or baggage
dū′ō, n., word form meaning two
dūpe, n., person easily fooled, -d
dū′plex, n., two-family house
dū-pli-cāte, v., exact copy, -cation
dū-plic′i-ty, n., deception
dū-râ-ble, a., of lasting quality, -bility
dū-rā′tion, n., length of existence
dū-ress′, n., pressure
dūr′ing, prep., in course of, while
dusk, n., twilight, -y
dust, n., small dirt particles
dū′ty, n., obligation, task, tax, -tiful
dwârf, n., small-sized
dwell, v., live, brood over, -ing, -er
dwin′dle, v., grow less, shrink
dye, v., change color of -ing
dy-nam′ic,a., active, energetic, forceful
dy′nà-mīte, n., explosive,

(coll.) dangerous

dy·ná·mō, *n.*, machine producing electric current, energetic person (coll.)

dy·nás·ty, *n.*, rulers of same family, **-tic**

dýs·én·ter·y, *n.*, diarrhea

dýs·func´tion, *n.*, abnormal action

dýs·pép·si·à, *n.*, improper digestion

E

ēach, *a.*, every one

ēa´gêr, *a.*, wanting anxiously, **-ly**

ēa´gêr bēa·ver (coll.), *n.*, anxious person

ēa´gle, *n.*, bird of prey

ēa´gle-eyed, *a.*, sharp in vision

ēar, *n.*, organ of hearing

ēar´drum, *n.*, ear part

ēarl, *n.*, nobleman

ēar´ly, *adv.*, before expected time

ēar´ly bírd (coll.), *n.*, early rising person

ēar´mark, *v.*, set apart, put sign on

ēarn, *v.*, deserve, gain, work for, **-ing**

ēar´nêst, *a.*, sincere

ēar´ring, *n.*, ear jewelry

ēar´shot, *n.*, close range

ēarth, *n.*, ground, globe, **-en**

ēarth´én·wâre, *n.*, heavy clay dishes

ēarth´quāke (kwayk), *n.*, earth tremor

ēarth´wôrm (wûrm), *n.*, soil worm

ēarth´ý, *a.*, relating to dirt, natural

ēase, *n.*, relaxed effort, comfort

ēa´sêl, *n.*, artist's stand for painting

ēas·i·ly, *adv.*, without effort, **-ness**

ēast, *n.*, direction of sunrise, **-ern**

ēas´y, *a.*, troublefree, effortless

ēas´y gō´ing, *a.*, relaxed, unworried

ēat, *v.*, consume food

ēaves´drop, *v.*, listen secretly

ebb, *v.*, lessen, flow away

eb´ön·y, *n.*, type of wood

é·bul´li·ênt (yint), *a.*, bubbling, lively

ec·cén´tric, *a.*, strange, **-ity**

ec·clē·si·as´tic, *n.*,

pertaining to church, clergyman, **-al**

ech´é·lon (esh), *n.*, step-like formation

ech´ō (ek-ōh), *n.*, repeated sound

e·clâir´ (ay-klayr), *n.*, filled pastry

ec·léc´tic, *a.*, choosing

è·clipse´, *n.*, temporary darkening of sun or moon

e·cól´ö·gy, *n.*, environmental study

ē·cö·nóm´i·cál, *a.*, thrifty, **-ze**

ē·cö·nóm´ics, *n.*, science of wealth, production and distribution

ē·con´ö·my, *n.*, distribution of wealth

ec·stá·sy, *n.*, intensely delighted feeling, **-tic**

ec·ū·men´i·cál, *a.*, universal

ec·zè·mà, *n.*, skin disease

ē·den´tāte, *a.*, toothless

edge, *n.*, margin, border, sharp side

edg´y, *a.*, nervous

ed´i·ble, *a.*, capable of being eaten

ē´dict, *n.*, order, proclamation

ed·i·fi·cā´tion, *n.*, moral improvement, enlightenment

ed´i·fice, *n.*, building

ed´it, *v.*, prepare for publication, **-or**

è·di´tion, *n.*, issue of book or newspaper

ed·i·tō´ri·ál, *n.*, written opinion, **-ize**

ed´ū·cāte, *v.*, train, teach, **-cable**

ed·ū·cā´tion·ál, *a.*, giving instruction

è·dūce´, *v.*, draw out

ēel, *n.*, snake-like fish

ef·fāce´, *v.*, erase, destroy

ef·fect´, *n.*, result

ef·féc´tive, *a.*, bringing results, impressive

ef-fec'tū-ȧl (choo), *a.*, bringing expected results, **-ate**

ef-fem'ı̆-nāte, *a.*, woman-like

ef-fēr-ent, *a.*, leading outward

ef-fēr-vesce', *v.*, bubble, **-nt**

ef-fēte', *a.*, worn out, jaded

ef-fı̆-cā'cious, *a.*, having desired result, **-cy**

ef-fı̆'cient, *a.*, working well

ef'fı̆-gy, *n.*, image

ef'flū-ent, *a.*, flowing out

ef'fôrt, *n.*, attempt to accomplish

ef-frŏn'tēr-y, *n.*, defiance, insolence, forwardness

ef-ful'gent, *a.*, bright, shining

ef-fūse', *v.*, spill forth, **-fusion**

e. g., for example

egg, *n.*, female reproductive cell

egg'-nog', *n.*, drink made of eggs and whiskey and cream

egg'-plant, *n.*, purple vegetable

ē'-gō, *n.*, self, **-ism**

è-grē'gious (jus), *a.*, unusually bad

ē'gress, *n.*, exit

eight (ayt), *n.*, cardinal numeral "8", **-h**

eight'ball, *n.*, pool ball, (coll.) difficult situation

eight'ēen, *n.*, ten plus eight

eight'y, *n.*, ten times eight

ēi'-thêr, *adj.*, one or the other

è-jac'ū-lāte (jak), *v.*, speak suddenly, **-lation**

è-ject', *v.*, discharge with force

ēke, *v.*, barely make do

è-lab'ôr-āte, *a.*, done in detail, fancy, **-ation**

è-lān' (ay), *n.*, spirit

è-lapse', *v.*, pass away

è-las'tic, *a.*, resilient

è-lāte', *v.*, make happy, **-lation**

el'bōw, *n.*, arm joint or bend

el'bōw rŏŏm, *n.*, plenty of space

eld'êr, *a.*, older, **-ly**

è-lect', *v.*, choose by voting, **-ion**

è-lec-tion-ēer', *v.*, speak on behalf of candidate

è-lec'tive, *a.*, chosen

è-lec'tôr-āte, *v.*, collective voters

è-lec'tric, *a.*, exciting energy

è-lec-tric'i-ty, *n.*, form of energy

è-lec'trı̆-fy, *v.*, excite, surprise

è-lec'trō-cūte, *v.*, kill with electricity

è-lec'tron, *n.*, negatively charged particle

è-lec-trŏn'ic brāin, *n.*, electronic computer

è-lec-trŏn'ics, *n.*, branch of science concerned with electrons

è-lec'trō-type, *n.*, printing plate

el-èe-mos'ȳ-nâr-y, *a.*, charitable

el'ē-gȧnce, *n.*, dignified richness, **-gant**

el'ē-gy, *n.*, mournful poem, **-giac**

el'ē-ment, *n.*, matter, basic part or principle, **-al**

el-ē-men'tȧ-ry, *a.*, simple to understand, beginning, basic

el'ē-phȧnt, *n.*, huge animal, **-ine**

el'ē-vāte, *v.*, raise, lift, **-vation**

el'ē-vā-tôr, *n.*, lifting device

è-lev'ẽn, *n.*, ten plus one, **-th**

elf, *n.*, tiny fairy-like being

è-lic'it, *v.*, bring forth

el'i-gi-ble, *a.*, having desired qualifications

è-lim'ı̆-nāte, *v.*, get rid of, remove, omit, **-nation**

è-līte' (lēet), *n.*, choice group

è-lix'îr, *n.*, magical drink, medicine

elk, *n.*, deer-like animal

è-lipse', *n.*, geometric curve

el-ō-cū'tion, *n.*, style of speech

è-lŏn'gāte, *v.*, make longer, **-gation**

è-lōpe', *v.*, run away in order to marry, **-ment**

el'ō-quence, *n.*, skillful speech, **-quent**

else, *a.*, different, more

else'where, *adv.*, in another place

è-lū'ci-dāte, *v.*, make clear, **-dation**

è-lūde', *v.*, escape from, **-lusive**

em, *n.*, printers' measure

è-mā'ci-ā-těd (she), *a.*, undernourished, thin

em'ȧ-nāte, *v.*, come from

è-man'ci-pāte, v., set free

é-mas'cū-lāte, v., castrate

ém-bälm', v., preserve dead body

ém-bänk'ment, n., slight hill

ém-bär'gō, n., restriction on trade

ém-bärk', v., begin journey

ém-bar'rass, v., shame, upset, -ment

em-bás'sy, n., ambassador's residence

ém-bat'tled, a., ready for fighting

ém-bel'lish, v., decorate, -ment

ém-bez'zle, v., steal

ém-bit'ter, v., make more unhappy or bitter

ém'blém, n., symbol, badge, -atic

ém-bod'y, v., give form

em'bō-lism, n., blood clot

ém-bóss', v., make raised design

ém-brāce', v., hug

em'brō-cāte, v., rub with soothing solution

ém-broi'dér, v., stitch fancy design in cloth, -y

ém-broil', v., involve in a fight

em'brȳ-ō, n., organism in early stage of development, -nic

è-mend', v., correct

em'ér-áld, n., green precious stone

è-mérge', v., come forth, -mersion

è-mér'gén-cy, n., sudden situation needing action

è-mer'i-tus, a., retired honorably

è-met'ic, a., causing vomiting

em'i-grāte, v., leave a country, -gration

em'i-nént, a., well known, important, -nence

em'is-sār'y, n., messenger

é-mit', v., send forth, give out

em'ol'li-ént, a., softening and soothing

è-mol'ū-ment, n., salary, payment

é-mōte', v., show emotion

é-mō'tion, n., feeling of love, hate, etc.

em'pá-thy, n., personality projection

em'pér-ór, n., king

em'phá-sīze, v., stress, -sis

em'pīre, n., countries under one rule

em-pir'ic, a., experimental, -al

ém-ploy', v., hire for work, use

ém-ploy'ér, n., one who hires, -ee

ém-ploy'ment, n., job, occupation

ém-pow'ér, v., give authority to

em'préss, n., queen

emp'ty, a., containing nothing, bare, hungry

em-pȳr'é-ál, a., heavenly

em'ū-lāte, v., imitate

é-mul'sion, n., undissolving chemicals

én-ā'ble, v., give power to do

én-áct', v., pass a bill, do, -ment

en-am'él, n., glossy paint, tooth coating

én-camp', v., make camp

en-ceph-à-lī'tis, n., brain inflammation

én-chant', v., cast spell, charm, -ment

en'chi-lä'da, n., filled tortilla (usually meat), in chili flavored sauce

én-cír'cle, v., surround

én-clōse', v., close in all around, -closure

en-cō'mi-um, n., praise

én-cóm'pass, v., surround, include

en'córe (ahn), n., request for another performance

én-coun'tér, v., meet someone, face in opposition

én-coûr'age (kûr), v., give confidence to, support, -ment

én-crōach', v., invade another's rights, etc., -ment

én-cum'bér, v., burden, block, -brance

én-cy-clō-pē'di-á, n., collection of general knowledge

end, v., last, limit, last part, purpose, finish, death

én-dān'gér, v., expose to danger

én-dēar', v., cause to love, -ment

én-deav'ör (dev), v., attempt

en-dem'ic, a., native to a region

end'ing, n., closing, death,

last part

end'less, *a.*, having no boundaries

en'dō-crine (krin) *n.*, type of body gland

en-dog'e-nous (doj) *a.*, from within

èn-dôrse', *v.*, approve, support, sign, **-ment**

èn-dow', *v.*, give gift, **-ment**

en-dūr'ance, *n.*, lasting power

èn-dūre', *v.*, allow, bear, suffer

è-ne'ma, *n.*, fluid injected into rectum

en'e-my, *n.*, person hated

en'er-gy, *n.*, strength, vigor, **-getic**

en-ēr'vāte, *v.*, weaken

èn-fôrce', *v.*, compel obedience

èn-gāge' (gayj) *v.*, pledge, involve, hire, be busy, fight, **-d**

èn-gāge'ment, *n.*, date, promise of marriage

èn-gen'dēr (jen) *v.*, cause, produce

en'gine (jin) *n.*, motor

en-gi-neer', *n.*, one in the engineering profession, train engine, **-ing**

Eng'lish (ing) *a.*, *n.*, pertaining to England, language

èn-grave', *v.*, cut deep impression, **-graving**

èn-gulf', *v.*, swallow up

èn-grōss', *v.*, occupy deeply

èn-hance', *v.*, add to, make better

è-nig'ma, *n.*, mysterious puzzle

en-join', *v.*, order, forbid

en-jōy', *v.*, be happy, **-ment**

èn-lärge', *v.*, increase size

èn-light'en, *v.*, teach, free from prejudice, **-ment**

èn-list', *v.*, join military group voluntarily, secure help, **-ment**

en masse', *adv.*, in a group

èn-mesh', *v.*, tangle

en'mi-ty, *n.*, feeling of hatred

en-nō'ble, *v.*, dignify

en'nui (ähn-wēe) *n.*, boredom

è-nôr'mous, *a.*, huge, **-mity**

è-nough' (nuff) *a.*, in sufficient quantity

èn-quire' (kwir) *v.*, ask, investigate

èn-quir'y, *n.*, question

èn-rāge', *v.*, make angry

èn-rōll', *v.*, sign up for, join, **-ment**

en-sconce', *v.*, fit in snugly

en-sem'ble (än-säm) *n.*, complete outfit

èn-shrine', *v.*, make sacred

en'sign (sin) *n.*, U. S. Navy officer, flag

èn-slāve', *v.*, make into slave

en-snāre', *v.*, trap, catch

en-sūe', *v.*, follow

èn-sure', *v.*, make certain

èn-tāil', *v.*, require, involve

èn-tan'gle, *v.*, involve, trap, **-ment**

en'tēr, *v.*, go into

èn-tēr-prise', *n.*, venture, undertaking

èn-tēr-prīs-ing, *a.*, energetic, bold

en-tēr-tain', *v.*, amuse, accept, **-ment**

èn-thrâll', *v.*, fascinate

èn-thrōne', *v.*, make king, place on throne

èn-thūse', *v.*, be inspired by

èn-thū'si-asm (zi-azm) *n.*, eagerness, intense interest, **-astic**

èn-tice', *v.*, lead on

èn-tire', *a.*, all, complete

èn-ti'tle, *v.*, allow, give right to act

en'ti-ty, *n.*, being, whole

èn-tomb' (tōōm) *v.*, bury in tomb

en-tō-mol'ö-gy, *n.*, study of insects

en'trance, *n.*, place or act of admission

èn-trance', *v.*, put under spell or trance

èn-trēat', *v.*, beg, **-y**

en'tree (ähn-tray) *n.*, meal's main course, freedom to enter

èn-trench', *v.*, establish firmly

en-trè-prè-neūr' (ähn) *n.*, person conducting own business

èn-trust', *v.*, trust with care of something

en'try, *n.*, listing, entrance

èn-twine', *v.*, wrap around

è-nū'mēr-āte, *v.*, count, **-ation**

è-nun'ci-āte, *v.*, speak clearly, **-ation**

èn-vel'öp, *v.*, surround, wrap,

-ment

en've-lope, n., letter container

en-vi'ron-ment, n., surroundings

en-vi'rons, n., neighborhood

en-vis'age, v., imagine, anticipate

en'voy, n., diplomatic messenger

en'vy, v., be jealous, **-viable**

en'zyme, n., body chemical

ep'au-let, n., military shoulder decoration

e-phem'er-al, a., short-lived

ep'ic, n., heroic long poem

ep'i-cen-ter, n., middle of earthquake

ep'i-cure, n., devotee of gourmet eating, **-an**

ep-i-dem'ic, n., widespread disease

ep'i-der'mis, n., outer skin

ep'i-gram, n., witty remark, **-matic**

ep'i-lep-sy, n., nerve disease, **-tic**

ep'i-logue, n., last part

e-pis'co-pal, a., governed by bishops, **-pacy**

ep'i-sode, n., event, part of whole story

e-pis-te-mol'o-gy, n., philosophy relating to knowledge

e-pis'tle, n., letter, writing

ep'i-taph, n., tombstone inscription

ep'i-thet, n., descriptive name

e-pit'o-me, n., summary, typical example, **-mize**

ep'och (uhk), n., period in history

e'qual (kwil), a., on even terms with, same, **-quable**

e-qual'i-ty, n., state of being equal

e-qua-nim'i-ty, n., calmness

e-qua'tion, n., expression of equal quantities, formula

e-qua'tor, n., imaginary circle around earth's center

e-ques'tri-an, n., horseback rider, **-enne**

e-qui-lib'ri-um, n., balance

e'quine, n., pertaining to horse

e'qui-nox, n., time when night and day are equal in length

e-quip', v., provide material needed

e-quip'ment, n., furnishings

eq'ui-ta-ble, a., fair, just

eq'ui-ty (ek-wi-ty), n., fairness, value

e-quiv'a-lent, a., equal, **-lence**

e-quiv'o-cal, a., misleading

e-quiv'o-cate, v., mislead, lie

e'ra, n., period of time

e-rad'i-cate, v., get rid of

e-rase', v., rub out, eradicate, **-r**

e-rect', v., build, **-ion**

er'e-mite, n., hermit

er'go, conj., therefore

er'mine, n., white fur

e-rode', v., wear away, **-rosion**

e-rot'ic, adj., arousing sexual desire

err, v., do or be wrong

er'rand (âir), n., trip, commission

er'rant, a., roving for adventure, straying

er-rat'ic, a., irregular

er-ro'ne-ous, a., mistaken

er'ror, n., mistake

er-sätz', a., artificial

er-u-dite', a., learned, **-dition**

e-rupt', v., burst forth, break out, **-ion**

es'ca-la-tor, n., moving steps

es'ca-pade, n., adventurous prank

es-cape', n., get free, avoid, run from

es-carp'ment, n., steep slope

es-chew', v., avoid

es-cort', v., go with, accompany

es-cu'lent, a., suitable for eating

e-soph'a-gus, n., tube leading to stomach

es-o-ter'ic, a., known to only a few

es-pe'cial-ly, adv., mainly, particularly, unusually

es'pi-o-näge (näj), n., spying

es-pouse', v., marry, support, adopt

es-prit' de corps (esprē di kōr), group spirit

es'quire (kwyr), n., title of courtesy

es'say, n., writing on a particular topic

es-say', v., try

es'sence, n., main part, flavor

es-sen'tial, a., important

es-tab'lish, v., settle, prove,

begin

ès-tab'lish-mènt, n., institution, household, business organization

ès-tāte', n., possessions, property

ès-tēem', v., value, consider

es'ti-mā-ble, a., worthy

es'ti-māte, v., guess roughly, judge

es'ti-māte, n., rough calculation

es-ti-mā'tion, n., regard, opinion

ès-trānge', v., become unfriendly

es'trō-gèn, n., female hormone

es'tū-ār-y, n., river mouth

et cet'èr-à, etc., and so forth

etch, v., engrave with acid, **-ing**

ètèr'nàl, a., endless, permanent, **-nity**

ē'thèr, n., chemical anesthetic, air

è-thē're-ál, a., heavenly

eth'ics, n., moral principles

eth'nic, a., racial, cultural

eth-nol'ō-ġy, n., study of the races of man

ē-ti-ol'ō-ġy, n., study of causes

et'i-quette (ket), n., behavior, manners

et-ỳ-mol'ō-ġy, n., study of word origins

eū-gen'ics, n., study of improvement of human qualities, heredity

eū'lō-ġy, n., praise for the dead

eū'nuch, n., castrated man

eū'phē-mism, n., use of pleasant word in place of distasteful one

eū'phō-ny, n., pleasing sound, **-nious**

eū-thà-nā'si-à, n., painless death, mercy killing

è-vac'ū-āte, v., empty, abandon, **-ation**

è-vāde', v., avoid, **-vasion**

è-val'ū-āte, v., appraise worth of, judge

ev-à-nes'cent, a., fleeting, fading quickly

è-van'ġel-ism (je), n., gospel preaching, **-list**

è-vap'ō-rāte, v., change to vapor, vanish

ēve, n., night before event

ē'vén, a., uniform, calm, level, equal, exact

ēve'ning, n., time before

night

è-vent', n., happening

è-vent'ū-ál, a., finally

ev'ér, adv., always, at all

ev-èr-grēen, n., tree, shrub

ev-ér-last'ing, a., forever

ev-èr-mōre', adv., always, forever

ev'èr-y, a., each one

ev'èr-y-bŏd-y, pro., every person

ev'èr-y-thing, pro., all things

ev'èr-y-where (wayr), adv., all places

è-vict', v., put out of home, **-ion**

evi-dence, n., proof

evi-dent, a., clear

ē'vil, a., wrong, wicked

ē'vil-eyed' (īd), a., having power to cause harm by glance

è-vince', n., show clearly

è-vis'cèr-āte, v., remove insides, deprive

è-vōke', v., call forth

ev-ō-lū'tion, n., development, formation over period of time

ev-ō-lū'tion-âr-y, a., gradually developing

è-volve', v., occur gradually

ewe (ū), n., female sheep

èx-act', a., correct, perfect

èx-act'ing, a., thorough, demanding

ex-ag'ġèr-āte (aj-jer-), v., overstate, enlarge upon, **-ation**

èx-ált', v., raise, praise, fill with joy, **-ation**

èx-am-i-nā'tion, n., test, search

èx-am'ine, v., test, look into, **-r**

èx-am'ple, n., model for imitation, sample

èx-as'pèr-āte, v., annoy, bother, make angry

ex'cà-vāte, v., dig out, make hollow, **-vation**

èx-cēed', v., do more than, go beyond, **-ing**

èx-cel', v., be better or greater than, outdo, **-lence, -lent**

ex'cél-lèn-cy, n., title of honor, high quality

èx-cept', prep., also, not including

èx-cep'tion, n., omission, particular instance,

objection

ĕx·cep'tion·ăl, *a.*, not ordinary, unusual

ex'cêrpt, *n.*, selection taken from book, etc.

ex·cess', *a.*, more than, immoderate, **-ive**

ĕx·change', *v.*, trade

ĕx·change' rē·ac'tion, *n.*, patterned movement of atoms

ex'cīse, *n.*, tax on certain articles

ex·cīse', *v.*, cut out, remove, **-cision**

ĕx·cīte', *v.*, stir emotions, **-ment**

ĕx·claim', *v.*, speak out suddenly

ex·cla·mā'tion, *n.*, sudden speech

ex·clūde', *v.*, keep out, refuse to admit, **-clusion**

ĕx·clū'sive, *a.*, selective, not shared

ex·cŏm·mū'ni·cāte, *v.*, expel from church

ĕx·cô'ri·āte, *v.*, denounce, **-ation**

ex'crē·ment, *n.*, waste material from bowels

ĕx·crēte', *v.*, expel waste matter from body

ĕx·crū'ci·āt·ing, *a.*, painful, torturous

ex'cul·pāte, *v.*, find innocent, **-pation**

ex·cûr'sion, *n.*, pleasure trip, round trip

ĕx·cūse' (kūz), *v.*, forgive, not blame

ĕx·cūse', *n.*, explanation

ĕx·e'cra·ble, *a.*, hateful

ĕx'e·crāte, *v.*, hate violently, **-cration**

ĕx'e·cūte, *v.*, put into effect, do, perform, kill as punishment, **-cution**

ĕx·ec'ū·tīve, *n.*, manager

ĕx·ec'ū·tŏr, *n.*, person who carries out terms of will, **-trix**

ĕx·ē·gē'sis (zis), *n.*, scholarly criticism of Bible

ĕx·em'plá·ry, *a.*, excellent

ĕx·em'pli·fy, *v.*, set example

ĕx·empt' (egs-emt) *a.*, excuse from participation

ex·êr·cīse (ĕk-sêr-syz), *v.*, use, do actively, practice, train

ĕx·êrt', *v.*, make effort,

perform, **-ion**

ĕx·hāle', *v.*, breathe out, **-halation**

ĕx·hāust', *v.*, tire, study completely, **-ion**

ĕx·hāust', *n.*, expelled burned engine gas

ĕx·hib'it, *v.*, show, demonstrate, **-ion**

ĕx·hil'a·rāte, *v.*, gladden, make merry, **-ration**

ĕx·hôrt', *v.*, urge, request, **-ation**

ĕx·hūme', *v.*, remove corpse from grave

ex'i·gĕn·cy, *n.*, need, demand

ex·ig'ū·ous, *a.*, small, little

ex'īle, *v.*, expel from native country

ĕx·ist', *v.*, live, be, **-ence**

ex·is·ten'tial·ism, *n.*, philosophy stressing personal worth in purposeless universe

ex'it, *n.*, door for leaving place

ex'ŏ·dus, *n.*, going forth

ĕx·on'êr·āte, *v.*, free from blame

ĕx·ôr'bi·tant, *a.*, extreme

ĕx·ôr·cīse, *v.*, drive out evil spirit, **-cism**

ĕx·ot'ic, *a.*, strangely beautiful, rare

ĕx·pand', *v.*, become larger

ĕx·panse', *n.*, broad space

ĕx·pan'sion, *n.*, enlargement

ĕx·pan'sive, *a.*, broad, generous

ĕx·pā'tri·āte, *v.*, exile from country

ĕx·pect', *v.*, look forward to, anticipate, **-ant, -ancy**

ĕx·pec'tŏ·rāte, *v.*, spit

ĕx·pē'di·ent, *a.*, advantageous, convenient

ex'pe·dīte, *v.*, speed up, make easy, **-r**

ex·pe·di'tion, *n.*, trip

ex·pe·di'tious, *a.*, quickly

ĕx·pel', *v.*, force out, remove

ĕx·pend', *v.*, use up

ĕx·pend'a·ble, *a.*, that which can be used up, replaceable

ĕx·pend'i·ture, *n.*, spending

ĕx·pense', *n.*, cost

ĕx·pen'sive, *a.*, of high price

ĕx·pē'ri·ence, *n.*, knowledge acquired by doing, something done

ĕx·per'i·ment, *n.*, test, trial, **-al**

ex·pêrt, n., skilled person

ex'pi·āte, v., atone for

ex·pīre', v., die, end, breathe out, **-piration**

ex·plāin', v., make clear

ex·plā·nā'tion, n., making clear

ex·plīc'it (sit), a., clearly clear

ex·plōde', v., burst violently, blow up, **-plosion**

ex'ploit, n., adventurous deed

ex·ploit', v., make use of

ex·plōre', v., search, look into, investigate

ex'pôrt, v., ship goods out of country

ex·pōse', v., show, leave unprotected, **-posure**

ex·pō·sē' (zay), n., disclosure

ex·pō·sī'tion, n., public showing

ex·pos'tū·lāte, v., argue

ex·pō'sure, n., uncovering, opening

ex'pound', v., make plain, **-ponent**

ex·press', v., say, put into suitable language, **-ion**

ex·press', n., quick transport of goods

ex·press'ly, adv., specifically

ex·press'way, n., superspeed highway

ex·prō'pri·āte, v., take away possessions

ex·pul'sion, n., forcing out, removing

ex'pûr·gāte, v., remove offensive words, censor

ex'qui·sīte (zit), a., delicately beautiful

ex'tânt, a., now in existence

ex·tem·pō·rā'nē·ous, a., not prepared, ad lib

ex·tem'pō·rīze, v., prepare as one goes along

ex·tend', v., give, reach, enlarge

ex·ten'sion, n., addition, **-sive**

ex·tent', n., amount, degree of

ex·ten'ū·ā·ting, a., explainable, excusing

ex·tē'ri·ôr, n., outside

ex·têr'mi·nāte, v., kill, destroy, **nator**

ex·têr'nal, a., outside, **-ly**

ex·tinct', a., no longer in existence, **-ion**

ex·tin'guish (gwish), v., put out, kill

ex'tîr·pāte, v., completely destroy, remove entirely

ex·tōl', v., praise highly

ex·tôrt', v., get money by threats, blackmail, **-ion**

ex'trā, a., special, additional

ex·tract', v., pull out, remove from, **-ion**

ex·trā·dīte, v., surrender prisoner to another state, **-dition**

ex·trā'nē·ous, a., not belonging to

ex·trāôr'di·nâr·y, a., very unusual

ex·trā·sen'sō·ry pêr·cep'tion, n., knowledge received through powers unexplainable scientifically

ex·trav'á·gànt, a., wasteful, **-gance**

ex·trēme', a., excessive, great, severe, **-tremist, -ly**

ex·trī·cāte, v., free from entanglement

ex·trin'sic (zik), a., from the outside

ex'trō·vêrt, n., outgoing person

ex·trūde', v., push out

ex·ū'bêr·ànt, a., profuse, gay, **-ance**

ex·ūde', v., ooze out

ex·ult', v., rejoice, be joyous, **-ation**

eye (ī), n., organ of vision

eye' glass·ès, n., lenses to improve vision

eye'tōōth, n., pointed upper tooth

eye'wit'nèss, n., one who actually sees occurrence take place

---

F

fā'ble, n., story with a moral, myth

fā'bled, a., made up, legendary

fab'ric, n., cloth, textile

fab'ri·cāte, v., make, lie, **-cation**

fab'ū·lous, a., marvelous,

unbelievable

fá-cáde' (såd), n., building front, false front

fāce, n., front part

fāce, v., squarely, meet

fac'ét, n., surface, part of gem

fá-cē'tious, a., funny, lightly joking

fac'ile, a., easily working

fá-cil'i-tāte, v., make easy, help, **-tation**

fá-cil'i-ty, n., ease of accomplishing

fac-sim'i-lē, n., exact copy of something

fact, n., reality, truth

fac'tion, n., group having same beliefs, **-al**

fac'tious, a., disagreeing, causing split

fac-ti'tious, a., artificial, made up

fac'tŏr, n., cause of something, mathematical part, agent

fac'tŏ-ry, n., place of manufacturing

fac-tō'tum, n., all-around worker

fac'tū-ál, a., real

fac'ul-ty, n., ability, staff of school instructors

fad, n., temporary fashion craze, **-dist**

fāde, v., disappear slowly, lose color

fagged (coll.), a., tired

fag'ŏt, n., bundle of sticks

fāil, v., lose power or strength, be unsuccessful, **-ure**

fāil-sāfe, adj., device which insures safety if primary system fails or malfunctions, esp. nuclear weapons

fāint, v., lose consciousness, swoon

fāint, a., weak

fâir, a., pleasant, clear, honest, light in color, beautiful

fâir'ly, adv., honestly, attractively, justly, **-ness**

fâir'y, n., elf, sprite

fāith, n., unquestioning belief, trust, **-ful**

fāke, v., fool, falsify, **-r**

fál'cŏn, n., hunting hawk

fáll, v., drop, lower, lose power, happen, **-en**

fál-lā'cious, a., wrong, misleading, **-cy**

fáll' guy (gī), (slang), n., easy victim, one who is blamed

fáll'out, n., radioactive particles

fal'lŏw, a., unplanted, inactive

fálse, a., untrue, artificial, **-hood**

fál'si-fy, v., misrepresent deliberately

fál'tēr, v., hesitate, stumble

fāme, n., reputation, glory

fá-mil'iar (yẽr), a., closely acquainted, friendly, known, **-ity**

fam'i-ly, n., related group of people

fam'ine, n., shortage of food

fā'mous, a., well known

fan, n., cooling machine, (coll.) admirer

fá-nat'ic, a., unreasonable in belief, **-ism**

fan'cy, a., not plain, decorated

fan'cy, n., imagination

fan'fâre, n., trumpet blast

fang, n., long pointed animal tooth

fan-tas'tic, a., strange, unheard of, unreal

fan'tá-sy, n., imagined thought, dream

fär, a., distant

färce, n., comedy

fär'ci-cál, a., funny, foolish, ridiculous

fâre'well', int., good-by

fär-fetched', a., indirect, improbable

färm, n., land for crop raising

färm, v., raise crops, rent out, **-ing, -er**

fâr-rā'gō, n., mixture

fär'sīght-ĕd, a., farseeing, wise

fär'thĕr, a., more distant

fär'thĕst, a., most distant

fas'ci-nāte, v., charm, attract powerfully, **-nation**

fas'cism (fa-shizm), n., government by dictatorship, extreme right wing, **-cist**

fash'ion, n., style, way of doing things, clothing design, **-able**

fast, a., quick, (coll.) immoral

fast, v., go without food

fas'tĕn (fas-in), v., fix tightly in place, attach

fas-tid'i-ous, a., difficult to

please, critical

fat, a., obese, **-ness**

fā'tal, a., causing death, **-ity**

fāte, n., destiny, **-ful**

fā'ther, n., male parent, priest, **-ly**

fath'om, v., understand

fath'om, n., six feet

fa·tigue' (tēg), n., exhaustion, **-d**

fa·tigues' (tēgz), n., military work clothes

fat'ū·ous, a., foolish, silly, **-ity**

fau'cĕt (sit), n., tap controlling water flow

fault, n., error, cause for blame, break in rock, defect, **-y**

fäu'ná, n., animals

faux' päs (fōh-pä), n., social error

fā'vor, v., like, prefer, look like, be fond of, etc.

fā'vor, n., kindness, gift

fā'vor·à·ble, a., pleasing, helpful

fā'vor·ite, n., preferred one

fawn, n., male deer

fē'al·ty, n., sworn loyalty

fear, n., feeling of danger, fright, **-ful**

fēa'si·ble, a., capable of being done, reasonable, **-bly**

fēast, n., rich meal, celebration

fēat, n., unusual accomplishment

feath'er (feth), n., bird covering, **-ed**

feath'er weight', n., boxer weighing less than 126 pounds

feath'er·y, a., light, soft as a feather

fēa'ture, n., face part, quality, special item

fē'brile, a., feverish

fē'cēs, n., waste from intestines

feck'less, a., careless

fē'cund (kund), a., fertile

fed'er·ál, a., pertaining to national government

fed'er·āte, v., unite in central government

fe·dô'rà, n., man's felt hat

fēe, n., money paid for service, admission, etc.

fē'ble, a., weak

fēe'ble mīnd'ĕd, a., low in mentality

fēed, v., give food, supply to

fēel, v., respond to, seem, assume, touch, think, **-ing**

feign (fayn), v., pretend

feint (faynt), n., false move

fe·lic'i·tāte, v., congratulate

fe·lic'i·ty, n., happiness, **-tous**

fē'līne, a., catlike

fell, v., bring down

fel'lōw, n., man, companion

fel'lōw·ship, n., friendliness

fel'ön, n., criminal, **-y**

fē'māle, n., woman, girl

fem'i·nine, a., womanlike

fence, n., enclosure, receiver of stolen goods (coll.)

fence, v., spar with swords or words

fend, v., defend, **-er**

fē'rál, a., wild

fêr'ment', v., react chemically, excite, **-ation**

fe·rō'cious, a., vicious, **-city**

fer'rĕt, v., search out

fer'rous, a., containing iron

fer'ry, n., boat for crossing river

fêr'tile, a., productive, **-tility**

fêr·ti·fīze', v., enrich, cause reproduction, **-r**

fêr'vent, a., enthusiastic, **-ly**

fêr'vid, a., highly emotional, **-ly**

fêr'vor, n., enthusiasm, intense feeling

fes'ter, v., become infected, swollen

fes'ti·vál, n., holiday, happy celebration, **-vity**

fetch, v., get, bring

fetch'ing, a., pleasing, attractive

fete (fayt), n., celebration

fet'id, a., smelling bad

fe'tish, n., symbol of magic power, **-ism**

fet'ter, v., chain

fet'tle, n., condition

fē'tus, n., child growing in womb

feūd, n., quarrel, fight

feū'dál, a., relating to Middle Ages

fē'vêr, n., rise in body temperature, excitement, **-ish**

few, a., not very many

fi·än·ce' (fee-ähn-say), n., engaged man, cēe

fi·as'cō, n., failure, ruin

fī'át, n., command

fib, n., lie, untruth

fi′bĕr, *n.*, thread, muscle tissue, character

Fi′bĕr-glas′, *n.*, yarn spun of fine glass filaments

fick′le, *a.*, changeable

fic′tion, *n.*, story, something imagined

fic-ti′tious, *a.*, made up

fid′dle, *v.*, play a violin, fool around (coll.), **-r**

fi-del′i-ty, *n.*, faithfulness

fidg′ĕt, *v.*, move uneasily, nervously

fiēld, *n.*, land area, vocation

fiĕnd, *n.*, cruel person, devil

fierce, *a.*, wild, untamed, **-ly**

fī′ĕr-y, *a.*, hot, like fire

fi-es′tà, *n.*, holiday

fife, *n.*, musical instrument

fif′tēen′, *n.*, ten plus five, **-th**

fifth, *n.*, after the fourth

fif′ty, *a.*, five times ten, **-tieth**

fig, *n.*, fruit

fight (fīt), *v.*, *n.*, battle, argument, **-er**

fig′mĕnt, *n.*, something imagined, **-ary**

fig′ūr-à-tive, *a.*, symbolic

fig′ūre, *n.*, form, shape, resemblance, design, amount

fig′ūre, *v.*, count, consider

fig′ūre-head, *n.*, leader in name only

fil′à-mĕnt, *n.*, fine thread

filch, *v.*, steal

file, *n.*, grinding tool, container for papers

file, *v.*, smooth away, arrange in order

fil′i-àl, *a.*, relating to daughter or son

fil′i-bus-tĕr, *n.*, excessive talk deliberately delaying legislation

fill, *v.*, supply, satisfy, make full, put into

film, *n.*, thin skin, chemically treated paper for photography

film′strip, *n.*, length of film containing images for projection on a screen individually

fil′tĕr, *v.*, purify, strain

filth, *n.*, dirt, **-y**

fin, *n.*, wing-like part

fi-nā′gle, *v.*, trick, cheat, connive

fi′nal, *a.*, last, end, **-ly**

fi-nä′lē, *n.*, ending

fi′nal-ist, *n.*, last remaining

contestant

fi′nance, *n.*, science of monetary affairs

fi-nan′cial, *a.*, pertaining to money, **-cier**

find, *v.*, locate, discover, **-ing**

fine, *a.*, desirable, good, **-ly**

fine, *n.*, payment for offense against law

fin′ĕr-y, *n.*, attractive wearing apparel

fi-nesse′, *n.*, subtle move, smooth action

fin′gĕr, *n.*, digit of hand

fin′ick-y, *a.*, over-concerned, particular

fin′is, *n.*, ending

fin′ish, *v.*, conclude

fi′nīte, *a.*, having body, within limits

fīr, *n.*, evergreen tree, pine

fire, *n.*, burning substance

fire, *v.*, burn, shoot, discharge from job (coll.)

fire′ärm, *n.*, gun

fire′bug, *n.*, person who sets fires

fire′ drill′, *n.*, routine practice in escaping fire

fire′màn, *n.*, fire fighter, furnaceman

firm, *n.*, business company

firm, *a.*, solid, unyielding, determined

fir′mà-mĕnt, *n.*, sky, heavens

first, *a.*, before all others

first′āid′, *n.*, temporary medical help

first′ rāte′, *a.*, excellent

fish, *n.*, animal living in water, **-erman**

fish stō′ry, *n.*, lie, tall tale

fish′y, *a.*, questionable, suspicious (coll.)

fis′sion (fish-in), *n.*, splitting into parts

fis′sūre, *n.*, crack, split

fist, *n.*, clenched hand

fit, *n.*, sudden upset, convulsion

fit, *v.*, prepare for, suit to, adapt, alter to size, shape, etc., **-ting**

five, *n.*, cardinal numeral "5"

fix, *v.*, repair

fix, *n.*, difficult situation, prearranged contest (coll.)

fix-ā′tion, *n.*, strongly formed habit

fix′ings, (coll.), *n.*, trimmings

fix′tūre, *n.*, something permanent

fiz'zle (coll.), v., fail

flab'bêr-gast, v., amaze, **-ed**

flab'by, a., fleshy, soft

flac'cid (flak-sid), a., limp, hanging loose

flag, n., banner

flag, v., wave, droop

flag-êl-lā'tion (flaj), n., whipping

flâ-gi'tious (ji), a., evil, shameful, criminally wicked

flā'grant, a., evil, blatantly wrong

flag'ship, n., fleet commander's ship

flak, n., pieces of exploded anti-aircraft shell

flāke, n., small thin slice

flam-bōy'ant, a., flaming, bold, brilliantly decorated

flāme, n., blaze, person loved (coll.)

flāme, v., burn

flām'ing, a., burning

flank, n., body part between rib and hip

flan'nêl, n., soft woolen or cotton cloth

flap, v., wave up and down

flap, n., piece hanging loosely

flap'pêr, n., flirting woman or girl

flāre, v., glow forth suddenly

flāre'-up, n., sudden burst of anger

flash, n., sudden burst of light, news report

flash'-back, n., showing of past events

flash'līght, n., battery powered hand light

flash'y, a., showy

flask, n., pocket bottle container

flat, n., a level, dull, **-ly**

flat, n., apartment

flat'câr, n., low freight car

flat'têr, v., praise insincerely, **-y**

flat'ū-lênt, a., gassy, empty: as speech

flā'tus, n., expelled gas, puff of wind

flâunt (flawnt), v., show openly, challenge

flā'vŏr, n., seasoning, **-ing**

flâw, n., defect, fault, **-less**

flax, n., linen plant

flēa, n., insect

fleck, n., spot

fledg'ling, n., young bird

flēe, v., run away from

flēece, v., rob

flēece, n., sheep's wool, **-y**

flēet, n., group of battleships

flēet, a., fast, quick, **-ing**

flesh, n., tissue under skin, **-y**

flex'i-ble, a., easily shaped

flīght (flyt), n., flying

flīght'y, a., silly, unstable

flim'sy, a., without strength, weak

flinch, v., shrink away from

fling, v., throw

fling, n., dance, (coll.) time of unrestrained pleasures

flip, v., move jerkily, quickly

flip, a., disrespectful, **-pant**

flirt, v., consider lightly

flit, v., move lightly from place to place

flōat, v., suspend in water, suspend freely

flōat'êr, n., one who moves from job to job

flock, n., group, crowd

flog, v., beat with whip

flōod, n., overflow of water

flōor, n., walking surface, building story

flōor (coll.) v., surprise

flop, n., failure, fall

flop'house, n., dormitory for vagrants

flō'ra, n., plants, **-l, -rist**

flŏr'id, a., rosy, ruddy, showy

flō-til'lâ, n., group of ships

flot'sâm, n., floating sea wreckage

flounce, n., skirt ruffle

floun'dêr, v., struggle helplessly

flour, n., ground product of wheat

flou̇r'ish (flêr), v., thrive, display

flout, v., treat with scorn

flōw, v., move smoothly, **-ing**

flow'êr, n., blossom, **-ing**

fluc'tū-āte, v., change irregularly

flū'ênt, a., flowing

fluff'y, a., soft

flū'id, n., liquid

flūke, n., chance happening

flunk (coll.), v., fail in school

flu-ö-res'cence, n., glow produced by energy reacting on gas, **-cent**

flū'ö-rine (rēen), n., gas

flush, v., grow red, cleanse with flood of water

flush, *a.*, excited, full, rich

flus'tered, *a.*, nervous, embarrassed

flute, *n.*, wind musical instrument

flut'ter, *v.*, move in jerky motions

flux, *n.*, flowing, change

fly, *v.*, move through air on wings, run, **-ing**

fly, *n.*, insect

foal, *n.*, new-born horse

foam, *n.*, mass of tiny bubbles, **-y**

foam' rub'ber, *n.*, soft rubber

fo'cus, *n.*, center, where points meet

fod'der, *n.*, horse food

foe, *n.*, enemy

fog, *n.*, heavy mist, **-gy**

foil, *n.*, thin sheet metal, fencing sword

foil, *v.*, prevent from doing

fold, *v.*, bend

fold, *n.*, group, flock

fold'er, *n.*, cardboard file container

fo'li-age, *n.*, leaves, **-ate**

fo'li-o, *n.*, book with large size pages

folk (fōhk), *n.*, group of people

folk'way, *n.*, people's habits and customs

fol'li-cle, *n.*, small body sac

fol'low, *v.*, pursue, go after, **-er**

fol'ly, *n.*, foolishness

fo-ment', *v.*, stir up rebellion

fond, *a.*, affectionate, loving, **-le**

font, *n.*, fountain, type face

food, *n.*, that which is eaten

fool, *n.*, silly person

fool, *v.*, play trick on, be lazy, **-ish**

foot, *n.*, base of leg, 12 inches

foot'ball, *n.*, game played with oblong ball

foot'ing, *n.*, place to stand, basis of establishment

foot'lights, *n.*, lights on stage front

foot'work, *n.*, action with feet

for, *prep.*, on behalf of, with purpose of, in the interest of, in honor of

for'age, *v.*, search for food supplies

for-bid', *v.*, prohibit, **-den**

force, *n.*, power, might, violence

force, *v.*, compel, make

unusual attempt, **-d**

for'ceps, *n.*, surgical pincers

ford, *v.*, cross a river

fore, *adv.*, front

fore, *int.*, golf warning

fore'cast, *v.*, predict

fore-go'ing, *a.*, previous, previous

fore-gone', *a.*, past, known

for'eign (in), *a.*, from outside, not native, not familiar, **-er**

fore'man, *n.*, supervisor of work

fore-see', *v.*, know in advance

fore-shad'ow, *v.*, be evident before happening

fore'sight, *n.*, knowing in advance, being careful

for'est, *n.*, woods, **-er**

fore-tell', *v.*, prophesy

for-ev'er, *adv.*, eternally, without an end

fore'word, *n.*, introduction to book

for'feit (fit), *v.*, give up, **-ure**

forge, *v.*, shape heated metal

for'ger-y, *n.*, counterfeiting another's signature

for-get', *v.*, cease to remember, **-ful**

for-give', *v.*, excuse, overlook fault, **-ness**

for-go', *v.*, give up

fork, *n.*, pronged utensil, division into branches

for-lorn', *a.*, alone, unhappy

form, *n.*, shape, pattern, outline, **-less**

for'mal, *a.*, strictly according to custom, **-ity**

for-ma'tion, *n.*, structure of

form'a-tive, *a.*, in process of being developed

for'mer, *a.*, before

for'mer-ly, *adv.*, in past time

for'mi-da-ble, *a.*, strong, powerful

for'mu-la, *n.*, set of rules, pattern

for'mu-late, *v.*, express, put into formula

for-ni-ca'tion, *n.*, sexual intercourse between unmarried persons

for-sake', *v.*, give up, **-n**

fort, *n.*, military establishment, place of defense, **-ress**

forte, *n.*, strong point

forth-right', *a.*, direct, honest in speech

fôr'ti-fy, *v.*, strengthen against enemy, **-fication**

fôr'ti-tūde, *n.*, strength, courage

fôrt'night'-ly, *adv.*, every two weeks

fôr-tū'i-tous, *a.*, by chance

fôr'tū-nāte, *a.*, lucky, **-ly**

fôr'tune (chin), *n.*, good luck, riches

fôr'um, *n.*, area for public discussion

fôr'ward, *a.*, onward, toward front

fôr'ward, *v.*, send mail ahead

fos'sil, *n.*, hardened form of ancient things

fôs'tèr, *v.*, help, encourage

fôs'tèr par'ent, *n.*, person who raises anothers children

foul, *a.*, dirty, unfair

foul, *n.*, breaking rules of game, **-ly**

found, *v.*, discover, establish base

foun-dā'tion, *n.*, base structure, support, fund for charity

foun'dèr, *v.*, sink, fail

found'ling, *n.*, abandoned infant which is found

foun'dry, *n.*, factory for casting metal

foun'tain, *n.*, stream of water

fôur, *n.*, cardinal number, "4", **-th**

fôur'tēen', *n.*, ten plus four

fôurth di-men'sion, *n.*, time in mathematical terms

fowl, *n.*, any bird

fox, *n.*, small animal

fox ter'ri-èr, *n.*, breed of dog

fox' trot, *n.*, dance

fox'y, *a.*, shrewd

frā'cás, *n.*, fight

frac'tion, *n.*, part of

frac'ture, *v.*, break

frag'ile, *a.*, delicate, **-ility**

frag'ment, *n.*, broken part, bit of something **-ary**

frā'grànt, *a.*, sweet-smelling, **-grance**

frāil, *a.*, weak

frāme, *n.*, shape, structure of

frāme-up, *n.*, dishonest arrangement in advance against someone

fran'chise, *n.*, right to operate a business

frank, *a.*, candid

frank, *n.*, postal mark giving privilege of free mailing

fran'tic, *a.*, excited, wild

frā-tèr'nál, *a.*, brotherly, **-nity, -nize**

fraud (frâwd), *n.*, dishonesty, hoax, **-ulent**

fray, *n.*, battle, fight

frēak, *n.*, queer person or strange happening

freck'le, *n.*, dark spot on skin

frēe, *n.*, not restricted, spontaneous, without cost, **-dom**

frēe'by, *n.*, something obtained free of charge, **-bie**

frēe' lance, *v.*, produce work for any buyer, **-r**

frēe' vèrse, *n.*, poetry without set meter

frēeze, *v.*, change into ice

frēez'èr, *n.*, machine that freezes, **ing**

freight (frayt), *n.*, method of shipping goods

freight'èr, *n.*, ship for carrying goods

French' fries, *n.*, deep-fried strips of potato

frē-net'ic, *a.*, frantic, **-al**

fren'zy, *n.*, wild, excitement, **-zied**

frē'quèn-cy, *n.*, taking place often, broadcasting cycles, **-t**

frē'quèn-cy mod-ū-lā'tion, *n.*, method of broadcasting

fresh, *a.*, recently made, **-ly**

fresh'màn, *n.*, first year student

fret, *v.*, worry, whine, **-ful**

fric'tion, *n.*, rubbing together, conflict

friend (frend), *n.*, close companion, **-ly**

fright'en, *v.*, scare, **-ful**

frig'id, *a.*, cold

frill, *n.*, unneeded ornament, luxury

fringe, *n.*, ornamental edging, border

frisk, *v.*, jump about, (coll.) search someone, **-y**

friv'ö-lous, *a.*, not serious, trivial, **-lity**

frock, *n.*, monk's robe, dress

frôg, *n.*, toadlike animal

frôm, *prep.*, starting with, out of, because of

frônt, *n.*, that which faces forward, false behavior, united action, **-al**

frön-tièr', *n.*, border where

two countries meet, wild part of country, **-sman**

fröst, *n.*, frozen vapor

fröst'ing, *n.*, icing for cake top

frown, *v.*, wrinkle brows together in disapproval, **-ing**

frō'zen, *a.*, changed into ice

frū'gál, *a.*, thrifty, saving, **-ity**

fruit, *n.*, edible plant part

fruit'ful, *a.*, bearing many, fertile

frū-i'tion, *n.*, completion

fruit'less, *a.*, without results, unsuccessful

frus'trāte, *v.*, keep from doing, be a failure, **-tration**

fry, *v.*, cook in fat

fry'ẽr, *n.*, chicken for frying

fūch'si-à (few-sha), *a.*, red-purple color

fudge, *n.*, type of candy

fū'el (fewl), *n.*, material burned for heat or energy

fū'gi-tive, *n.*, one who runs away, criminal

fūgue (fewg), *n.*, musical composition

ful-fill', *v.*, bring about, cause to occur, **-ment**

full, *n.*, filled, not able to eat any more, round, **-ness**

full dress', *n.*, formal evening clothes

full'y, *adv.*, completely

ful'mi-nāte, *v.*, express violently against, **-nation**

fum'ble, *v.*, seek awkwardly

fūme, *v.*, emit fumes, grow angry

fū'mi-gāte, *v.*, disinfect

fun, *n.*, good time, **-ny**

func'tion, *n.*, job, duty, purpose, task

fund, *n.*, collection of money

fun-dà-men'tal, *a.*, basic, essential, **-ism**

fū'nêr-ál, *n.*, ceremony of burying of dead

fū-nē'rē-ál, *a.*, pertaining to funeral, **-ly**

fun'gus, *n.*, spongy plant

fun'nël, *n.*, pouring utensil wide at one end, narrow at other, chimney

fũr, *v.*, animal hair covering

fū'ri-ous, *a.*, angry

fũr'nàce, *n.*, mechanical device for providing heat

fũr'nish, *v.*, provide, put furniture into, **-ings**

fũr'ni-ture, *n.*, tables, chairs, lamps, beds, etc.

fū'rôr, *n.*, commotion, anger

fũr'ri-ẽr, *n.*, dealer in furs

fũr'rōw, *n.*, groove plowed in ground

fũr'thêr, *a.*, more distant

fũr'thêr, *v.*, promote cause

fũr'tive, *a.*, stealthy, **-ly**

fūse, *n.*, device to protect wires against overheating, device to light explosive material

fūse, *v.*, melt together

fū'sē-läge (ij), *n.*, body of airplane

fū-sil-läde', *n.*, gun fire

fū'sion, *n.*, uniting together, blending

fuss, *v.*, argue, bother

fuss'y, *a.*, over-particular

fū'tile, *a.*, without success, hopeless

fū'ture, *n.*, that which is to come

fuzz, *n.*, loose, lintlike material

G

gab (coll.), *v.*, chatter

gab'ár-dine (dēen), *n.*, type of cloth

gā'ble, *n.*, pointed roof

gad'à-bout', *n.*, one who moves constantly about

gadg'ét, *n.*, work-easing device

gag, *n.*, object stuffed into mouth, joke (coll.)

gāi'é-ty, *n.*, fun, merriment

gāin, *v.*, acquire, increase

gāin-say', *v.*, deny

gāit, *n.*, style of walking

gā'là, *n.*, gay occasion, merry entertainment

gal'ãx-y, *n.*, enormous system of star groups, group of famous people

gāle, *n.*, strong wind

gãll, *n.*, bile, (coll.) daring

gal'lànt, *a.*, brave, chivalrous, **-ry**

gal'lẽr-y, *n.*, upstairs seats in auditorium, building projection, exhibit hall gal'ley, *n.*, kitchen on ship

gal'lon, *n.*, four quarters

gal'lop, *n.*, fast running pace

gal'lows, *n.*, device for hanging people

ga-losh'es, *n.*, high rubber overshoes

ga-lumph', *v. i.*, word invented by Lewis Carroll to denote triumphant marching along heavily or triumphantly

gam'bit, *n.*, chess move

gam'ble, *v.*, take a chance, play game for money, **-bling**

gam'bol, *v.*, frisk about playfully

game, *n.*, sports contest, hunted animals

game, *a.*, willing, courageous (coll.)

gam'ut, *n.*, fullness, inclusiveness

Gan'dhi-ism, *n.*, the political theories of Mohandas (Mahatma) Gandhi which employ passive resistance and civil disobedience to achieve a goal

gang, *n.*, group having similar interests

gan'gli-on, *n.*, nerve cells

gan'grene, *n.*, flesh decay

gang'ster, *n.*, member of criminal gang

gap, *n.*, *n.*, split, opening

gape, *v.*, stare open-mouthed

ga-rage' (räjh), *n.*, building for housing automobiles

gar'bage (bijh), *n.*, trash

gar'ble, *v.*, purposely confuse

gar'den, *n.*, ground for raising plants

gar-dē'ni-a, *n.*, fragrant white flower

gar'gle, *v.*, wash the throat with antiseptic

gar'goyle, *n.*, grotesque animal figure projecting from building

gar'lic, *n.*, strong tasting plant

gar'ment, *n.*, article of clothing

gar'nish, *v.*, decorate, **-ment**

gar'ret, *n.*, attic

gar'ri-sön, *n.*, fortified military place

gar'ru-lous (ri-lis), *a.*, talking overly much

gar'tēr, *n.*, elastic piece to hold up stockings

gas, *n.*, invisible vaporous element, **-eous**

gas-ö-line' (lēen), *n.*, engine fuel

gasp, *v.*, catch breath quickly

gas'tric, *a.*, relating to stomach

gas-trö-nm'ic, *a.*, relating to eating, **-y**

gate, *n.*, frame mounted on fence, opening, (coll.) attendance

gath'er, *v.*, collect, bring together, **-ing**

gau'dy, *a.*, brilliantly showy

gauge, *n.*, measurement

gaunt, *a.*, extremely thin

gauze, *n.*, thin cotton fabric

gav'el, *n.*, mallet of presiding officer

gawk, *v.*, gaze open-mouthed

gay, *a.*, happy, merry, **-ly**

gaze, *v.*, stare intently

ga-zette', *n.*, sensational newspaper

gear, *n.*, toothed wheel

Gei'ger count'ēr, *n.*, device that detects radioactivity

gel'ā-tin, *n.*, substance which jells, **-ous**

gem (jem), *n.*, precious stone

gēn-e-al'-ö-gy (oli-ä-gēe), *n.*, person's ancestry

gen'er-ăl, *a.*, concerning everything, common, all-inclusive

gen'er-ăl-ly, *adv.*, usually, ordinarily

gen'er-āte, *v.*, begin, produce, **-ator**

gen-er-ā'tion, *n.*, persons of same era

gĕ-ner'ic (je), *a.*, pertaining to a genus, inclusive

gen'ĕr-ous, *a.*, giving freely, **-osity**

gĕ-net'ics, *n.*, study of heredity

gen'ial, *a.*, friendly

gēn'i-tăls, *n.*, reproductive organs

gēn'ius, *n.*, person with superior intellect or talent

gen'ö-cīde, *n.*, planned killing of races of people

gen-tēel', *a.*, polite

gen'tīle, *n.*, non-Jewish person

gen'tle, *a.*, mild, easygoing, quiet, **-tly**

gen'tle-man, *n.*, good mannered male, **-woman**

gen'ū-ine (win), *a.*, real,

sincere

gē'nus (jee), n., specific class

gē-og'ra-phy, n., study of
earth surface and shape,
countries, -phic

gē-ol'ō-gy, n., study of
earth's composition, -gical

gē-om'e-try, n., mathematics
of lines, angles, surfaces

ger-i-at'rics, n., study of the
elderly

gêrm, n., microscopic
organism, seed

gêr-māne', a., related closely
to, having connection with

gêr'mi-cīde, n., germ killing
preparation

gêr'und, n., verb made into
noun

ges-tic'ū-lāte, v., make
gesturing motion

ges'ture (jes), n., motion of
expression

get, v., receive, possess,
obtain

get'-up (coll.), n., outfit worn

ghast'ly, a., frightening,
terrible

ghost, n., spirit, -ly

ghost wrīter, n., person
writing for another

gī'ant (jy), a., extremely large

gib'bŏn, n., type of ape

gībe (jyb), v., ridicule, sneer

gid'dy, a., dizzy

gift, n., present

gift'ed, a., born with skill,
capable

gī-gan'tic (jy), a., huge,
tremendous

gig'gle, v., laugh foolishly

gild, v., cover with gold

gim'mick, n., helpful device,
trick

gin, n., alcoholic drink

gin'ger āle, n., soft drink

gin'ger-ly, a., carefully

gi-raffe', n., long-necked
animal

gîrd, v., prepare for action,
arm

gîr'dle, v., surround, engirth

gîrl, n., young female, -ish

gist (jist), n., significant part
of

give, v., present to, grant

glā'cier (shir), n., slowly
moving ice mass, -cial

glad, a., delighted, joyful, -ly

glam'our (êr), n., fascinating
allure, -ous

glance, n., brief look

gland, n., body organ

controlling secretion, -ular

glāre, v., shine very brightly

glass, n., hard, brittle,
transparent substance

glass'y, a., resembling glass,
expressionless

glāze, n., smooth, shiny
finish

glē am, n., ray of light

glē an, v., collect grain, collect
bit by bit

glee, n., fun, joy

glee' club, n., choir of singers

glib, a., fluent, smooth

glīde, v., flow smoothly, move
gracefully

glīd'êr, n., motorless airplane

glim'mêr, n., passing light

glimpse, v., suddenly see

glis'těn, v., sparkle

glōb'ăl, a., relating to the
globe

glōbe, n., round map of world

glōbe'-trot'ter, n., a person
who frequently travels all
over the world

glōom, n., darkness, sadness

glō'ri-fy, v., give honor to

glō'ri-ous, a., splendid

glō'ry, n., splendor, honor,
fame, wonder

glos'sā-ry, n., dictionary of
special words

glōve, n., covering worn on
hand

glōw, v., shine brightly

glū'cōse, n., sugar-type
liquid

glūe, n., substance for
holding things together

glum, a., unhappy

glut, v., over-fill

glut'tŏn, n., one who eats
excessively, -ous

gnash (n), v., crush together

gnat (n), n., insect

gnaw (n), v., eat away slowly

gnū (n), n., buffalo-like
animal

gō, v., move, work, depart,
act, reach, pass

gōal, n., aim, purpose

gōat, n., domesticated animal

gōat-ēe', n., pointed beard

gob, n., sailor, (coll.) mass

gob'lět, n., long-stemmed
glass

God, n., deity, creator of
universe, -ly

god'par-ěnt, n., sponsor at
baptism

gō'-get'ter, n., enterprising
person

gōld, n., precious yellow metal, **-en**

golf, n., sport involving hard ball and club, **-er**

gôn'êr, n., one who is beyond help (coll.)

gon-ör-rhē'à, n., venereal disease

good, a., desirable, correct, enjoyable, pleasant, **-ly**

gōō'ey, adj., sticky, messy, or overly sweet or sentimental

gōōse, n., large webfooted fowl

gō'phêr, n., burrowing rodent

gôre, n., clotted blood

gôr'geous (jus), a., splendid, beautiful

gö-ril'là, n., largest ape

Gos'pël, n., preachings of Jesus

gos'sip, n., idle or malicious talk about people

gos'sà-mêr, a., thin, filmy

gouge (gouj), v., dig deep into, cheat (coll.)

gout, n., painful disease of joints

göv'êrn, v., rule, direct, guide

göv'êrn-ment, n., method of rule of nation or state

göv'êr-nör, n., head of state government, device which controls speed of motor

gown, n., woman's dress

grab, v., take hold of suddenly

grāce, n., polish, beauty, short prayer, favor, **-ful**

grā'cious (shis), a., kind, polite, **-ness**

grā-dā'tion, n., slow change,step by step

grāde, v., sort out, mark, arrange by steps, level or slope ground

grad'ū-àl, a., by slow degrees

grad'ū-āte, v., complete school, mark off, **-ation, -d**

grad'ū-āte, n., one who has completed schooling

graf-fī'tī, n., words written on walls in public places

graft, n., transplant of skin or plant, political dishonesty

grāin, n., wheat, etc., fiber arrangement

gram, n., unit of weight

gram'mär, n., structure and usage of a language, **-matical**

gran'à-ry, n., warehouse for storing grain

grand'child, n., son or daughter's child, **-ren**

grand'däugh-têr, n., son or daughter's daughter

gran'dêur (jêr), n., imposing appearance, splendor

grand'fä-ther, n., parent's father

grand'möth-êr, n., parent's mother

grand'sön, n., son or daughter's son

grand'stand, n., seating area in stadium

gran'ite, n., hard rock

grant, v., give

grāpe, n., fruit

grāpe'frūit, n., citrus fruit

graph, n., chart showing relative figures

graph'ic, a., real, vivid, relating to printing

grap'ple, v., wrestle

grasp, v., seize, hold, learn

grasp'ing, a., selfish, greedy

grass, n., green lawn plant, **-y**

grass wid'ōw, n., divorced woman

grāte, v., grind into shreds, irritate

grāte'ful, a., thankful

grat'i-fy, v., satisfy

grā'tis, a., free

grat'i-tūde, n., thankfulness

grà-tū'i-tous, a., free

grà-tū'i-ty, n., gift of money, tip

grāve, n., burial place, **-yard**

grāve, a., serious, sad, **-ly**

grav'ël, n., small bits of rock

grav'i-tāte, v., move toward

grav'i-ty, n., attraction of one object on another

grā'vy, n., meat sauce

grāy, n., color between white and black

grāze, v., eat grass, touch lightly

grēase, n., thick lubricating substance

grēat, a., large, important, main, wonderful, **-ness**

grēed, n., selfish desire, **-y**

grēen, n., color resembling grass

green'-eyed, a., jealous (coll.)

grēen'house, n., glass building for growing plants

grēet, v., welcome, meet warmly, **-ing**

gre·gâr'i·ous, *a.*, fond of company, sociable

gre·nāde', *n.*, hand type bomb

grey'hound (gray), *n.*, breed of dog

grid'dle, *n.*, flat pan for cooking

grid'i·ron, *n.*, football field

grief, *n.*, sadness, grief

griev'ance, *n.*, complaint

grieve, *v.*, feel sorrow

grill, *v.*, broil, question intensely

gri·māce', *v.*, twist facial expression

grime, *n.*, dirt

grind, *v.*, rub harshly together

grip, *v.*, hold tightly

gripe (coll.), *n.*, complaint

grippe, *n.*, severe cold or flu

grit, *n.*, sand, courage, **-ty**

griz'zly, *a.*, grayish

grōan, *n.*, low moaning sound

grō'cêr, *n.*, food dealer, **-y**

grog'gy, *a.*, dizzy

grōom, *n.*, man being married, one in charge of horse's care

grōove, *n.*, rut, routine

grōov'y, *adj.*, highly pleasing, attractive (coll.)

grōpe, *v.*, feel, search hesitantly

grōss, *a.*, *n.*, large, entire amount

grō·tesque' (tesk), *a.*, ugly or strange in appearance

grouch, *n.*, mean person, **-y**

ground, *n.*, earth, dirt, area of land, reason or basis

ground'less, *a.*, having no reason

ground'work (wûrk), *n.*, preceding effort, foundation

group, *n.*, several people together

grov'el, *v.*, crawl, beg

grow, *v.*, become larger, come to life, spread, raise, **-th**

grudge, *n.*, ill will, dislike

grue'sōme, *a.*, ugly, horrible

grum'ble, *v.*, complain half aloud

grunt, *n.*, short, low sound in throat

G'-sūit, *n.*, pressurized suit for astronauts or pilots

guar·an·tēe', *n.*, promise of satisfactory performance,

-tôr, *v.*, watch over, control, protect

guärd'i·ân, *n.*, one appointed to look after another

guess (ges), *v.*, estimate without basis of fact, **-ing**

guest (gest), *n.*, one entertained

guid'ance, *n.*, direction, leadership, **-e**

guīle, *n.*, deceit, dishonesty, **-ful**

guilt (gilt), *n.*, culpability, feeling ashamed, breech of conduct, **-y**

guin'ēa, *n.*, English coin, domestic fowl

gui·tär', *n.*, stringed musical instrument

gulf, *n.*, large, round bay, wide distance

gul'li·ble, *a.*, easy to fool

gulp, *v.*, swallow suddenly

gum, *n.*, flesh surrounding teeth, sticky substance

gun, *n.*, weapon for firing bullet

gung' hō', *adj.*, wholeheartedly enthusiastic, often naïvely so

gun'nêr, *n.*, one who fires guns, **-y**

gup'py, *n.*, small tropical fish

gûr'gle, *v.*, make bubbling sound

gush, *v.*, spurt out

gust, *n.*, strong rush of wind, sudden, **-y**

gus'tō, *n.*, enthusiasm

gut, *v.*, *n.*, destroy entirely, intestine

gut'têr, *n.*, groove for draining off water

gut'tûr·ál (têr), *a.*, deep in the throat

guy (gī), *n.*, person, rope for securing

gym·nā'si·um (zēe), *n.*, place for athletic activity

gy·ne·col'ō·gy, *n.*, study of women's diseases

gyp (jip), *v.*, steal from, cheat (coll.)

gyp'sum, *n.*, material for making lime products

gyp'sy (sēe), *n.*, migratory person

gy'rāte (jy), *v.*, spin

gy'rō·scōpe, *n.*, stabilizing device

— H —

hä, *inter.*, exclamation

hā'bē-us côr'pus, *n.*, order to produce prisoner in court

hab'ēr-dash-ēr, *n.*, dealer in men's clothing, **-y**

hab'it, *n.*, constant practice, **-ual**

hab'i-tat, *n.*, natural living place, **-ion**

hack, *v.*, chop, cough

hack'nĕyed, *a.*, worn out, overused

had'dŏck, *n.*, fish

hag, *n.*, ugly old woman

hag'gärd, *a.*, worn, tired looking

hag'gle, *v.*, quarrel over terms of bargain

hāil, *v.*, greet, salute

hāil, *n.*, frozen rain

hāir, *n.*, growth on body, **-y**

hāir'do (dōō), *n.*, way of setting hair, coiffure

hal'cy̆-ŏn (si-un), *a.*, peaceful, happy

hāle, *a.*, healthy, hearty

half, *n.*, one of two equal parts

half heärt'ĕd, *a.*, disinterested, discouraged, desultory

half-wit'tĕd, *a.*, not intelligent, mentally deficient

hal'i-but, *n.*, large fish

hâll, *n.*, passageway, public room, **-way**

hâll'märk, *n.*, stamped design, mark of something genuine

hal'lōwed, *a.*, holy

hal-lū'ci-nāte, *v.*, visualize unreal things, **-nation**

hā'lō, *n.*, ring of light around object, or head of holy person

hâlt, *v.*, stop, pause

hăl'tēr, *n.*, woman's short blouse, rope to lead animal

ham, *n.*, meat from pig's thigh, amateur radio operator (coll.)

ham'bûrg-ēr, *n.*, ground beef

ham'lĕt, *n.*, small village

ham'mēr, *n.*, tool for pounding nails

ham'mŏck, *n.*, suspended canvas bed

ham'pēr, *v.*, hinder

hand, *n.*, end part of arm, worker

hand, *v.*, give

hand'bag, *n.*, woman's purse

hand'cuff, *n.*, wrist fetter

hand'i-cap, *n.*, equalization of a contest, physical distortion, difficulty, **-ped**

hand'kēr-chief (chif), *n.*, cloth for blowing nose

han'dle, *v.*, feel, touch, grasp, sell

hand'sōme, *a.*, good looking, **-ly**

hand'y, *a.*, clever with hands, convenient

handy'man, *n.*, general repairman

hang, *v.*, suspend, execute

hang'ār, *n.*, airplane shelter

hang'dŏg, *a.*, sneaky, miserable

hang'out, *n.*, familiar meeting place

hang'ō-vēr, *n.*, headache in morning from drinking

han'kēr, *v.*, desire very much, long for, **-ing**

hap'haz-ärd, *a.*, accidental, confused

hap'pēn, *v.*, occur, take place, **-ing**

hap'py, *a.*, enjoying peace and comfort, glad

há-rangue' (rang), *n.*, defaming, accusing speech

há-rass', *v.*, bother, annoy

här'bin-gēr, *n.*, sign of coming events

här'bŏr, *n.*, shelter for ships

härd, *a.*, difficult, solid, tough

härd'ēn, *v.*, make hard, become cruel

härd'ly, *adv.*, barely

härd'ship, *n.*, difficult circumstance, extreme discomfort

härd'wâre, *n.*, metal household articles

hâre, *n.*, rabbit

här'ēm, *n.*, residence of sultan's wives

här'lŏt, *n.*, prostitute

härm, *n.*, injury, danger, **-ful**

här-mon'i-cá, *n.*, mouth organ

här′mō-ny, n., pleasant agreement, **-nious**

härp, n., stringed instrument

härp′si-chôrd, n., piano-like instrument

har′rōw, n., instrument for breaking up soil

härsh, a., hard, rough, unpleasant, **-ly**

här′vĕst, n., gathering of a crop, **-er**

hash, n., chopped meat and vegetable dish, mixture

has′sŏck, n., padded footstool

hāste, n., speed, **-n**

hat, n., covering for head

hatch, v., bring forth from eggs, plan, **-ery**

hatch′et, n., hand axe

hāte, v., dislike extremely, **-ful**

häugh′ty, a., vainly proud, arrogant

häul, v., pull, drag

häunt, v., visit some place often, **-ed**

have, v., hold in one's possession, own

hā′vĕn, n., place of safety

hav′ŏc, n., wreckage, destruction

häwk, n., eagle-like bird

hay, n., grass used for cattle food

haz′ärd, n., danger, risk, **-ous**

hāze, n., mist

hā′zĕl, n., tree, nut, greenish color

H′-bomb′, n., bomb powered by thermonuclear fusion of hydrogen isotopes (hydrogen bomb)

hē, pro., referring to male

head (hĕd), n., top part of body, leader, main part

head′mas′tēr, n., head of private school

head′quär-tērs (kwôr), n., center of operations

head′strŏng, a., stubborn

head′y, a., intoxicating

hēal, v., cure

health, n., physical well-being, toast, **-y**

hēap, n., pile

hēar, v., perceive sounds, listen to, learn, **-ing**

hēarse (hĕrs), n., car for transporting dead

hēart, n., blood-pumping body organ, main part, courage

hēart′āche, n., sorrow, grief

hēart′ĕn, v., cheer, inspire

hēart′fĕlt, a., honest, sincere

hēarth, n., floor of fireplace

hēart′lĕss, a., cruel, cold

hēart′-tō-hēart′, a., direct, honest

hēart′y, a., sincere, healthy

hēat, n., warmth, excitement

hē′at′ĕd, a., excited, warm

hē′a′thĕn, n., one without religion

hēave, v., throw forcefully

heav′ĕn, n., sky, paradise

heav′ĕn-ly, a., pleasant, delightful

heav′y, a., weighing much, sorrowful

Hē′brew, n., language of Israel, **-braïc**

heck′le, v., bedevil, **-r**

hedge, n., evade taking definite position

hedge′hop, v., fly airplane near ground

hē′dŏn-ism, n., entire devotion to pleasure

hēed, v., watch, pay attention, **-ful**

hēel, n., under back part of foot, worthless person, (coll.) shoe part

hēeled (coll.), a., rich

hef′ty, a., heavy, large

heif′ĕr (hĕf), n., young cow

hēight (hyt), n., degree of tallness, **-en**

hei′nous (hay-nus), a., cruel, evil

heir (ayr), n., person who inherits, **-ess**

hel′i-cŏp-tēr, n., plane able to go straight up and hover

hē′li-um, n., gaseous element

hell, n., abode of damned souls

hel-lō′, int., greeting

helm, n., ship's steering wheel

hel′mĕt, n., protective head covering

help, v., assist, aid, serve, **-ful**

help′lĕss, a., unable to assist self

hem, n., sewn edge of garment

hem′i-sphēre, n., half of earth

hem′lŏck, n., evergreen tree

hē-mō-phil′i-à, n., disease characterized by uncontrollable bleeding

hem'ör-rháge (rij), n., heavy bleeding

nem'ör-rhoids (hemroids), n., swollen blood vessels near anus

hemp, n., fibrous plant

hen, n., female of fowl (coll.) woman

hence, adv., from now on

hen'pecked, a., dominated by wife

hêr, pro., referring to female possession

her'áld, v., announce

hêrb, n., plant used for seasoning

hêrd, n., group of animals

hēre, adv., in this place

hēre-af'têr, adv., after this time, after death

hēre-by', adv., in this way

hē-red'i-ty, n., transmission of characteristics from parent to child, **-tary**

her'ē-sy (hayr), n., opinion contrary to religious belief, **-tic**

her'it-áge, n., that which is passed on to descendants

hêr-maph'rö-dīte, n., animal with characteristics of both sexes

hêr'mit, n., person who lives alone

hêr'ni-â, n., rupture

hē'rō, n., man admired for qualities and deeds, ideal, model, **-ic, -ism, -ine**

her'ō-in, n., narcotic

hêr-pè-tol'ö-gy, n., study of reptiles

her'ring, n., fish

hes'i-tāte, v., pause, **-tation**

het-êr-ö-gē'nē-ous, a., different, varied, **-ity**

hew, v., cut down

hex'á-gon, n., six-sided figure

hey (hay), int., greeting, call

H'-hour, n., time set for planned attack

hi-ā'tus, n., break, pause

hi-bā'chi, n., little Japanese charcoal stove

hī'bêr-nāte, v., sleep during winter, **-nation**

hic'cup, n., spasm in throat

hick'ō-ry, n., tree, nut

hīde, v., conceal, stay out of sight

hid'ē-ous, a., ugly

hī'êr-ärch-y, n., system of rank or order

hī-êr-ö-glyph'ics, n., ancient Egyptian writing

hīgh (hy), a., far up, almost drunk (coll.)

hīgh'báll, n., whiskey and mixer

hīgh'boy, n., tall furniture chest

hīgh'brow, n., intellectual snob

hīgh'fa-lū'tin, adj., (coll.) pretentious, pompous, haughty

hīgh'-fi-del'i-ty, n., true reproduction of sounds

hīgh'-frē'quèn-cy, a., broadcast in higher signal ranges

hīgh'-hat, v., snub (coll.)

hīgh'līght, n., main point

hīgh'-pres'sure, a., using forceful means

hīgh'-strung', a., excited, nervous

hīgh'way, n., wide road

hī'jack, v., steal goods from trucks

hīke, n., long walk

hi-lār'i-ous, a., humorous, boisterous, merry, **-ty**

hill, n., raised part of land, **-y**

hill'bil-ly, n., native of mountain area

hilt, n., sword handle

him, pro., objective case of he

hīnd, a., rear part

hin'dêr, v., keep from doing, stop, **-drance**

hīnd'sīght, n., considering past happenings

hinge (hinj), n., movable joint

hint, v., subtly suggest

hip, n., projecting part of thigh

hip-pö-pot'á-mus, n., large animal

hīre, v., employ, pay for services

hīr'sūte, a., hairy

his, pro., possessive of him

his'tá-mine (mēen), n., body chemical affecting allergies

his-tol'ö-gy, n., study of tissues

his-tor'i-cál, a., pertaining to history

his'tö-ry, n., study of past events and people

his-tri-on'ic, a., relating to acting and drama

hit, v., strike

hitch, v., tie to something

hitch'hīke, v., ask for auto ride

hith'êr, adv., here

hīve, n., place for keeping bees

hīves, n., skin rash

hōar, a., white with age

hōard, n., collection of that which is saved

hōarse, a., rough sounding, **-ly**

hōax, n., deception, fraud

hob'ble, v., limp

hob'by, n., activity for recreation

hō'bō, n., tramp, bum

hock, n., animal leg joint

hock'ēy, n., game played with sticks on ice or field

hōe, n., garden tool

hōg, n., pig

hōgs'head, n., barrel

hoi'pol-loi', n., the masses, common people

hoist, v., pull up

hō'kum, n., lie, foolish talk

hōld, v., grasp, contain, defend, stick to

hōle, n., empty space, opening

hol'i-day, n., day of celebration

hō'li-nèss, n., state of being holy

hol'lōw, a., empty, of little value

hol'lō-wâre, n., tableware, esp. silver, which is hollow or concave (dishes, bowls, etc.)

hol'ly, n., evergreen plant

hol'ō-cäust, n., complete destruction by fire

hōl'stêr, n., pistol case

hō'ly, a., pertaining to Godly virtues, sacred

hom'áge, n., consideration for, respect

Hom'bûrg, n., style of man's hat

hōme, n., place of residence

hōme'ly, a., ugly, unattractive

hōme'sick, a., yearning to be home

hom'i-cīde, n., killing a person

hom'i-ly, n., sermon

hom'i-ny, n., type of corn

hō-mō-gē'nè-ous, a., alike,

-ity

hō-mo'gèn-īze, v., blend together

hom'ō-nÿm, n., word pronounced like another, but with different meaning and spelling

Hō'mō sā'pi-ens, n., relating to mankind

hō-mō-sex'ū-àl, n., one attracted by person of same sex

hon'èst (on), a., truthful, sincere

hon'ēy (hun), n., sweet liquid produced by bees, term of endearment

hon'ēy-mōōn, n., newly-wed's trip

hon'ôr (on-êr), n., respect, credit, **-able**

hood, n., covering for head

hōōd'lum, n., rough person, gangster

hood'wink, v., cheat, trick

hōōp, n., circular band

hōōt'en-an'ny, n., informal concert of folk music

hop, v., jump on one foot

hōpe, v., wish for earnestly, anticipate

hôrde, n., large group or crowd

hō-rī'zòn, n., apparent meeting line of earth and sky, **-tal**

hôr'mōne, n., stimulating chemical discharged from body glands

hôrn, n., tough growth on animal's head, musical instrument

hō-rol'ō-gy, n., measurement of time

hor'ō-scōpe, n., prediction of future based on stars

hor'ri-ble, a., terrifying

hor'rid, a., terrible

hor'rör, n., great fear

hôr'ti-cul-ture, n., cultivation of a garden

hōse, n., rubber water pipe, women's stockings

hos'pi-tàl, n., institution for treating sick

hos-pi-tal'i-ty, n., friendly welcome

hōst, n., one who entertains, large group, **-ess**

hos'tàge, n., person held as a pledge in kidnapping

hos′tile, *a.*, unfriendly, **-tility**

hot, *a.*, great amount of heat

hot′foot′, *adv.*, in a hurry, also prank of match in person's shoe sole

hō-tel′, *n.*, large inn

hot′house, *n.*, a glasshouse used for growing plants

hot′rod′, *n.*, ordinary car modified to be extremely fast

hound, *v.*, follow closely

hour, *n.*, 60 minutes, time of day, **-ly**

house, *n.*, place of living, business institution, legislative division of government

house′ break, *v.*, train pet in self-control

house′hold, *n.*, members of family

hous′ing, *n.*, dwelling place

höv′ël, *n.*, poor, deteriorated house

höv′ër, *v.*, remain in one place, linger

how, *adv.*, in what way, manner, condition, etc.

how-ev′ër, *adv.*, nevertheless, in what manner, even so

howl, *n.*, long, mournful cry

hua-rä′chēs, *n.*, Mexican sandal of woven leather strips

hub, *n.*, center

huck′stër, *n.*, person who sells from house to house, one in advertising

hud′dle, *v.*, crowd together

hūe, *n.*, color, loud noise

huff′y, *a.*, insulted, angry

hug, *v.*, embrace tightly

hūge (hewj) *a.*, extremely large

hulk, *n.*, massive person or object

hull, *n.*, framework of ship

hum, *n.*, low, sing-song tone

hū′mán, *a.*, relating to man, **-ity, -ly**

hū-man-i-târ′i-án, *n.*, one who loves mankind

hum′bly, *adv.*, in an unimportant position or manner, **-ble**

hum′bug′, *n., v.*, hoax, nonsense, impostor

hum′drum, *a.*, dull, commonplace

hū′mid, *a.*, moist, damp, **-ity**

hū-mil′i-āte, *v.*, shame painfully, **-ation**

hū-mil′i-ty, *n.*, absence of pride, meekness

hū′mör, *n.*, something amusing, disposition, **-ist**

hū′mör-ous, *a.*, amusing

hump, *n.*, small rise

hū′mus, *n.*, soil containing vegetable mold

hun′drëd, *n.*, ten times ten

hun′gër, *n.*, need for food, desire, **-gry**

hunt, *v.*, look for, search, **-er**

hûr′dle, *n.*, obstacle

hûrl, *v.*, throw with force

hur′ray′, *inter.*, cry of appreciation and enthusiasm

hûr′ry, *v.*, go quickly, move speedily

hûrt, *a.*, wounded, **-ful**

hus′bánd, *n.*, male spouse

hus′bánd-ry, *n.*, farming

hush, *v.*, quiet

hush′-hush′, *adj.*, highly secret

husk′y, *a.*, strong, having hoarse sound

hus′tle, *v.*, move quickly

hut, *n.*, small house

hy′á-cinth, *n.*, spring flower

hy′brid, *n.*, of mixed breed

hy′dránt, *n.*, fire plug

hy-drâu′lic (drâw), *a.*, relating to water in motion

hy′drö-gĕn, *n.*, gaseous element

hy′drö-gĕn bomb, *n.*, bomb of tremendous destructive force, employing the fusion of hydrogen atoms

hy-drö-phō′bi-á, *n.*, rabies in man

hy-drö-thêr′á-py, *n.*, use of water to cure

hy-ē′ná, *n.*, animal resembling wolf

hy′giëne (jēen), *n.*, science of health

hymn (him), *n.*, song of praise, **-al**

hy′pêr, *prefix*, forms compounds with the meaning of "excessive." *Example:* **hy-pêr-crit′i-cál**, *a.*, excessively critical

hy-pêr′bö-lē, *n.*, exaggeration

hy′phĕn, *n.*, short mark connecting two related

---

rod ōld wŏn fôr tōō good out oil owl pup ūnit ûrn

words

hýp'nö-tīze, v., put into a trance-like state, **-tism**

hy'pö-, prefix, forms compounds with the meaning "beneath" or "under." Example:

hy-pö-dêr'mic, n., injection under skin by needle

hy-pö-chon'dri-å (kon), n., unrealistic fear of illness, **-c**

hýp'ö-crite (krit), n., one who deceives others by false actions, **-critical**

hy-poth'é-sis, n., unproven belief, theory, **-tical**

hýs-tē'ri-å, n., uncontrolled emotional outburst, **-cal**

I

I, pro., first person singular

īce, n., frozen water

īce' crēam, n., frozen flavored cream

ich-thy-ol'ö-gy (ik-thi), n., science of fish

ī'ci-cle, n., long, sharp piece of ice

īc'ing, n., sugar frosting on cake

ī-con'ö-clast, n., image destroyer, attacker of conventional beliefs

ī'cy, a., frosty, frigid

ī-dē'å, n., imagined image, belief

ī-dē'ål, a., perfect, model, **-ism**

ī-dē'ål-ly, adv., perfectly

ī-den'ti-cal, a., exact

ī-den'ti-fy, v., show as similar, recognize, **-fication**

ī-den'ti-ty, n., specific individuality

id-ê-ol'ö-gy, n., science of ideas and beliefs, **-gical**

id'i-öm, n., mode of expression, **-atic**

id-i-ö-sýn'cra-sy, n., unusual way of behavior, **-tic**

id'i-öt, n., person with defective mentality, fool, **-ic**

ī'dle, a., unemployed, inactive

ī'döl, n., worshipped image, hero, **-atry**

ī'döl-īze, v., adore

ī'dýll (dil), n., poem

if, conj., on condition, in case, although, whether

ig'lōō, n., Eskimo house of ice

ig-nīte', v., start fire, **-nition**

ig-nö'ble, a., low, unworthy

ig-nö-min'i-ous, a., shameful, dishonorable, **-ly**

ig-nö-ra'mus, n., stupid person

ig'nö-ránt, a., lacking

knowledge, unlearned, **rance**

ig-nôre', v., shun, disregard

il-, prefix, same as **in-** before "l"

ilk, a., n., kind, type

ill, a., sick, bad

il-lē'gál, a., unlawful, not accepted, **-gitimate**

il-lic'it, a., not legal, improper

il-lit'êr-āte, a., unable to read or write, **-acy**

il-lū'mi-nāte, v., brighten, **-nation**

il-lū'sion, n., false appearance, impression, **-sive**

il'lus-trāte, v., draw picture for, tell, explain, **-tration**

il-lus'tri-ous, a., well known, famous

im-, prefix, same as **in-** before "m", "b", and "p", in, not

im'āge, n., mental picture, similar reproduction, **-ry**

i-mag'ine (maj), v., picture mentally, guess, **-ination**

im'bē-cile, n., mentally deficient person, **-cilic**

im-bībe', v., drink

im-brö'glīö (brohl-yoh), n., contention, difficult situation

im-būe', v., encourage

im'i-tāte, v., copy, be like, **-tation**

im-mac'ū-lāte, a., perfect, sinless

im-má-tē'ri-ål, a., unimportant

im-mē'dī-āte, a., at once, **-ly**

im-mē-mô'ri-ål, a., longer time than can be remembered

im-mense', a., huge, **-ly**

im-mêrse', v., dip into a liquid

im'mi-grāte, v., come to

---

at bāy ákin fâre cär ăll end hē défy hêr ill īce sîr

another country to live, **-gration, -grant**

im'mi·nent, *a.*, about to occur

im·mō'bile, *a.*, inactive, **-bilize**

im·mor'al, *a.*, sinful, indecent

im·mor'tal, *a.*, being eternally, **-ity**

im·mune', *a.*, free from disease, not subject to, **-munity**

im·mūre', *v.*, lock up in prison

im·mū'ta·ble, *a.*, not changeable

im'pact, *n.*, force of contact

im·pair', *v.*, weaken, damage, **-ment**

im·pal'pa·ble, *a.*, imperceivable to touch, hard to understand

im·part', *v.*, give, pass on to

im·par'tial, *a.*, fair, without prejudice, **-ity**

im·passe', *n.*, deadlock

im·pas'sioned, *a.*, showing deep emotion

im·pas'sive, *a.*, showing little emotion

im·pā'tient, *a.*, not able to stand waiting, restless, **-tience**

im·pēach', *v.*, convict of wrongdoing in public office, **-ment**

im·pec'ca·ble, *a.*, without error, **-bly**

im·pē·cū'ni·ous, *a.*, without money

im·pēde', *v.*, obstruct

im·ped'i·ment, *n.*, obstruction

im·pel', *v.*, drive, push

im·pend', *v.*, occur immediately

im·per'a·tive, *a.*, extremely important

im·per'fect, *a.*, incomplete, not perfect, **-ion**

im·pē'ri·al, *a.*, pertaining to sovereign or empire, **-ism**

im·per'il, *v.*, place in danger

im·pē'ri·ous, *a.*, domineering, dictatorial

im·pêr'sōn·al, *a.*, relating to no one in particular, **-ly**

im·pêr'sōn·āte, *v.*, imitate

im·pêr'ti·nent, *a.*, rude, **-nence**

im·pêr·tûrb'a·ble, *a.*, calm, cool, **-bly**

im·pêr'vi·ous, *a.*, impenetrable, not affected

by

im·pet'ū·ous, *a.*, acting suddenly, **-ity**

im'pē·tus, *n.*, force of movement

im·pinge' (pinj), *v.*, come in to contact with, encroach

im'pi·ous, *a.*, unholy, evil, **-ety**

im·plā'ca·ble, *a.*, unforgiving, **-bly**

im'plē·ment, *n.*, tool, utensil

im'plē·ment, *v.*, do, accomplish

im'pli·cāte, *v.*, involve, infer, **-cation**

im·plic'it, *a.*, without question

im·plōre', *v.*, beg, plead

im·ply', *v.*, suggest indirectly

im·pō·līte', *a.*, rude

im·pon'dêr·a·ble, *n.*, something that cannot be measured exactly

im'pôrt, *v.*, bring merchandise into country, **-ation**

im·pôr'tant, *a.*, having value, very significant, **-tance**

im·pôr'tu·nāte, *a.*, persistent, demanding

im·pôr·tūne', *v.*, request time and again

im·pōse', *v.*, place obligation upon, tax, **-position**

im·pos'si·ble, *a.*, unable to occur, **-bility**

im·pos'tor, *n.*, fraud, cheat

im'pō·tent, *a.*, ineffective, powerless, **-tence**

im·pov'êr·ish, *v.*, cause to be poor, **-ed**

im·preg'na·ble, *a.*, powerful

im·preg'nāte, *v.*, saturate, make fruitful

im·press', *v.*, affect deeply, cut mark into, **-ive, -ion**

im·pres'sion·ism, *n.*, school of art that emphasizes feelings rather than detail

im·pris'ŏn, *v.*, lock in jail, confine

im·promp'tū, *a.*, suddenly, without prior thought

im·prove' (prōōv), *v.*, make better, change in desirable way, **-ment**

im'prō·vīse, *v.*, create spontaneously without prior thought

im'pu·dent, *a.*, rude, unmannerly, **-dence**

im·pugn' (pewn) *v.*, cast doubt upon by disagreeing with

im'pulse, *n.*, sudden idea, thoughtless behavior, **-pulsive**

im·pure', *a.*, not clean, **-purity**

in, *prep.*, within, inside of, regarding

in-, *prefix*, forms compounds, with its other forms, **il-**, **im-**, **ir-**, that give negative meanings to the simple word. *Example:*
in·con'stant, *a.*, not constant.
Where the meaning can easily be found from the simple word, the compound words have been omitted

in·ad·vert'ent, *a.*, unintentional

in·al'ien·a·ble, *a.*, incapable of being taken away

in·ane', *a.*, silly, ridiculous, foolish, **-anity**

in·as·much, *conj.*, since

in·au'gu·rate, *v.*, swear into public office, **-ral**

in·aus·pi'cious, *a.*, unfavorable, unpromising

in'bred, *a.*, natural trait, developed from related parents

in·cal'cu·la·ble, *a.*, more than can be counted, valuable

in·can·des'cent, *a.*, glowing with heat

in·can·ta'tion, *n.*, magic spell

in·ca·pac'i·tate, *v.*, cause to be disabled, **-ity**

in·car'cer·ate, *v.*, lock in jail, confine

in·cen'di·ar·y, *a.*, inflammatory, causing fire

in'cense, *n.*, fragrant smoke given off from perfumed solid

in·cense', *v.*, cause anger

in·cep'tion, *n.*, beginning

in·ces'sant, *a.*, ceaseless, **-ly**

in'cest, *n.*, sexual relations between members of same family, **-uous**

inch, *n.*, 1/12 part of foot

in·cho'ate (koh·it), *a.*, not developed

in'ci·dent, *n.*, occurrence, event

in·ci·den'tal, *a.*, occurring accidentally, **-ly**

in·cin'er·ate, *v.*, burn, **-ator**

in·cip'i·ent, *a.*, beginning

in·ci'sion, *n.*, cut, slot

in·cite', *v.*, encourage to act

in·clem'ent, *a.*, rough, stormy

in·cline', *v.*, want to do, lean toward

in'cline, *n.*, slope

in·clude', *v.*, contain, consist of, be within limits of, **-clusive**

in·cog·ni'to (nēe), *a.*, hidden, disguised

in·co·her'ent, *a.*, mixed up, not clear, **-ence**

in'come, *n.*, money received

in·com·men'su·rate (shi·rit), *a.*, not satisfactory, out of proportion, **-rable**

in·com·mū·ni·cā'do, *a.*, out of contact

in·com'pa·ra·ble, *a.*, unequalled, excellent

in·con'gru·ous, *a.*, not in keeping, unsuitable, **-ity**

in·con·sist'ent, *a.*, contradictory, not logical

in·con·vēn'ient, *a.*, difficult, bothersome, uncomfortable

in·cor'po·rate, *v.*, unite, bring about corporation

in·cor'ri·gi·ble, *a.*, bad beyond control

in·crease', *v.*, add to, make more of, multiply, extend

in·cred'i·ble, *a.*, difficult to believe

in·cred'ū·lous, *a.*, not believing

in'crē·ment, *n.*, addition, raise in salary

in·crim'i·nate, *v.*, involve in crime, accuse, **-nation**

in'cū·bāte, *v.*, hatch eggs, develop, **-bation**

in'cul·cāte, *v.*, teach by intensive drilling, **-cation**

in·cum'bent, *n.*, one who holds office

in·cur', *v.*, cause to happen

in·debt'ed, *a.*, owing, obligated, **-ness**

in·dē'cent, *a.*, crude, vulgar

in·dē·ci'sion, *n.*, inability to decide

in·dec'o·rous, *a.*, unmannerly, undignified, **-rum**

in·dēed', *adv.*, actually, truly

in·dē·fat'i·ga·ble, *a.*, continuous in effort, untiring

in-def'i-nite, a., not clear, vague, **-ly**

in-del'i-ble, a., cannot be erased

in-dem'ni-fy, v., give security against loss, **-fication**

in-dent', v., make a dent, **-ation**

in-de-pend'ent, a., secure in oneself, standing alone, free to do as one pleases, **-ence**

in-depth', adj. thorough, profound, complete

in-de-tẽr'mi-nā-ble, a., unsettled, not decisive, **-te**

in'dex, n., summary of topics in book, indication, sample of study

in'di-cāte, v., show, demonstrate, **cation**

in-dĩct' (dite), v., present as having committed crime, **-ment**

in-dif'fer-ent (dif-rint), a., not reacting to, unconcerned, **-ence**

in'di-gẽnce, a., poverty, need, **-gent**

in'di-gé-nous (dij), a., native

in-di-ges'tion, n., pain due to poor digestion

in-dig'nant, a., angry, upset, **-nation**

in-dig'ni-ty, a., insult

in'di-gō, n., dark bluish color

in-dis-crēet', a., careless, foolish, **-cretion**

in-dis-pōsed', a., sick, not well, **-position**

in-dis-pū'tà-ble, a., without dispute

in-dis-tinct', a., not clear, confused

in-di-vid'ū-àl, n., a., one person, each, **-ly**

in-di-vid'ū-àl-ist, n., independent person

in-di-vid'ū-àl-īze, v., make with special traits

in-doc'tri-nāte, v., teach, impress upon, **-nation**

in'dō-lent, a., lazy, **-lence**

in-dom'i-tà-ble, a., undefeatable, **-bly**

in-dū'bi-tà-bly, adv., without doubt

in-dūce', v., convince, cause, **-ment**

in-duct', v., install, initiate, **-ion**

in-dulge', v., engage in, allow, **-nce**

in-dus'tri-ous, a., making much effort, conscientious

in'dus-try, n., production and distribution of goods, showing interest in work, **-trial**

in-ē'brī-āt-ĕd, a., drunk

in-ef'fà-ble, a., indescribable, not able to be expressed in language

in-ĕf-fec'tū-ál, a., weak, useless, **-ly**

in-ĕf-fi'cient, a., not capable, lacking in ability, wasteful, **-ly**

in-ept', a., not capable, unskilled, **-ly**

in-ē'qui-tà-ble (ek-wi), a., unjust, unfair, **-bly**

in-ẽrt', a., not moving, not active, **-ly**

in-ẽr'tia (shà), n., property of staying still or remaining in motion until changed by outside forces

in-es'ti-mà-ble, a., of great value, not to be estimated

in-ev'i-tà-ble, a., certain to occur, inescapable

in-ex'ō-rà-ble, a., not forgiving, inflexible, **-bly**

in-ex'pi-à-ble, a., cannot be atoned for

in-ex-pli'cà-ble, a., unexplainable, **-bly**

in-ex'tri-cà-ble, a., impossible to escape from, **-bly**

in-fal'li-ble, a., without mistake, **-bility**

in'fà-mous, a., evil, wicked, notorious, **-ly**

in'fà-my, n., disgrace, dishonor, notoriety

in'fànt, n., baby, **-fancy**

in'fàn-try, n., foot soldiers

in-fat-ū-ā'tion, n., foolish love

in-fect', v., contaminate, spread, **-ion, -ious**

in-fe-lic'i-ty, n., unhappiness

in-fẽr', v., conclude as a result of facts, **-ence**

in-fē'ri-ŏr, a., lower than, degraded, **-ity**

in-fẽr'nál, a., hellish

in-fest', v., overrun

in'fil-trāte, v., come secretly into place, **-ion**

in'fi-nite, a., boundless, without beginning or end, **-nity**

in-fin-i-tes'i-màl, a.,

extremely small, tiny, **-ly**

in-fin'i-tive, *n.*, verb part in grammar

in-firm', *a.*, sickly

in-fir'ma-ry, *n.*, hospital

in-flam'ma-ble, *a.*, easy to burn

in-flam-ma'tion, *n.*, infection marked by redness and swelling, stimulation, **-tory**

inflate', *v.*, fill with air

infla'tion, *n.*, swelling, excess of money in circulation

in-flec'tion, *n.*, change in tone

in-flict', *v.*, give, impose

in'flu-ence, *n.*, power, authority, prestige, **-ential**

in-flu-en'za, *n.*, infectious disease

in'flux, *n.*, that coming in

in-form', *v.*, give information about, tell on, **-er**

in-for'mal, *a.*, apart from strict rules, easy-going, **-ity**

in-for-ma'tion, *n.*, facts

in-frac'tion, *n.*, violation

in-fre'quent (kwent), *a.*, happening seldom

in-fu'ri-ate, *v.*, make extremely angry, **-ation**

in-fuse', *v.*, pour into, fill, **fusion**

in-ge'ni-ous (jēen-yus), *a.*, very clever

in-ge-nu'i-ty, *n.*, skill, cleverness

in-gen'u-ous, *a.*, honest, sincere

in-gest', *v.*, absorb food into body, **-ion**

in'got, *n.*, metal bar

in'grained, *a.*, what is deep inside one

in'grate, *n.*, ungrateful individual

in-grat'i-tūde, *n.*, absence of appreciation

in-gre'di-ent, *n.*, part of a whole

in-group, *n.*, a group of people bound by shared interests, often exclusive of others

in-hab'it, *v.*, dwell, **-ant**

in-hāle', *v.*, breathe in

in-her'ent, *a.*, inborn, **-ly**

in-her'it, *v.*, receive by law the possessions of others, **-ance**

in-hib'it, *v.*, stop, suppress, **-ition**

in-im'i-cál, *a.*, unfriendly, hostile

in-im'i-tà-ble, *a.*, unable to be imitated

in-iq'ui-tous, *a.*, sinful, wicked, **ty**

in-i'tial, *a.*, beginning, first, **-ly**

in-i-ti-ā'tion, *n.*, ceremony of admission to society, club, etc.

in-i'ti-à-tive, *n.*, taking the lead

in-ject', *v.*, introduce liquid into, remark, **-ion**

in'jure (jėr), *v.*, hurt, harm **-jury**

in-jus'tice, *n.*, inequity

ink, *n.*, liquid used for writing

ink'ling, *n.*, hint

in'lànd, *a.*, away from sea

in'-läw', *a.*, relative of husband or wife

in'māte, *n.*, one confined to institution

in'nāte, *a.*, natural

in'nēr, *a.*, inside

in'ning, *n.*, change of team in baseball

in'nō-cênt, *a.*, free of guilt, **-cence**

in'nō-vāte, *v.*, start, change, **-vation**

in-nū-en'dō, *n.*, subtle reference

in-nū'mêr-à-ble, *a.*, countless

in-oc'ū-lāte, *v.*, protect against disease by vaccination

in-ôr'di-nàte-ly, *adv.*, exceedingly

in-ôr-gan'ic, *a.*, non-living elements

in'quest, *n.*, coroner's inquiry into death

in-quīre' (kwīr), *v.*, look for, **-quiry**

in-sāne', *a.*, mentally ill, crazy, **-sanity**

in-sā'ti-à-ble (shi-bil), *a.*, not able to be satisfied

in-scrībe', *v.*, write words upon or into, **-scription**

in-scrū'tà-ble, *a.*, difficult to comprehend

in'sect, *n.*, tiny animal such as ant, flea, etc.

in-sem'i-nāte, *v.*, sow seeds, make fertile, **-nation**

in-sen'sàte, *a.*, not feeling

in-sen'si-ble, *a.*, unaware, unconscious

in-sert', v., place inside or among, **-ion**

in'side, a., within, (coll.) secret

in-sid'i-ous, a., operating mysteriously

in-sight', n., understanding

in-sig'ni-à, n., mark of rank or group

in-sig-nif'i-cànt, a., unimportant, of no value

in-sin'ū-āte, v., suggest, imply, **-ation**

in-sip'id, a., tasteless uninteresting, boring

in-sist', v., strongly request, **-ent**

in'sö-lènt, a., insulting

in-sol'ū-ble, a., not to be solved

in-som'ni-à, n., inability to sleep

in-sou'ci-ànt (sōō), a., carefree, **-ance**

in-spect', v., search thoroughly, **-ion**

in-spīre', v., excite to action, fill with emotional or spiritual strength, **-spiration**

in-stâll', v., place in office or position, **-ation**

in-stâll'mènt, n., payment of debt at certain intervals

in'stànce, n., example, specific occasion

in'stànt, n., specific time, moment, **-ly**

in-stàn-tā'nē-ous, a., immediate, **-ly**

in-stead' (sted), adv., in place of, rather

in'sti-gāte, v., excite, arouse, cause, **-gation**

in-still', v., teach gradually, inspire

in'stinct, n., unlearned action, intuition, **-ive**

in'sti-tūte, v., begin, create

in-sti-tū'tion, n., accepted custom, school, hospital, etc., establishment, **-te**

in-struct', v., teach, **-ion**

in'stru-mènt, n., tool, implement

in-stru-men'tàl, a., assisting, necessary in

in-sub-ôr'di-nàte, a., opposing law or authority, **-nation**

in-suf'fèr-à-ble, a., difficult to accept or live with

in'su-lāte, v., protect by covering, **-lation**

in'su-lin, n., medicine taken for diabetes

in'sult, n., indignity

in-sult', v., abuse verbally

in-sūre', v., guarantee against loss, **-surance**

in-sûr'gènt, a., rebellious, **-gence**

in-sur-rec'tion, n., rebellion, revolution

in-tact', a., complete, whole

in-tan'gi-ble, n., not solid or material

in-tē'grál, a., essential, entire, full

in-tē'grāte, v., fuse together, **-gration**

in-teg'ri-ty, n., honest character

in'tèl-lect, n., ability to reason and understand, **-ual**

in-tel'li-gènce, n., ability to learn, **-gible**

in-tem'pèr-āte, a., going to extremes, immoderate

in-tend', v., propose to do

in-tense', a., showing strong concentration, powerful, **-tensity**

in-ten'si-fy, v., increase in degree

in-tent', n., aim, purpose, **-ion**

in-tent', a., earnest, engrossed

in'têr, prefix, forms compounds meaning among, mutually, or between, *Examples:*

in-têr-chānge', v., exchange among each other, **in-têr-fēre'**, v., bother in someone else's affairs.

Where the meaning can easily be found from the simple word, the compound words have been omitted

in-têr-cēde', v., make a plea for someone else, **-cession**

in'têr-course, n., relationship with

intêr-cept', v., prevent completion, interfere

in-têr-dict', n., order to prohibit, **-ion**

in'têr-èst, v., attract attention of, become concerned about, **-ed**

in'têr-èst, n., fee paid for use

in·ter·im, *a.*, temporary time

in·te′ri·or, *n.*, inside

in·ter·jec′tion, *n.*, exclamation

in·ter·loc′u·tô·ry, *a.*, pending

in′ter·lōp·êr, *n.*, one who intrudes

in′ter·lūde, *n.*, period of time between

in·ter·mē′di·ate, *n.*, go-between, in the middle

in·têr′mi·nä·ble, *a.*, without end, **-bly**

in·ter·mis′sion, *n.*, period between acts of play

in·ter·mit′tènt, *a.*, stop and start, periodic

in′têrn, *n.*, student-doctor working in hospital

in·têrn′, *v.*, keep within bounds

in·têr′nál, *a.*, inside

in·têr·nē′cine, *a.*, destroying both sides

in·têr′pō·lāte, *v.*, change or alter words in translation

in·têr·pōse′, *v.*, place between

in·têr′prêt *v.*, translate, give meaning, **-ation**

in·ter·rö·gā′tion, *n.*, asking questions, **-tory**

in·têr·rupt′, *v.*, break in activity

in·ter·sect′, *v.*, divide, cross, **-ion**

in·têr·spêrse′, *v.*, divided among or between

in′têr·val, *n.*, period of time in between, musical pause

in·têr·vēne′, *v.*, come between

in′têr·view (vū), *n.*, meeting arranged for one person to question another, *v.*

in·tes′tāte, *a.*, leaving no will at death

in·tes′tine, *n.*, bowel part below stomach, **-tinal**

in′ti·māte, *a.*, personal, private, **-ly**

in′ti·māte, *v.*, hint, **-mation**

in·tim′i·dāte, *v.*, overpower, threaten, **-dation**

in′to (tōō), *prep.*, inside, to form of

in·tol′êr·a·ble, *a.*, difficult to tolerate, hard to bear, **-bly**

in·tol′êr·ant, *a.*, prejudiced, narrow-minded, **-ance**

in·tō·nā′tion, *n.*, manner of speaking

in·tox·i·cā′tion, *n.*, drunkenness

in·trac′ta·ble, *v.*, difficult to manage, stubborn

in·trá·mū′rál, *a.*, within the limits of

in·tran′si·gènt, *a.*, not willing to yield, stubborn

in·trá·stāte′, *a.*, within a state

in·trá·vē′nous, *a.*, within veins

in·trep′id, *a.*, courageous, fearless

in′tri·cāte, *a.*, complicated, twisted, **-cacy**

in′trigue (trēeg), *v.*, fascinate

in′trigue, *n.*, conspiracy, mystery

in·trin′sic (zik), *a.*, inborn, true

in·trö·dūce′, *v.*, bring into, have persons meet, begin, **-duction**

in·trö·spec′tion, *n.*, self-analysis

in′trö·vêrt, *n.*, extremely reserved person

in·trūde′, *v.*, break into, interrupt, **-trusion**

in·tū·i′tion, *n.*, insight, **-tive**

in′un·dāte, *v.*, flood, overflow, **-dation**

in·ūre′, *v.*, become accustomed to, make tough, **-d**

in·vāde′, *v.*, enter forcefully, **-vasion**

in′vá·lid, *n.*, person who is sick for long time

in·val′id, *a.*, not valid, void, **-ate**

in·val′ū·á·ble, *a.*, of great value

in·vâr′i·á·bly, *adv.*, unchangingly, constantly

in·vec′tive, *n.*, scorn, insult, verbal attack

in·vei′gle (vay), *v.*, lure

in·vent′, *v.*, create, coax, make, **-ion**

in·ven′tôr, *n.*, one who creates new process or product

in′vèn·tö·ry, *n.*, count of, list

in·vêrse′, *a.*, turned around, reversed, **-version**

in·vest′, *v.*, put money into business, stocks, etc., with hope of profit, put forth effort, empower, install,

-ment

in·ves'ti·gāte, v., examine, search, **-gation**

in·vet'êr·ȧte, a., habitual, of long standing

in·vid'i·ous, a., hateful

in·vig'ŏr·āt·ėd, a., refreshed, **-ing**

in·vin'ci·ble, a., unbeatable

in·vī'-ō·lāte, a., untouched, not harmed

in·vis'i·ble, a., cannot be seen

in·vīte', v., request to attend, ask comments, tempt, **-vitation**

in·vīt'ing, a., tempting, pleasurable

in·vōke', v., request blessing of, **-vocation**

in·vol·un·tā·ry, a., unintentional, automatic, **-rily**

in·volve', v., include in activity, be concerned with, complicate, entangle, **-ment**

in·vul'nêr·a·ble, a., not capable of being hurt

in'wȧrd, a., within, toward inside

ī'ō·dīne, n., non-metallic element, chemical used as antiseptic

ī'on, n., electrically charged particle

ir-, prefix, same as in- before "r"

i·ras'ci·ble, a., quickly angered, **-bility**

īre, n., anger

ir·i·des'cėnt, a., of many colors

ī'ris, n., flower, part of eye

ĩrk, v., annoy, bother, **-some**

ī'rŏn (ẽrn), n., strong metal, pressing device

ī·ron'i·cȧl, a., sarcastic

ī'rŏn lŭng', n., machine to enforce breathing

ī'rō·ny, n., sarcastic statement or fateful happening

ir·rā·di·ā'tion, n., enlightenment, illumination

ir·rel'ė·vȧnt, a., not related to the subject at hand

ir·rep'ȧ·rȧ·ble, a., cannot be fixed

ir'ri·gāte, v., supply with water, **-gation**

ir'ri·tȧ·ble, a., easily annoyed, excitable, **bility**

ir'ri·tāte, v., annoy, disturb, **-tation**

īs'lȧnd, n., land surrounded by water

īsle (ile), n., little island

ism (izem), n., theory, doctrine, system

ī'sō·lāte, v., keep alone, separate, **-lation**

ī'sō·tōpe, n., element form

is·sūe' (ish-ew), v., give forth, send, publish

is·sūe', n., offspring, result, disputed matter, something published

isth'mus, n., narrow connecting strip of land

it, pro., something particular, something referred to

ī·tal'ic, a., slanted type face, **-ize**

itch, n., skin irritation

ī'tėm, n., specific thing

ī'tėm·īze, v., make list

it·êr·āte, v., repeat

ī·tin'êr·ȧnt, a., traveling, **-ary**

ī'vŏ·ry, n., elephant tusk, creamy color

ī'vy, n., climbing vine

J

jab, v., punch, poke

jack, n., lifting device

jack'ȧl, n., wild dog

jack'ȧss, n., donkey

jack'ėt, n., short coat

jack'pot, n., highest winnings

jāde, n., green stone

jag, n., spree

jag'gėd, a., rough, uneven

jag'uär (währ), n., S. Am.

leopard

jai'a·lai' (hi-li), n., game similar to handball, played with long baskets strapped to players' wrists

jāil, n., place of imprisonment

jam, v., squeeze tightly together, crowd

jam, n., difficulty, jelly

jan'gle, n., harsh ringing

sound

jan'i-tŏr, n., building caretaker

jär, n., glass container

jär, v., disturb, shock

jär'gŏn, n., confused language

jäun'dice, n., liver disease

jäunt, n., short journey

jäw, n., bones that make up bottom part of mouth

jazz, n., type of music

jeal'ous, a., suspiciously watchful, envious, **-y**

jēep, n., small automotive vehicle

jēer, v., make fun of, mock

jė-jūne', a., dull, uninspiring

jell, v., crystallize, set

jel'ly, n., fruit cooked with sugar

jeop'ärd-y, n., danger, **-ize**

jêrk, v., pull suddenly

jêrk (coll.), n., stupid person

jêrk'watêr, adj., off the main line, out of the way, insignificant

jêr'sėy, n., clinging knitted cloth

jest, n., joke, prank

jet, n., powerful spray, mineral

jet prö-pul'sion, n., forward motion as result of gases being expelled under pressure

jet'ti-sŏn, v., lighten a load, discard

jet'ty, n., landing pier

Jew, n., believer in Judaism, **-ish**

jew'ėl, n., gem, watch bearing, **-ry**

jībe (coll.), v., agree

jif'fy, n., moment, instant

jig'gle, v., move back and forth slightly

jilt, v., cast off loved one

Jim Crow, adj., practice of discriminating against or segregation of Negroes

jin'gle, n., musical bell-like sound

jin'gō-ism, n., extreme nationalism

jinx (coll.), n., bad luck

jīve, n., v., jazz, kid, tease

job, n., work, occupation, position

job'bêr, n., distributor of goods

jock'ėy, n., race horse rider

jock'strap, n., support for male genitals, worn during athletics

jō-cōse', a., joking, humorous

joc'ū-lär, a., playful

jodh'pûrs (jod), n., tight fitting riding pants

jog, v., push, run slowly

jog, n., push

join, v., unite, become part of

joint, n., where things meet, (coll.), low class entertainment place

jōke, n., funny activity or story, jest

jol'ly, a., gay, merry, **-lity**

jŏlt, v., knock against, upset, hurt slightly

jon'quil (kwil), n., flower

jos'tle, v., push into or against, **-tling**

jot, v., write down

joûr'nal, n., record of happenings, newspaper, diary, periodical

joûr'nal-ism, n., writing articles and reporting for mass media, **-ist**

joûr'nėy, n., trip

joûr'nėy-man, n., experienced, reliable worker

jō'vi-ál, a., in good spirits, **-ity**

jowl, n., lower jaw

joy (joi), n., happiness, delight, **-ful**

jū'bi-lant, a., exceedingly happy, **-lation**

jū'bi-lēe, n., special anniversary

Jū'da-ism, n., religion developed by ancient Hebrews

judge, v., settle dispute, determine guilt, present opinion, **-ment**

jū-di'ci-ár-y, a., relating to judges

jū-di'cious, a., judging wisely

jū'dō, n., self-defense without weapons, based on jujitsu

jug, n., small pitcher

jug'gle, v., perform skillful tricks, **-r**

jūice, n., liquid of fruit or vegetable

jū jit'sū, n., system of weaponless fighting

jūke' box, n., coin operated record player

jum'ble, v., confuse, mix

---

at bāy ákin fâre cär ăll end hē dėfy hêr ill īce stir

together

jump, v., leap

junc'tion, n., meeting place

junc'ture, n., crisis, point of meeting

jun'gle, n., thickly grown tropical forest

jūn'ĭŏr (yŭr), a., youthful, younger, lower in position

jūn-ĭŏr col'lēge, n., two year college

junk, n., small Chinese boat, trash

jun'kėt, n., official trip

jun'ta (hun´ta), n., group who controls a government

jū-ris-dic'tion, n., power, authority, control

jū-ris-prū'dĕnce, n., system of law

jū'rist, n., authority in law, -ic

jū'ry, n., citizens who sit in judgment in court, -ror

just, a., fair, right, truthful

just, adv., shortly, precisely, almost, only

jus'tice, n., fair judgment, correct treatment, judge

jus'tĭ-fy, v., prove as being correct, make excuse for, -fication

jut, v., stick out, project

jūte, n., tough material for making rope

jū'vėn-īle, a., young, relating to youth, childish

jux-tȧ-pōse', v., place next to each other, -position

K

---

kaī'sėr, n., former German emperor

kāle, n., a cabbage-like vegetable

kà-lĕī'dŏ-scōpe, n., optical tube showing colored glass, constant change, -scopic

kan-gȧ-rōō', n., leaping mammal

kā'ty-dĭd, n., grasshopper

kay'ak (kī), n., Eskimo canoe

kēel, n., bottom of ship

kēen, a., sharp, eager

kēen, n., sound of mourning, -er

kēep, v., preserve, maintain, support, -ing

kēep'sȧke, n., souvenir

keg, n., small barrel

kelp, n., seaweed

kel'vin (k), n., unit of temperature change

ken, n., knowledge

ken'nėl, n., house for dogs

kept, a., supported

kêr'chief (chĭf), n., head covering

kêr'nėl, n., grain, seed, core

ker'ö-sēne, n., oil fuel

ketch, n., two-masted ship

ket'tle, n., pot for boiling

ket'tle drum, n., large drum

kēy, n., unlocking device, tone, solution, lever

kēy'bŏard, n., keys on piano, typewriter, etc.

kēy'hōle, n., hole in lock

kēy'nōte, n., main note, central idea

kēy'stōne, n., something on which associated things depend

khak'ĭ (ē), n., yellowish brown cloth

khän, n., ancient Chinese emperor

Kib-butz, n., collective farm in Israel

kib'ĭtz, v., advise, meddle, -er

kick, v., strike with foot, resist, rebel

kick'back (coll.), n., money returned illegally

kick'off, n., opening kick in football or soccer

kid (coll.), v., joke, fool, tease

kid'nap, v., steal person by force

kid'nĕy, n., body organ

kid'nĕy bēan, n., dark red bean

kill, v., cause to die, defeat

kill'ėr, n., anything that kills, -ing

kill'joy, n., spoiler of fun

kiln, n., drying oven

kĭl'ö-gram, n., 2.2046 pounds

kĭl'ö-mē-tėr, n., 3,280.8 feet

kĭl'ö-watt, n., 1000 watts

kilt, n., short, pleated skirt

ki-mō'nŏ, n., loose Japanese robe

kin, n., relatives

kīnd, n., sort, quality

---

kīnd, a., loving, gentle, agreeable

kin'dêr-gär-ten, n., school for young children

kīnd'heärt'ed, a., tender

kin'dle, v., light, arouse

kīnd'li-ness, n., kindly act

kin'dling, n., wood shavings for starting fire

kīnd'ly, a., friendly, natural

kīnd'ness, n., favor, affection

kin'drĕd, a., related

kin-ė-mat'ics, n., study of pure motion

kin-ĕs-thet'ic, a., relating to muscular activity

ki-net'ics, n., study of forces causing motion changes

king, n., hereditary male ruler

king' bîrd, n., large bird, flycatcher

king' bŏlt, n., front-axle bolt

king' crab, n., large crab

king'dŏm, n., realm

king' fish (coll.), n., undisputed ruler

king'ly, a., like a king

king'pin, n., center pin in bowling, headpin

kink, n., quirk, whim, **-y**

kins'fŏlk, n., relatives

kin'ship, n., relationship

kī'osk, n., small open-sided building

kip, n., small animal's hide

kip'pêr, n., dried smoked herring

kīs'mĕt, n., fate

kiss, v., touch lips together

kit, n., small carrying case

kitch'ĕn, n., room for cooking

kitch-ĕn-ette', n., small kitchen

kīte, n., paper on wood frame flown in air, a bird

kit'tĕn, n., young cat, **-ish**

kit'ty, n., kitten

Klēe'n'ex, n., trade name for disposable tissue

klep-tō-mā'ni-å, n., uncontrollable desire to steal, **-c**

knack (nak), n., ability

knap'sack, n., bag carried on back

knāve, n., rascal, **-ry**

knĕad, v., squeeze, press, mold

knee, n., joint between thigh and leg

knee' cap, n., bone in front of knee

knēe'-dēep' (coll.), a., deeply involved

knēe'hīgh', a., reaching to the knees

knēel, v., rest on knee

knēe' pad, n., pad to protect knees

knell, n., sound of funeral bell

knick'êrs, n., pants gathered at knees

knick'-knack, n., trifling decoration, ornament

knīfe, n., tool for cutting, **-ives**

knīght, n., heroic fighter

knīght' er'rant, n., knight searching adventure, **-ry**

knīght'hood, n., rank of a knight

knīght'ly, a., chivalrous

knit (nit), v., interweave thread, unite, **-ting**

knŏb, n., knob, knot

knock, v., hit, rap

knock'å-bout, a., n., boisterous, sailboat

knock'êr, n., knob for rapping on door

knock'-knēed, a., knees turned inward

knock'out, n., punch causing unconsciousness

knŏll, n., small round hill

knot, v., tie together, entangle

knot'hōle, n., hole in board

knot'ty, a., difficult, complex

knōw, v., be aware of, be familiar with

knōw'-how, n., skill, ability

knōw'ing, a., smart, deliberate

knowl'ĕdge (nol-ij), n., understanding of facts, **-able**

knuck'le, n., joint of finger

knuck'le down', v., exert earnest effort

knûrl, n., knob, knot

kō-ä'lå, n., furry Australian animal

Kō'dak, n., trade name for small camera

kohl-rä'bi, n., cabbage-like vegetable

kō'lå, n., African nut tree

kö-lin'sky, n., Asian mink

kō'pĕck, n., Russian coin

kō'shêr, a., sanctioned by Jewish law

krääl (krähl), *n.*, South African village

Krem'lin, *n.*, Russian government headquarters

krō'nē, *n.*, Danish and Norwegian coin

kryp'ton, *n.*, inert gas

kū'dōs, *n.*, fame, glory

Kū Klux Klan, *n.*, secret society

kū-läk', *n.*, prosperous Russian farmer

kūl-tūr', *n.*, German understanding of culture

kum'mēl (ki-mil), *n.*, caraway flavored liqueur

kum'quat (kwot), *n.*, smallish orange

kväss, *n.*, Russian drink

L

---

lā'bēl, *n.*, description, title, name tape

lā'bör, *n.*, work, **-er**

lā'bör, *n.*, job, childbirth pains, task, group of workers

lab'ö-rá-tō-ry, *n.*, place for performing research

lab'y-rinth, *n.*, intricacy, maze

lāce, *n.*, decorated material of delicate threads

lac'ēr-āte, *v.*, tear, mangle, hurt, **-ation**

lach'rý-mál (lak), *a.*, relating to tears, **-mose**

lack, *v.*, do without, be in need, **-ing**

lack-á-dāi'sí-cál, *a.*, without energy, lazy, languid

lá-con'ic, *a.*, speaking little

lá-crōsse', *n.*, game using webbed sticks

lac-tā'tion, *n.*, secretion of milk

la-cū'na, *n.*, gap, missing part

lad, *v.*, do without

lad'dēr, *n.*, device with rungs for climbing upward

lā'ding, *n.*, loading, cargo, freight

lā'dle, *n.*, long-handled spoon

lā'dy, *n.*, woman, well-mannered lady

lag, *v.*, go slowly, fall behind

lá-gōōn', *n.*, shallow lake or pond

lâir, *n.*, animal's den

lais-sez fâire' (les-ay), *n.*, non-interference

lā'i-ty, *n.*, non-cleric people

lāke, *n.*, body of water surrounded by land

lam (coll.), *v.*, run away

lamb, *n.*, young sheep

lāme, *a.*, crippled

lá-ment', *v.*, grieve over, mourn for, **-ation**

lam'i-nāte, *v.*, compress into a thin plate

lamp, *n.*, light-giving device

lam-pōōn', *v.*, ridicule

lance, *n.*, type of spear

land, *n.*, earth, ground, area of ground, **-ing**

land'lörd, *n.*, property leaser

land'scāpe, *n.*, view of countryside, vista

lāne, *n.*, narrow path

lan'guáge (gwij), *n.*, contents of speech, way of speaking

lan'guid, *a.*, lacking energy, weak, listless

lan'guish, *v.*, lose strength, fall away, long, suffer with longing

lan'guör (gēr), *n.*, weakness, lack of interest

lank'y, *a.*, tall and thin

lan'ö-lin, *n.*, oil from wool

lan'tērn, *n.*, portable device which gives off light

lap, *n.*, legs above knees when seated, fixed distance in race

lap, *v.*, enfold, wash against

lá-pel', *n.*, folded part of coat

lapse, *v., n.*, forget temporarily, interval, interruption

lär'cē-ny, *n.*, theft

lärge, *a.*, big, many, broad, **-ly**

lar'i-át, *n.*, rope with loop at end, lasso

lärk, *n.*, song bird, (coll.) fun

lar'va, *n.*, early form of insect

lar'ÿnx (lar-inx), *n.*, top part of windpipe

lás-civ'í-ous, *a.*, lewd, lustful, immoral

lash, *v.*, beat, insult, tie

lass, *n.*, girl

las'si-tūde, *n.*, laziness,

---

weakness

las'sō, *n.*, rope with a noose

last, *a.*, at the end, most nearly recent, final

last'ing, *a.*, that which endures, permanent

lāte, *a.*, delayed, recently dead

lāte'ly, *adv.*, recently

lā'tent, *a.*, hidden, dormant

lā'tex, *n.*, plant liquid

lāthe, *n.*, machine for shaping

lath'ēr, *n.*, froth, foam

lat'i-tūde, *n.*, distance measured north and south from equator, freedom to act

lat-i-tū-di-nâr'i-an, *n.*, tolerant person

lat'tēr, *a.*, second of two

lat'tice, *n.*, criss-crossed wooden pieces

lăud, *v.*, praise, **-atory**

laugh (laf), *n.*, oral expression of glee, **-ter**

launch, *v.*, send into water or air, begin

lăun'dēr, *v.*, wash and iron clothes, **-dry**

lâu'rĕl, *n.*, evergreen tree

lā'vä, *n.*, hot volcanic liquid

lav'a-tō-ry, *n.*, wash room

lav'en-dēr, *n.*, purple color, sweet smelling perfume

lav'ish, *v.*, spend freely, pay much attention to, squander

lăw, *n.*, rules to live by, **-ful**

lăwn, *n.*, ground covered with grass

lax, *a.*, loose, not strict, **-ity**

lax'a-tive, *n.*, substance to loosen bowels

lay, *v.*, place, put down, produce eggs

lay, *a.*, not professional

lay'ēr, *n.*, single thickness of matter

lay-ette', *n.*, outfit for infant

lay'man, *n.*, person not of the clergy

lay'out, *n.*, design, plan

lā'zy, *a.*, sluggish, indolent

lēad, *v.*, guide, conduct, go first, **-er**

lead (led), *n.*, metallic element, graphite

lēaf, *n.*, plant foliage, sheet of paper

lēague (lēeg), *n.*, federation, category

lēak, *n.*, hole, crack

lēan, *a.*, thin, spare

lēap, *v.*, jump

lēarn, *v.*, gain understanding, discover

lēarn'ing, *n.*, knowledge, facts

lēase, *v.*, rent, hire

lēast, *a.*, in the smallest degree, unimportant, slightest

leath'ēr (leth), *n.*, processed animal skin

lēave, *v.*, *n.*, depart, desert, vacation period

lec'ture, *v.*, talk to group, reprimand

ledge, *n.*, narrow edge or shelf

ledg'ēr, *n.*, account book

lēe, *n.*, protected side, **-ward**

left, *a.*, opposite of right

left'ist, *n.*, one holding radical political iews

leg, *n.*, limb for walking, support, part

leg'a-cy, *n.*, something inherited, bequest

lē'gál, *a.*, relating to law, **-ize**

lē-gā'tion, *n.*, diplomatic mission

leg'end (lej), *n.*, tale, myth, map key, **-ary**

leg-ēr-dē-māin', *n.*, sleight of hand, skill

leg'i-ble, *a.*, able to be read, plain, **-bly**

lē'gion, *n.*, division of army, many

leg'is-lāte, *v.*, enact laws, **-lation**

leg'is-lā-ture, *n.*, law-making body

lē-git'i-māte, *a.*, proper, within law, **-macy**

lēi'sure, *n.*, time of rest, free time, **-ly**

lem'ŏn, *n.*, citrus fruit, **-ade**

lend, *v.*, give temporary use of, **-er**

length (lenth), *n.*, measurement of the long part, distance

length'en, *v.*, extend

lē'ni-ent, *a.*, kind, easy, tolerant, indulgent

lens, *n.*, camera glass part, image-creating part of eye

leop'ard (lep), *n.*, wild cat-like animal

lep'rō-sy, *n.*, disease of skin

les'bi-an, *n.*, homosexual female

s'sion, n., body injury, harm

ess, a., not as much as, minor in position, smaller in size or degree, **-en**

ess, prep., minus, diminished by

es'sön, n., fact or knowledge taught

et, v., allow, permit to occupy, give out under contract, hire

et'down, n., fatigue, failure, disappointment

ē'thäl, a., deadly

eth'är·gy, n., sleepiness, inactivity, indifference **-gic**

let'tër, n., written message, alphabet symbol

let'tuce, n., leafy vegetable

leū-kē'mi·ā, n., surplus of white cells in blood

lev'ēe, n., high bank of river, pier

lev'el, a., precisely horizontal, balanced, even, (coll.) honest

lev'ēr, n., bar used to apply force easily

lē-vī'a·thän, n., something enormous

lev'i·ty, n., absence of proper manners, silliness, foolish action, lightness

lev'y, n., amount of taxes

lewd, a., sexually indecent, obscene

lex·i·cog'ra·phy, n., compilation of dictionary, **-pher**

lī'a·ble, a., responsible for, owing, most likely, **-bility**

li·āi'son (lee-ay-zon), n., union, relationship, connection

lī'bel, n., insult to one's reputation, **-ous**

lib'ēr·al, a., fair, charitable, tolerant, loose, generous, **-ity**

lib'ēr·āte, v., free, release, **-ation**

lib'ēr·tine (tēen), n., immoral individual, freethinker

lib'ēr·ty, n., freedom, right to do something, chance

li·bid'i·nous, a., sexually immoral, lascivious

lī'brar·y, n., collection of books, **-ian**

li·bret'tō, n., words of song or opera, **-tist**

Lib'ri·um, n., trade name for chlordiazepoxide, a sedative

lī'cënse, n., formal permission

lī·cen'tious, a., lacking moral or legal restraints

lic'it, a., permissible

lick, v., pass tongue over, (coll.) beat, defeat

lid, n., container top

lie, v., make dishonest statement, rest in flat position

lieū, n., instead of

lieū·ten'ant, n., military officer

life, n., living, total number of person's years, activity, **-less**

life'guärd, n., bathing beach guard

lift, v., raise, (coll.) steal, plagiarize

lig'a·ture, n., bond

light, n., device or means by which we see, understanding

light, a., not heavy, gay

light, v., set fire to, cause illumination

light'ën, v., make easier, produce light

light'ēr, n., ship, barge, device for lighting

light'ly, adv., easily, without concern, not heavily, gently

light'ning, n., electricity flash in sky

lig'nē·ous, a., resembling wood

līk'a·ble, a., pleasant, agreeable

līke, v., enjoy, want

līke, a., similar

līke'ly, adv., in all probability, suitable

līke'ness, n., resemblance, copy

līke'wīse, adv., also, similarly

lī'lāc, n., purple flower

lil'y, n., bulbous flower

limb, n., arm or leg, tree branch, extension

lim'bēr, a., flexible, agile

līme, n., alkaline substance, greenish citrus fruit

līme'līght, n., spotlight, center of attention

lim'it, v., restrict, confine, **-ing**

lim·i·tā'tion, n., restriction,

lim'ou·sine' (zeen), n., large, luxurious car
limp, v., walk unevenly
limp, a., drooping, weary
lim'pid, a., clear, transparent
lin'den, n., type of tree
line, n., piece of string or rope, boundary mark, edge of row, mark, direction
lin'e·al, a., relating to descent, hereditary
lin'e·ar, a., relating to lines, straight
lin'en, n., cloth manufactured from flax
lin'ger, v., remain behind, stay, tarry, delay
lin'ge·rie (lähn-zhi-ray), n., women's underwear
lin'gual (gwil), a., relating to speech or language, **-guist**
lin'i·ment, n., soothing liquid
lin'ing, n., inside covering
link, n., connection, bond
links, n., golf course
li·no'le·um, n., type of floor covering
lin'o·type, n., typesetting machine, **-r**
li'on, n., wild animal of cat family
li'on·ize, v., treat with special importance
lips, n., mouth edges, edge of something
lip'stick, n., chemical used by women for coloring the lips
liq'uid (kwid), a., substance resembling water in form, **-uefy**
liq'ui·date (wi), v., settle, wipe out, murder
liq'uor (lik-ẽr), n., alcoholic drink
lisp, v., pronounce "s" as "th"
list, v., n., catalog, shift to one side, series
lis'ten, v., hear, heed, pay attention to, **-er**
lit'er·al, a., exact wording, actual, **-ly**
lit'er·ar·y, a., relating to literature, **-ily**
lit'er·ate, a., able to read and write, educated, lucid
lit'er·a·ture, n., artistic effort
li·thog'ra·phy, n., printing process, **-grapher**
lit'i·gate, v., bring lawsuit against someone, **-gation**

lit'ter, n., group of animals just born, trash, stretcher
lit'ter-bug, n., one who litters public places with trash
lit'tle, a., small, unimportant, narrow
live, v., be alive, exist upon, reside
live, a., showing life, being alive, unclosed
live'li·hood, n., way of earning living
live'ly, a., active, spirited, energetic, animated
liv'er, n., body organ that secretes bile
live'stock, n., domestic or farm animals
live'wire (coll.), n., energetic person
liv'id, a., pale in color, enraged
liv'ing, a., having life, alive
liz'ard, n., small reptile
lla'ma (lä-ma), n., S. Am. beast of burden
load, n., burden, weight, amount, trouble, cargo
load, v., place weight in vehicle or container, heap
loaf, v., fool time away, **-er**
loaf, n., mass of baked bread
loan, n., something lent
loath, a., unwilling, reluctant, **-some**
loathe, v., hate, detest
lob'by, n., hallway, foyer, group influencing law making
lob'ster, n., edible crustacean
lo'cal, a., relating to immediate environment
lo·cal'i·ty, n., place
lo'cate, v., find, establish, place
lo·ca'tion, n., place where established, position
lock, v., fasten, link
lock, n., fastening device, canal section, tuft of hair
lo·co·mo'tion, n., movement
lo·co·mo'tive, n., train engine
lo'cust, n., crop destroying insect, grasshopper
lodge, v., rest, stay in rented rooms, file, **-r**
loft'y, a., exceedingly high, superior, supercilious
log, n., section of fallen tree, ship's diary
log'i·cal (loj), a., orderly,

lo·gis'tics (jis), *n.*, military transportation of materials

loi'ter, *v.*, wait idly, linger nearby, dawdle

lone, *a.*, single, alone, solitary

lone'ly, *a.*, alone, by oneself, desolate

long, *a.*, great length

lon·gev'i·ty, *n.*, living long life to old age, seniority

long'ing, *n.*, sentimental desire for, craving

lon'gi·tūde, *n.*, distance measured east and west across earth, length, **-tudinal**

long'shöre·män, *n.*, dock worker

look, *v.*, *n.*, see in a particular direction, seek for, search, expression for weaving

loom, *n.*, machine for weaving

loop, *n.*, line, rope, etc. curved into circle, circular effect

loose, *a.*, untied, unfastened, slack, relaxed, immoral, **-n**

loot, *n.*, stolen material, money

lop, *v.*, sever

lope, *n.*, easy, steady pace

lop'sid'ed, *a.*, out of balance, crooked

lo·quā'cious, *a.*, talkative, **-city**

lôrd, *n.*, God, royal ruler, knighted person, **-ly**

lose (lōōz), *v.*, put someplace and forget, give up, be defeated

lôss, *n.*, something misplaced, something given up

lôst, *a.*, not present, not in possession of, gone away, desperate

lot, *n.*, much of something, fortune, land parcel

lō'tion, *n.*, soothing liquid

lot'tēr·y, *n.*, game of chance

loud, *a.*, noisy

loud'spēak'ēr, *n.*, device which amplifies sound

lounge (lounj), *v.*, *n.*, loaf, be lazy, couch, recreation room

louse, *n.*, insect, contemptible person

lous'y, *a.*, having lice, (coll.) terrible, disgusting

love, *n.*, *v.*, emotion of affection, be devoted to, cherish, **-ing, -r**

love'ly, *a.*, beautiful

low, *a.*, unhappy, not expensive, beneath a particular level, immoral, common, **-ly**

low'êr·ing, *a.*, gloomy

loy'äl (loi), *a.*, faithful to, believing, trusting, **-ly**

lū·au' (ow), *n.*, Hawaiian feast

lū'bri·cāte, *v.*, grease, **-cant**

lū'cênt, *a.*, luminous, clear

lū'cid, *a.*, easy to understand, sane, clear, **-ity**

luck, *n.*, good fortune, **-y**

lū'crā·tive, *a.*, profitable

lū·cū·brā'tion (kyōō), *n.*, arduous learning, meditation

lū'di·crous, *a.*, foolishly funny, laughable

lug'gáge (gij), *n.*, traveler's baggage

lu·gū'bri·ous, *a.*, mournful

lūke'wärm, *a.*, tepid

lul'lá·by, *n.*, child's sleeping song

lum'bêr, *n.*, building wood

lū'mi·nous, *a.*, shining, bright, clear

lump, *n.*, something swollen or enlarged, mass, **-y**

lū'när, *a.*, relating to moon

lū'nä·tic, *a.*, insane person

lunch, *n.*, noon meal, **-eon**

lung, *n.*, breathing organ in body

lunge, *v.*, thrust forward

lûrch, *v.*, twist sideways, pitch forward, stagger

lū'rid, *a.*, gruesome, horrible, sensational

lûrk, *v.*, hide, sneak, skulk

lus'cious, *a.*, pleasant, seductive, rich in appearance

lust, *n.*, sexual desire, strong craving, **-ful**

lus'trous, *a.*, shining

lus'ty, *a.*, robust, powerful

lūte, *n.*, ancient stringed instrument

lux'u·ry, *n.*, material thing beyond ordinary needs, **rious**

lye, *n.*, alkaline solution

ly'ing, *n.*, speaking falsehood

lynch, *v.*, hang unlawfully

lyr'ic, *a.*, songlike, **-al**

M

ma-cab're (käb), *a.*, gruesome

māce, *n.*, official staff

ma-caw', *n.*, South American parrot

mac'ēr-āte, *v.*, make soft, wear away

mach-i-nā'tion (mak), *n.*, plot, intrigue

mà-chine' (shēēn), *n.*, device using power to do work, -ry

mà-chin'ist, *n.*, one who makes or repairs machines

Mäch' num'ber (mähk), *n.*, ratio of the speed of a body to the speed of sound at various altitudes

mack'ēr-ėl, *n.*, fish

mac'rō-cosm, *n.*, universe, large-scale reproduction

mad, *a.*, angry, insane, rabid, senseless, -ly

mad'ām, *n.*, married woman, polite form of address to women

mad'ri-gàl, *n.*, song

maes'trō (mys-trōh), *n.*, composer, orchestra conductor, master

Mä'fi-à, *n.*, secret crime organization, chiefly Sicilian or Italian

mag-à-zine' (zēēn), *n.*, periodical, explosives storehouse

mag'got, *n.*, insect larva

mag'ic, *n.*, tricks, illusions, -ian

mag'is-trāte, *n.*, judge, -terial

mag-nan'i-mous, *a.*, forgiving, generous, -ly

mag'nėt, *n.*, something that attracts, -ic

mag-nif'i-cėnt, *a.*, splendid, grand appearance, -cence

mag'ni-fy, *v.*, make larger, exaggerate

mag'ni-tūde, *n.*, size, quantity

mag-nō'li-à (ya), *n.*, tree, flower

mag'num, *n.*, half gallon

mà-hog'à-ny, *n.*, type of wood

māid'ėn, *n.*, young girl, -hood

māid'ėn-head, *n.*, vaginal membrane

māil, *n.*, letters sent through

postoffice, armor, -man

māim, *v.*, cripple, disfigure

māin, *a.*, outstanding, principal, most significant, -ly

māin-tāin', *v.*, keep in working condition, assert, support, -tenance

māize, *n.*, Indian corn

maj'ès-ty, *n.*, nobility, dignity, grandeur

ma'jŏr, *a.*, *n.*, main, army officer

mà-jŏr'i-ty, *n.*, greater number

māke, *v.*, cause, build, arrange, do, create

māke'-bė-liēve (lēv), *a.*, imagined

māke'shift, *a.*, temporary

māke'-up, *n.*, composition, personality, cosmetics

mal-àd-just'ėd, *a.*, unable to adapt to one's environment, -ment

mal-à-droit', *a.*, inept, awkward

mal'à-dy, *n.*, disease

mà-lār'i-à, *n.*, type of disease, -l

mal'cön-tent, *n.*, dissatisfied person

māle, *n.*, relating to the man

mà-lef'i-cėnt, *a.*, harmful, dangerous, -cence

mal-fŏrmed', *a.*, misshapen

mal'ice, *n.*, harm, spite, ill will, -icious

mà-lig'nànt, *a.*, diseased, harmful, tending to infiltrate

mà-lin'gėr, *v.*, pretend illness and loaf, -er

mal'làrd, *n.*, type of duck

mal'lėt, *n.*, wooden hammer

mal-nu-tri'tion, *n.*, lack of proper food

mal-prac'tice, *n.*, criminal act by professional person

mält, *n.*, barley used in brewing

mal-trēat', *v.*, treat badly, abuse

mam'mŏth, *n.*, huge

man, *n.*, adult male, the human race, -ly

man'à-cle, *v.*, handcuff

nan'áge, v., handle, conduct, operate, -r

nan'áge-ment, n., administrative group

nan'dáte, n., order, directive

nan'dá-tō-ry, a., obligatory

nan-dō-lin', n., musical instrument

nāne, n., animal's neck hair

ná-neū'vêr, n., military exercises, **-able**

nān'gêr, n., trough for animal food

man'gle, v., crush, maim

mān'gy, a., seedy, shabby

man'han-dle, v., handle roughly

man'hood, n., condition of being an adult male

mā'ni-a, n., craze, -c

man'i-cūre, v., clean and file fingernails

man'i-fest, n., catalogue of cargo

man-i-fès-tā'tion, n., display, demonstrate

man'i-fōld, a., many, varied

má-nip'ū-lāte, v., utilize, control to one's own advantage, **-lation**

man'kīnd, n., human beings

man'ly, a., strong, virile, **-liness**

man'nêr, n., way, behavior, **-ly**

man'nêrs, n., social behavior

man'ör, n., estate, mansion

man'sion, n., large house

man'släughter (släwt), n., accidental killing

man'tra, n., chant to be recited or sung

man'ū-ál, a., n., relating to hands, handbook

man-ū-fac'ture, v., make with hands or machine, invent, **-r**

má-nūre', v., animal refuse used as fertilizer

man'ū-script, n., author's written composition

mǎn'y, a., large number of

map, n., flat representation of an area

mā'ple, n., tree

mar'á-thon, n., long race, endurance contest

mär'ble, n., ornamental limestone

märch, v., walk in measured steps

mâre, n., female horse

mär'gá-rine, n., butter substitute

mär'gin, n., edge, border

mar'i-gōld, n., flower

ma-ri-juä'ná (wä), n., wild tobacco, hemp

má-rine' (rēen), a., relating to sea

mar-i-ö-nette', n., puppet operated by strings

mar'i-tál, a., relating to marriage

mar'i-tīme, a., relating to sea

märk, n., visible impression, target, outstanding achievement

mär'kèt, n., place for buying and selling goods

mär'lin, n., large fish

mär'má-lāde, n., fruit preserves

má-rōōn', v., leave in isolation

mar'rōw, n., bone tissue

mar'ry, v., join as husband and wife, **-ried, -riage**

märsh, n., swampy land

mär'shál, n., title of officer

märsh, n., swampy area

mär'shál, n., title of officer

märsh'mal-lōw (mel), n., candy

mär'tiál (shäl), a., relating to war or military, military

mär-ti-net', n., strict disciplinarian

mär-ti'ni (tēe-nee), n., drink made with gin and vermouth

mär'tyr (tir), n., one who suffers for a cause, victim, **-dom**

mär'vel, v., be astounded

mär'vel'ous, a., astonishing, wonderful, unusual

Märx'ism, n., political creed of Karl Marx

mas'cot, n., team pet

mas'cū-line, a., relating to male

mash, v., crush

mask, n., cover for face

mas'öch-ism (i-kizm), n., enjoyment of being abused

mā'sön, n., stone builder, **-ry**

mass, v., n., gather together large group of, bulk, size

mas'sá-cre (kèr), v., slaughter

mas'säge (säzh), n., rubbing

of muscles, **-seur, -seuse**

mast, *n.*, ship's sail support

mas'tĕr, *n.*, one who rules another, employer, skilled worker, **-y**

mas'tĕr-pīece, *n.*, work of art

mas'ti-cāte, *v.*, chew

mas'tiff, *n.*, huge dog

mas-tûr-bā'tion, *n.*, sexual stimulation without intercourse

mat, *n.*, small rug, pad, tangled mass

match, *n.*, small stick that ignites, contest, alikeness

match, *v.*, be alike, pit one against another

māte, *n.*, husband or wife, ship officer, winning chess move

mà-tē'ri-àl, *n.*, goods, fabric, things that exist, **-istic**

mà-tē'ri-àl-īze, *v.*, happen, take actual shape

mà-tē'ri-àl-ly, *adv.*, to a great degree

mà-tē'ri-el', *n.*, military equipment

mà-tēr'nàl, *a.*, relating to mother, **-ly**

mà-tēr'ni-ty, *n.*, state of motherhood

math-ē-mat'ics, *n.*, science of numbers, **-ical**

mat-i-nee' (nay), *n.*, afternoon performance

mā'tri-cīde, *n.*, killing of mother by her child

mà-tric'ū-lāte, *v.*, enroll in college, **-lation**

mat'ri-mō-ny, *n.*, uniting in marriage, **-nial**

mā'trŏn, *n.*, dignified married woman, female supervisor, **-ly**

mat'tĕr, *n.*, composition of all life, basic substance of things, meaning, importance

mat'trĕss, *n.*, stuffed case for bed

mà-tūre', *a.*, grown up, ripe, adult, **-turity**

matz'ŏ, *n.*, thin, unleavened bread for Jewish Passover

maud'lin, *a.*, excessively sentimental

maul, *n.*, large hammer

mau-sō-lē'um (maw), *n.*, large tomb

max'i-mum, *n.*, upper limit; largest, highest, greatest

may, *v.*, be allowed to, hope for, shall

may'bē, *adv.*, perhaps

Māy'dāy, *n.*, international distress signal

may-ŏn-nāise', *n.*, salad dressing

may'ŏr, *n.*, head of local government, **-alty**

māze, *n.*, confusing network

mead'ōw, *n.*, grassy land area

mēa'gēr, *a.*, thin, scant

mēal, *n.*, ground grain, food eaten at one time

mēan, *a., v.*, low, vulgar, stingy, bad-tempered, intend, signify, middle

mē-an'dēr, *v.*, ramble

mēa'sles (zilz), *n.*, disease

mēa'sly (zly), *a.*, small

meas'ure (mezh-ĕr), *v.*, determine quantity, size, regulate, **-ment**

mēat, *n.*, flesh of animal, meaning, **-y**

mē-chan'ic (kan-ik), *n.*, one skilled with machinery, **-al**

mech'à-nism, *n.*, structure of machinery, working system, **-nize**

med'àl, *n.*, metal disc used for an award

med'dle, *v.*, pry into other's affairs

mē'di-àn, *n.*, middle point

mē'di-āte, *v.*, act to settle dispute, **-ator**

med'ic (coll.), *n.*, doctor, corpsman

Med'i-cāid, *n.*, government financed medical care for certain income groups

med'i-càl, *a.*, relating to medicine, **-cate**

Med'i-cāre', *n.*, government financed medical care for the elderly

med'i-cine, *n.*, science of disease and health, drug administered, **-cinal**

me-di-ē'vàl, *a.*, relating to Middle Ages (700-1400 A.D.)

mē-di-ō'cre (kĕr), *a.*, plain, ordinary

med'i-tāte, *v.*, think about, reflect on, **-tation**

mē'di-um, *a.*, middle, means, surroundings

med'lēy, *n.*, mixture, hodgepodge

mēek, a., mild, submissive, **-ly**

mēet, v., come together, encounter in person, satisfy, assemble, **-ing**

mel'an-chol-y, a., sad, depressed, **-ic**

mē'lǐo-rāte, v., make better, improve

mėl-lif'lū-ous, a., smooth, sweetly flowing, **-ent**

mel'lōw, a., fully ripe, smooth, full, agreeable

mel'ŏ-dy, n., tuneful musical sound, **-dic**

mel'ŏn, n., gourd shaped fruit

melt, v., dissolve, change form, vanish, soften

mem'bêr, n., one who officially belongs, part of a whole

mem'brāne, n., thin skin layer

mė-men'tō, n., reminder, souvenir

mem'oir (währ), n., writings of personal experiences, biography

mem'ŏ-rā-ble, a., worth remembering, notable

mem-ŏ-ran'dum, n., note to remind

mė-mô'ri-ál, n., monument, memento, **-ize**

mem'ŏ-rīze, v., commit to memory

men'āce, n., threat, danger, **-acing**

mè-nag'êr-ïē (naj), n., collection of animals

mend, v., fix, repair

men-dā'cious, a., dishonest, **-city**

men'di-cánt, n., beggar

mē'ni-ál, a., relating to menial class, lowly, subservient

men-in-gī'tis, n., inflammation of tissue surrounding brain

men'ŏ-pause, n., end of menstruation

men-stru-ā'tion, n., monthly discharge of blood from uterus

men-sū-rā'tion, n., measurement of things

men'tal, a., relating to mind, intellectual, **-ity**

men'tion, v., talk of, cite

men'ū, n., listing of foods served

mêr'cán-tile (teel), a.,

relating to business

mêr'cè-nār-y, a., interested only in money, greedy

mêr'chán-dīse, n., articles bought and sold

mêr'chánt, n., one who operates store

mêr'cū-ry, n., heavy chemical element

mêr'cy, n., kindness, charity, clemency, **-ciful**

mēre, a., only

mer-è-trī'cious, a., flashy, gaudy

mêrge (mèrj), v., unite, combine, **-r**

mė-rid'i-án, n., point in direct line with earth's poles

mer'it, n., v., value of worth, virtue, deserve, earn

mer'ry, a., full of fun, jolly, **-riment**

mesh, n., net, network

mes'mer-īze, v., hypnotize, fascinate

mess, n., disorder, jumble, unpleasant situation, **-y**

mes'ságe, n., written or spoken communication

mes'sèn-gêr, n., one who carries message

met'ál, n., chemical element, *i.e.*: tin, iron, silver, etc., **-lic**

met-à-môr'phŏ-sis, n., change in form

mē'tè-ôr, n., particle in the solar system, **-ic**

mē'têr, n., measuring machine, unit of length

meth'ŏd, n., way of accomplishing something, **-ic**

met'rŏ-nōme, n., device for measuring musical time

met-rŏ-pol'i-tàn, a., relating to a large city

met'tle (met-il), n., courage, stamina

mez'zō (met-zō), a., medium, moderate

mī-as'má (az), n., poisonous mist

mī'crōbe, n., minute living matter

mī'crō-film, n., film used for recording, reduced printed material

mī'crŏ-phŏne, n., device which transmits sound

mī'crŏ-scŏpe, n., device that enlarges objects

mī-crŏ-scop'ic, a., very small

mid, *a.*, between, in middle of

mid'dle, *a.*, in between, center, intermediate

midg'ét, *n.*, tiny person, dwarf

mid'night, *n.*, twelve A.M.

mid'ship·män, *n.*, student of U. S. Naval Academy

might, *n.*, power, strength, **-y**

mi'gräte, *v.*, move from one locality to another, **-gration**

mild, *a.*, soft, gentle, temperate

mile, *n.*, 5,280 feet

mi'lieu (mil-yū'), *n.*, environment, setting

mil'i-târ·y, *a.*, relating to armed forces

mi·li'tia (sha), *n.*, militarily trained civilians

milk, *n.*, liquid excreted from breasts of female animals

milk run, *n.*, routine military flight

mill, *n.*, grinding machine, factory

mil·len'ni·um, *n.*, 1000 years, period of universal peace

mill'ér, *n.*, one who manufactures flour

mil'li·nêr, *n.*, one who deals in women's hats, **-y**

mil'lión (mil-yin), *n.*, a thousand thousand, **-aire**

mill'wright (ryt), *n.*, mill mechanic or builder

mim'ē·ö·graph, *n.*, duplicating machine

mim'ic, *n.*, one who imitates, **-ry**

mince, *v.*, cut up into small pieces

mind, *n.*, organ of thought in humans, will power

mind, *v.*, care, pay attention

mine, *pro.*, belonging to me

mine, *n.*, excavation to get minerals

min'êr·ál, *n.*, material found in earth, inorganic matter

min'gle, *v.*, unite together, intermix

min'i·a·ture, *n.*, something on a small scale

min'i·mum, *n.*, least

min'i·skirt, *n.*, very short skirt

min'is·têr, *n.*, church official, diplomatic representative, **-ial**

mink, *n.*, animal valued for fur

min'nŏw, *n.*, fish

mi'nŏr, *a.*, *n.*, unimportant, less, one under legal age

mi·nŏr'i·ty, *n.*, smaller number

mint, *n.*, pleasant tasting plant, place where money is coined

mi'nus, *a.*, less than, taking away from, deprived of

min'ute (it), *n.*, sixty seconds, one sixtieth of hour

mi·nūte', *a.*, tiny, small

mi·nū'ti·ae (shē·eye), *n.*, unimportant matters, trivia

mir'á·cle, *n.*, unusual splendid occurrence, **-culous**

mi·räge' (räzh), *n.*, imagined sight

mir'rŏr, *n.*, glass that reflects images

mirth, *n.*, fun, humor, **-ful**

mis'án·thrŏpe, *n.*, one who hates mankind

mis·bē·häve', *v.*, act improperly

mis·car'riage, *n.*, noncompletion, failure

mis·cel·lā'nē·ous, *a.*, varied, many, mixed

mis'chief (chif), *n.*, troublesome or playful conduct, **-chievous**

mis·cŏn·strūe', *v.*, misinterpret

mis·dē·mēan'ŏr, *n.*, bad conduct, minor law violation

mi'sêr, *n.*, stingy person, **-ly**

mis'êr·à·ble (miz-ri-bil), *a.*, very unhappy, wretched

mis'fit, *n.*, one poorly adjusted

mis·fôr'tune (chin), *n.*, bad luck, trouble

mis·giv'ing, *n.*, doubt, fear

mis·lēad', *v.*, deceive

mis·nō'mêr, *n.*, incorrect title or name

mi·sog'y·ny, *n.*, hatred of females

miss, *n.*, title of unmarried woman, young girl

miss, *v.*, fail to hit, fail to achieve, omit, avoid

mis'sile, *n.*, object thrown or shot

miss'ing, *a.*, lost, lacking

mis'sion, *n.*, special assignment, religious errand, **-ary**

mis'sive, *n.*, letter

mist, *n.*, thin water vapor

mis-tāke', *n.*, error, **-n**

mis'tle-tōe, *n.*, plant, Christmas decoration

mis'tress, *n.*, female in command, unmarried woman living with a man

mis-trust', *v.*, have no faith in, doubt

mis-un-dēr-stood', *a.*, grasped incorrectly, not appreciated

mīte, *n.*, tiny insect

mit'i-gāte, *v.*, lessen, moderate, **-gation**

mitt, *n.*, baseball glove

mit'tĕn, *n.*, glove without fingers

mix, *v.*, join together, unite, get along with, combine, **-ture**

mixed, *a.*, different, varied

mix'-up, *n.*, disorder, confusion

mne-monic, *adj.*, aiding the memory

mōan, *n.*, low sound of pain

mob, *n.*, large, uncontrolled mass of people

mō'bile, *a.*, movable

mō'bi-līze, *v.*, put into action

mock, *v.*, ridicule, make fun of, imitate, **-ery**

mock'-up, *n.*, imitation, dummy

mod'ȧ-cryl'ic, *adj.*, synthetic fiber used for wool substitutes, etc.

mōde, *n.*, method, fashion, style

mod'el, *n.*, representation to be copied, design, poser for artist, clothing displayer

mod'ēr-āte, *a.*, within fair limits, temperate, **-ed**

mod'ēr-āte, *v.*, preside, make calm

mod'ērn, *n.*, representative of present time, up-to-date, **-ize**

mod'est, *a.*, humble, shy, reserved, **-y**

mod'i-fy, *v.*, change, lessen, limit, **ification**

mod'ū-lāte, *v.*, change tone, regulate, **-lation**

moist, *a.*, slightly damp, wet, **-en**

mō'lȧr, *n.*, chewing tooth

mōld, *n.*, pattern, shape, fungus

mōle (mol), *n.*, molecular weight of substance, gram molecule

mol'ė-cūle, *n.*, smallest part of an element

mō-lest', *v.*, bother, harm **-ation**

moll (coll.), *n.*, woman

mol'li-fy, *v.*, calm, appease

molt, *v.*, shed feathers

mō'ment, *n.*, brief time, importance, **-ary**

mō-men'tous, *a.*, extremely important

mō-men'tum, *n.*, impetus of body in movement

mom'ism, *n.*, over-dependence on the mother

mon'ȧrch, *n.*, ruler of kingdom, **-y**

mon'ȧs-ter-y, *n.*, place where monks live and work

mon'e-târ-y, *a.*, pertaining to money

mŏn'ēy, *n.*, medium of value or exchange, **-ed**

mon'grel, *a.*, of mixed breed

mŏnk, *n.*, man of religious order

mŏn'kēy, *n.*, animal of ape family

mon'o-cle, *n.*, single eyeglass

mō-nog'ȧ-my, *n.*, marriage to only one person at a time

mon'o-graph, *n.*, literary composition on one subject

mon'o-lōgue, *n.*, dramatic act for one person

mon'o-plāne, *n.*, plane with single wing

mō-nop'o-ly, *n.*, exclusive control, **-lize**

mon'o-rāil, *n.*, single rail train track

mon'o-thē-ism (izm), *n.*, belief in one god

mon'o-tōne, *n.*, unchanging single tone

mō-not'o-ny, *n.*, dullness, boredom, sameness, **-nous**

mon-sōōn', *n.*, periodic wind in Indian Ocean

mon'stēr, *n.*, huge thing, grotesque creature, **-strous**

mŏnth, *n.*, one-twelfth of year

mŏnth'ly, *n.*, every month

mon'ū-ment, *n.*, structure created in memory of person or event

mon-ū-ment'ȧl, *a.*, weighty, significant

rod ōld wŏn fôr tōō good out oil owl pup ūnit ûrn

mōōch (coll.), v., steal, sneak, beg, sponge

mōōd, n., temper, feeling, **-y**

mōōn, n., planet's satellite

mōōr, v., hold in place, anchor

mōōse, n., large animal resembling deer

mōōt, a., open to argument

mop, n., device for cleaning floors

mōpe, v., be gloomy, quietly unhappy

mop'pet, n., small child

mor'al, n., standard of right or wrong, lesson, **-ity**

mō-rale', n., spirit of group

mō-rass', n., low swampy ground

mōr-à-tō'ri-um, n., delay

mōr'bid, a., gloomy, scary, **-ity**

mōre, a., in addition to, larger in amount or degree, again

mōre-ō'vēr, adv., besides

mō'rēs, n., customs of group of people

mōrgue, n., place for unidentified corpses

mōrn'ing, n., beginning of daylight

mō'ron, n., person of low intelligence

mō-rōse', a., sad, unhappy, gloomy

mōr'phine (fēn), n., pain relieving drug

mōr'tàl, a., of this earth, deadly, fatal, **-ity**

mōr'tàr, n., cannon, bowl, cement

mōrt'gàge (mōr-gij), n., pledge of property to a creditor for payment

mōr-ti'cian, n., undertaker

mōr'ti-fy, v., cause to feel shame

mōr'tū-ar-y, n., place for keeping corpses

mō-sā'ic, n., inlaid design of stone, etc

mōs-quī'tō (kēē), n., biting insect

mōss, n., small, soft plant

mōst, a., greatest amount of

mō-tel', n., roadside hotel for motorists

mōth, n., insect

mōth'ēr, n., female parent, **-ly**

mōth'ēr-in-lāw', n., spouse's mother

mō-tif' (tēf), n., theme

mō'tile, a., capable of moving alone, **-tility**

mō'tion, n., movement

mō'tive, n., reason for action, **-tivate**

mō'tōr, n., engine that provides power

mō'tōr-cy-cle (kil), n., two-wheeled motor bike

mot'tled, a., streaked

mot'tō, n., saying, proverb, principle

mound, n., small hill

mount, v., climb, fasten

moun'tain (tin), n., very high hill, **-ous**

moun'tè-bank, n., clown, quack, impostor

mōurn, v., grieve, lament, **-ing**

mouse, n., small rodent

mouth, n., opening in face for eating, talking

move (mōōv), v., change position, change address, inspire, **-ment**

mov'ìe (mōōv-ēē), n., moving picture

mōw, v., cut down

moz'zá-rèl'la, n., an Italian cheese

much, a., large quantity, great amount

mū'ci-làge, n., glue, **-laginous**

muck, n., filth, slime

muck'rāke', v. i., to expose corruption or scandal

mū'cus, n., slimy body secretion

mud, n., wet ground, **-dy**

mud'dle, n., confusion

muf'fin, n., small, round type of bread

muf'fle, v., deaden sound, wrap snugly, **-r**

mug, n., drinking cup with handle, (coll.) face

mul'ber-ry, n., berry tree

mulch, n., rotted matter used to protect plants

mūle, n., descendant of donkey and horse, stubborn individual

mull, v., think over

mul'ti- prefix, many, several, various

mul-ti-fâr'i-ous, a., of great variety

mul'ti-ple, a., having many parts

mul'ti-ply, *v.*, increase in amount or number, **-plication**

mul'ti-tūde, *n.*, huge crowd, many, **-tudinous**

mum, *a.*, quiet, not giving information (coll.)

mum'ble, *v.*, talk indistinctly

mum'my, *n.*, embalmed Egyptian body

mumps, *n.*, disease involving glandular swelling

munch, *v.*, eat steadily, crunch

mun-dāne', *a.*, of this earth, worldly

mū-nic'i-pāl, *a.*, relating to civic affairs, **-ity**

mū-nif'i-cĕnt, *a.*, very generous, **-cence**

mū-ni'tions, *n.*, military weapons

mū'rāl, *n.*, painting on a wall

mûr'dĕr, *v.*, kill illegally, **-ous**

mûr'ky, *a.*, gloomy, obscure

mûr'mûr, *n.*, low, continuing partly heard sound

mus-cä-tel', *n.*, sweet white wine

mus'cle (mus-il), *n.*, body tissue that produces motion, strength

mus'cle-bound, *a.*, having overdeveloped muscles

mūse, *v.*, dream, think of

mū-sē'um, *n.*, building for displaying works of art

mush'rŏŏm, *n.*, fungus plant

mush'y, *a.*, sickly sweet, sentimental

mū'sic (zic), *n.*, sounds produced in harmonious, rhythmic combinations, **-ian**

mus'kĕt, *n.*, type of gun, **-eer**

mus'lin (muz), *n.*, type of firm cotton cloth

muss, *v.*, mess up

must, *a.*, of necessity

mus-tache', *n.*, upper lip hair

mus'tärd, *n.*, hot seasoning

mus'tĕr, *v.*, gather

mū-tā'tion, *n.*, change in genes affecting heredity

mūte, *a.*, silent, unable to speak

mū'ti-lāte, *v.*, mar, disfigure, **-ation**

mū'ti-ny, *n.*, organized revolt against authority

mut'tĕr, *v.*, speak in low, grumbling tone

mut'tŏn, *n.*, sheep meat

mū'tū-ál (choo-il), *a.*, shared jointly, interchangeable

muz'zle, *n.*, guard for mouth of animal

my, *pro.*, possessive case of "I"

my-ō'pi-ä, *n.*, nearsightedness

myr'i-ǎd, *n.*, *a.*, countless, many

mys-tē'ri-ous, *a.*, hidden, unknown

mys'tĕr-y, *n.*, unexplainable matter

mys'tic, *n.*, believer in secret happenings, **-ism**

mȳth, *n.*, tale of gods and heroes, **-ical**

mỳ-thŏl'ŏ-gy, *n.*, collection of myths

N

---

nab, *v.*, suddenly catch, seize

nä-celle', *n.*, enclosed part of airplane

nā'cre (kĕr), *n.*, mother-of-pearl, **-ous**

nā'dir, *n.*, lowest point

nag, *v.*, annoy by continual scolding

nag, *n.*, horse (coll.)

nai'ad, *n.*, water nymph

nāil, *n.*, pointed slender metal piece for holding wood, horny skin growth on fingers and toes

nä-ive' (ēēv) *a.*, simple, unsophisticated, gullible, **-te**

nā'kĕd, *a.*, undressed, nude

nam'by-păm'by, *a.*, simple, weak, dull

nāme, *n.*, words identifying person or thing, **-less**

nāme'ly, *adv.*, that is, as follows

nāme'sāke, *n.*, person named for another

nap, *n.*, short sleep, fuzzy surface on cloth

nāpe, *n.*, back of neck

naph'thä, *n.*, chemical

solvent

nap′kin, n., cloth used at meals for cleaning hands

na-pō′lē-ŏn, n., old French coin, pastry

năr′cis-sism, n., love of one's self

năr-cis′sus, n., bulbous plant

năr-cŏt′ic, n., habit-forming drug

när′ghi-lē, n., Oriental form of pipe smoking

nar-rāte′, a., relate a story, repeat details, **-ration**

nar′ra-tive, n., tale, story, **-tor**

nar′rŏw, a., small in width, prejudiced

nā′sal, a., pertaining to nose, **-ly**

nās′cent, a., starting to exist

na-stûr′tium, n., flower

nas′ty, a., disgusting, unpleasant

nā′tal, a., pertaining to one's birth

nā′tant, a., swimming, floating, **-tatory**

nā′tion, n., people organized as a state, **-al**

na′tion-ăl-ism, n., devotion to nation's interests, **-ist**

na-tion-al′i-ty, n., belonging to a particular nation, **-ize**

nā′tion-wīde, a., throughout entire nation

nā′tive, a., belonging to or originating in a place, natural

nā-tiv′i-ty, n., birth

nat′ty, a., neat, stylish in appearance

nat′û-rál, a., as nature, at ease, normal

nat′û-rál gas, n., fuel gas naturally formed in earth

nat′û-rál-ism, n., action based on instinct, realism, **-ist**

nat′û-rál-īze, v., become a citizen

nat′û-rál-ly, adv., by nature, of course

nā′ture, n., everything created, temperament, type

nâug′a-hyde, n., trade name of a synthetic leather

nâught (nàwt), n., zero, nothing

nâugh′ty, a., bad, disobedient, improper

nâu′sĕ-á, n., sick feeling in stomach, disgust, **-ted**

nâu′ti-cál, a., pertaining to

ships or sailors

nāve, n., middle part of church, wheel hub

nā′vel, n., hole in abdomen

nav′i-gá-ble, a., deep enough for ship passage

nav′i-gāte, v., guide ship or plane, plot course, travel, **-gation**

nav′i-gā-tŏr, n., one who charts course

nā′vy, n., fleet of warships, nation's sea force, **-val**

nāy, adv., no

Nä′zi (nät-si), n., member of German National Socialist Party

nēar, a., close, intimate

nēar′ly, adv., almost

nēar′-sīght′ĕd, a., seeing only at short distance

nēat, a., clean, tidy

neb′ū-lā, n., star cluster, luminous gas mass, **-losity**

neb′ū-lous, a., cloudy, confused, vague

nec-ĕs-sâr′i-ly, adv., due to need

nec′ĕs-sâr-y, a., required, needed

nē-ces′si-tāte, v., compel, require

nē-ces′si-ty, n., absolute need to do, compulsion

neck, n., connection between head and shoulders

neck′ĕr-chief, n., scarf worn around neck

neck′lace, n., ornaments worn around neck

neck′tīe, n., band worn around shirt collar

neck′wear, n., ties, scarves

ne-crŏl′o-gy, n., death notice

nec′rō-man-cy, n., magic using corpses

ne-crŏp′o-lis, n., cemetery

ne-crō′sis, n., decay of body or plant tissue

nec′tar, n., delicious drink, drink of the gods, **-ine**

nee (nāy), a., indicates woman's maiden name

nēed, n., requirement, necessity, **-ful**

nee′dle, n., sharp sewing device, indicator

nēed′less, a., not needed

nee′dle-wôrk, n., embroidery, sewing, knitting

nēed′y, a., in need, poor

ne'er-do-well (nâr-dōō), *n.*, worthless person, bum, drifter

ne-fâr'i-ous, *a.*, extremely wicked, **-ly**

ne-gāte', *v.*, deny, refuse, **gation**

neg'a-tive, *a.*, opposite of positive, denying, implying "no", **-tivism**

neg'a-tive, *n.*, picture in reverse

neg-lect', *v.*, ignore, not care for, disregard, **-ful**

neg-li-gee' (zhāy), *n.*, loose informal robe worn at home

neg'li-gence, *n.*, lack of care, failure, to do, **-gent**

neg'li-gi-ble, *a.*, of minor importance

ne-gō'ti-à-ble, *a.*, transferable

ne-gō'ti-āte, *v.*, arrange certain terms by meeting, **-ation**

Ne'grō, *n.*, member of black race

neigh'bor (nāy), *n.*, person living near another, **-hood**

nē'i-ther, *conj.*, not either

nem'a-tōde, *n.*, slender worm

nē'ō, *combining form*, new

nē-ō-lith'ic, *a.*, later stone age

nē-ol'ō-gism, *n.*, use of new words or meanings

nē'on, *n.*, gas used in lighted signs

nē'ō-phyte, *n.*, new convert, beginner

ne-pen'thē, *n.*, drug causing forgetfulness

neph'ew, *n.*, brother or sister's son

ne-phrī'tis, *n.*, kidney inflammation

nep'ō-tism, *n.*, favoring relatives in politics or jobs

nêrve, *n.*, bundle of fibers sending impulses to and from the brain, courage, **-less**

nêrv'ous (vus), *a.*, relating to nerves, excitable, tense

nes'ci-ence (nesh-ins), *n.*, ignorance, **-cient**

nest, *n.*, warm place for raising young

nes'tle, *v.*, snuggle closely

nest'ling, *n.*, young bird or child

net, *n.*, close woven mesh

net, *v.*, catch

net, *a.*, amount remaining after expenses and taxes

neth'êr, *a.*, below, under, **-most**

net'ting, *n.*, meshed fabric

net'tle, *v.*, disturb, irritate

net'wörk (würk), *n.*, any group of connected things

Neuf'châ-tel (nōō), *n.*, soft white cheese

neu'ral (nōō), *a.*, relating to nervous system

neu-ral'già (ja), *n.*, nerve pain

neu-rás'thē'ni-á, *n.*, emotional weakness

neu-rī'tis, *n.*, nerve inflammation

neu-rol'ō-gy, *n.*, study of nervous system

neu-rō'sis, *n.*, emotional sickness, **-tic**

neu'têr, *a.*, of neither sex, sexless

neu'tral, *a.*, not joining either side, **-ity**

neu'tron, *n.*, neutral electrical particle

nev'êr, *adv.*, not at any time

nev'êr-môre', *adv.*, not ever again

nev-êr-thê-less', *adv.*, even so, in spite of that

new, *a.*, first created, not familiar, just acquired, **-ly**

new'cŏm-êr, *n.*, person newly arrived at a place

new'êl, *n.*, top or bottom post of stair rail

new-fan'gled (gild), *a.*, new in concept

news, *n.*, report of recent happenings

news'let-têr, *n.*, bulletin

news'pā-pêr, *n.*, daily paper printing news

news'rēel, *n.*, moving picture of events in news

newt, *n.*, amphibious salamander

new'yēar, *n.*, beginning of another year

next, *a.*, beside, time following, nearest to

nex'us, *n.*, connection

nī'à-cin, *n.*, nicotinic acid

nib'ble, *v.*, take small bites

nib'lick, *n.*, golf club

nīce, *a.*, pleasing, agreeable, good, **-ness**

nī'cē-ty, *n.*, special delicacy

niche (nitch), *n.*, wall hollow,

place

nick, *n.,* notch, groove, small cut

nick'el, *n.,* white metallic element, coin

nick-el-ō'dé-ón, *n.,* phonograph operated by inserting coin

nick'nāme, *n.,* substitute or shortened name

nic'ō-tine (tēen) *n.,* poison in tobacco, **-tinic**

nic'ti-tāte (nik), *v.,* wink

nièce, *n.,* daughter of brother or sister

nig'gárd-ly, *a.,* stingy, mean

nīgh, *adv., a.,* near

night, *n.,* period of darkness after daylight

night' blínd'néss, *n.,* poor night vision

night'-cap (coll.) *n.,* drink at bedtime

night' club, *n.,* place of entertainment, drinking, dancing

night'fall, *n.,* approach of night

night'in-gāle, *n.,* European songbird

night' let'têr, *n.,* night telegram

night'māre, *n.,* frightening dream

night' walk-êr, *n.,* earthworm

nī'hil-ism, *n.,* non-acceptance of religion, law, etc.

nim'ble, *a.,* quick, alert, agile

nim'bus, *n.,* halo around head of a saint, type of cloud

nin'cöm-pōōp, *n.,* fool

nīne, *n.,* cardinal number, "9"

nīne'fōld, *n.,* nine times as much

nīne'tēen', *n.,* nine more than ten

nīne'ty, *n.,* nine times ten

nin'ny, *n.,* fool

nip, *v.,* minor bite

nip, *n.,* cold, chill, **-py**

nip'pêr, *n.,* pincers, claw

nip'ple, *n.,* breast part giving milk, rubber cap for infant feeding bottle

nîr-va'na, *n.,* state of Buddhist perfect blessedness

nit, *n.,* egg of louse

nī'trāte, *n.,* nitric acid salt

nī'tric ac'id, *n.,* corrosive chemical

nī'trō'gén, *n.,* gas making up

4/s of air

nī-trō-glýc'êr-in, *n.,* explosive oil

nī'trous, *a.,* relating to nitrogen

nit'wit, *n.,* stupid or silly person

nō, *adv.,* not any, not at all

nō-bil'i-ty, *a.,* of high social rank, being noble

nō'ble, *a.,* famous, lofty, superior, **-man, -woman**

nō'bod-y, *n.,* no one, unimportant person

nock, *n.,* notch in bow or arrow

noc-tûr'nàl, *a.,* pertaining to night

noc'tûrne, *n.,* dreamy night music

nod, *v.,* bob head

nōde, *n.,* knot, knob

nod'ūle, *n.,* lump, knob

No'el, *n.,* Christmas

nog'gin (coll.) *n.,* head

noise, *n.,* sound made, **-less**

nois'y, *a.,* making noise

nō'mad, *n.,* homeless wanderer, **-ic**

nom' dé plūme, *n.,* pen name

nō'mén-clā-ture, *n.,* system of names

nom'i-nàl, *a.,* in name only, trifling

nom'i-nāte, *v.,* propose for office, **-nee**

nom'i-nā-tive, *a.,* indicating verb's subject

nō-mis'tic, *a.,* based on holy law

non-, *prefix,* meaning not, negative of, *Example:*
non-aggressive, *a.,* (see aggressive), not aggressive,
non-payment, *n.,* no payment

nonâge, *n.,* not of legal age

non-à-gé-nâr'i-àn, *n.,* one 90 years old

nonce, *n.,* only for present occasion

non'chá-lánce, *n.,* cool unconcern, **-lant**

non'com, *n.,* non-commissioned officer

non-com'bát-ánt, *n.,* one not involved in combat

non-com-mit'tàl, *n.,* not revealing position, not making definite statement

non'dé-script, *a.,* hard to describe

nōne, *pro.,* not any

non-en'ti-ty, *n.,* unimportant person

non-ès-sen'tial, *a.,* unnecessary, not needed

non-mor'ál, *a.,* neither moral nor immoral

non-pá-reil' (rel), *a.,* having no equal

non'plus, *v.,* confuse beyond ability to act or think

non-sec-târ'i-àn, *a.,* of no religious sect

non'sense, *n.,* foolishness, silliness, **-sensical**

nŏŏ'dle, *n.,* thin dough strip used in soup

nook, *n.,* corner

nŏŏn, *n.,* 12 o'clock daytime, midday

nŏŏse, *n.,* rope loop, trap

nôr, *conj.,* not either, used with neither

nôrm, *n.,* standard, average pattern

nôr'mál, *a.,* average, **-ly**

nôrth, *n.,* to right when facing setting sun, **-ern**

nôrth-ēast', *a.,* halfway between north and east, **-ern**

nôrth-ēast'êr, *n.,* storm from N. E. direction, **-ly**

nôrth-wèst', *a.,* halfway between north and west, **-ern**

nōse, *n.,* facial feature bearing nostrils, organ for detecting odors

nōse' dīve, *n.,* sudden downward plunge by plane

nōse'gay, *n.,* small bunch of flowers

nos-tal'gi-á (ja), *n.,* longing for the past

nos'tril, *n.,* nose orifice

nos'trum, *n.,* favorite remedy

nōs'y, *a.,* curious, prying

not, *adv.,* negative expression, in no way

nō'tà-ble, *a.,* important

nō'tà-rīze, *v.,* witness officially

nō'tà-ry, *n.,* document certifier

nō-tā'tion, *n.,* observation, note, system of symbols (algebra, music, etc.)

notch, *n.,* cut, degree

nōte, *n.,* short letter, reminder

nōte, *v.,* observe, pay attention

nōt'ĕd, *a.,* famous

nōte' pā'pêr, *n.,* paper for writing letters

nōte'wôr'thy, *a.,* worth noticing, significant

nŏth'ing, *n.,* not anything, **-ness**

nō'tice, *v.,* observe

nō'tice, *n.,* declaratory document

nō'tice-à-ble, *a.,* worth noticing, easily seen

nō-ti-fi-cā'tion, *n.,* notice given or received

nō'ti-fy, *v.,* inform

nō'tion, *n.,* idea, small useful article, **-al**

nō-tō'ri-ous, *a.,* widely and unfavorably known, **-ety**

not-with-stand'ing, *conj.;prep.,* nevertheless, in spite of

noū'gát, *n.,* candy with nuts

noun, *n.,* person, place, thing

noûr'ish, *v.,* feed, develop growth, **-ment**

nou'veaux riche (noo-vo-resh), *adj.,* someone newly rich

nov'èl, *a.,* unusual

nov'èl, *n.,* book length fiction, **-ette, -ist**

nov'èl-ty, *n.,* newness, unusualness, gadget

Nō-vem'bêr, *n.,* 11th month

nō-vē'nà, *n.,* 9 days' religious devotion

nov'ice, *n.,* beginner

nō-vi'ti-àte, *n.,* beginner in religious order

nō'vò-cāine, *n.,* local injected anesthetic

now, *adv.,* at present time, immediately, next, very recently

now'á-days, *adv.,* during these days, at present

nō'way, *adv.,* in no manner

nō'where (wayr), *adv.,* not at any place

nox'ious (shus), *a.,* harmful

noz'zle, *n.,* spout of hose, pipe, etc.

nū-ánce', *n.,* shade of difference, variation

nub, *n.,* main point

nū'bi-à, *n.,* woman's scarf

nū'bile, *a.,* marriageable

nū'clè-ár, *a.,* pertaining to nucleus

nū'clé·àr fis'sion, n., splitting of atoms

nū'clé·àr fū'sion, n., combining of atoms

nū'clé·us, n., central thing surrounded by others

nūde, a., naked

nudge, v., push slightly

nū'di·ty, n., nakedness

nŭg'ga·tō·ry, a., worthless

nug'gét, n., small lump, as gold

nūi'sànce, n., annoyance, inconvenience

null, a., not binding, void

nul·li·fi·cā'tion, n., making null

nul'li·fy, v., make void, ineffective

nul'li·ty, n., invalidity

numb, a., without sense of feeling, -ly

num'bêr, n., amount of, counting symbol

num'bêr, v., count

num'bêr·less, a., without number, countless

nū'mêr·à·ble, a., countable

nū'mêr·ál, n., symbol for number

nū'mêr·ā·tōr, n., fraction part, counter, **-tion**

nū·mêr'i·càl, a., pertaining to numbers

nū'mêr·ous, a., many

nū·mis·mat'ics, n., coin, medal collecting

num'skull, n., ignorant person

nun, n., woman living in convent

nun'ci·ō (shee), n., Pope's representative

nun'nêr·y, n., where nuns live

nup'tial, a., pertaining to marriage

nûrse, n., person who takes care of sick or young

nûrse'māid, n., woman hired to take care of children

nûrs'êr·y, n., children's room, place for cultivating plants, man

nûrs'êr·y schōōl, n., play school for young children

nûr'tûre, v., feed, nourish

nut, n., hard-shelled fruit

nut'crack·êr, n., tool for cracking nuts

nut'hatch, n., nut eating bird

nut'meg, n., spice

nū'tri·ént, a., nourishing

nū'tri·mént, n., food

nū·tri'tion, n., utilization of food for growth, health, etc., **-tious**

nut'ty (coll.), a., crazy

nuz'zle, v., rub nose against, snuggle

ny'lon, n., strong synthetic material

nymph, n., beautiful maiden

nym·phō·mā'ni·à, n., oversexuality in women

O

ōaf, n., clumsy person

ōak, n., kind of tree

ō·ā'sis, n., fertile spot

ōar, n., rowing implement

ōat, n., cereal grain

ōath, n., vow

ob'dū·rāte, a., stubborn

ō·bē'di·ént, a., following orders, **-ence**

ō·bei'sànce (bay), n., showing of respect, deference

ō·bēse', a., very fat

ō·bey' (bay), v., follow orders, do as told

ob·fus'cāte, v., confuse, bewilder, **-cation**

ō·bit'ū·âr·y, n., death announcement

ob'ject, n., person or thing, purpose, **-ive**

ŏb·ject', v., oppose, disagree, **-ion**

ob'jûr·gāte, v., criticize, scold, **-gation**

ob·li·gā'tion, n., responsibility, duty, indebtedness, **-tory**

ō·blīge', v., do a favor for, compel

ŏb·lique' (lēek), a., slanting

ŏb·lit'êr·āte, v., wipe out, destroy, **-ation**

ŏb·liv'i·ous, a., completely unaware, **-on**

ob'lō·quy (li·kwēe), n., blame, public criticism

ŏb·nox'ious, a., hateful,

---

unpleasant

ō'bōe, n., wind musical instrument

ob-scēne', a., immoral, lewd

ob-scūre', a., not clear, hidden, **-scurity**

ob-sē'qui-ous, a., over-polite, servile

ob-sêrv'ance, n., keeping of a custom

ob-sêrv'a-tô-ry, n., building for observing stars

ob-sêrve', v., see, examine, say, follow custom, **-servation**

ob-sess', v., persistently dwell in the mind, **-ion, -ive**

ob-sö-les'cent, a., not in current use

ob'sö-lēte, a., out of date

ob'sta-cle, n., hindrance

ob-ste-tri'cian (shin), n., doctor who delivers babies, **-cs**

ob'sti-nāte, a., stubborn, **-nacy**

öb-strep'êr-ous, a., loud, noisy, unruly

öb-struct', v., block, hinder, clog, **-ion**

öb-tāin', v., get possession, reach, **-able**

öb-trūde', v., force oneself upon, **-trusion**

öb-tūse', a., dull

ob'vi-āte, v., become unnecessary, remove, dispense with, **-ation**

ob'vi-ous, a., readily apparent, easy to understand, **-ly**

öc-cā'sion, n., specific time, happening

öc-cā'sion-al, a., occurring infrequently, **-ly**

oc'ci-dent, n., the West

öc-clūde', v., close, **-clusion**

öc-cult', a., mystical, hidden

öc-cū-pā'tion, n., job, work, being busy, **-al**

öc'cū-py, v., possess, live in, fill, busy, hold, **-pant**

öc-cûr', v., happen, come into mind, **-rence**

ō'cean (shin), n., large body of salt water, sea

ō'chêr (kêr), n., clay with iron ore, dark yellow color

oc'ta-gön, n., eight-sided geometric figure

oc-tet', n., group of eight

Oc-tō'bêr, n., 10th month

oc'tö-pus, n., eight-armed sea animal

oc'ū-lâr, a., by eyesight

oc'ū-list, n., eye doctor

odd, a., left over, extra, strange, **-ity**

odds, n., betting difference, advantage

ōde, n., long poem

ō'di-ous, a., unpleasant, disgusting

ō'dôr, n., smell, aroma, **-ous**

of, prep., showing possession, from, relating to

öff, a., prep., distant, away from

öf-fend', v., anger, displease, insult

öf-fense', n., wrong doing

öf-fen'sive, a., displeasing, irritating

of'fêr, v., propose, present, bid

of'fêr-ing, n., gift, presentation

of'fice, n., place of business, position held

of'fi-cêr, n., one in command, policeman

öf-fi'cial, a., authorized, formal, **-ly**

öf-fi'cious, a., pushy, meddlesome

ôff'set, n., v., method of printing, balance

öff'spring, n., child

ôf'tén (offin), adv., frequently, many times

ō'gle, v., look at with desire

ōh, inter., exclamation of surprise, fear, pain

ōhm, n., unit of electrical resistance

oil, n., liquid fuel, **-y**

oint'ment, n., soothing salve

O.K., adj., satisfactory, all right

ōld, a., aged, shabby, former

ōld'fash'ioned, a., of the past, out-of-date

ō-lē-ō-mär'ga-rine (ji), n., butter substitute

ōl-fac'tö-ry, a., sense of smell

ol'i-gärch-y (ärk), n., government by select few

ol'ive, n., tree, fruit

om'e-let, n., egg dish

ō'mén, n., sign

om'i-nous, a., threatening

ō-mit', v., leave out, **-mission**

om'ni-bus, n., collection, bus

om-nip'ö-tent, a., of

unlimited power

om-nis'cient (nishint), a., knowing all, **-cience**

om-niv'ō-rous, a., devouring all

ôn, prep., upon, ahead

once (wuns), adv., at a single time, in the past

one (wun), n., single item, whole

on'êr-ous, a., troublesome

ŏn'ion (unyin), n., edible pungent bulb

ōn'ly, a., adv., single, merely, but

ôn'wârd, adv., going forward

ōōze, v., n., leak slowly, slime

ō'pál, n., gem

ō-pâque', a., not transparent, clouded

ō'pĕn, a., v., not closed, fair, frank, not occupied, begin, pry or lift up

ō'pĕn-ing, n., beginning, hole

op'êr-á, n., musical drama, **-etta**

op'êr-āte, v., function, work, perform surgery, **-ator**, **-ation**

op'êr-á-tive, a., is effective, **-ble**

oph-thál-mol'ō-gy, n., study of eye

ō'pi-āte, n., sleep inducing drug

ö-pin'ion, n., evaluation, belief, judgment

ö-pin'ion-āt-ĕd, a., fixed in opinion

ō'pi-um, n., narcotic

öp-pō'nĕnt, n., adversary, one opposing

op-pör-tūne', a., well chosen, favorable

op-pör-tū'ni-ty, n., chance

öp-pōse', v., be against, resist

op'pö-site (zit), a., different, facing, **-sition**

öp-press', v., overpower, **-ion**

öp-prō'bri-ous, a., disgraceful, shameful, **-um**

or'á-cle, n., prophecy

op'tic, a., pertaining to eye, **-al**

op-ti'cian, n., eye glass maker

op'ti-mism, n., belief that good prevails, hope, **-mistic**

op'tion, n., right to buy or sell, choice

op'tion-ál, a., elective

op'tom'ĕ-try, n., examination of eyes, **-trist**

op'ū-lĕnt, a., rich, splendid, **-lence**

ō'pus, n., artistic work

ôr, conj., alternative

ō'rál, a., relating to mouth, spoken, life

or'ange, n., citrus fruit

ô-rā'tion, n., lecture, speech, **-tor**

ôrb, n., eye, circular object

ôr'bit, n., path of a heavenly moving body

ôr'chârd, n., farm for raising fruit trees

ôr'chĕs-trá (kis), n., musicians playing together, section of theater seating

ôr'chĕs-trāte, v., arrange music, chat

ôr'chid (kid), n., tropical flower, color

ôr-dāin', v., order, appoint, admit to ministry, **-dination**

ôr-dēal', n., painful experience

ôr'dêr, n., v., position, plan, condition, request, arrange, command, **-ly**

ôr'di-nánce, n., law

ôr'di-nâr-y, a., plain, usual, common, **-ily**

ôrd'nánce, n., military materials

ōre, n., natural source of an element

ôr'gán, n., body part, musical instrument

ôr-gan'ic, a., relating to life, organs or carbon

ôr'gán-ism, n., living thing

ôr'gán-īze, v., place in orderly arrangement, unite, **-ization**

or'gasm, n., climax of sexual excitement

ôr'gy (ji), n., wild party, debauchery

ō'ri-ĕnt, n., the East

ō'ri-ĕnt, v., adjust, adapt, **-ation**

or'i-gin, n., beginning, source, **-ate**

ö-rig'i-nál, a., freshly created, new, **-ity**

ō'ri-ōle, n., kind of bird

Or'lon, n., trade name for synthetic textile fiber

ôr'ná-mĕnt, n., something decorative, **-al**

ôr-nāte', a., elaborate, fancy, showy

ôr-ni-thol'ō-gy, n., study of birds

ôr'phan, n., child with dead parents, **-age**

ôr-thō-don'tist, n., dentist who straightens teeth

ôr'thō-dox, a., following established practice, **-y**

ôr-thog'rȧ-phy, n., spelling

ôr-thō-pē'dics, n., bone surgery

os'cil-lāte, v., move back and forth, **-lation**

os'cū-lāte, v., kiss, **-lation**

os-mō'sis, n., passage of fluid through membrane

os'si-fy, v., change to bone

os-ten'si-ble, a., apparent, **-bly**

os-ten-tā'tion, a., pompous, outward display, **-tious**

os-tē-ol'ō-gy, n., study of bones

os'tē-ō-path, n., doctor who treats disease by massage, **-y**

os'trȧ-cīze, v., ban from society

os'trich, n., large bird

ŏth'ér, a., indicating something else, different, remaining

ŏught (ôt), n., v., should be required to, zero

ounce, n., 1/16 part of pound

our, pro., possessive plural of "I", **-selves**

oust, v., throw out, remove from, expel

out, a., adv., n., not inside, not in possession of, used up, excuse, **-side**

out'cast, n., ostracized person

out'door, a., outside of building

out'fit, n., v., equip, furnish, organization, costume

out'gō-ing, a., leaving, friendly

out'house, n., outdoor toilet

out'lȧw, n., v., criminal, declare to be beyond law

out'let, n., market for goods, way out, passage

out'līne, n., brief summary, outward line of figure

out'look, n., attitude, prospect

out'rāge, n., violent act, deep offense, **-ous**

out-rīght', adv., openly, fully, immediately

out'spō'ken, a., direct, blunt in speech

out-stand'ing, a., prominent, unpaid

out'wȧrd, a., visible, outside, **-ly**

out-weigh' (wāy), v., be more important

ō'val, a., egg-shaped

ō'vȧ-ry, n., female egg-producing organ

ō-vā'tion, n., enthusiastic applause

ŏv'en, n., device for baking foods

ō'vêr, a., prep., n., adv., higher than, greater than, about, around, upon, more than necessary, excess, remainder, above

ō'vêr-, prefix, meaning more than, too much, higher, greater than

ō'vêr-äll', a., widely inclusive, total

ō'vêr-älls, n., work clothes

ō'vêr-bear'ing, a., domineering, arrogant

ō'vêr-cast, a., cloudy

ō'vêr-coat, n., heavy topcoat

ō-vêr-hȧul', v., repair completely

ō-vêr-lap', v., extend past, cover

ō-vêr-sēas', adv., across ocean, abroad

ō'vêr-sēe', v., supervise

ō-vêr-sīght', n., failure to see, inadvertent omission

ō-vêrt', a., openly, outward, forthright

ō-vêr-tāke', v., catch up with and pass

ō'vêr-ture, n., offer, musical introduction

ō-vêr-whelm', v., make helpless, crush, conquer, **-ing**

ō'vum, n., female egg cell

ōwe, v., be in debt to

owl, n., night bird

ōwn, v., a., admit, possess, belonging to oneself

ox, n., bovine beast of burden

ox'fôrd, n., type of shoe or cotton cloth

ox'īde, n., oxygen combined with another chemical

ox'i-dīze, v., combine with oxygen

ox'ў-gėn, n., gas necessary for breathing and life

oys'tėr, n., bivalve shellfish

ō'zōne, n., form of oxygen

— P —

pāce, n., v., walking step, rate of speed, walk with measured step

pach'ў-dẽrm, n., elephant

pȧ-cif'ic, a., peaceful, not quarrelsome, **y**

pack, v., put into box or bag, store, crowd together

pack, n., bundle, package, group of animals

pack'age, n., bundle

pact, n., treaty between nations

pad, n., soft stuffing, paper sheets for writing, **-ding**

pad'dle, n., oar, beat, swim

pad'dŏck, n., enclosure for horses

paē'ȧn, n., hymn of praise or joy

pā'gȧn, n., unbeliever in God, **-ism**

pāge, n., one side of a leaf in book, attendant

pag'eȧnt, n., colorful exhibition, mass drama, **-ry**

pāid, a., hired to do, given in payment, past tense v., pay

pāil, n., bucket

pāin, n., v., physical hurt, distress, **-ed**

pāins'tāk-ing, a., extremely careful

pāint, n., colored pigment, **-ing**

pāir, n., two things alike, couple

pāis'ley, adj., detailed, intricate design for fabric

pȧ-ja'mȧs, n., sleeping garments

pal, n., friend (coll.)

pal'ȧce, n., residence of royalty

pal'ȧt-ȧ-ble, a., pleasant tasting

pal'ȧte, n., top of mouth

pȧ-lā'tiȧl, a., luxurious

pāle, a., lacking color

pā-lē-ō-lith'ic, a., pertaining to Stone Age

pā-lē-ŏn-tol'ō-gy, n., study of fossils

pal'ētte, n., artist's color

board

pall, v., become bored with

pal'li-āte, v., excuse, lessen, ease

pälm, n., inside of hand

pälm'is-try, n., fortune telling by lines in hand

pal'pi-tāte, v., beat rapidly, tremble, **-tātion**

pȧl'sy (zy), n., trembling of body

pam'phlėt, n., small, printed booklet

pan, n., cooking utensil

pan (coll.), v., criticize adversely

pan-ȧ-cē'ȧ, n., cure-all

Pan'-A-mer'i-can, adj., pertaining to North, Central, and South America

pan'crē-ȧs, n., digestion-aiding gland, **-atic**

pāne, n., glass window section

pan-ė-gýr'ic (jir-ik), n., statement in praise, **-al**

pan'ėl, n., wooden section, discussion group

pang, n., sudden pain, spasm

pan'ic, n., sudden terror

pan-ō-ram'ȧ, n., vast picture

pan'sy (zy), n., flower

pan'thėr, n., large feline animal

pan'try, n., kitchen closet

pants, n., trousers

panty hōse, n., women's one piece undergarment consisting of panties and hose

pā'pal, n., relating to the Pope

pā'pėr, n., thin sheet for writing

pȧ-py'rus, n., plant used for paper in ancient times

pär, a., equal, average

par'ȧ-ble, n., story with moral

par'ȧ-chūte, n., device for dropping safely from airplane

pȧ-rāde', n., v., march in

---

public

par'á-dīse, n., heavenly place

par'á-dox, n., statement that contradicts itself

par'á-gon, n., example of excellence, model

par'á-graph, n., related sentences placed together in group

par'al-lel, a., lines running side by side

pá-ral'ý-sis, n., inability to move or feel, **-ze**

par'á-mount, a., main, above all others

par-á-noi'á, n., mental disease

par-á-pher-nā'li-à, n., collection of things, apparatus

par-á-plē'gi-à, n., paralysis from waist down

par'á-sīte, n., one that lives by another

pär'cel, n., package

pärched, a., dry and hot

pärch'ment, n., skin used for writing

pär'don, v., forgive, excuse

pär'ent, n., father or mother

pá-ren'thé-sis, n., curved lines enclosing phrase placed in sentence

pá-rī'áh, n., outcast

pari-mū'tu-el (muchil), n., method of race track betting

par'ish, n., church district, **-ioner**

par'i-ty, n., equality

pärk, n., public outdoor recreation area

pärk, v., place temporarily, (coll.) deposit

pärk'way, n., wide highway

pär'lance, n., way of talking, speech

pär'lay', v., place winnings on another bet

pär'lēy, n., discussion

pär'lia-ment, n., government group of lawmakers, **-ary**

pär'lôr, n., living room

pär'lôr cär, n., first class railroad car

pär'lous, a., clever, dangerous

pá-rō'chi-ál (ki-al), a., narrow, relating to religious institutions

par'ö-dy, n., humorous imitation

pá-rōle', n., freedom from jail prior to serving full term

par'ri-cīde, n., murder of parent

par'rot, n., bird that can be taught to imitate speaking

pär-si-mō'ni-ous, a., needlessly economical, miserly

pär'sön, n., religious minister, **-age**

pärt, n., section, portion, piece

pär-tāke', v., share in, eat or drink

pär'tial, a., prejudiced, incomplete, partly, **-ity**

pär-tic'i-pāte, v., do, take part in, **-pation**

pär'ti-cle, n., small amount of, part of grammar

pär-tic'ū-lär, a., special, unusual, hard to please

pärt'ing, n., leaving, departure

pär-ti'tion, n., division

pärt'ly, adv., to some extent

pärt'nêr, n., one who shares, **-ship**

pär-tū'ri-ent, a., giving birth

pär'ty, n., political group, social gathering, group of people, (legal) one side of people involved

pass, v., move by, approve, occur

pass, n., right to go by, state of affairs, narrow opening in mountains

pas'sage, n., voyage, fare, part of reading matter, entrance or exit, hallway

pas'sèn-gêr, n., traveler in vehicle

pas'sing, a., temporary, not of long duration

pas'sion, n., powerful emotion, strong love, **-ate**

pas'sive, a., not active, quiet, receptive

pass'pôrt, n., document proving right to travel in foreign country

past, a., that which is gone

pāste, n., mixture for gluing

pas'tôr, n., minister of church, **-ate**

pās'try, n., fancy baked goods

pas'ture, n., grassy meadow for animal grazing

pat, v., touch lightly

patch, v., mend hole in

clothing

pāte, n., head

pat'ent, a., n., obvious, exclusive copyright to invention

pa-tēr'nal, a., fatherly, **-ly**

path, n., narrow footway, course to follow

pa-thet'ic, a., sad, moving

pa-thŏl'ö-gy, n., study of disease

pā'thos, n., emotion of pity, sadness

pā'tience, n., ability to endure calmly, wait

pā'tient, a., n., steady, calm, person under medical treatment

pat'i-nȧ, n., surface coating or color

pa'ti-ō, n., rock or brick courtyard

pā'tri-ärch (ärk), n., elderly, loved family figure, father

pa-tri'cián, a., noble, high in social scale

pat'ri-cīde, n., killing of father

pā'tri-ŏt, n., one faithful to his country, **-ism**

pȧ-trōl', n., group for guarding or reconnoitering

pā'trŏn, n., one who lends support, **-ize**

pā'trŏn-āge, n., support

pat'tĕr, n., informal chatter

pat'tĕrn, n., design, model

pau'ci-ty (pàw-si), n., scarce in number

pǎunch (pàwnch), n., prominent belly

pau'pĕr (pàw), n., poor, destitute person

pause (pàwz), v., n., hesitate, stop

pāve, v., to surface a roadway

pāve'ment, n., sidewalk

pǎw, n., animal foot

pǎwn, n., goods to secure borrowed money, chess piece

pāy-load, n., cargo carried by space vehicle, made up of items necessary to purpose of flight

pēace, n., ease, freedom from war, **-ful**

pēach, n., fruit

pēak, n., highest point, hill top

pēak'ĕd, a., fatigued

pēal, n., ringing sound

pē'a'nut, n., edible seed pod

peâr, n., fruit

pêarl (pêrl), n., white, spherical gem

peas'ant (pes-int), n., uncultured person, ignorant farmer

peb'ble, n., tiny stone

peck, n., v., ¼ bushel, strike with beak, kiss

pec'ū-lāte, v., steal, defraud, **-lation**

pė-cū'liar (pi-kyul-yèr), a., odd, strange, **-ity**

ped'ȧ-gogue (gog), n., teacher, **-gogy**

ped'ant, n., strict teacher, **-ry**

ped'dle, v., sell goods, **-r**

pė-dès'tri-ȧn, n., person on foot

pė-di-ȧ-tri'cian, n., baby doctor, **-cs**

ped'i-grēe, n., descent from ancestors

pēel, v., remove outer covering from object

pēep, n., bird cry, brief look

pēer, n., one of same rank, nobleman

peg, n., small wooden pin

pe-lag'ic (laj-ik), a., pertaining to ocean

pěl'la'grȧ, n., disease caused by poor diet

pė-lū'cid, a., clear

pelt, n., v., animal fur, throw missiles

pen, n., writing device, cage

pē'nȧl, a., pertaining to punishment, **-ize**

pen'ȧnce, n., repentance for sin

pen'chȧnt, n., strong desire, inclination

pen'cil, n., writing device

pend'ing, a., until, awaiting decision

pen'ė-trāte, v., pierce, **-tration**

pen-i-cil'lin, n., antibiotic drug

pė-nin'su-lȧ, n., strip of land projecting into water

pē'nis, n., male sex organ

pen'i-tènt, a., sorry for sins, **-tence**

pen-i-ten'tiȧ-ry (chi-rēe), n., jail, prison

pen'mȧn-ship, n., handwriting

---

at bāy ȧkin fâre cär ăll end hē dèfy hêr ill īce sîr

pen'nant, n., banner
pen'ny, n., one cent piece
pē-nol'ö-gy, n., study of crime and prisons
pen'sion, n., payment for past services, **-er**
pen'sive, a., thoughtful
pen'tà-gon, n., five-sided geometric figure
pent'up, a., held in, closed-in
pen'u-ry (ye-ree), n., poverty
pē'ön-āge, n., forced work to pay debt
pē'ö-ny, n., showy flower
pēo'ple (pee-pil), n., whole groups of persons, members of groups
pep, n., vigor, **-py**
pep'pêr, n., hot food seasoning
pep'pêr-öni, n., Italian sausage
pep'tic, a., pertaining to digestion
pêr, prefix, by, through
pêr an'num, a., by the year
pêr'cale', n., type of cotton cloth
pêr-cēive', v., know through senses
pêr cent', n., in, to, or for each hundred, **-age**
pêr-cep'ti-ble, a., able to be understood through senses
pêrch, v., sit upon
pêr-cip'i-ent, a., perceiving easily
pêr'cö-lā-tör, n., coffee maker
pêr- di'êm, a., by the day
pêr'e-gri-nāte, v., journey, travel, wander
pêr-emp'tö'ry, a., positive, absolute
pêr-en'ni-àl, a., lasting from year to year, forever
pêr'fêct, a., without mistake, excellent, complete, **-ion**
pêr'fi-dy, n., falseness, **-dious**
pêr'fö-rāte, v., punch holes in, **-ration**
pêr-förm', v., accomplish, do, act, **-ance**
pêr'fume', n., pleasant smelling liquid or cream
pêr-func'tö-ry, a., done indifferently, without interest
pêr'haps', adv., maybe
per'il (pair), n., danger, **-ous**
pér-im'ē-tēr, n., measurement of outer edge
pē'ri-öd, n., time,

punctuation mark ending sentence, duration
pē-ri-od'ic, a., from time to time
pē-ri-od'i-càl, n., regularly published magazine
per-i-pà-tet'ic, a., walking around
pê-riph'êr-y, n., edge, outside surface
per'i-scöpe, n., device in submarine for viewing at different levels
per'ish, v., be destroyed, die, **-able**
pêr'ju-ry, n., deliberate telling of a lie under oath
pêrk'y, a., active, vigorous
pêr'mà-nent, a., lasting forever, **-nence**
pêr'mē-āte, v., saturate, soak into, **-able**
pêr-mis'sion, n., giving consent, allowing, **-sible**
pêr-mit', v., n., allow, give consent, written authorization
pêr-ni'cious, a., harmful, deadly
pêr-pèn-dic'ū-làr, a., upright, perfectly straight
pêr'pê-trāte, v., commit undesirable act, **-tration**
pêr-pet'ū-àl, a., constant, lasting forever, **-ly**
pêr-pet'ū-āte, v., remember forever, **-ity**
pêr-plex'i-ty, n., puzzling condition
pêr se' (say), a., itself
pêr'sē-cūte, v., oppress, **-cution**
pêr-sē-vēre', v., work at something consistently, **-verance**
pêr-sist', v., continue steadily, **-ent**
pêr'sön, n., human being
pêr'sön-à-ble, a., attractive
pêr-sön-àl, a., individual, intimate, private, relating to self
pêr'sön-àl-ly, adv., by, for oneself
pêr-sön'i-fy, v., stand for, represent, **-fication**
pêr-sön-nel', n., employees, group of individuals
pêr-spec'tive, n., at a distance, in proper proportion
pêr-spic'ū-ous, a., clearly

understood

pêr-spi-rā'tion, n., sweat, -re

pêr-suāde' (swayd), v., convince to accept one's side, -suasion

pêr-tāin', v., relate to, belong

pêr-ti-nā'cious, a., persistent, -ity

pêr'ti-nent, a., relating to, bearing on

pêr-tûrb', v., disturb, cause worry

pê-rūse', v., read carefully, study

pêr-vāde', v., go through, influence, -vasion

pêr-vêrse', a., contrary, stubborn, -ness

pêr-vêrt', v., twist, misuse

pes'si-mism, n., hopeless outlook on things, -mist

pest, n., nuisance, -er

pes'ti-lence, n., widespread disease

pet, n., v., kept animal or person, caress

pet'ál, n., flower part

pet'it (petty), a., little, small, minor

pé-ti'tion, n., written request, court document demanding action

pet'ri-fy, v., change into stone, frighten, -fied

pé-trō'lē-um, n., oil

pet'ti-cōat, n., female undergarment

pet'ty, a., small, trivial

pet'ū-lánt, a., irritated, peeved, -lance

pew, n., church bench

phal'lus, n., image of male reproductive organ

phan'tasm, n., apparition, vision

phan'tōm, n., ghost

phär'má-cy, n., drugstore, -cist

phāse, n., part of development, section

phé-nom'é-non, n., strange happening, -nal

phi-lan'thrō-py, n., love of mankind, generous giving to charity, -pic

phi-lat'é-ly, n., hobby of stamp collecting

phi-lol'ö-gy, n., study of languages

phi-los'ö-phy, n., laws relating to truth, natural happenings, cause and

effect, -pher

phlegm (flem), n., mucus discharge

phleg-mat'ic, a., cold, reserved, dull

phō'bi-à, n., extreme fear

phōne, n., telephone

phō'nō-graph, n., record player

phos'phāte, n., chemical fertilizer, soft drink

phos'phō-rus, n., substance which shines in dark

phō-tō-é-lec'tric, a., of electric effects obtained by light

phō'tö-graph, n., v., picture, take picture of, -y

phrāse, n., certain group of words

phrè-net'ic, a., insane, frantic

phrè-nol'ö-gy, n., fortune telling by feeling skull

phy'lum, n., division of animal kingdom

phys'i-cál (fiz), a., relating to material things, of the body

phy-si'cian (fi-zi), n., doctor

phys'ics (fiz-iks), n., science of matter and energy

phys-i-ol'ö-gy, n., science of how animals function

phy-sique' (fi-zēk), n., body build

pī, n., mixed up type, π (3.1416)

pi-an'ö, n., musical instrument, -ist

pi'ca, n., type size

pic-ä-yūne', n., trivial, unimportant

pic'cö-lö, n., type of flute

pick, n., sharp-pointed tool, choice

pick, v., choose, dig at

pick'êr-el, n., fish

pick'êt, n., pointed wood slat, striker at job

pick'le, n., cucumber seasoned with vinegar

pic'nic, n., food served outdoors

pic'ture, n., image reproduction, painting

pic-tur-esque' (esk), a., beautiful, like a picture

pie, n., baked crusted dish

pīece, n., part, section

piêr, n., bridge support, dock

pī'é-ty, n., religious devotion

pig, n., hog

pi′geon (pij-in), n., bird

pig′ment, n., coloring matter, **-ation**

pike, n., pointed stick, road, fish

pik′er, n., stingy person

pile, n., things laid on top of each other, large beam, atomic reactor, soft surface

pil′fer, v., steal

pil′grim, n., wanderer, traveler for religious reasons, **-age**

pill, n., tiny disc used as medicine, (coll.) dull person

pil′lar, n., upright column of support

pil′low, n., cushion for head

pi′lot, n., guider of ship, aviator

pi-men′to, n., type of pepper

pin, n., pointed fastener

pin′a-fore, n., sleeveless dress like apron

pinch, v., squeeze between finger and thumb, (coll.) arrest

pinch′ hit′ter, n., substitute baseball batter

pine, n., evergreen tree

pine, v., yearn for

pine′ap-ple, n., fruit

pink, n., light red shade, communist sympathizer

pin′na-cle, n., peak

pi′noch-le (pee), n., card game

pint, n., half quart

pin′to, n., small horse

pin′-up, n., sexy picture of girl

pi-o-neer′, n., early settler, discoverer

pi′ous, a., holy, religious

pipe, n., tube through which substances pass

pi′quant (pee-kint), a., stimulating, exciting

pi′rate, n., robber of ships, thief, **-racy**

pis-ca-to-ry, a., relating to fisherman

pis-ta′chi-o (shē), n., nut

pis′til, n., part of flower

pis′tol, n., hand gun

pit, n., hole, fruit seed

pitch, n., tar, music tone, throw, degree of slope

pitch, v., throw, lurch

pitch′er, n., container for holding liquids, baseball player

pith, n., main part

pit′y, v., n., feel sorry for, sympathy

piz′za, n., Italian pie made of dough, tomato sauce, cheese, meat

piz-zi-ca′to (pi-tzi-kä-toh), a., plucking motion in music

plā′cāte, v., appease, soothe

place, v., put

place, n., particular area, spot, street, position

pla-cen′ta, n., organ formed for nourishment of fetus, which is discharged after birth

plac′id, a., peaceful, **-ity**

plā′gi-a-rīze (ji-ryz), v., steal from written work of another, **-rism**

plague, n., widespread disease

plaid (plad), n., checked pattern

plain, a., simple, easy to understand, not fancy

plain, n., flat, vast area of land

plain′tiff, n., person who initiates law suit

plain′tive, a., sad, melancholy

plan, v., arrange scheme, design for building, **-ning**

plane, n., flat surface, carpenter's tool, airplane

plan′et, n., heavenly body circling sun

plank, n., board

plant, n., v., natural growth, factory, put into soil for growing

plan-tā′tion, n., large farm

plaque (plak), n., tablet honoring someone

plas′ter, n., lime mixture for covering walls, **-er**

plas′tic, n., a., hard, molded synthetic material, easy to form, **-ity**

plate, n., dish

plate, v., coat with metal

pla-teau′ (to), n., raised area of land

plat′form, n., stage, political policy

plat′i-num, n., precious metal

plat′i-tude, n., common, trite statement, **-tudinous**

plat′ter, n., large dish

plau′dit, n., praise, approval, applause

plau′si-ble, a., seeming to be true, reasonable, **-bility**

play, v., engage in recreation,

have fun, act or perform, -ful

play, n., recreation, dramatic piece, **-er**

plä′za, n., public or open space in city, shopping center

plē′a, n., appeal, request

plēad, v., ask for, request, beg, **-ing**

pleas′ant, a., agreeable, kind, giving pleasure

plē′ase, v., satisfy, be agreeable

pleas′ure (yēr), n., satisfaction, enjoyment, happiness, **-able**

plē′be, n., service school freshman

plē-bē′ian (in), a., lower social class, common

pleb′i-scīte, n., vote

pledge, v., n., make promise, vow

plen-i-pö-ten′ti-ār-y, a., having full authority

plen′ti-ful, a., enough, full supply

plen′ty, n., enough, prosperity

pleth′ō-rà, n., excess

Plex′i-glas′, n., synthetic thermoplastic resin, transparent for windows, lenses, etc.

plī′a-ble, a., easily influenced, **-bility**

plī′êrs, n., pincers

plīght, n., v., difficult situation, pledge

plod, v., walk in tired way, work steadily

plot, n., course of events, scheme, land

plow, n., machine for turning over soil

pluck, v., pick

pluck′y, a., brave

plug, n., v., hole stopper, advertise (coll.)

plum, n., fruit

plumb, v., determine perpendicular, determine water depth

plumb′êr, n., installer and repairer of water and gas fixtures, pipes, etc., **-ing**

plum′mēt, v., fall, drop down

plump, a., fat

plun′dêr, v., attack and rob

plunge (plunj), v., force, jump into

plū′rál, a., more than one, word form

plus, prep., added to

plush, a., luxurious, thick and velvety

ply, v., n., work diligently, ask, travel, layer of material

p. m., noon to midnight

pneū-mō′nì-à (noo), n., lung disease

pōach, v., cook egg in water, steal

pock′êt, n., pouch sewed into clothing

pod, n., seed holder

pō′di-um, n., musical conductor's platform

pō′êm, n., verse composition

pō′êt, n., composer of poems, **-ry**

pō′gō-stick, n., a pole with footrests, handle, and spring, on which one may be propelled by bounds

pō-gröm′, n., organized massacre of certain people

poign′ânt (poin-yint), a., painful, sharp

point, n., sharp end, characteristic, fact

point, v., show, direct, make sharp

point′êd, a., significant, direct

point′êr, n., suggestion, breed of dog

poise, n., balance, ease of manner, **-d**

poi′sōn (zin), n., deadly chemical, **-ous**

pōke, v., push into

pōk′êr, n., card game, fire tool

pōk′êr fāce, n., face without expression

pōle, n., long stick, earth's axis

pō-lem′ic, n., argument, debate, **-al**

pō-lĩce′ (lēes), n., law officers, cops, **-man**

pol′i-cy, n., means of procedure, insurance contract

pō-li-ō-my-ē-lī′tis, n., nerve damaging virus disease

pol′ish, v., make glossy, smooth, shine

pō-līte′, a., having good manners, considerate

pŏl′i-tics, n., government party connections, scheming within group, **-tician**

pōl′ká, n., lively dance

pōll, n., number of votes, head, relating to voting, voting place

pol'lèn, n., fertilizing dust produced by flowers

pōl-lūte', v., make unclean, defile, **-lution**

poly-, prefix, many

po-lō-nāise', n., dance

pol'ý-an'dry, n., having more than one husband

pö-lýg'á-my, n., having more than one wife

pol'ý-mēr', n., synthetic substance having giant molecules

pōme, n., apple-like fruit

pome'gran-āte, n., fruit

pomp, n., stateliness, courtly display

pon'chō, n., loose capelike garment

pond, n., small body of water

pon'dēr, v., think, carefully consider

pon'dēr-ous, a., heavy

Pon'tiff, n., the Pope

pōny, n., small horse

pō'ny-tāil', n., hairstyle in which hair is drawn back, fastened at neck, allowed to hang free

pōōch, n., (coll.) dog

pōōl, n., small body of water, joint funds

pōōl, v., join together in effort

poor, a., lacking material things, needy

pop, n., sudden, loud sound, father (coll.)

Pōpe, n., head of Catholic Church

pop'lär, n., kind of tree

pop'ū-lâce, n., common people

pop'ū-lär, a., liked by many, having wide acceptance, **-ity**

pop-ū-lā'tion, n., count of people

pop'ū-lous, a., crowded with people

porch, n., covered outside entrance to building

pôre, n., skin opening

pôre, v., study, meditate

pôrk, n., hog meat

pôr'nog'ra-phy, n., obscene art or literature

pôrt, n., harbor, left side of ship, wine

pôrt'a-ble, a., able to be carried

pôr'tal, n., entrance, doorway

pôr-tend', v., predict, warn

pôr-ten'tous (tus), a., threatening of tragedy

pôr'tēr, n., attendant, janitor

pôr'tēr-house, n., cut of steak

pôrt-fō'li-ō (lee-ōh), n., portable carrying case for papers

pôr'tion, n., part of, share of

pôrt'ly, n., fat, dignified

pôr'trait (trit), n., person's picture

pôr-trāy', v., make picture of, describe

pōse, v., assume a specific position, show off

pō-si'tion, n., spot where situated, job, certain place

pos'i-tive, a., certain, direct, plus

pos'i-tive-ly, adv., without doubt

pŏs-sess', v., own, be in control, **-ion**

pos'si-ble, a., likely to happen, **-bility**

pōst, n., upright piece of wood, military camp, mail

pōst'àge, n., cost of mailing letters, etc.

pos-tē'ri-ôr, n., rear part

pos-ter'i-ty, a., future time

post'hū-mous (choo-mus), a., occurring after death, **-ly**

pōst-môr'tĕm, a., after death, autopsy

pôst-pōne', v., delay, **-ment**

pos'tū-lāte (choo), n., statement without any proof, assumption

pos'ture, n., body position, pose

pot, n., container, utensil

pö-tā'tō, n., root vegetable

pō'tĕnt, a., powerful, strong

pō-ten'tial, a., capacity, undeveloped potential

pot'tēr-y, n., earthenware

pŏt'pour-rī' (pō-poor-rē), n., mixed, dried flower petals and spices in jar for perfume

pouch, n., bag

pōul'try, n., domestic fowl

pounce, v., suddenly fall upon, take hold of

pound, v., hammer, **-age**

pōur, v., empty out, flow

pov'êr-ty, n., need, destitution

pow'der, n., solid matter ground to very fine substance

pow'er, n., strength, force, ability, **-ful**

pow'wow, n., discussion (coll.)

prac'ti-ca-ble, a., possible, usable, **-bly**

prac'ti-cal, a., useful, doing as opposed to thinking, sensible

prac'ti-cal-ly, adv., almost, virtually

prac'tice, n., way of doing, custom, habit, professional occupation

prag'ma-tism, n., philosophy emphasizing practical behavior, **-tic**

praise, n., approval, honor

prank, n., mischievous trick, joke

prat'tle, n., foolish chatter

pray, v., ask of God, **-er**

preach, v., discuss moral issue in public, proclaim in sermon, give advice

pre-ca'ri-ous, a., dangerous, risky, **-ly**

pre-cau'tion, n., preceding caution or care

pre-cede', v., go before, **-nce**

pre'ce-dent, n., previous happening used as rule

pre'cinct (seenkt), n., geographical district

pre'cious, a., of great value

pre-cip'i-tate, v., start suddenly, cause to happen, **-tation**

pre-cise', a., exact, correct, **-cision**

pre-clude', v., keep from, prevent, **-clusion**

pre-co'cious, a., mature at early age, **-city**

pre-con-ceive', v., form opinion beforehand

pre-cur'sor, n., one who comes before

pred'a-tô-ry, a., preying on others

pred'e-ces-sôr, n., one who has gone before

pre-des-ti-na'tion, n., decree in advance, fate

pre-dic'a-ment, n., confused or unfortunate situation

pred'i-cate, n., grammar part

pred'i-cate, v., make statement, base on fact

pre-dict', v., prophesy, foretell the future, **-ion**

pre-di-lec'tion, n., desire for, preference

pre-dom'i-nate, v., exert greater power, rule

pre-empt', v., take possession of before another, **-ion**

preen, v., clean feathers, primp

pre'fab, adj., n., prefabricated (coll.)

pre-fab'ri-cate, v., manufacture sections in mass for single assembly

pref'ace, n., introduction, beginning to book

pre-fer', v., desire above others, **-able**

pre'fix, n., root at beginning of word

preg'nant, a., carrying child in womb, fruitful

pre-hen'sile, a., able to grasp

pre-his-tor'ic, a., before recorded history

prej'ü-dice, n., unfair dislike, **dicial**

prel'ate, n., minister

pre-lim'i-när-y, a., introductory, beforehand

pre-ma-türe', a., before time due, early

pre-mier' (mēer), n., head of government, prime minister

pre-mière', n., first public performance

pre'mi-um, n., reward, prize

pre-mö-ni'tion, n., forewarning, hunch

pre-na'tal, a., before birth

pre-pâre', v., make ready for, **-paration**

pre-pon'dêr-ance, n., greater amount, size, power, etc.

prep-o-si'tion, n., part of speech

pre-pos'têr-ous, a., impossibly ridiculous

pres'age, n., warning, feeling of danger

pre-sci-ence (shi-ins), n., having previous knowledge

pre-scribe', v., write medical directions, **-scription**

pres'ence, n., be in company of, personality

pres'ent, a., being here, at this place now

pres'ent, n., gift

pre-sent' (zent), v., give to,

introduce

pre·sent'a·ble (zent), *a.*, attractive, suitable to be given or seen

pres·en·ta'tion, *n.*, giving

pres'ent·ly, *adv.*, soon

pre·serve' (zèrv), *v.*, keep from spoiling, save for future

pre·side' (zyd), *v.*, be in charge over

pres'i·dent, *n.*, head officer

press, *v.*, push against, squeeze, force, urge

press, *n.*, publications business, printing machine

press box, *n.*, section where members of press are seated at sporting event

pres'sure (shir), *n.*, applied force, influence, duress

pres'sure suit, *n.*, inflatable suit for use against low pressure, as for aviators

pres·tige' (tēej), *n.*, honor, influence, position

pre·sume' (zōōm), *v.*, take for granted, **-sumption**

pre·sump'tu·ous, *a.*, over-bold, too forward

pre·tend', *v.*, make believe, **-tense**

pre·ten'tious, *a.*, showing false superiority, showy

pre'text, *n.*, false reason

pret'ty, *a.*, attractive to the eye, to a degree, **-tily**

pre·vail', *v.*, exist, be in force

pre·var'i·cate, *v.*, lie, **-cation -ion**

pre·vent', *v.*, stop from doing

pre'vi·ous, *a.*, occurring before, earlier

prey (a), *n.*, something or someone hunted

price, *n.*, cost

prick, *v.*, pierce lightly

pride, *n.*, dignity of self

priest, *n.*, religious minister, **-ly**

pri·mâr'i·ly, *adv.*, mainly

pri'mâr·y, *n.*, first, most important, interparty election

prime, *a.*,*v.*, main, chief, best, prepare for immediate action

pri·me'val, *a.*, most ancient

prim'i·tive, *a.*, ancient, simple, crude

primp, *v.*, dress up

prince, *n.*, son of a king, **-ss**

prin'ci·pâl, *a.*, *n.*, main, chief, school director, money loaned with interest, **-ly**

prin·ci·pal'i·ty, *n.*, prince's territory

prin'ci·ple, *n.*, basic truth, moral standard, basis of reasoning

print, *n.*, impression made by use of type or other patterns, **-ing**

print·out, *n.*, material produced by computer

pri'ôr, *a.*, before, coming first

pri·ôr'i·ty, *n.*, preferential rating

pris'ôn, *n.*, jail, **-er**

pris'sy, *a.*, finicky, prudish

pris·tine' (tēen), *a.*, as at beginning, unspoiled

pri'vate, *a.*, limited to selected persons, secret, **-vacy**

priv'et, *n.*, kind of hedge

priv'i·lège, *n.*, particular right or favor

priv'y, *n.*, *a.*, outhouse, secret

prize, *n.*, *v.*, reward won in competition, value

prō, *n.*, *adv.*, short for professional, in sympathy with

prob'a·ble, *a.*, likely to take place, **-bility**

prō·ba'tion, *n.*, test period of behavior, **-ary**

probe, *v.*, search for, examine

prob'lem, *n.*, unsolved question or situation

prō·ce'dûre, *n.*, method of doing

prō·ceed, *v.*, go ahead

prō'cess, *v.*, *n.*, develop, fix, method of procedure

prō·ces'sion, *n.*, group moving in fixed order, parade

prō·claim', *v.*, declare publicly

proc·la·ma'tion, *n.*, official announcement

prō·cliv'i·ty, *n.*, tendency

prō·cras'ti·nāte, *v.*, delay, put off, **-nation**

prō'crē·āte, *v.*, give birth to, bring forth, produce, **-ation**

prō·cûre', *v.*, get, obtain for

prod, *v.*, push to activity, urge

prod'i·gàl, *a.*, wasteful, **-ity**

prō·di'gious (jus), *a.*, huge, tremendous, **-ly**

pro-dūce', v., create, manufacture, grow, **-r**

prod'ūce, n., vegetables, food

prod'uct, n., something which is made, result of effort, **-ion, -ive**

prō-fāne', a., unreligious, in poor taste, **-fanity**

prō-fess', v., declare

prō-fes'sion, n., belief, learned occupation, **-al**

prō-fes'sŏr, n., college teacher

prō-fi'cient, a., very capable, skilled, **-ciency**

prō'file, n., outline, side view

prof'it, n., v., amount earned beyond expenses, benefit, **-able**

prof'li-gāte, a., wild, corrupt, **-gacy**

prō-found', a., deep in feelings, **-fundity**

prō-fū'sion, n., many, abundance, excess

prog'e-ny (proj), n., children, offspring

prog-nos'ti-cāte, v., forecast, **-cation**

prō'gram, n., listing of events, plan to be followed

prog'ress, n., development, growth, improvement

prō-gres'sive, a., going forward, advanced

prō-hib'it, v., forbid, stop, **-ion**

proj'ect, n., proposed plan

prō-ject', v., protrude, send forward, **-ion**

prō-lē-tār'ī-āt, n., the working people, masses, **-an**

prō-lif'ic, a., rapidly producing, fruitful

prō-lix', a., long-winded

prō-lŏng', v., lengthen time of, **-ation**

prom-ĕn-āde', n., leisurely walk

prom'i-nĕnt, a., well known, projecting, highly noticeable, **-nence**

prō-mis'cū-ous, a., immoral without discrimination, **ity**

prom'ise, n., agreement to do something, possible future excellence

prō-mōte', v., advance in position, work toward goal

prompt, a., v., on time, inspire to action, **-ly**

pro-mul'gāte, v., declare, announce, **-gation**

prōne, a., likely, lying face down

prō'noun, n., replacement for noun

prō-nounce', v., say clearly, speak

prō-nounced', a., very strongly marked

prō-nounce'mĕnt, n., official statement

prōōf, n., act of proving, evidence

prop, n., support

prop-á-gan'dá, n., widely organized effort to educate others to one's beliefs, **-dize**

prop'á-gāte, v., bear offspring, spread

prō-pel', v., cause to move forward

prō-pen'si-ty, n., strong tendency

prop'êr, a., suitable, correct

prop'êr-ty, n., particular attribute, goods which are owned

proph'ĕt, n., one who foretells future events, **-esy**

prō-phy-lac'tic, n., a., guarding against disease

prō-pin'qui-ty, n., nearness, kinship

prō-pi'ti-āte, v., win favor of, calm anger

prō-pi'tious, a., favorable, fortunate

prō-pôr'tion, n., comparative relation between connected things, part

prō-pōse', v., offer for consideration, ask for hand in marriage

prop-ō-si'tion, n., offer, undertaking

prō-prī'ĕ-tŏr, n., owner

prō-prī'ĕ-ty, n., suitable behavior

prō-sā'ic, a., resembling prose, ordinary

prō-sci-ūt'to (prō-shōō-tō), n., Italian ham

prō-scrībe', v., outlaw, prevent from doing, **-scription**

prōse, n., spoken or written words

pros'ĕ-cūte, v., institute legal charges against, **-cution**

pros'ĕ-lyte, n., convert to another belief

pros'pect, n., outlook, chance, potential customer

prō-spec'tus, n., summary of proposed plan

pros'pêr, v., enjoy good fortune, thrive, **-ity**

pros'tāte, n., male gland

pros'ti-tūte, n., woman who has sexual relations for a fee

pros'trāte, a., flattened, helpless

prō-tect', v., guard against, shield, defend, **-ion**

prō'test, n., strong objection, complaint

Prot'es-tänt, n., any western Christian other than Catholic

prō'tö-col, n., treaty, correct diplomatic procedure

prō'tö-plasm, n., basic substance of living tissues

prō'tö-type, n., original type, first model

prō-tract', v., delay, prolong

prō-trūde', v., stick out, project, **-trusion**

proud, a., having pride, haughty, **-ly**

prove (proov), v., demonstrate as true, test

prov'êrb, n., short wise saying, **-ial**

prō-vīde', v., supply with, take care of, require

provi-dent, a., looking ahead

prov'ince, n., geographical district

prō-vin'cial, a., countryish, limited, **-ism**

prō-vi'sion, n., certain arrangement, requirement, food

prō-vōke', v., incite to anger, stir up, arouse

prō'vō-lō'nē, n., Italian cheese

prow, n., front of ship

prow'ess, n., courage, daring, ability

prowl, v., move stealthily, **-er**

prox'i-māte, a., near, **-mity**

prox'y, n., substitute, authority to vote

prūde, n., overly modest person

prū'dént, a., careful, wise, sensible

prūne, n., dried plum

prū'ri-ént, a., having lewd desires

pry, v., look inquisitively, raise up, force up

psälm (sählm), n., religious song of praise

pseū'dō (sōō-dō), a., false

psy-che-del'ic, adj., heightened sensory perception, sometimes hallucination, distortion

psy-chī'á-try (sye-kye-i-trēe), n., science of treatment of emotional illness, **-trist**

psy-chō-à-nal'y-sis, n., deep examination of emotional disturbances, **tical**

psy-chol'ö-gy, n., study of human behavior and emotions

psy'chō-neu-rō'sis, n., manifestation of physical or emotional disorder without any cause or disease

psy-chō'sis, n., severe mental illness

psy-chō-sō-ma'tic, a., physically affected by emotions

psy-chō-ther'á-py, n., treatment of emotionally disturbed person

ptō'māine (tōh), n., poisonous matter found in food

pū'bêr-ty, n., physical beginning of sexual development

pu'bic, adj., pertaining to pubes

pub'lic, a., open to all people

pub-li-cā'tion, n., book, magazine, newspaper

pub-lic'i-ty, n., broadcast, published, or otherwise spread

pub'lish, v., prepare and print book, etc. for sale, **-er**

pū-den'da, n., external genitals

pud'ding, n., type of dessert

pu'êr-ile, a., boyish, child-like

puff, v., breathe fast, hard, swell

pū'gil-ism, n., art of fist fighting, **-ist**

pug-nā'cious, a., argumentative, fighting

pū'is-sänt, a., powerful, **-sance**

pul'chri-tūde, n., physical beauty

pull, v., draw or haul

pull, n., influence, (coll.)

device for pulling	pûr'loin, v., steal
pul'let, n., young hen	pûr'ple, n., red-blue color, violet
pul'mö-nâr-y, a., relating to lungs	pûr'pôrt, n., meaning
pulp, n., soft mass	pûr'pöse, n., aim, goal, -ly
pul'pit, n., church podium	pûrse, n., container for carrying money
pul-sā'tion, n., throbbing	pûr-sūe', (vay) v., chase, -suance
pulse, n., throb of blood flow as felt in arteries	pûr-sūit', n., chase, vocation
pul'vêr-īze, v., grind into powder	pûr-vey' (vay) v., obtain, supply with food, -ance
pump, v., force liquids or gases into or out of something	pus, n., discharge from infection
pump'er-nick-ĕl, n., dark, sour rye bread	push, v., press against with force, continuous energy
pump'kin, n., fruit of gourd type	push'ö-vêr, n., (coll.) goal easy to accomplish, person easily persuaded
pun, n., play on words	pū-sil-lan'i-mous, a., servile, cowardly
punch, v., n., beat, hit, cut through, fruit drink, blow	put, v., place, express, guess, apply
punc-til'i-ous, a., noting every detail, exact	pū-tre-fy, v., decay, -faction
punc'tū-ǎl, a., on time	pū'trid, a., rotten, corrupt
punc'tū-āte, v., place correct grammatical symbols, emphasize, -ation	putt, n., golf stroke
	put'ty, n., material used to hold glass, or for patching walls
punc'ture (punk), v., punch hole in	puz'zle, n., difficult problem
pun'gĕnt, a., strong, biting, sharp	pyg'mý, n., very short person
pun'ish, v., penalize, -ment	py'lon, n., tall signal tower
punt, n., flat-bottomed boat, football kick	py-ör-rhē'ǎ, n., gum disease
pū'ny, a., tiny, weak	pyr'ȧ-mid, n., geometrical form with triangular sides meeting in point
pup, n., baby dog, -py	
pū'pil, n., one being educated at school, part of eye	pyre (pīr), n., fire for burning of dead body
pup'pĕt, n., animated doll	Py'rex, n., heat resistant glass
pûr'châse, v., buy	
pūre, a., clean, free from evil, -ly	py-rö-mā'ni-ȧ, n., craving to start fires
pûr'gȧ-tive, n., laxative	py-rö-tech'nics (tek-niks), n. display of fireworks
pûrge, v., cleanse of impurities, execute political opponent	py'thon, n., enormous non-poisonous snake

<hr>

Q

qu, pronounced as kw except where shown	quǎd'rū-ped, n., four-footed animal
quack, n., duck sound, false professional practitioner	quǎd-rū'ple, v., to multiply by a factor of four
quǎd'ran-gle, n., square area surrounded by buildings	quaff, v., drink enormously
quǎd'rȧnt, n., fourth part of circle, instrument for measuring altitude	quail, n., v., bird, be frightened
quá-drille', n., dance by four couples	quaint, a., unusual, interesting due to age
	quāke, v., shake
	quāke, n., earthquake

qual'i-fy, v., achieve fitness for position, etc., meet requirements, alter, **-fication**

qual'i-ty, n., characteristic, trait

qualm, n., inner disturbance, general uneasy condition, twinge

quan'da-ry, n., confusion, puzzled condition

quan'ti-ty, n., amount of, number

quan'tum, n., amount

quar'an-tine (teen), n., sanitary cordon

quar'rel, n., v., argument, spat, tiff, squabble

quar'ry, n., place from which stone is obtained, object of a chase

quart (kwärt), n., quarter of a gallon, a vessel of said capacity

quar'ter, n., one fourth of something, fourth part

quar'ter-back, n., football signal caller

quar'tered, a., cut into four parts

quar-tet', n., group of four, musical composition for four pieces

quartz, n., silica type mineral

qua'sar, n., distant celestial object which emits radio waves

qua'si, a., not actual, seemingly

qua'ver, v., tremble

quay (kee), n., loading place for ships

queen, n., royal female ruler

queer, a., strange, unusual, different, odd, homosexual

quell, v., bring order out of confusion, quiet state of disorder

quench, v., slake thirst, drown out

quer'u-lous (i-lus), a., critical, fretful, peevish

que'ry, n., v., question, raise doubt

quest, n., search, investigation

ques'tion, v., ask of, raise

doubt, **-able**

queue, n., line of waiting people, hair braid

quib'ble, v., carp, bicker

quick, a., fast, alive, intelligent, impatient, **-ly**

quick'freeze', v., freeze food for preserving

quick'sand, n., loose sand into which heavy objects sink

qui-es'cence, n., condition of being quiet, **-cent**

qui'et, a., without noise, peaceful, **-ude**

quilt, n., colorful bed covering

qui'nine, n., anti-malarial drug

quin-tes'sence, n., good example of, purest type

quin-tet', n., group of five

quin-tu'ple, a., five times something, five times as much

quin'tu-plet, n., one of five children born at one birth

quip, n., v., clever remark, joke

quire, n., 24 sheets of paper

quirk, n., unusual behavior, mannerism

quit, v., leave, resign, go, die

quite, adv., very, extremely

quit'ter, n., one who cannot face difficult situation

quiv'er, v., n., tremble, arrow case

qui'vive, n., challenge, alert

quix-ot'ic, a., foolishly romantic, impractical

quiz, n., school test, examination

quiz'zi-cal, a., strange, humorous

quod, n., prison

quon'dam, a., prior, previous

quo'rum, n., number necessary at a meeting to legally act

quo'ta, n., number allowed, share of

quo-ta'tion, n., repeated remark, current price

quote, v., to repeat verbatim

quo'tient, n., result of dividing one number by another, quota, share

---R---

rab'bī, n., Jewish minister, **-nical**

rab'bit, n., member of the hare family

rab'ble, n., noisy mob

rab'id, a., violent, affected with rabies

rā'bīes, n., disease caused by bite of warm-blooded animals

rac-cōōn', n., fur-bearing animal

rāce, n., speed contest, people with related ancestry

rack, n., v., torture instrument, framework, torment

rack'et, n., dishonest occupation, loud noise, stringed frame for tennis, **-eer**

rack up', v., score

ra'con, n., radar beacon

rāc'y, a., risqué, suggestive

rā-där, n., radio detecting and ranging device

ra'di-an (rad), n., plane angle (circle)

rā'di-ā'tion, n., energy emitted in waves or particles

rā'di-ance, n., degree of brilliance

rā'diāte, v., emit, **-ation**

rā'di-ā-tor, n., auto part for cooling water, device for heating homes, a transmitting antenna

rad'i-cál, a., basic, extreme

rā'di-ō, n., instrument for sending any receiving sound by electrical impulse

rā-di-ō-ac'tive, a., giving off alpha, beta, or gamma rays

rā-di-ol'o-gy, n., the use of radiant energy in medicine

rā-di-ō-sonde', n., instrument bearing radio transmitter, sent into atmosphere to send back information

rad'ish, n., plant of the mustard family

rā'di-um, n., radioactive element

rā'di-us, n., line from center to edge of circle

rā-dōme, n., housing for radar antennae

rā'don, n., radioactive gaseous element created by disintegration of radium

raf'fle, n., sale of tickets for prize, to conduct sale

raft, n., floating framework of boards, logs, etc., large number, any large number, host

raft'er, n., roof support

rag, n., old, worn cloth

rāge, n., extreme anger, to storm

rag'ged, a., worn, in tatters

rag'tīme, n., syncopated melody with strict two-four accompaniment (piano)

rāid, n., surprise attack, to conduct such an attack

rāil, n., v., metal or wood bar, reproach, **-ing**

rāil'lēr-y, n., banter

rāil'rōad, n., transportation system

rāi'mėnt, n., habiliments

rāin, n., water dropping to earth, flow, **-y**

rāin'bōw, n., colored semi-circle in sky

rāin'check, n., repeat invitation

rāise, v., pick up, promote in job

rāi'sin (zin), n., dried grape

rāke, n., gardening tool, useless person

rāke'off, n., kick-back

rāk'ish, a., jaunty

ral'ly, n., mass meeting, gathering

ram, n., male sheep

ram'ble, v., roam about, talk incoherently

ram-bunc'tious, a., confused, noisy

ram-i-fi-cā'tion, n., subdivision, result

ram'jet, n., jet engine

ramp, n., inclined walkway

ram'pāge, n., violent behavior

ranch, n., animal farm

ran'cid (sid), a., smelling rotten, decomposed

ran'côr, n., abhorrence, **-ous**

ran'döm, *a.*, without pattern

ränge, *n.*, *v.*, extent, stove, distance, wander, classify

rank, *n.*, *a.*, classification, position, offensive, extreme

ran'kle, *v.*, cause pain, annoy

ran'sack, *v.*, search

ran'söm, *n.*, sum demanded to free kidnapped person

rá-pä'cious, *a.*, greedy, plundering, **-ly**

räpe, *n.*, sexual intercourse by force

rap'id, *a.*, fast, quick

rap'id, *n.*, fast, shallow river current

rap-pôrt', *n.*, mutual understanding

rapt, *a.*, paying close attention

rap'ture, *n.*, strong delight, happiness, **-turous**

râre, *a.*, unusual, scarce, **-ly**

râr'e-fy, *v.*, make pure, **-faction**

râr'i-ty, *n.*, scarcity

ras'cál, *n.*, mischievous person, imp

rash, *n.*, spots on skin

rash, *a.*, too hasty

rasp'ber-ry, *n.*, edible berry

rat, *n.*, rodent

rat, *v.*, to inform on

räte, *n.*, *v.*, amount of, degree, evaluate

rath'êr, *adv.*, preferably, to some degree

rat'i-fy, *v.*, approve

rä'ti-ō, *n.*, one thing in comparison to another, proportion

rä'tion, *n.*, allotment

ra'tion-ál, *a.*, reasonable, making sense, **-ize**

rationale, *n.*, reasons for

rat'tle, *v.*, make quick, sharp sounds

rat'tle-trap, *n.*, old-type vehicle

rău'cous, *a.*, harsh or strident

rav'äge, *n.*, damage

rav'äge, *v.*, lay waste, wantonly destroy

räve, *v.*, shout uncontrollably

răv'el, *v.*, disentangle

räv'ën, *n.*, corvine bird

răv'ën, *a.*, black and lustrous

rav'e-nous, *a.*, extremely hungry, rapacious

rá-vine' (vēen), *n.*, long narrow valley

rav-i-o'li, *n.*, Italian dish

rav'ish, *v.*, carry off, enrapture, **-ing**

râw, *a.*, uncooked, racy

ray, *n.*, thin stream of light, line of invisible beams

ray'on, *n.*, synthetic fabric

räze, *v.*, destroy

rä'zör, *n.*, shaving device

razz, *v.*, criticize lightly, heckle

rē-, *prefix*, to do again

rēach, *v.*, touch, achieve, arrive

rē-act', *v.*, respond to, **-ion**

rē-ac'tion-âr-y, *n.*, extreme political conservative

rē-ac'tör, *n.*, device that produces atomic energy

rēad, *v.*, understand printed words, interpret

rēad'out, *n.*, display of information from computer, recorded by tape or typewriter

read'y (red), *a.*, prepared, prompt, at hand

read'y rōōm, *n.*, place where aircraft crews receive briefing and orders

rē'ál, *a.*, actual, existing, **-ity**

rē'ál-ize, *v.*, bring into existence, understand, profit, **-ization**

rē'ál-ly, *adv.*, actually, in truth

realm (relm), *n.*, region, area of influence

rēal time, *n.*, time in which occurrence and recording of an event are nearly simultaneous

rē'ál-tör, *n.*, real estate broker

rēam, *n.*, 500 sheets of paper

rēap, *v.*, gather crop, receive results, **-er**

rēar, *n.*, *v.*, end part, back, raise, bring up

rēa'sön (zuhn), *n.*, excuse for doing, motive, ability to think

rēa'sön-á-ble, *a.*, fair, sensible, moderate

rēa'sön-ing, *n.*, thought behind actions

rē-ás-sūre', *v.*, express faith in, **surance**

rē'bäte, *n.*, returned money

reb'ël, *n.*, *v.*, one who revolts, to revolt, **-lion**

rē-bound', *v.*, bounce back

rė-buff', v., halt, turn aside

rė-būke', v., take to task, scold

rē-bus, n., puzzle

rė-but'tȧl, n., refuting arguments in debate

rė-cal'ci-trȧnt, a., rebellious

rė-cȧll', v., call back, remember

rė-cant', v., take back

rē-cȧ-pit'ū-lāte, v., summarize

rė-cēde', v., lessen, ebb

rė-cēipt'(sēet), v., n., receive, written proof of obtaining

rė-cēiv'ȧ-ble, a., capable of being received

rė-cēive', v., get, take, accept, -r

rēcent, a., happening in near past, -ly

rė-cep'tȧ-cle, n., container

rė-cep'tion, n., getting, party, greeting, -ist

rė-cess', n., period of rest, wall opening

rė-ces'sion, n., moving backward, drop in business

re-cher'che, a., rare

re-cid'i-vism, n., return to crime

rec'i-pē, n., formula for preparing food

rė-cip'i-ėnt, n., one that receives

rė-cip'rō-cȧl, a., mutual, in return, -ly

rė-cip'rō-cāte, v., give in return, -city

rec-i-tā'tion, n., performing speech aloud

rė-cīte', v., narrate to an audience, -cital

reck'less, a., dangerous, not careful

reck'ȯn, v., add, consider, -ing

rė-clāim', v., call back, ask return of, -clamation

rė-clīne', v., lie down

rė-clūse', n., one hidden away, hermit

rec'ȯg-nīze, v., know, notice, -nition

rė-col-lect', v., recall

rec-ȯm-mend', v., speak well of, advise, entrust, -ation

rec'ȯm-pense, v., pay for services

rec'ȯn-cīle, v., settle on friendly terms, -ciliation

rec'ȯn-dīte, a., secret, hidden, unknown

rė-con'nais-sánce (nisintz), n., exploration, survey

rec'ȯrd, n., listing of events in written form, phonograph disc

rė-cȯrd', v., write down, list

rė-cȯv'êr, v., get back, become well again, -y

rec'rė-āte, v., have fun, relax, refresh

rē-crė-āte', v., create once more

rec-rė-ā'tion, n., diversion, sport

rė-crim-i-nā'tion, n., return of accusation, countercharge

rė-crūit', n., v., enlistee, enlist

rec'tan-gle, n., certain four-sided geometrical figures

rec'ti-fy, v., to make right, -fication

rec'ti-tude, n., quality of being correct

rec'tum, n., end part of large intestine

rė-cū'pêr-āte, v., recover from illness or surgery, -ation

rė-cûr', v., happen again, repeat, -rence

red, a., primary color

Red, n., Communist

re-dact', v., prepare for publication, edit

red-cär'pet, adj., ceremonial courtesy, display of deferential treatment

rė-dēem', v., get back by payment, -demption

red'eye, n., cheap whiskey

red gum, n., eucalyptus gum

red'han'ded, a., caught in the act of a misdeed

red'head, n., a person having red hair

red heat, n., state of being red-hot

red her'ring, n., diversion from real issue

red'ō-lent, a., sweet smelling, lence

rė-doubt' (dout), n., fortress

rė-dound', v., contribute

rė-dress', v., make right, fix

red tāpe', n., confusing details, excessive paper work, routine

rė-dūce', v., decrease in size, lessen, degrade, -duction

rė-dun'dȧnt, a., repetitious

rēed, n., hollow type grass, woodwind vibrator

rēef, *n.*, hazardous obstruction

rēef′ẽr (coll.), *n.*, narcotic cigarette

rēel, *n.*, winding apparatus, dance

re-en′try, *n.*, return to earth's atmosphere from spaceflight

re-fec′to-ry, *n.*, dining hall

rê-fẽr′, *v.*, submit to decision, allude to, **-ral**

ref′ẽr-ēe′, *n.*, sports official

ref′ẽr-ence, *n.*, recommendation, information, regard, mention

ref-ẽr-en′dum, *n.*, submission of an issue to popular vote

rê-fīne′, *v.*, make pure, **-ry**

rê-fīned′, *a.*, polished, genteel

rê-flect′, *v.*, cast back light, meditate, **-ion**

rê-flect′, *n.*, mirrored image

rē′flex, *a., n.*, returned, involuntary response

rê-fôrm′, *v.*, change, correct, improve, **-er**

rê-fôrm′ä-tô-ry, *n.*, correctional institution for juveniles

rê-frāin′, *v., n.*, hold back, repeated verse

rê-fract′, *v.*, bend rays in passing

rê-frac′to-ry, *a.*, resistant

rê-fresh′, *v.*, revive

rê-fresh′ment, *n.*, light snack, food

rê-frig′ẽr-āte, *v.*, keep cold, **-ator**

ref′ūge, *n.*, protective haven

ref-ū-gēe′, *n.*, one who seeks relief from difficult conditions

rē′fund, *n.*, repayment

rê-fūse′, *v.*, turn down

ref′ūse, *n.*, unwanted material, trash

rê-fūte′, *v.*, show as false, **-futation**

rê-gāin′, *v.*, get back

rē′gal, *a.*, royal, stately

rê-gāle′, *v.*, entertain, delight

rê-gärd′, *v., n.*, consider, care about, esteem

rê-gärd′ing, *prep.*, concerning

rê-gärd′less, *a.*, in spite of

rē-gen′ẽr-āte (jen), *v.*, form again, **-ation**

rē′gent, *n.*, one governing for another

reg′i-men, *n.*, regulated system

reg′i-ment, *n.*, military unit, **-al**

reg′i-ment, *v.*, organize

reg-i-men-tā′tion, *n.*, severe control

rē′gion, *n.*, place, particular area, **-al**

reg′is-tẽr (rej), *v.*, enroll, record, indicate, match in range, **-tration**

reg′is-trär (rej), *n.*, college record keeper

rê-gress′, *v.*, go backward

rê-gret′, *v.*, feel sorrow, **-ful**

reg′ū-lär, *a.*, usual, steady, **-ity**

reg′ū-lāte, *v.*, control, adjust, **-lation**

rê-gûrgi-tāte (ji), *v.*, vomit

rē-hä-bil′i-tāte, *v.*, make useful, healthy, change

rē-hash′, *v.*, go over

rē-hẽarse′, *v.*, go through trial run

reign (rayn), *n.*, time of rule

rē-im-bûrse′, *v.*, pay back, **-ment**

rein (rayn), *n.*, strap for guiding horse, any controlling device

rē-in-cär-nā′tion, *n.*, rebirth into new body

rē-in-fôrce′, *v.*, make stronger, **-ment**

rē-it′ẽr-āte, *v.*, repeat, **-ation**

rē-joice′, *v.*, revel

rē-join′, *v.*, join again

rē-join′dẽr, *n.*, answer, comeback

rē-lapse′, *v.*, fall back

rê-lāte′, *v.*, tell, connect

rê-lāt′ed, *a.*, of same family, akin, **-ion**

rê-lā′tion-ship′, *n.*, a particular connection, closeness

rel′á-tive, *n.*, person in same family, loosely connected with a particular group

rel′á-tive, *a.*, being connected, bearing upon, comparative, **-ly**

rel-á-tiv′i-ty, *n.*, spacetime relationship of two or more moving objects

rê-lax′, *v.*, be at ease, **-ation**

rē′lay, *v.*, send on

rê-lēase′, *v.*, turn loose, emancipate

rel′ê-gāte, *v.*, banish, assign to lower position, **-gation**

rê-lent′, *v.*, become less severe

rê-lent′less, *a.*, cruel, severe

rel′ê-vant, *a.*, meaningful

re-lī′à-ble, a., trustworthy, -nce

rel′ic, n., keepsake, memento

re-lief′, n., help, that which lessens

re-lieve′, v., lessen, assist

re-li′gion, n., system of belief and worship

re-lin′quish, v., give up

rel′ish, v., like taste of, seasoning

re-luc′tance, n., hesitancy

re-main′, v., stay, continue to be, -der

re-mand′, v., return

re-mark′, n., comment

re-mark′a-ble, a., worthy of note

rem′e-dy, n., cure, -dial

re-mem′ber, v., recollect, recall, -brance

re-mind′, v., freshen memory, -er

rem-i-nisce′ (nis), v., recollect the past, -nce

re-miss′, a., thoughtless, incomplete

re-mis′sion, n., forgiveness

re-mit′, v., forgive, send money, -tance

rem′nant, n., part left over

re-mod′el, v., make over

re-mon′strate, v., offer protest, take stand against, -strance

re-morse′, n., deep sense of guilt

re-mote′, a., far away, not likely to occur

re-move′(moov), v., take away, get rid of, -moval

re-mū′ner-āte, v., reimburse, -ation

ren-ais-sance′, n., revival, rebirth

re-nas′cent, a., reborn

rend, v., tear apart

rend′er, v., give help, make report, pay in return, cause

ren′dez-vous (rähn-di-voo), n., meeting place or time

ren′e-gade, n., deserter, traitor

re-new′, v., make new again, give fresh start, -al

re-nounce′, v., reject, give up claim to

ren′ö-vāte, v., make new, refurbish

re-nown′, n., fame, popularity

rent, n., payment for property or goods used, torn place

re-ōr′gan-īze, v., form again, -ization

re-pâir′, v., fix, mend, go away to, -parable

rep-a-rā′tion, n., payment for harm done, fixing

rep-är-tee′ (tay), n., clever retorts

re-past′, n., dinner

re-pay′, n., compensate

re-pēal′, v., revoke, rescind

re-pēat′, v., do again, speak again, -er

re-pel′, v., force back, repulse, -lent

re-pent′, v., be sorry for, change ways, -ance

re-pêr-cus′sion, n., reaction

rep′êr-toire (twär), n., catalogue of artistic works available for performance

rep-e-ti′tion, n., repeating, -tious

re-plen′ish, v., supply

re-plēte′, a., full

re-ply′, v., answer

re-pôrt′, n., v., account, rumor, sound, summary, tell

re-pôrt′êr, n., newspaper writer

re-pōse′, n., rest, peace, sleep

re-pōs-sess′, v., reestablish ownership

rep-re-hend′, v., criticize, accuse, blame, -hensive

rep-re-sent′, v., take place of, show, be symbol for, -ative

re-press′, v., keep down, -ion

re-priēve′, n., delay of punishment

rep′ri-mand, n., severe reproof

re-prīs′al, n., taking revenge

re-prōach′, n., harm done, censure, criticism

rep′rö-bāte, n., v., scamp, criticize

rē-prö-dūce′, v., give birth, do again, copy, -duction

re-proof′, n., blame, scolding

re-prove′ (proov), v., blame, criticize

rep′tile, n., crawling animal

re-pub′lic, n., representative type government, -an

Rē-pub′li-can, n., major American political party

re-pū′di-āte, v., refuse, reject, -ation

re-pug′nant, a., extremely distasteful

re-pulse′, v., beat back

rep-ū-tā′tion, n., opinion people hold of one, -ble

re-pūte′, n., value, fame

re-quest′, n., v., something asked, ask

Re′qui-em, n., Mass for the

Dead, dirge

re-quire' (kw), v., ask, demand of, need, -ment

req'ui-site (zit), a., essential, need

req-ui-si'tion (rek-wi), n., formal order, request

re-quite', v., repay

re-scind', v., cancel, revoke

res'cue, v., save, free

re-search', n., investigation to get facts

re-sem'ble, v., appear similar

re-sent', v., be angry about, feel hurt, -ment

re-ser'pine, n., a drug

res-er-va'tion, n., something held back, land put aside, tickets put aside, place kept

re-serve', v., n., hold apart, money for special use, civilian military member

re-served', a., cool, modest, set apart

res'er-voir (vwähr), n., place for storing water

re-side', v., live, dwell

res'i-dence, n., domicile, home, -dent

res'i-due, n., remainder, residuum, -dual

re-sign', v., leave job, quietly accept conditions, -ation

re-sile', v., spring back

re-sil'i-ent, a., able to bounce back, -ence

res'in, n., natural gum

re-sist', v., fight against, oppose, -ance

res'o-lute, a., determined, steadfast, -ly

res-o-lu'tion, n., determination, solution

re-solve', v., answer, decide upon, agree to do, promise

res'o-nance, ,n., quality of echoing, -nant

re-sort', n., v., vacation place, turn to

re-sound', v., echo, reverberate

re-source', n., assistance, place where help is found, wealth

re-source'ful, a., capable, smart

re-spect', v., be considerate of, esteem, -ful

re-spec'tive, a., each, several, -ly

res-pi-ra'tion, n., breathing

air, -tory

res'pite, n., reprieve, postponement of sentence

re-splend'ent, a., brilliant, lustrous

re-spond', v., answer, -sponse

re-spon'si-ble, a., liable for, having obligations, capable of trust, mature, -bility

rest, v., n., stop activity, repose, remainder, prop, -ful

res'tau-rant, n., public eating place

res-ti-tu'tion, n., compensation for loss

res'tive, a., hard to control, balky

re-store', v., repair, renew, re-establish, -storation

re-strain', v., prevent from doing, -t

re-strict', v., limit, -ion

re-sult', n., consequence, conclusion, -ant

re-sume', v., start after stopping, -sumption

res-ur-rect', v., bring back to life, -ion

re'tail, n., sale of goods to ultimate consumer, -er

re-tain', v., keep in possession, -tention

re-take', v., take again

re-tal'i-ate, v., get revenge, strike back, -ation

re-tard', v., delay, impede

ret'i-cent, a., quiet, reserved

ret'i-na, n., part of eye

ret'i-nue', n., escort, suite

re-tire', v., leave job at old age, go to bed, leave, -ment

re-tir'ing, a., reserved

re-tort', n., answer, response

re-tract', v., take back, -ion

re-treat', n., withdrawal, safe place

re-trench', v., reduce, economize

ret-ri-bu'tion, n., deserved punishment or reward

re-trieve', v., get back

ret-ro-ac'tive, a., affecting things past

ret'ro-fire, n., ignition of retro-rocket

ret'ro-gress, v., move backward, deteriorate

ret'ro-rock'et, n., auxiliary rocket engine producing backward thrust for deceleration

ret'rō-spect, n., review of past events

rē-tûrn', v., come back, revert, answer, bring back

rē-ūn'ion (yin), n., gathering together again

rē-vēal', v., show, tell, divulge

rev'ē-lā'tion, n., unexpected display, disclosure

rē-venge', v., get back at, **-ful**

rev'ē-nūe, n., money, income

rē-vēre', v., show honor to

rev'êr-ence, n., deep respect, deference, **-ent**

rē-vêrse', a., n., backward, opposite, bad luck, **-versal**

rē-vêrt', v., turn back to

rē-view', v., reconsider, revise, examine, write report on, go over

rē-vīle', v., insult

rē-vīse', v., change, correct, edit, **-vision**

rē-vīve', v., cause to return to life, **-vivify**

rē-vōke', v., repeal, recall, **-vocation**

rē-volt', v., rebel, disgust

rē-volt'ing, a., disgusting, abhorrent

rev-ō-lū'tion, n., sudden change, rebellion against, full circle, **-ary**

rē-volve', v., go around in circle, rotate

rē-volv'êr, n., hand gun

rē-vūe', n., theatrical production

rē-vul'sion, n., drawing away in disgust

rē-wârd', n, recompense

rhap'sō-dy, n., exciting feeling, musical composition, **-dic**

rhet'ō-ric, n., effective use of language, **-al**

rheū'ma-tism, n., joint disease

Rh fac'tor, n., group of antigens in blood, presence or absence Rh positive or Rh negative persons

rhī-noc'ĕr-ōs, n., huge mammal

rhō-dō-den'drŏn, n, evergreen shrub

rhū'bärb, n., plant used as vegetable, (coll.) argument

rhyme (rīm), n., verse with endings having similar

sounds

rhythm (rith-im), n, regular movement, flow or beat, syncopation, **-ical**

rib, n., chest bone

rib'ald, a., crude, offensive

rib'bŏn, n., narrow band of fine cloth

rīce, n., cereal grass

rich, a., having wealth, well supplied, **-es**

rick'ets, n., bone disease

rid, v., be free from, **-dance**

rid'dle, n., involved question

rīde, v., be carried, **-r**

ridge, n., raised strip

ri-dic'ū-lous, a., nonsensical, absurd, **-le**

rīfe, a., full of, happening often

riff'raff, n., unworthy people, hoi polloi

rī'fle, n., v., long gun, search through

rift, n., opening, crack, split

rig, v., n., furnish ship, dress, ship sails

right, a., truthful, good, correct, desirable, away from left, correctness, opposite of wrong, straight, **-eous**

right' of way, n., land strip through another's property

rig'id, a., stiff, firm, severe, **-ity**

rig'ŏr-ous, a., strict, precise

rim, n., edge

ring, n., v., circular ornament or device, circle edge, make bell sound, encircle

rink, n., skating arena

rinse, v., wash lightly

rī'ŏt, n., noisy confusion of crowd, civil disorder, **-ous**

rip, v., tear, cut apart

rīpe, a., brought to maturity, fully developed, **-n**

rip'ple, n., small wave, **-pling**

rīse, v., raise up, get up, be promoted, rebel against, **-n**

risk, n., danger, chance taken, **-y**

ris-que', a., verging on indecency

rīte, n., ceremony

rit'ū-al, n., religious act, ceremony, **-istic**

rī'val, n., competitor, **-ry**

riv'êr, n., large stream of running water

riv′ét, n., metal bolt
road, n., pavement for vehicles, -way
roam, v., wander about
roan, n., horse, color
roar, n., loud, full noise
roast, v., n., cook, heat, criticize, cut of meat
rob, v., steal, -ber
robe, n., long, loose garment
rob′in, n., bird
ro′bot, n., mechanical man
ro-bust′, a., healthy, strong
rock, n., stone, -y
rock, v., sway, vibrate, -er
rock′and′roll′, n., popular music style
rock′ét, n., high speed device propelled by fuel having own oxygen supply
rock′et-ry, n., science of rocket design
rod, n., long narrow, round bar, 5½ yards, weapon
ro′dént, n., any rat-like beast
roe, n., type of deer, fish eggs
rogue, n., scoundrel
rogues′ gal′lèr·y, n., picture file of criminals
roil′, v., stir up
role, n., part taken in play, function
roll, v., n., move by revolving, sway, bun, money, full sound, list, cylinder
roll bar, n., overhead safety bar in automobiles
rol′lick-ing, a., gay, lively
rö-mance′, n., tale of love or adventure, love interest, -mantic
romp, n., boisterous play
ron′dō, n., type of poem or musical piece
roof, n., top cover of building
rook, n., chess piece, crow
rook′ie, n, recruit, novice
room, n., division of house, spacer, -er
room′y, a., large
roost, v., n., rest on perch, pause in spot
roost′ér, n., male chicken, cock
root, n., plant part under earth, beginning, take hold, cheer
rope, n., strong twisted cord
rö′sā-ry, n., holy beads
rose, n., flower
ros′in, n., pine gum
ros′tér, n., list, roll

ros′trum, n., speaker's stand
rot, v., crumble, decay, -ten
ro′tāte, v., go around, take turns, -tation
rote, n., routine or repetition
ro-tis-ser-ie, n., motor-driven spit for grilling
rouge (rüzh), n., red cosmetic or polish
rough (ruf), a., uneven, crude
rough′age, n., food high in fiber
round, a., n., shaped like circle, surrounding, tour, number of shots, musical form
rouse, v., awaken, move to act
rout, n., v., mob, defeat
route, n., line of travel
rou-tine′ (een), a., n., regular, unchanging, daily duties, -ly
rove, v., wander aimlessly
row, n., v., use oars in boat, things in a line
row, n., dispute, -dy
roy′ál, a., relating to kings, etc., -ty
rub, v., wipe off with force, apply pressure
rub′bér, n., material that stretches, -y
rub′bérs, n., over-shoes
rub′bish, n., garbage, trash
rub′ble, n., broken building material
rub′down, n., massage
ru′by, n., red precious stone
rud′dér, n., steering part
rud′dy, a., reddish
rude, a., discourteous, not polished, rough
ru′di·mént, n., origin, beginning, fundamental
rue, v., regret, -ful
ruf′fi·án, n., brutal, cruel person
ruf′fle, v., roughen, vex
ru′fous, a., reddish
rug, n., floor covering
rug′géd, a., rough, strong
ruin, n., damage, destroy, -ous
rule, n., v., law, standard, principle, yardstick, govern, pass decision on, measuring stick, -r
rum′ba, n., v., dance
ru′mi-nāte, v., chew cud, meditate, -nation
rum′mage, v., look for

carefully

rū'mŏr, n., hearsay

rump, n., hind part, buttocks

rum'ple, v., crush, wrinkle

run, v., move at fast pace, flee, become political candidate, operate

rung, n., step of ladder, degree

run'nêr-up', n., next to winner

runt, n., animal below usual size

rup'ture, n., v., break, split, hernia

rū'răl, a., relating to the country

rūse, n., trick, subterfuge

rush, v., move speedily, attack

rus'sĕt, a., reddish brown

rust, n., russet oxidation, -y

rus'tic, a., of country, rural, plain, -ity

rus'tle, n., soft, rubbing sound, -tling

rut, n., groove, routine, hollow in earth

rūth'lĕss, a., without mercy, cruel

rye, n., grain, type of bread

S

Sab'bàth, n., day of rest

sàb-bat'i-cál, a., bringing period of rest

sā'bĕr, n., sword

sā'ble, n., animal valued for fur

sab'ŏ-tāge' (tazh), n., willful destruction to hinder, -teur

sac'chá-rin (sak-ir-in), n., sugar substitute

sac'chá-rin (sak-ir-in), a., ingratiatingly agreeable

sa-chet' (shay), n., small perfumed bag

sack, n., v., paper or cloth bag, dismiss from job

sac'rá-ment, n., religious ceremony, -al

sā'crĕd, a., holy, worthy of veneration

sac'ri-fice, v., give up something valuable, incur loss, -ficial

sac'ri-lege (lij), n., destroying or not honoring something holy, -legious

sac'rō-sanct, a., holy, sacred, inviolable

sad, a., unhappy, downcast

sad'dle, n., leather seat for riding animals, burden

sād'ism (izm), n., pleasure from inflicting pain on another, -ist

sāfe, n., strong container for protecting possessions

sāfe, a., free from danger, -ty

sag, v., sink, droop

sā'gá, n., story

sá-gā'cious, a., wise, -city

sāil, n., v., cloth that catches

wind to propel ship, travel by water, glide

sāil'ŏr, n., seaman

sāint, n., holy person, angel, kind person, -ly

sāke, n., purpose, behalf

sá-lā'cious, a., lustful, lascivious

sal'àd, n., cold dish

sá-lā'mi, n., spiced delicatessen meat

sal'á-ry, n., money received for work done

sāle, n., exchange of something for money, offering of goods

sāles'tax, n., tax on purchase price of goods

sā'li-ĕnt, a., noticeable, main, prominent

sā'līne, a., containing salt

sá-lī'vá, n., liquid in mouth, -te

sal'lŏw, a., of a sickly yellow color, murky

sal'ly, n., witticism, quip

salm'ŏn (sam-in), n., game fish

sá-lon', n., large meeting room, beauty shop, exhibit gallery

sá-lōōn', n., place where whiskey and beer are sold and drunk

sält, n., sodium chloride used as seasoning, -y

sá-lū'bri-ous, a., healthful, beneficial

sá-lūte', v., n., greet, sign of recognition

sal'vàge, n., goods saved

---

sal·vā'tion, n., deliverance

salve (sav), n., v., healing ointment, soothe

sāme, a., alike, similar

sam'ple, n., v., copy, model, examine, try

san·ā·tō'ri·um, n., hospital, rest home

sanc'tion, v., agree to, allow, ratify

sanc'ti·mō'ny, n., insincere show of holiness, **-nious**

sanc'ti·ty, n., holiness, **-fy**

sanc'tū·ar'y, n., holy place, refuge

sand, n., fine bits of rock, **-y**

san'dal, n., type of footwear

sand'wich, n., meat, etc. between slices of bread

sāne, a., sensible

San'for·īzed, adj., made shrink-resistant (fabric)

sang-froid, n., coolness, aplomb, equanimity

san'guine (gwin), a., ruddy, cheerful, healthy, **-guinary**

san·i·tā'tion, n., cleanliness, **-ry**

san'i·ty, n., mental well-being, health of mind

sans, prep., without

sap, n., liquid from tree or plant, (coll.) fool

sap, v., destroy, weaken

sā'pi·ence, n., wisdom, **-ent**

sap'phīre (saf), n., precious blue stone

sa·ran', n., transparent vinyl wrapping

sär'casm (kazm), n., gibe, biting remark, **-castic**

sär'dine (deen), n., tiny fish

sär·don'ic, a., bitter, mocking

sā·rong', n., wrap-around garment

sar·sā·pa·ril'la (sas-pá-ril-la), n., soft drink

sär·tō'ri·al, a., relating to tailoring

sash, n., wide ribbon, window frame

sa·shāy', v., walk mincingly, glide

sas'sy, a., disrespectful, saucy

satch'el, n., carrying case

sat'el·līte, n., small body revolving around larger one, moon

sā'ti·āte (shi), v., satisfy, glut

sat'in·y, a., smooth, shiny

sat'īre, n., ridicule and sarcasm, **-irical**

sat·is·fac'tō·ry, a., meeting need of, adequate

sat'is·fy, v., please, fulfill wants, **-faction**

sat'ū·rāte, v., impregnate, soak, fill, **-ration**

sauce, n., food accompaniment

sau'cer, n., dish

sau'cy, a., flippant, sassy

sau'na, n., Finnish steam bath

saun'ter, v., walk casually, stroll

sau'sāge, n., chopped meat in thin casing

sau·tērne', n., semisweet white wine

sav'age, n., a., wild, uncivilized person, cruel, **-ry**

sāve, v., deliver from harm, rescue

sāv'ings, n., money accumulated over a period of time, bank deposit

sāv'ior (yòr), n., person who rescues

sa·voir-fāire' (savwär), understanding, tact

sā'vòr·y, a., pleasant to taste

sàw, n., edged tool for cutting

sàw'dust, n., tiny bits of wood

sax'ō·phōne, n., reed instrument

say, v., express in words

say'ing, n., wise statement, aphorism

scab, n., crust over wound, strike breaker

scā'brous, a., rough

scads, n., many

scaf'fold, n., temporary platform for workers, gallows

scäld, v., burn with boiling liquid or steam, scorch

scāle, n., machine for weighing, graded steps

scāle, v., climb, strip

scäl'löp, n., type of shellfish, decoration

scalp, n., head skin, trophy of victory

scalp, v., charge high price for tickets

scam'pêr, v., move hurriedly away

scan, v., examine lightly

scan'dal, n., result of disgraceful actions, **-ize**, **-ous**

scant, a., not enough, lacking, **-y**

scant'ling, n., small quantity

scāpe'gōat, n., one taking blame due others

scär, n., mark left by healed wound

scärce, a., rare, unusual

scärce'ly, adv., not quite, hardly

scär'ci-ty, n., shortage

scäre, v., frighten, intimidate

scäre'crōw, n., figure to frighten birds from crops

scär'let, a., brilliant red color

scär'let fē'vêr, n., disease

scāthe', v., harm, injure

scāth'ing, a., bitterly severe

scát'têr, v., spread about loosely, strew, disperse

scav'en-gêr, n., animal living on decayed matter, user of refuse

scē-nā'ri-ō (si), n., outline or synopsis

scēne (seen), n., place where something happens, play division, view

scēn'êr-y, n., visual surroundings

scent, n., smell

sched'ule (sked-jil), n., routine, list, inventory, timed plan

schēme, n., plan, proposal, dishonest purpose

schēm'ing, a., given to plotting dishonestly

schism, n., division, **-atic**

schiz-ö-ö-phrē'ni-á (skitz-u-free-nee-eh), n., mental disorder, **-c**

schlē-miel' (shli-meel), n., fool, dumb person

schol'ár, n., educated person, **-ly**

schol'ar-ship, n., aid to help student continue study

schö-las'tic, a., relating to schools, **-ism**

schööl, n., place for learning, group of fish, **-ing**

sci'ence, n., system of knowledge

sci'en-tist, n., one doing research in facts, **-tific**

sci'on (sy), n., offspring, bud from plant

scis'sörs (siz-zêrs), n.,

two-handled cutting tool

scoff-law, n., one who disregards law

scōld, v., criticize, censure

scōōp, v., dig out, take

scōōt'êr, n., small two-wheeled vehicle

scōpe, n., area covered, distance, understanding

scôrch, v., burn, singe

scôre, n., result, mark, cut

scôrn, v., n., ignore, contempt, **-ful**

scoun'drêl, n., bad person, villain

scour', v., clean by hard rubbing, search for

scoûrge (skûrj), n., v., punishment, whip

scout, n., one sent to reconnoiter

scowl, n., threatening look

scram, inter., go away, scat

scram'ble, v., mix up, climb

scrap, n., small piece, fight

scrāpe, v., rub over roughly, collect with difficulty

scratch, v., cut surface, remove horse from race, **-y**

scrawl, v., write aimlessly

scrēam, n., sudden shrill cry

scrēen, n., protection, partition, coarse mesh, surface for movie showing, examine, hide, shelter, sift

screw, v., twist, squeeze, fasten

scrib'ble, v., write illegibly

scrībe, n., writer

scrimp, v., be frugal, save, **-y**

script, n., written alphabet figures, short for manuscript

scrip'ture, n., written word of God

scrounge (coll.), v., beg and pilfer

scrub, v., wash vigorously, eliminate

scrū'ple, n., moral guide, qualm

scrū'pū-lous, a., honorable, upright in actions

scru'ti-ny, n., close examination, **-nize**

scuff, v., scrape feet in walking, scrape

scuf'fle, n., fight, altercation

sculp'tör, n., artist who carves figures

sculp'ture, n., carved figures

scum, n., refuse, rabble

scŭr'ril-ous, *a.*, vulgar, -lity

scŭr'vy, *n.*, disease

scŭt'tle, *v.*, sink ship, jettison

scythe (syth) *n.*, mowing implement

sēa, *n.*, large area of water, ocean, vastness

sēal, *n.*, design used as mark of authority, mammal with flippers

sēal, *v.*, agree, conclude, close, mark as authoritative

sēa li'ŏn, *n.*, type of Pacific seal

sēa'măn, *n.*, sailor, mariner

sēam'strĕss, *n.*, woman who sews

sēam'y, *a.*, unpleasant, sordid

sē'ănce (say-ähns) *n.*, meeting of spiritualists

sear, *v.*, burn, parch

search, *v.*, look for, seek

sēarch'ing, *a.*, closely examining, penetrating, exploring

sēarch'light, *n.*, device for radiating a beam of light

sēa'sŏn, *n.*, spring, summer, autumn, or winter, special time

sēa'sŏn, *v.*, flavor, improve, mature, -ing

sēat, *n.*, place to sit, person's rear where he sits, buttocks

sēat belt, *n.*, straps for securing passengers in vehicle

sēa'wŏr-thy, *a.*, capable of going to sea

sē-cēde' (seed), *v.*, withdraw from, -cession

sē-clūde, *v.*, hide, stay away from, -clusion

sec'ŏnd, *a.*, immediately after first, -ary

sec'ond, *n.*, 1/60 of a minute, assistant

sec'ŏndăry-schōōl, *n.*, high school

sec'ŏnd hand', *a.*, used, not original, borrowed

sē'crĕt, *a.*, hidden, covert, mysterious, -ive

sē'crĕt, *n.*, something no one else knows, mystery

sec'rē-tăr-y, *n.*, governmental department head, one who types letters taken in shorthand and assists executive, -ial

sē-crēte', *v.*, hide, put away, -cretion

sē'crĕ-tive, *a.*, kept from others, hidden

sect, *n.*, group believing alike

sec'tion, *n.*, part of, -al

sec'ū-lăr, *a.*, mundane, non-spiritual, -ism

sē-cūre', *a.*, safe, tight, sure of self, -curity

sē-dan', *n.*, four-doored auto

sē-dāte', *a.*, quiet, calm, placid

sed'ă-tive, *n.*, drug that induces sleep or calmness

sed'ĕn-târ-y, *a.*, sitting

sed'i-mĕnt, *n.*, matter that settles to bottom of liquid

sē-dūce', *v.*, entice, -duction

sē-dū'lous, *a.*, taking pains at work, steadfast, -lity

sēe, *v.*, observe with eyes, examine, understand, -ing

sēe, *n.*, official jurisdiction of bishop, Rome

sēed, *n.*, plant part that grows other plants, origin, offspring

sēed'y, *a.*, poor looking, unattractive, shabby

sēek, *v.*, look for, search

sēem, *v.*, appear to be -ing

sēep, *v.*, ooze through

sē'ēr, *n.*, one who can tell future, prognosticate

sēethe, *v.*, boil, foam over

seg'mĕnt, *n.*, section, portion, -ation

seg'rē-gāte, *v.*, set apart, -gation

seīs-mol'ŏgy (syz), *n.*, study of earthquakes

sēize, *v.*, catch hold of, capture, take advantage of, -seizure

sel'dŏm, *adv.*, not often, -ly

sē-lect', *v.*, *a.*, choose, best of

sē-lect-ēe', *n.*, male drafted to military service

sē-lec'tion, *n.*, something picked, -tive

se'le-nog'ra-phy, *n.*, study of the moon

self, *n.*, one's own person, ego

self'ish, *a.*, interested only in one's own wishes

self-pŏs-sessed', *a.*, having control of one's emotions

self'sāme, *a.*, same as

self-suf-fi'cient, *a.*, having confidence in one's own powers, viable

sell, v., give something for payment received

sell'-out, n., everything already purchased

se-man'tics, n., study of words and meanings

sem'blance, n., likeness of, resemblance

se-mes'ter, n., portion of school year

semi', (sem-ee) prefix, half, partly

sem-i-an'nu-al, a., twice a year, -ly

sem'i-när, n., class involving research or advanced study

sem'i-när-y, n., women's college, college for ministry students

Sen'ate, n., upper house of Congress, -ator

send, v., cause to go

se-nes'cent, a., aged, growing old

se'nile, a., being mentally weak in old age, -nility

sen'ior (yŭr), a., older, of greater age, in oldest school class, -ity

sen-sa'tion, n., perception, emotion, the senses, impression, -al

sense, n., touch, taste, hearing, sight, smell, understanding, feeling

sense'less, a., unintelligent, wanton

sen'si-ble, a., wise, sagacious

sen'si-tive, a., susceptible to, easily affected, responsive

sen'su-ous (shoo), a., relating to feelings, tactile, -al

sen'tence, n., judge's decision, complete thought in grammar

sen-ten'tious, a., wise in speech, sounding like an authority

sen'tient, a., relating to sensation

sen'ti-ment, n., feelings, emotions, -al

sen'ti-nel, n., watchman, guard, vigilante

sen'try, n., guard

sep'a-räte, v., divide, take apart, part, -ration

sep'a-räte, a., apart, unrelated, distinctive

sep'tic, a., diseased, infected, decomposed

sep'ul-chër (kër), n., burial vault, -chral

se'quel (kw), n., continuation, effect

se'quence (kw), n., one thing following another, order, -quential

se'quin (kw), n., bright dress ornament

ser-e-näde', n., wooing music

ser'en-dip'i-ty, n., accidental desirable discovery

se-rēne', a., calm, quiet, august, tranquil, -renity

serf, n., slave, member of servile class

ser'geant (sär'gent), n., non-commissioned officer

se'ri-al, n., continued installment

se'ries, n., number of things, one after another

se'ri-ous, a., in earnest, important, -ly

ser'mon, n., religious lecture, homily

ser'pent, n., snake, malicious person

se'rum, n., fluid injected to prevent disease

serv'ant, n., person hired to wait on others

serve, v., give assistance, spend time, start tennis volley

serv'ice, n., use, benefit, ceremony

serv'ice-man, n., repairman, member of armed forces

ser'vile, a., similar to slaves, low, common, humble, -vitude

ses-qui-cen-ten'ni-al, n., 150th anniversary

ses'sion, n., meeting of a group, term

set, v., fix, place, determine, hatch, put, bear fruit

set, n., collection, firmness, position, part of tennis game, stage scenery

set'back, n., discouragement, reversal of progress, defeat

set'ter, n., large bird dog

set'tle, v., arrange, decide upon, make payment, move to a place, -ment

set'up, n., plan for, organization of

sev'en, n., cardinal number "7", -th

sev-en-teen', n., ten plus

seven, -th

sev'en-ty, n., ten times seven

sev'êr, a., v., cut, separate, divide

sev'êr-ål, a., more than one

sè-vēre', a., strict, grievous

sew (soh), v., unite with needle and thread, -ing

sew'åge (soo), n., waste matter

sew'êr (sōō), n., underground pipes for carrying off waste

sex, n., division into male or female, relating to reproductive organs, -ual

sex'y (coll.), a., sexually stimulating, erotic

shab'by, a., worn out, ragged

shack'le, v., n., tie together, fasten, manacle, fetter

shade, n., degree of color, device for keeping out sun

shad'ow, n., dark image caused by something intercepting light rays, ghost, follower

shake, v., tremble, vibrate, quaver

shake'down, n., getting money by threat

shāk'y, a., tottering, feeble, undependable

shal'low, a., not deep

sham'bles, n., scene of destruction, wreckage

shame, n., feeling of guilt, disgraceful act, -ful

sham-pōō', n., hair cleaner

shape, n., v., figure, outline, form, -ly

share, v., n., divide, section, portion

share'crop-pêr, n., farmer who works for a share of the crop

shärk, n., predatory fish, skilled player

shärp, a., able to cut easily, smart, pointed, biting, -en

shat'têr, v., break, ruin, destroy

shāve, v., pare away, remove hair, plane, -d

shē, n., pro., woman, girl, 3rd person singular

shēar, v., cut with sharp object, gather wool

shēars, n., large scissors

shēath, n., close fitting case

shed, v., allow to fall, drop, shake

shed, n., small, narrow storage building

shēep, n., wool producing mammal

shēep'ish, a., shy, timid

shēer, a., extremely thin, utter, pure

shēet, n., bed covering, broad piece of thin material

shēik, n., Arab leader

shelf, n., wood, metal support for storing items

shell, n., v., covering, thin racing boat, remove from shell

shel'têr, n., v., protection against nature's forces, sanctuary, protect

shelve, v., put on shelf, put away, lay aside

shē-nan'i-gån, n., trickery, mischief

shep'hêrd (êrd), n., tender of sheep, -ess

sher'iff, n., law enforcement officer

sher'ry, n., wine

shield, n., protection, screen, guard

shift, v., alter, change, move

shift'less, a., lazy, unambitious

shift'y, a., dishonest, untrustworthy

shim'mêr, v., shine in trembling way

shin, n., front of lower leg

shin'dig, n., party, fete

shine, v., send forth light, perform well

shin'êr, n., black eye, small silver fish

shin'ing, a., bright, -y

ship, n., vessel large enough for sea travel

ship, v., send by freight, board ship, -ment

ship'shape, a., in good order

ship'wright (ryt), n., ship repairman

ship'yärd, n., place for repairing or building ships

shirk, v., evade, try to avoid, -er

shirt, n., garment

shiv'êr, v., n., shake

shock, n., v., impact, violent damage, upset emotionally

shock ther'a-py, n., electrical shock treatment of mental illness

shoe (shoo), n., foot covering, protective plate

shoot, v., fire a gun or bow,

move swiftly and suddenly

shop, v., look for articles in stores

shop, n., store for selling or repairing things, mart

shop'lift, steal from store, **-er**

shôre, n., v., land touching water: river, sea, etc., support

shôrt, a., not tall, small, not long, lacking, rude, **-age**

shôrt-chánge', v., cheat by not returning enough money

shôrt'cóming, n., failure, deficiency, defect

shôrt'én-ing, n., grease for baking or frying

shôrt'hand, n., speed writing using lines and curves

shôrt'hand'éd, a., lacking adequate number of people

shôrt'ly, adv., soon, anon

shot, n., lead pellets, missile, act of shooting, dose, attempt, alcoholic drink

shoûl'dér, n., v., place where arm is attached to body, accept responsibility

shout, n., loud call, yell

shöve, n., v., push forward

shöv'él, n., tool for excavating

show, n., exhibition, act, presentation

show, v., allow to be seen, indicate, explain, be third in horse race, guide

show'down, n., conclusion, revelation, disclosure of facts, type of card game

show'ér, n., slight rain, bath, party for special occasion

show'-off, n., person who goes out of way to attract attention

shrap'nél, n., contents of exploding shell

shrew, n., argumentative woman, nocturnal mammal

shrewd, a., clever, wily

shriék, n., high, piercing yell

shrill, a., high, piercing in tone

shrimp, n., crustacean, tiny person

shrîne, n., holy place, sanctuary

shrink, v., avoid, pull back, draw up, become small, **-age**

shriv'él, v., dry up, wither

shroud, n., burial clothes, screen

shrub, n., small bush, **-bery**

shrug, v., shake shoulders

shuck, v., remove inner contents from, shell, husk

shud'dér, v., shake with fright, shiver

shuf'fle, v., drag feet, mix

shun, v., ignore, avoid

shunt, v., rid oneself of, put aside, shift

shut, v., close, lock up

shut'down, n., closing

shut'-in, n., sick person confined indoors, invalid

shut'out, n., game with one scoreless team

shut'tér, n., device for keeping out light

shy, a., uneasy in a crowd, bashful, diffident

shy, v., draw back from

shy'stér, n., unethical lawyer

sib'ling, n., brother or sister

sick, a., ailing, ill, not well, tired, upset, **-ness**

sîde, n., boundary surrounding somehing, surface of, right or left part, (act of) being for or against

sî-dē're-ál, a., relating to stars, astral

sîd'ing, n., railroad track off of main route, shingles

siège, n., placing under continuing attack

sieve (siv), n., kitchen utensil with many holes, strainer

sigh (sy), v., long breath expressing emotion, grieve, yearn

sight (syt), n., ability to see, view, look

sight'sëe-ing, n., act of viewing places of interest

sign (syn), n., v., advertising board or plaque, signal, portent, presage, mark, write name

sig'nál, n., sign, notice, indication, **-ing**

sig'na-ture, n., written name of person, part of a book

sig-nif'i-cánt, a., having meaning, **-cance**

sig'ni-fy, v., intend, mean, show

sî'lénce, n., quiet, absence of noise, **-lent**

sil-hoū-ette' (oo-et), n.,

outline of an object seen against the light

silk, *n.,* product of silkworm

sil'ly, *a.,* foolish, giddy

sil'vêr, *n.,* metallic element, **-y**

sil'vêr-wâre, *n.,* household articles made of silver or other metal

sim'i-ăn, *a.,* apelike

sim'i-lâr, *a.,* resembling, like, **-ity**

sim'mêr, *v.,* boil gently or slowly

sim'ö-ny, *n.,* buying or selling church property

sim'ple, *a.,* easy to know, unaffected, not complex, honest, **-ton**

sim'pli-fy, *v.,* make easy

sim'ply, *adv.,* just, merely, without show

sim'ū-lāte, *v.,* copy, be like, pretend, **-lation**

sī-mul-tā'nē-ous, *a.,* occurring at same time

sin, *v.,* break moral laws, **-ful**

since, *prep.,* until present, for some time past

sin-cēre', *a.,* honest, genuine, real, **-cerely**

sin'ew-y, *a.,* tough, strong, muscular

sing, *v.,* produce music with voice, **-er**

sin'gle (gil), *a.,* one, one only, unmarried, not married

sin'gū-lâr, *a.,* unique

sin'is-têr, *a.,* dangerous, threatening

sink, *v.,* fall, drop down or beneath, grow weak

sink'êr, *n.,* lead weight, (coll.) doughnut

sī'nus, *a.,* opening in skull above nose

sip, *v.,* drink in little bits, taste

sîr, *n.,* title of respect, address to a man

sī'rĕn, *n.,* female enticer, warning signal or whistle

sîr'loin, *n.,* good cut of meat, from loin

sis'sy, *n.,* timid or cowardly person

sis'têr, *n.,* female offspring of same parents

sis'têr-in-lâw, *n.,* wife of husband's sister, brother's wife

sit, *v.,* seat oneself, rest in a

spot, fit, stay with

sīte, *n.,* foundation place

sit'ū-āt-ĕd, *a.,* located in place, working

sit-ū-ā'tion, *n.,* job, place, condition, happening

six, *n.,* cardinal 6, **-th**

six-tēen', *n.,* ten plus six, **-th**

six'ty, *n.,* ten times six

sīze, *n.,* capacity, amount of space covered, length, width, depth

skāte, *n.,* shoe attachment for rolling or gliding, fish

skel'ē-ton, *n.,* bone structure of body

skep'tic, *n.,* one who doubts, **-al**

sketch, *n.,* informal drawing, rough draft

ski (skee) *n.,* wooden slat for gliding on snow or water, **-ing**

skid, *v.,* slide, slip

skill, *n.,* ability to do something, **-ful**

skin, *n.,* outer covering, **-ny**

skip, *v.,* omit, jump from leg to leg

skip'pêr, *n.,* ship captain, leader

skîr'mish, *n.,* slight battle

skîrt, *n.,* woman's dress from waist down, (coll.) woman or girl

skit, *n.,* brief comic sketch

skull, *n.,* bony structure of head

skunk, *n.,* small mammal, obnoxious person

sky, *n.,* heavens, area overhead

sky'-dīve, *v.,* jumping from plane with delayed opening of parachute

sky'jack, *v.,* illegal seizure of airplane

slack, *a.,* slow, loose, **-en**

slack'êr, *n.,* lazy person

slāke, *v.,* satisfy, quench

slam, *v.,* throw down, close noisily

slan'dêr, *n.,* false or malicious statement about someone, **-ous**

slang, *n.,* argot, jargon

slant, *v.,* lean, slope

slap, *v., n.,* hit with open hand, insult

slap'stick, *n.,* comedy attained by action

slash, *v.,* cut, beat

slăugh'tĕr, *n.*, killing

slāve, *n.*, person who is property of and subject to another, **-ry**

slay, *v.*, kill, murder

sled, *n.*, vehicle with runners, **-ding**

slēek, *a.*, smooth, nice looking

slēep, *n., v.*, rest without conscious activity, go in that state, **-y**

slēeve, *n.*, part of garment covering arm

sleigh (slay), *n.*, passenger vehicle with runners

slen'dĕr, *a.*, small in width, not thick, **-ize**

slēuth, *n.*, detective

slīce, *n.*, cut thin piece from, hit golf ball at angle

slīde, *v.*, glide smoothly on surface

slīght (slyt), *a.*, tiny, unimportant

slim, *a.*, thin, small, scanty

slink, *v.*, move quietly or in stealthy manner

slip, *v.*, lose footing, go easily, weaken

slip, *n.*, mistake, woman's undergarment, ship's docking spaces

slip'pĕr, *n.*, low-cut shoe

slip'pĕr-y, *a.*, easy to slip on, dishonest

slip'shod, *a.*, careless, slovenly

slob, *n.*, offensive person

slō'găn, *n.*, motto

slōop, *n.*, type of sailboat

slop, *n.*, dirt, garbage

slōpe, *n., v.*, upward or downward incline, slant

slot, *n.*, slit, notch

slouch, *v.*, droop

slŏv'ĕn-ly, *a.*, dirty, untidy

slōw, *a.*, gradual, not fast, not active, uninteresting

slug, *v.*, hit hard

slug, *n.*, inactive animal without shell, coin imitation, printer's metal, bullet

slug'gish, *a.*, inactive, moving slowly, indolent, torpid

slum, *n.*, poor, overcrowded, rundown section of city

slum'bĕr, *v.*, sleep, doze

slump, *n., v.*, fall, droop, economic decline

slŭr, *n.*, insult, connected notes in music

slush, *n.*, dirty melting snow

slut, *n.*, slattern

sly, *a.*, secret, underhanded, tricky, **-ly**

smack, *n.*, loud kiss, sailboat, slap

smăll, *a.*, little, tiny, limited in size

smăll fry, *n.*, little children

smăll'pox, *n.*, febrile virus disease

smärt, *v.*, pain, **-ing**

smärt, *a.*, keen, clever, severe, painful, attractive, **-ly**

smash, *v.*, break into pieces, batter, hit

smat'tĕr-ing, *n.*, small amount

smēar, *v.*, rub, spread

smell, *v.*, detect by use of nose, give off odor

smī'lax, *n.*, vine

smīle, *n.*, pleased facial look

smock, *n.*, loose garment

smog, *n.*, fog, smoke mixture

smōke, *n.*, mixture given off by something burning, smudge

smōk'ĕr, *n.*, informal social gathering for men

smōl'dĕr, *v.*, burn without flame, **-ing**

smōŏch, *v.*, kissing or petting

smōŏth, *a.*, easy, calm, even surfaced, level, polished in manner **-ly**

smŏr'găs-bôrd, *n.*, Swedish buffet meal

smŏth'ĕr, *v.*, suffocate, asphyxiate

smug, *a.*, highly self-satisfied, **-ly**

smug'gle, *v.*, import or export illegally and secretly

smut'ty, *a.*, dirty, indecent

snack, *n.*, light meal

sna'fū (slang), *a.*, completely confused (situation normal all fouled up)

snag, *v.*, catch, damage, tear

snāke, *n.*, reptile

snap, *v.*, answer angrily, bite at, make sharp sound, **-py**

snāre, *n.*, noose type trap, lure, type of drum

snärl, *v.*, tangle, mix-up

snärl, *n.*, growl, angry retort

snēak, *v.*, move in quiet, secret way

neak, n., dishonest person, cheat, **-y**

neer, v., n., express contempt, look of contempt

neeze, n., exhale, breath in sudden explosive action of nose and mouth

nif'fle, v., sniff often to clear nose due to crying or head cold

nitch, v., steal, inform

nob, n., one judging by rank and wealth rather than merit, **-bery**, **-bish**

nŏŏp, v., pry or peer into, meddle

nŏŏze, n., short sleep, doze

nôr'kél, n., air obtaining mechanism for a submerged submarine or diver

snōw, n., thin, frozen crystals of rain, **-y**

snōw'mō-bile, n., vehicle for traveling on snow

snuff, n., v., tobacco for inhaling, put out

snug, a., cozy, comfortable, trim, neat

snug'gle, v., cling closely, cuddle

sō, adv., in this manner, to a certain degree, very much

sōak, v., wet completely, permeate

sōap, n., cleansing agent, **-y**

sōar, v., fly upward, glide

sob, v., cry in gasps

sō'bêr, a., abstemious, temperate, **-briety**

soc'cêr (sok-er-), n., team football game

sō'cia-ble (shi-bil), a., friendly, enjoying other's company

sō'cial, a., relating to individuals or groups of people

sō'cial-ism, n., Marxist economic system, **-ize**

sō-ci'e-ty, n., group of people living together, **-tal**

sō-ci-ol'ō-gy (shi), n., study of human groups

sock, n., v., foot covering, hit

sod, n., grass covered earth

sō'dà, n., alkali, soft drink

sō'di-um, n., metallic element

sod'ŏm-y, n., sexual relations not widely accepted

sō'fà, n., upholstered couch

sôft, a., giving way easily to touch, gentle, smooth, easily influenced

sôft'bâll, n., type of baseball

sôft drink, n., non-alcoholic effervescent drink

sôft'-sōap', v., praise, flatter

sôft'ware, n., programs, charts, etc., for computer

sog'gy, a., damp and heavy

soil, n., dirt, earth

soil, v., make, dirty

sō-joûrn (jern), v., stay for short time

sol'áce, v., comfort, console

sōlär, a., relating to sun

sol'dêr (so-dèr), n., alloy used to join metal

sōl'dièr (jèr), n., combatant

sōle, n., foot or shoe bottom, flat fish

sōle, a., single, one, only, **-ly**

sol'émn (sol-um), a., holy, serious, **-ity**

sō-lic'it, v., seek, ask for, request, **-ation**

sō-lic'i-tous, a., apprehensive, eager, **-tude**

sol'id, a., hard, united, smart, having three dimensions, **-ity**

sō-lil'ō-quy (kwēe), n., dramatic monologue, **-quize**

sol'i-tāire, n., one-person card game, single stoned ring

sol'i-târ-y, a., single, alone

sol'i-tūde, n., seclusion, isolation

sō'lō, n., performance by one, **-ist**

sol'ū-ble, a., able to be solved or dissolved

sō-lū'tion, n., answer to problem, chemical combination

solve, v., find answer

sō-mat'ic, a., relating to the body

som'bêr, a., serious, melancholy

sōme, a., unknown, unspecified; approximate, remarkable

sōme'bod'y, pro., a person

sōme'how, adv., in an uncertain manner

sōme'ōne, n., a person

sōme'thing, n., uncertain thing

sōme'time, adv., uncertain time

sōme′tīmes, *adv.,* occasionally

sōme′what, *adv.,* to a certain degree, slightly

sōme′where (wayr) *adv.,* in some place

som-nam′bū-lism, *n.,* sleep walking, **-list**

sŏn, *n.,* male offspring

sō′nánce, *n.,* sound, **-nant**

sō-nā′tä, *n.,* piece of music

sŏng, *n.,* tune, musical piece including words

sŏn′ic, *a.,* pertaining to sound, capable of perception by the human ear

sŏn′-in-lȃw, *n.,* daughter's husband

sŏn′nĕt, *n.,* 14 line poem, with varying rhymes

sö-nō′rous, *a.,* resonant, **-ly**

sööthe, *v.,* comfort, calm, pacify, humor

sŏph′ism, *n.,* argument, intended to deceive, **-istry**

sō-phĭs′tĭ-cāt-ĕd, *a.,* worldly-wise, complex, **-ion**

sŏph′ö-mȯre, *n.,* second year student, **-moric**

sö-prä′nō, *n.,* highest singing voice

sŏr′cēr-y, *n.,* magic, **-er**

sŏr′did, *a.,* common, squalid, dirty, **-ly**

sōre, *a.,* painful, distressing, infection, affliction

sö-rŏr′i-ty, *n.,* girl's club

sŏr′rĕl, *n.,* reddish-brown horse

sŏr′rōw, *n.,* sadness, unhappiness, grief, **-ful**

sŏr′ry, *v.,* mournful, sad

sȯrt, *n.,* kind, type, arrange, classify

sōul, *n.,* person's inner spiritual self, **-ful**

sound, *n.,* that which is heard, **-less**

sound, *a.,* orthodox, valid

sound track, *n.,* sound on movie film

sōup, *n.,* liquid food

sour, *a.,* bitter in taste, unpleasant, bad tempered

sȯurce, *n.,* start, origin

souse, *v., n.,* soak, drunkard, sot, **-d**

south, *n.,* opposite of north, to right facing rising sun, **-ern**

south′pȧw, *n.,* left-handed person

soū-vē-nir′ (nēer) *n.,* keepsake, memento

sou′-west′ér, *n.,* rain hat

sov′ér-eign (sov-rin) *n.,* person supreme in power, king or queen, **-ty**

sō-vī′ĕt, *n.,* elected communist official

spāce, *n.,* unlimited area expanding in all directions, room, empty place

spāce′ ship′, *n.,* vehicle for travel outside earth's atmosphere

spāce′ walk′, *v.,* activity outside of spacecraft

spā′cious, *a.,* roomy, **-ly**

spāde, *n.,* digging tool, card suit

spä-ghĕt′ti, *n.,* long noodles

span, *n.,* hand measurement, space of time, measurement of space

Span-glish, *n.,* Spanish combined with English

span′iel (yil), *n.,* type of dog, servile person

spank, *v.,* hit with open hand, **-ing**

spär, *n.,* thick pole

spar, *v.,* box with fists

spāre, *v., a.,* have mercy for, save, held in reserve, extra, not in use

spär′ing, *a.,* meager, bare

spärk, *n., v.,* small particle of fire, inspire

spär′kle, *v.,* glisten, effervesce

spärse, *a.,* thinly spread out, not thickly grown or settled

spasm, *n.,* sudden involuntary muscular contraction, **-odic**

spā′tial, *a.,* relating to space

spat′tér, *v.,* splash, defame

spȧwn, *v.,* produce eggs, give birth, generate

spēak, *v.,* say, talk, **-ing, -er**

spēar, *n.,* weapon with sharply pointed head

spē′ar-head′, *v.,* thrust forward in attack, leading element

spe′cial, *a.,* noteworthy, particular, unusual, **-ist**

spec′-ial-īze, *v.,* study or practice particular subject, **-ty**

spē′cie (she), *n.,* money in

coin

spē'ciēs (shēs), n., group having common appearance, etc.

spe·cif'ic, a., accurate, precise

spec·i·fi·cā'tion, n., description

spec'i·fy, v., describe, name explicitly

spec'i·men, n., sample, lot, sort

spē'cious, a., seemingly so, sophistical

speck, n., v., bit, spot, particle

spec'tā·cle, n., noteworthy exhibition

spec'tā·cles, n., eye glasses

spec·tac'ū·lär, a., dramatic, thrilling

spec'tā·tor, n., one who watches, onlooker

spec'trum, n., band of colors

spec'ū·lāte, v., guess, thing, lation

spec'ū·lā·tör, n., gambler

spēech, n., talk, -less

spēed, n., quick movement, -y

spēed·om'é·têr, n., device showing rate of speed

spēed'-up, n., quickening movement

spell, v., repeat letters of word in order, -er

spell, n., magic, charm, fascination, incantation

spend, v., give money for, wear out, time

spêr·ma·tö·zō'á, n., male reproductive cells

sphēre (sfeer), n., globe, solid ball, province

spīce, n., zest, seasoning, perfume

spīc'y, a., containing seasoning, sexy

spī'dêr, n., insect, -y

spiēl, n., speech, talk

spīke, v., add alcoholic beverage, pierce

spīke, n., large nail, plant stalk

spill, v., drop, flow, fall

spin, v., make into thread, twirl around, -ning

spin'ách, n., leafy vegetable

spin'dly, a., thin and long

spīne, n., backbone

spin'ét, n., compact upright piano

spin'off, n., corporate redistribution of stock

spī'rál, a., like coil or curve

spīre, n., pointed top part of steeple

spir'it, n., soul, ghost, frame of mind, intangible self in man, courage, liveliness, distillate, alcoholic drink, -ual

spir·it·ū·ál·ism, n., contact by living people with dead

spit, n., v., pointed stick, force saliva from mouth

spit'fīre, n., hot-tempered person

splash, v., scatter liquid over, -ing

splash'down, n., ocean landing of spacecraft

splen'did, a., colorful, glorious, wonderful, -dor

splīce, v., join together, marry

splin'têr, n., n., break into pieces, small piece

split, v., divide, cut apart

splûrge, v., spend excessively, show off

spoil, v., become rotten, damage, -ed

spōke, n., bar to center of wheel, rung of a ladder

spōkes'mán, n., one who talks for others

spönge, n., skeleton of sea animal used for absorbing liquids, absorbent material

spon'sör, v., underwrite success of, promote

spon·tā'nē·ous, a., occurring naturally or impulsively

spööf, v., deceive, hoax

spöök, n., ghost, specter

spööl, n., reel

spöön, n., eating utensil, fishing lure

spô·rad'ic, a., happening at scattered intervals, -ally

spört, n., athletic game, fun, frolic, -ing

spot, n., mark, small bit of, fault

spot, v., find, locate, stain

spot'ty, a., irregular, unusual, uneven

spouse, n., husband or wife

spout, n., v., tube for pouring liquid out, pour out

sprāin, v., twist or wrench

spray, n., liquid in fine drops, liquid mist

spread, *v., n.*, extend over large area, stretch apart, food display, bed covering

spright'ly, *a.*, very active, bright, lively, spirited

spring, *n.*, season of year, water coming from earth, elastic device, leap

spring, *v.*, jump up, grow up

spring fē'vêr, *n.*, restlessness around springtime

sprin'kle, *v.*, scatter in drops

sprint, *n., v.*, race, run fast

sprout, *v.*, start growing, young plant

sprûce, *n.*, evergreen tree

spry, *a.*, brisk, agile

spu-mo'ni, *n.*, Italian ice cream

spunk, *n.*, courage, mettle

spûr, *v., n.*, urge on, metal attachment for horseman's heel, projecting mountain range, extension

spū'ri-ous, *a.*, false, counterfeit

spûrn, *v.*, ignore scornfully, refuse, trample

spûrt, *v., n.*, gush outward, sudden show of energy or liquid

sput'nik, *n.*, Russian man-made satellite

spy, *v., n.*, catch sight of, gather secret information, secret agent

squâb'ble, *v.*, argue noisily, wrangle

squâd, *n.*, small group of soldiers, policemen, etc.

squâd' cär, *n.*, police car

squâd'rŏn, *n.*, naval or military unit

squäl'id, *a.*, miserable, dirty, sordid

squâll, *n.*, sudden wind gust, raucous cry, scream

squâl'ôr, *n.*, dirt, filth

squän'dêr, *v.*, spend wastefully, dissipate

squâre, *n., a.*, figure with four equal sides, open section in city, even, honest

squâre dē al', *n.*, fair transaction

squâsh, *n.*, edible gourd, tennis type game

squâsh, *v.*, crush, silence

squât, *v., a.*, sit in crouch, low and wide

squâw, *n.*, Indian woman

squâwk, *v.*, complain, make harsh sound

squê'al, *n.*, shrill cry

squê am'ish, *a.*, made sick easily, queasy

squêeze, *v.*, press firmly

squelch, *v.*, suppress

squint, *v.*, strain eyes

squîr'rêl, *n.*, rodent

stab, *v.*, wound with something pointed, effort, try

stā'ble, *n.*, place where domestic animals are housed

stā'ble, *a.*, firm, mature, secure, **-bility**

stack, *n., v.*, pile

stā'di-um, *n.*, open air arena

staff, *n.*, rod, body of workers

stag, *n.*, deer, party only for men

stāge, *n.*, platform, phase

stag'gêr, *v.*, move unsteadily, astonish, arrange alternately

stag'nânt, *a.*, motionless, inactive, dull, diseased, **-nate**

stāid, *a.*, dignified, settled, sedate

stāin, *n.*, spot, dye, stigma

stāir, *n.*, step of a series

stāke, *n.*, pointed rod, bet, prize

stà-lac'tîte, *n.*, lime deposit hanging down in cave

stā-lag'mîte, *n.*, lime deposit sticking up in cave

stāle, *a.*, no longer fresh, tedious from familiarity

stâlk, *n., v.*, plant stem, follow quietly

stâll, *n., v.*, division of stable, delay, hold up

stal'lion (yin), *n.*, male horse not castrated

stâl'wârt, *a.*, courageous, valiant, resolute, strong, **-ly**

stamp, *n.*, decorated insignia placed on letters for mailing, mark placed on something, sign

stamp, *v.*, lower foot forcefully, cut out, affix postage

stand, *n.*, position, platform, container of something

stand, *v.*, rise up, have rank, allow, be in vertical position, tolerate, bear

stan'dârd, *n.*, flag, accepted rule, pattern, norm

stand′ăr-dīze, v., make uniform, bring into conformity

stan′dărd tīme, n., regional mean solar time

stand′-by, n., substitute

stand′-in, n., substitute for actor

stand′ing, n., reputation, position, location

stand′still, n., complete halt, stop

stā′ple, n., a., main commodity, U-shaped wire fastener, main, regular

stär, n., heavenly body, five or six pointed object, outstanding performer

stärch, n., carbohydrate food matter, clothes stiffener

stāre, n., steady look, gaze

stärk, a., strong, complete, utter, fully, **-ly**

stär′lĕt, n., young actress

stär′ling, n., passerine bird

stärt, v., begin, move suddenly

stär′tle, v., surprise, frighten

stärve, v., suffer from hunger

stash (slang), v., hide

stāte, n.,v., condition of being, territory, political unit, express in words

stāte′ly, a., dignified, haughty

stāte′mĕnt, n., something said or written, account, summary proposition

stātes′măn, n., one wise and experienced in government

stat′ic, n., a., noise produced by electricity, unmoving

stā′tion, n., assigned place, designated building, position, posture

stā′tion-âr-y, a., fixed, still, unmoving

stā′tion-êr-y, n., writing materials

stā′tion wag′ŏn, n., type of automobile

stà-tis′tics, n., collection of numerical data, **-tical**

stat′ūe, n., carved figure

stat-ū-esque′ (esk), a., stately

stat′ūre, n., height

stā′tus, n., condition, position, stature

stā′tus quō (kwō), n., existing state of affairs

stat′ūte, n., law

stat′ū-tô-ry, n., relating to law, legal

stay, v., remain, be located, stop

stay, n., firm support, delay, time spent

stead (sted), n., place, position

stead′fast, a., permanent

stead′y, a., regular, uniform, **-ily**

steāk, n., cut of meat

stēal, v., take dishonestly from someone, move quietly

stealth (stelth), n., furtiveness, slyness, **-y**

stēam, n., water vapor

stēed, n., spirited horse

stēel, n., strong metal of iron and carbon

stēep, a., extreme in slope, high in cost

stēe′ple, n., high tower on building

stēe′ple-chāse, n., horse race over obstacles

stēer, n., ox, castrated bull

stēer, v., guide, direct

steīn, n., beer mug, quantity of beer that a stein holds

stem, n., branch, plant part, stalk, stock

stem, v., stop, originate

stench, n., unpleasant smell

sten′cil, n., pattern, printing process

stè-nog′ra-phêr, n., person who takes dictation, **-phy**

sten′ö-typ-y, n., shorthand using letters

sten-tô′ri-ăn, a., extremely loud

step, v., n., move one foot at a time, foot print, short distance, foot rest, level

step-, prefix, relates to relative gained by marriage, not birth. Example: **step′sŏn**

ste-rā-di-ăn (sr), n., solid angle (sphere)

ster-e-ö-phŏn′ic, a., two (or more) dimensional sound

ster′e-ö-type, n., something conforming to a fixed pattern

ster′ile, a., not able to reproduce, free from germs, barren, impotent, **-ilize**, **-ility**

stêr′ling, n., genuine silver

stêrn, a., strict, hard

stêr'tôr, n., act of snoring

steth'ŏ-scōpe, n., device to hear heart and lung sounds

stē'vĕ-dōre, n., laborer who loads and unloads ships

stew, n., v., meat and vegetables cooked together, worry, boil

stew'ârd, n., attendant, manager, **-ess**

stick, n., piece of wood

stick, v., push into, puncture, stay, attach, remain firm

stick'êr, n., thorn, burr, gummed label

stick'lêr, n., insistent person, poser

stick shift, n., type of manual transmission

stick'y, a., adhesive, muggy

stiff, a., firm, hard, **-en**

stī'fle, v., halt breathing, deter, discourage

stig'má, n., sign of disgrace, brand, stain, plant part

still, a., quiet, inactive, motionless

still, n., device for distilling liquids, distillery

still'bôrn, a., dead at birth, abortive

stilt'ĕd, a., artificially formal, stiff

stim'ū-lāte, v., rouse, excite, provoke, **-lant**

stim'ū-lus, n., something that causes or increases activity

sting, n., insect bite

stin'gy (jēe) a., miserly, niggardly

stink, n., offensive smell, stench

stint, n., limit, task

stī'pend, n., fixed payment, wage

stip'ū-lāte, v., specify, arrange for, **-lation**

stîr, v., move around, rouse, **-ring**

stitch, v., sew, do needlework

stock, n., goods on hand, descent, interest, company shares on financial market, type of flower

stock-āde', n., jail, strong enclosure

stock'brō-kêr, n., dealer in securities

stock'hōld-êr, n., owner of company shares

stock'ing, n., covering for foot or leg, sock

stock'pīle, v., buy and store for future use

stock'y, a., short and broad

stodg'y, a., heavy, dull, hidebound

stō'gy, n., cigar, brogan

stō'i-câl, a., not expressing feelings, **-ly**

stōke, v., feed fuel, stir up a fire

stōle, n., type of scarf, robe

stol'id, a., showing little or no emotion, impassive

stŏm'ách, n., v., digestive organ of body, tolerate, put up with

stōne, n., rock, gem

stōōge, n., comedian's assistant, straight man

stōōl, n., seat without back

stōōl' pi'geon, n., decoy, informer

stōōp, v., bend, lower oneself

stop, v., bring an end to, prevent, block, cease

stop'gap, n., temporary substitute, makeshift

stôr'áge, n., place for keeping goods

stôre, n., place for selling, supply, abundance

stôre, v., put away in reserve

stôre'kēep-êr, n., small retailer

stôrk, n., bird

stôrm, n., atmospheric disturbance of wind, rain, snow, lightning, thunder, etc., disturbance, **-y**

stô'ry, n., tale, account, rumor, horizontal building division

stout, a., fat, obstinate, sturdy

stout'-heärt-ĕd, a., brave

stōve, n., cooking or heating device

stōw, v., pack, confine

strá-bis'mic, a., cross-eyed

strad'dle, v., be astride

stráfe, v., attack with gunfire at close range

strag'gle, v., wander from group, rove, stray

strāight (strayt), a., having no curves, bends or curls, honest, proper, **-en**

strāight fôr'wârd, a., direct, honest

strāin, v., pull tight, filter, hurt, strive

strāin, n., race, tune, effort

strāit, n., narrow waterway

strand, n., v., thread, run aground

strange, a., unusual, not known, queer, **-r**

stran'gle, v., choke, stifle

strap, n., leather strip

strap'ping, a., strong

strat'á-gèm, n., trick, planned deception, artifice

strá-tē'gic, a., essential

strat'é-gy, n., plan

strat'ö-sphēre, n., upper atmosphere

strā'tum, n., layer, level

strāw, n., hollow grain stem, drinking device

strāw'ber-ry, n., edible red fruit

stray, v., wander, roam

strēak, n., stripe, trace

strēam, n., steady flow or series, small river

strēam'līned, a., built for greatest efficiency

strēet, n., paved road

strēet'cär, n., vehicle operating on rails

strength (strenth), n., power, force, **-en**

stren'ū-ous, a., requiring effort or energy

stress, n., worry, pressure, importance, accentuation

stretch, v., pull, reach

stretch'êr, n., device for carrying the injured or disabled

strew, v., scatter

strī'āt-èd, a., striped, grooved

strict, a., severe, exact, harsh

stric'ture, n., adverse criticism, closing

strīde, n., long step, advancement

strī'dent, a., noisy, harsh, grating

strīfe, n., conflict

strīke, v., hit, stop work to enforce demands, discover, injure, hit at, attack, **-r**

string, n., cord, row or series

string-bēan, n., green podded vegetable

strin'gènt, a., strict, severe, **-gency**

strip, v., undress, make bare, deprive, **-per**

strip, n., long narrow piece, airstrip

strīpe, n., long narrow mark

strīve, v., make great effort

strōke, n., blow, movement

strōll, v., walk casually, saunter

strông, a., powerful

strông'ärm, v., use physical force

struc'ture, n., building, construction, **-tural**

strug'gle, n., fight, great effort

strut, v., walk pompously, swagger

strych'nine, n., poisonous alkaloid

stub, n., remaining piece

stub, v., hit against an object

stub'börn, a., unwilling to change, obstinate

stuck'-up, a., snobbish, affected

stud, n., breeding horse, buttonlike ornament, building support

stū'dent, n., one who studies, scholar

stu'di-ō, n., workshop for artists, performers, etc.

stū'di-ous, a., fond of or engaged in study

stud'y, n., learning facts and ideas, examination, room for reading, writing, etc.

stuff, n., raw material, goods, foolishness

stuff, v., fill, pack, load

stuff'y, a., poorly ventilated, old fashioned, dull

stul'ti-fy, v., appear foolish, useless, **-fication**

stum'ble, v., trip, move unsteadily

stump, n., v., remaining part, repair, tour making speeches, puzzle

stun, v., make unconscious, surprise, shock, **-ned**

stun'ning, a., exceedingly attractive, striking, surprising

stunt, n., v., hinder growth, daring act

stū'pè-fy, v., amaze, make senseless, **-faction**

stū-pen'dous, a., immense, overwhelming, prodigious

stū'pid, a., dull, lacking intelligence, **-ity**

stū'pör, n., loss of senses, lethargy

stûr'dy, a., strong, solid, **-diness**

stut'têr, v., speak haltingly,

stammer, **-ing**

sty, *n.*, animal enclosure, filthy place, eyelid swelling

style, *n.*, manner or distinction of dress, expression, art, etc., design, manner, distinction, type

styl′ish, *a.*, fashionable, chic, smart

sty′mie, *v.*, block, check

suàve, *a.*, smoothly gracious, urbane

sub-, *prefix*, meaning under or below, a division of, lower than. *Example:*
sub-ăl′tĕrn, *a.*, lower in rank, **sub-branch′**, *n.*, branch division,
sub-con′scious, *a.*, below conscious level,
sub-di-vīde′, *v.*, separate into parts

sub-dūe′, *v.*, vanquish, curb

sub′ject, *n.*, topic, citizen, study of study

sub-ject′, *v.*, expose, put under control, enslave

sub′ju-gāte, *v.*, bring under control

sub′li-māte, *v.*, substitute better activity, **-mation**

sub-līme′, *a.*, noble, splendid, exalted

sub-jec′tive, *a.*, affected by inner level

sub-má-rine′ (reen) *a.*, *n.*, underwater, underwater vessel

sub-mérge′, *v.*, go under water, hide

sub-mit′, *v.*, yield

sub-ôr′di-nâte, *a.*, dependent, inferior

sub-scrībe′, *v.*, give order for, support, agree to terms, **scription**

sub′sè-quent, *a.*, following, later, **-ly**

sub-sér′vi-ênt, *a.*, humbly yielding, **-ence**

sub-sīde′, *v.*, lessen, abate

sub′si-dì-âr-y, *n.*, thing giving aid, support, or service, company controlled by another

sub′si-dy, *n.*, money for aid, **dize**

sub-sist′, *v.*, exist, live, **-ence**

sub′stânce, *n.*, matter, character, reality, contents

sub-stan′tial, *a.*, important, considerable

sub-stan′ti-āte, *v.*, give evidence

sub′sti-tūte, *n.*, replacement, **-tution**

sub′tĕr-fûge, *n.*, evasive trick

sub-tĕr-rā′nè-ân, *a.*, hidden

sub′tle (sut-il), *a.*, delicate, clever, **-ty**

sub-tract′, *v.*, deduct

sub′urb, *n.*, outlying part of city or town, **-an**

sub-vért′, *v.*, destroy, undermine, **-version**

sub′way, *n.*, subterranean transportation system

suc-cēed′ (suk-seed), *v.*, follow, reach goal

suc-cess′, *n.*, favorable result, gain, **-ful**

suc-ces′sive, *a.*, following in order, **-sor**

suc-cinct′ (sinkt), *a.*, short and clear, **-ly**

suc′cör, *n.*, aid, relief

suc′cū-lent, *a.*, juicy, tasty

suc-cumb′, *v.*, die, yield

such (sutch), *a.*, of this or that kind, so much, similar

suck, *v.*, draw into or from, **-ing**

suck′ĕr, *n.*, fish, one who is fooled, lollipop

suck′le, *v.*, feed at breast

suc′tion, *n.*, adherence

sud′dèn, *a.*, not expected, quick, **-ly**

suds, *n.*, soapy water, beer

sūe, *v.*, take legal action against, plead

suede (swayd), *n.*, soft leather or cloth

suf′fĕr, *v.*, experience pain, sadness, etc., allow, endure, **-ing**

suf-fi′cient, *a.*, enough, meeting need, **-ciency**

suf-fîce′, *v.*, be enough

suf′fix, *n.*, word ending

suf′fö-cāte, *v.*, cause to stop breathing, **cation**

suf′frâge, *n.*, right to vote, enfranchisement

sug′ǎr, *n.*, sweetener, a unit of sugar

sug-gest′, *v.*, offer, propose, hint, **-ion**

sū′i-cīde, *n.*, killing of self, one who kills self

sūit, *n.*, set of clothes, legal action, playing card division

suit'a·ble, *a.*, correct, satisfactory

suit'case, *n.*, traveling bag

suite (swēt), *n.*, group of related things

sul'fa, *n.*, infection fighting drug

sulk, *v.*, become sullen, mope

sul'len, *a.*, silent, resentful, ill-tempered

su·ki·yā'ki, *n.*, Japanese stew

sul'ly, *v.*, soil

sul'try, *a.*, hot and humid, titillating

sum, *n.*, amount, total

sum'ma·ry, *n.*, brief account, digest, **-rize**

sum'mer, *n.*, hot season of year

sum'mit, *n.*, topmost point, apex

sum'mon, *v.*, call for presence of

sum'mons, *n.*, order to appear

sump'tu·ous, *a.*, splendid, costly, **-ly**

sun, *n.*, body around which planets revolve, source of light, heat, energy, **-ny**

sun'dae', *n.*, ice cream topped with syrup

sun'dry, *a.*, various

sun'ken, *a.*, below normal level

sun'ny, *a.*, warm, bright, cheerful

sup, *v.*, eat supper

su'per, *n., a.*, extra actor, extra-special, extreme

su'per, *prefix*, meaning higher, greater, more than, above. *Ex:* **su·per·flu'ous**, *a.*, more than necessary, **su'per hū'man**, *a.*, greater than human

su·perb', *a.*, excellent, splendid, majestic

su·per·cil'i·ous, *a.*, scornful, haughty

su·per·fi'cial, *a.*, surface, easily seen, shallow, skin deep

su·per·im·pose', *v.*, put on top of

su·per·in·tend'ent, *n.*, manager, head administrator

su·pe'ri·or, *a.*, higher, greater, better, excellent,

ity

su'per·jet, *n.*, large jet airplane

su·per'la·tive, *a., n.*, exceeding all else, highest degree of comparison

su'per mär'ket, *n.*, large self-service retail outlet

su·per·nat'u·ral, *a.*, outside nature, miraculous

su·per·nū'mer·ār·y, *n., a.*, extra

su·per·sēde', *v.*, replace with something superior

su·per·son'ic, *a.*, faster than speed of sound

su·per·sti'tion, *n.*, irrational belief, **-tious**

su'per·vise, *v.*, direct, oversee, manage, **-vision, -visor**

su·pīne', *a.*, inactive, lying on back

sup'per, *n.*, evening meal

sup·plant', *v.*, displace through force

sup'ple, *a.*, flexible, pliant

sup'ple·ment, *n.*, added part, **-ary**

sup'pli·cāte, *v.*, ask humbly, **-cation, -ant**

sup·ply', *v.*, provide, furnish, purvey

sup·ply', *n.*, amount, stock

sup·port', *v.*, hold up, take side of, provide for, help

sup·pose', *v.*, assume, consider as possible, expect

sup·press', *v.*, put down by force, stop, **-ion**

su·pra', *adv.*, above

su·prem'a·cist, *n.*, believer in supremacy of certain group

su·prēme', *a.*, highest, ultimate, utmost, **-premacy**

sūre (sh), *a.*, certain, without doubt, positive

sūre'ly, *adv.*, indeed, certainly

sūre'ə·ty, *n.*, certainty, guarantee, insurance

surf, *n.*, shore waves, breakers

sur'face, *a.*, top or outside, rise to top

sur'feit (fit), *n.*, excess, intemperate indulgence

surge, *n.*, rush

sur'geon (jin), *n.*, doctor who operates, **-gery**

sur'ly, *a.*, rude, arrogant

sur·mīse', *v.*, guess, infer on

slight grounds

sûr-mount', v., overcome, rise over

sûr'nāme, n., family name

sûr-pass', v., exceed

sûr'plus, n., amount left over

sûr-prīse', n., v., sudden unexpected event, amaze, **-prising**

sur-rē'al-ism, n., abstract expression of mental activities

sur-ren'dêr, v., give up, give in

sûr-rep-ti'tious, a., secret, stealthy

sur-round', v., enclose, **-ing**

sûr-veil'lance (vayl), n., observation

sûr'vey' (vay), v., view from a distance, examine, set boundaries, poll

sûr'vey, n., study, poll

sûr-vīve', v., continue living, **-vival**

sus-cep'ti-ble, a., easily affected

sus'pect, n., person believed to have committed crime

sus-pect', v., distrust, presume, **-picion**

sus-pend', v., hang, remove from position, stop temporarily, cancel, **pension**

sus-pense', n., uncertainty, anxiety

sus-tāin', v., support, nourish, keep alive, **-ing**

sus'tê-nance, n., that which keeps one alive, food, provision

su'ture, v., sew wound

svelte, a., slender, lithe

swāb, v., clean, medicate

swäd'dle, v., wrap in cloth, bandage

swag'gêr, v., strut, boast, **-ing**

swäl'lōw, n., small passerine bird

swäl'lōw, v., pass food through throat, take

swämp, n., wet land, marsh den

swämp, v., flood, overwhelm

swän, n., water bird

swank, a., stylish, showy, **-y**

swän' sông, n., one's last act

swäp, v., trade

swärm, v., crowd

swärth'y, a., dark

swät, v., hit, smack

swätch, n., sample of goods

sway, v., move back and forth, influence

swear, v., promise on oath, take an oath, use profanity

sweat (swet), v., perspire

sweat'êr, n., knitted garment

sweep, v., n., clean with broom, move smoothly, extent, win

sweep'ing, a., complete, comprehensive

sweet, a., pleasing to senses, kind, pleasant, **-en**

sweet'heärt, n., darling, lover

swell, v., grow larger

swell, (slang), a., wonderful, nifty

swel'têr, v., suffer from intense heat

swêrve, v., turn aside

swift, a., fast moving, rapid

swim, v., move through water, become dizzy

swin'dle, v., cheat, **-r**

swīne, n., hog

swing, v., turn, sway, do, move freely

swīpe, v., hit, steal

swirl, v., twist

swish, v., rustle

switch, n., stick for beating, controlling device, change, abrupt movement

swiv'êl, v., rotate

swōōn, v., faint

swōōp, v., descend suddenly, snatch

swôrd (sôrd), n., sharp pointed weapon

sýb'a-rīte, n., one liking luxuries

sýc'ō-phant, n., seeker of favor by flattery, parasite

sýl'la-ble, n., pronouncing division of word, **-bize**

sýl'la-bus, n., course of study, compendium

sylph, n., slender, graceful woman

sýl'van, a., relating to woods

sým'bōl, n., sign, representation, **-ism**, **-ic**

sým'mê-try, n., balance in arrangement, **-trical**

sým'pá-thy, n., understanding, sharing another's feelings, **-thetic**

sým'phö-ny, n., harmony, long composition for full

orchestra

sým-pō'si-um, *n.,* discussion meeting

sýmp'tõm, *n.,* outward sign, indication, **-atic**

sýn'ȧ-gogue (gog) *n.,* Jewish house of prayer

sýn'chrō-nīze, *v.,* make move together, **-nization**

sýn'cō-pāte, *v.,* shift regular beat, abbreviate, **-pation**

sýn'di-cȧte, *n.,* union of companies, **-d**

sýn'drōme, *n.,* symptoms occurring together characterizing a disease or condition

sýn'ŏd, *n.,* meeting of Church authorities, council

sýn'ō-ným, *n.,* word with same meaning as another, **-ous**

sýn-op'sis, *n.,* summary, abstract

sýn'tax, *n.,* sentence structure

sýn'thē-sis, *n.,* uniting parts into whole, **-size**

sýn-thet'ic, *a.,* created artificially, man-made

sý-ringe' (rinj), *n.,* device for drawing in and expelling liquid, concentrated juice

sýr'up, *n.,* sweet liquid

sýs'těm, *n.,* series, orderly plan, procedure, method, bodily function

---

— T —

tab, *n.,* flap, (coll.) bill

tab'êr-nac-le, *n.,* tent, place of worship

tā'ble, *n.,* furniture with flat surface and legs, list, source of food

tā'ble, *v.,* delay, tabulate

tab'leau (lō), *n.,* scene, picture

tā'ble-spoon, *n.,* large serving, eating, measuring spoon

tab'lět, *n.,* flat slab, writing pad

tab'loid, *n.,* newspaper, digest, summary

tȧ-boo', *a.,* forbidden, banned

tab'ū-lāte, *v.,* list

tac'it, *a.,* quiet, unspoken, implied

tac'i-tûrn (tas), *a.,* habitually silent, **-ity**

tack, *n.,* short nail, course of action, ships course

tack'le, *n.,* lifting and lowering device, football position, gear

tact, *n.,* diplomatic behavior, savoir faire, **-ful, -less**

tac'tics, *n.,* skillful plan, **-tical**

tac'tile, *a.,* relating to touch, tangible

tad'pōle, *n.,* frog larva

tag, *n., v.,* label, touch, follow

tāil, *n.,* end, rear part

tāil'gate, *v.,* drive too close behind other vehicle

tāi'lŏr, *n.,* person who makes or mends clothing

tāi'lŏred, *a.,* fitted

tāil wind, *n.,* wind coming behind ship

tāint, *v.,* spoil

tāke, *v.,* get, use, accept, receive, subtract, carry

tāke'-hōme pay, *n.,* salary after deductions

tāke'-ŏff, *n.,* imitation, start

tāle, *n.,* story, lie

tal'ent, *n.,* native ability

tal'is-mȧn, *n.,* charm

tȧlk, *v., n.,* say, speak, discuss, gossip, **-ative**

tȧll, *a.,* high

tal'lōw, *n.,* animal fat

tal'ly, *v.,* count, agree

Tal'mud, *n.,* Jewish books of laws

tȧ'lŏn, *n.,* claw

tȧ-mä'lē, *n.,* Mexican food

tam-bou-rine' (reen), *n.,* hand drum

tāme, *a.,* gentle, subdued

tamp, *v.,* pack down

tam'pêr, *v.,* bother with, interfere

tan, *v.,* make hide into leather, whip, sunburn

tan'děm, *adv.,* one behind another

tang, *n.,* strong taste or smell

tan'gent, *a.,* touching at a point, irrelevancy

tan-gē-rine' (rēen), *n.,* citrus fruit, mandarin

---

tan'gi·ble, *a.,* actual, having substance

tan'gle, *v.,* mix up, confusion

tan'gō, *n.,* Spanish dance

tank, *n.,* container, armored military car, prison cell

tan'tà·līze, *v.,* provoke then dash hope

tan'tà·mount, *a.,* equal, equivalent in effect

tan'trum, *n.,* display of bad temper, fit

tap, *v.,* pat gently, drain liquid from

tāpe, *n.,* narrow strip of cloth or metal

tā'pêr, *n.,* candle, decrease gradually

tap'ès·try, *n.,* artistically woven fabric

tap·i·ō'cà, *n.,* dessert

tär, *n.,* thick liquid derived from coal, seaman

tà·ran'tu·là (chi·leh), *n.,* spider

tär'dy, *a.,* late, delayed, sluggish

tär'get, *n.,* object aimed at, goal

tar'iff, *n.,* tax on imported goods

tär'nish, *v.,* become dull, discolor, stain, vitiate

tär·pău'lin, *n.,* heavy canvas covering

tar'ry, *v.,* linger, stay, sojourn

tärt, *a.,* sharp, sour

tärt, *n.,* pastry, prostitute

task, *n.,* difficult work, assigned job, chore

task förce, *n.,* military group on special mission

tāste, *n.,* flavor, small amount, preference, sense of beauty, propriety, etc., experience, **-less**

tat'tle, *v.,* tell tales

tăunt, *v.,* make fun of, insult, ridicule

tăut, *a.,* tight, tense

tău·tol'ō·gy, *n.,* unnecessary repetition

tav'êrn, *n.,* bar, place for selling, drinking alcoholic drinks, inn

tăw'dry, *a.,* showy, cheap

tax, *n.,* payment required by government, assessment, **-ation, -able**

tax'i (ee), *n.,* auto for hire, **-cab**

tax'i, *v.,* coast, glide

tēa, *n.,* beverage, afternoon meal

tēach, *v.,* instruct, impart knowledge, **-er**

tēak, *n.,* Indian hardwood

tēal, *n.,* gray-blue color, duck

tēam, *n.,* group working together, athletic group

tēam'stêr, *n.,* truck driver, horse driver

tēar, *n.,* fluid of eye, **-y**

tēar, *v.,* force apart, wound, split, hurry

tēase, *v.,* annoy persistently, comb out

tē'spŏŏn, *n.,* small eating, measuring spoon

tēat, *n.,* nipple, small projection

tech'ni·càl (tek), *a.,* relating to mechanical processes, skilled in certain area, **-ity**

tech·ni'cian, *n.,* one having special skill or knowledge

tech·nique' (nek), *n.,* method

tech·nol'ō·gy, *n.,* science of industrial processes

tē'di·ous, *a.,* tiresome, boring

tēē shirt (T), *n.,* man's undershirt

tēem, *v.,* pour, swarm

tēen'āg·êr, *n.,* a person in his teens

tēethe, *v.,* grow teeth

tē·tō'tàl·êr, *n.,* one who abstains from alcoholic drink

tel'é·cast, *v.,* television broadcast

tel'é·côurse, *n.,* televised course for credit

tel'é·graph, *n.,* device for sending message by electricity, **-gram**

tē·lep'à·thy, *n.,* thought transference

tel'é·phōne, *n.,* electrical device for transmitting sound

tel'é·print·er, *n.,* printing telegraphic device

Tel'é·prompt·êr, *n.,* electronic prompter

tel'é·scōpe, *n.,* instrument for making objects appear nearer

Tel'é·type, *n.,* telegraph device like typewriter

tel'é·vi·sion (zhin), *n.,* sending and receiving pictures over distances without wires

tell, v., express in words, reveal, order

tell'êr, n., bank clerk, counter

tell'tāle, a., indicating, informing

tē·mer'i·ty, n., recklessness, foolish courage, audacity

tem'pêr, n., tendency to anger easily, disposition

tem'pêr, v., restrain, mollify

tem'pêr·à·ment, n., makeup, complexion

tem·pêr·à·men'tàl, a., high-strung, unpredictable

tem'pêr·ance, n., moderation, abstinence from alcohol, self-control

tem'pêr·à·ture, n., degree of heat or cold

tem'pêst, n., storm, tumult, uproar, **-uous**

tem'plate (plit), n., pattern, mold

tem'ple, n., place of worship, side of head

tem'pō, n., rate of speed, pace

tem'pō·rál, a., worldly, not spiritual, secular

tem'pō·rār'y, a., occurring for a limited time

tem'pō·rīze, v., delay action, compromise

tempt, v., persuade, attract, provoke, **-er**

ten, n., nine plus one, **-th**

ten'à·ble, a., defensible, reasonable

tē·nā'cious, a., holding firmly, retentive, **-city**

ten'ant, n., dweller, occupant

tend, v., manage, lead to, incline

tend'en·cy, n., disposition for, inclination

ten'dêr, a., loving, soft, frail, **-ness**

ten'dêr·loin, n., fillet of beef or pork

ten'é·ment, n., substandard crowded housing

ten'êt, n., belief, doctrine

ten'nis, n., court game

ten'ôr, n., highest natural male voice, tendency

tense, a., pulled tight, high-strung, nervous, (verb form denoting time)

ten'sion, n., stress, tautness, anxiety

tent, n., canvas shelter

ten'tà·tive, a., temporary, provisional, hesitant

ten'ū·ous, a., slender, thin, flimsy, weak

ten'ure (yêr), n., length of time in position, grasp, hold

tē'pēe, n., Indian tent

tep'id, a., lukewarm, halfhearted

têr·cen'tē·nâr·y, n., 300 years

têrm, n., designated period of time, condition of contract, expression, **-inology**

têr'mi·nàl, n., railroad station, extremity

têr'mi·nāte, v., end, **-nation**

têr'mite, n., insect

ter'race, n., raised flat land, paved garden area

têr'rà cot'tà, n., glazed clay ware

têr·rāin', n., land contour

Ter·rà·my'cin, n., antibiotic drug

têr·râr'i·um, n., enclosed small garden without water

têr·res'tri·àl, a., relating to earth, land

ter'ri·ble, a., tragic, dreadful, severe

ter'ri·êr, n., small dog boldly bred for hunting

ter'ri·fy, v., overwhelm with fear, intimidate

ter'ri·tō·ry, n., land belonging to country, land area, **-rial**

ter'rôr, n., intense fear, brat

têrse, a., short, direct, succinct

test, n., examination, trial, proof

tes'tà·ment, n., will, Bible section, credo

tes'tāte, a., having made a will, **-tator**

tes'ti·cle, n., male reproductive gland

tes'ti·fy, v., give evidence, indicate, prove, profess

tes·ti·mō'ni·àl, n., honor, statement of recommendation

tes'ti·mō·ny, n., evidence

tes'ty, a., irritable, irascible

tet'à·nus, n., lock-jaw disease

teth'êr, n., rope, scope

text, n., book, topic, wording

tex'tīle, n., woven or knit cloth

tex'ture, n., make-up, feel of something

than, conj., denoting comparison

thank, v., express gratitude

that, pro., a., designating person or thing

thaw, v., melt, warm, abandon hostility

the, a., used to indicate a particular thing, person, or place

the'a·têr, n., building where shows are presented, drama, **-trical**

theft, n., stealing, larceny

theirs (thayrs), pro., belonging to them

the'ism, n., belief in God, **-istic**

theme, n., written composition, main topic, main tune

then, adv., at a particular time, thereafter, likewise

the-ol'ö·gy, n., study of God, **-gical**

the'ö·ry, n., supported principle, educated guess, mental plan rather than actual practice

ther'a·py, n., remedial treatment of a disorder, **-peutic**

there (thâr), adv., at, to, in, toward, particular place, now, in that respect

there-af'têr, adv., after that

there·by', adv., by that means

there·of', adv., from that

there·up·on', adv., at once, as a result

thêr'mál, a., relating to heat

thêr'mö-, prefix, heat

thêr·mö-dy-nam'ics, n., relationship of heat and mechanical power

thêr·mom'ê·têr, n., device for measuring degrees of heat

thêr-mö-nü'clē-âr, a., relating to heat released in nuclear fusion

thêr'mö·stat, n., device for regulating amount of heat

the·sau'rus, n., treasury of information, storehouse

the'sis, n., hypothesis, dissertation

they (ay), pro., persons or things mentioned, **them**

thick, a., deep, dense, close, husky

thick'êt, n., dense growth of shrubbery or trees

thief, n., one who steals

thiev'êr·y, n., stealing

thigh, n., upper part of leg, femur

thim'ble, n., finger protection while sewing

thin, a., slender, slight, tenuous

thing, n., object without life, event, single entity, item

think, v., give mental image to, imagine, consider, **-ing**

think tank, n., research group, institute

third, a., after second

thirst, n., craving for water, longing, **-y**

thir-teen', n., ten plus three, **-th**

thir'ty, n., ten times three

this, pro., thing near or present

this'tle, n., plant with sharp points

thôrn, n., sharp plant part, something causing distress or irritation

thôrn'y, a., difficult, ticklish, having thorns

thôr'öugh (-oh), a., complete, exact

thôr'öugh'bred, n., pedigreed animal

thou, pro., you

thöugh, conj., despite, nevertheless

thôught, n., thinking, reasoning, idea, opinion, consideration, mental process, **-ful**

thous'and, n., ten times hundred, very large number

thrash, v., beat, move about violently

thread, n., fine cord, yarn, groove on screw

thread'bâre, a., worn, shabby

threat, n., promise of harm

threat'ên, v., portend, menace

three, n., cardinal numeral "3"

thresh, v., remove grain from wheat, forge

thresh'öld, n., doorway, entrance, gate

thrift, n., saving, frugality, management of money, **-y**

thrill, n., excitement

thrill'êr, n., mystery story

thrive, v., prosper, flourish, grow

throat, n., front of neck, neck passage

throb, v., beat steadily

throes, n., struggle, pang, spasm

throne, n., sovereign's chair of state

throng, n., crowd

throt´tle, n.,v., lever controlling power flow, choke, suppress

through, n.,v., from end to end or side to side, among, as result

through, a., ended, complete, by way of

through-put, n., production of computer

throw, v., cast, hurl, fling

thrush, n., song bird, fungal disease

thrust, v., push with force

thud, n., dull sound

thug, n., thief, murderer

thumb (thum), n., first digit of human hand

thun´dêr, n., sound following lightning, **-ous**

Thûrs´day, n., fifth day of week

thwärt, v., oppose

thy´mus, n., gland of body

thy´roid, n., body gland

ti-âr´á (tēe), n., semi-crown worn on head

tic, n., uncontrolled body twitch

tick, n., clock sound, parasitic insect

tick´èt, n., card entitling privileges, label, list of candidates

tick´le, v., cause laughter by stroking body part, amuse, **lish**

tīde, n., regular rise and fall of ocean, current

tīde´wä-têr, n., water affected by tide

tī´dings, n., news

tī´dy, a., neat, orderly

tīe, n.,n., join with rope, string, etc., unite, equal score, neckwear

tiêr, n., row, rank

tiff, n., argument, petty quarrel

tī´gêr, n., animal of cat family

tīght, a., close-fitting, firm, stingy, taut, **-en**

tīle, n., flat roof or floor covering

till, prep., to such a time

till, n., v., money drawer, cultivate

tilt, v., slant, incline

tim´bêr, n., lumber, wood suitable for building

tim´ber-līne, n., line of a mountain above which trees do not grow

tim´på-ni (bêr), n., sound quality

tīme, n., duration, period, precise moment, measured interval, **-less**

tīme-shäring, n., shared use of computer

tim´id, a., shy, diffident, **-ity**

tim´ôr-ous, a., fearful, afraid

tim´på-ni, n., set of two or three drums

tin, n., metallic element, **-ner**

tin´dêr, n., very flammable substance

tin´gle, v., sting, prickle

tin´kle, n., bell-like sound

tint, n., delicate color, hue

tin-tin-nab-ū-lā´tion, n., sounding of bells

tī´ny, a., small, minute

tip, n., edge, top, cap

tip, v., give money for service, tilt

tip´-ôff, v., give information

tip´sy, a., drunk, fuddled

tī´rade, n., argumentative, vicious speech

tīre, n., v., rubber wheel for vehicle, lose strength, bore

tīre´sôme, a., boring, tedious

tis´sūe, n., body substance, thin paper or cloth, paper handkerchief

tīthe, v., give 1/10th of income to church

tī´tian, a., of a brownish-orange color

tit´il-lāte, v., tickle

tī´tle, n., name, designation, right to ownership, **-tular**

tit´têr, v., giggle

to (too), prep., toward, as far as, on until, with

tōad, n., frog-like animal, contemptible person

tōast, v., brown the surface, warm, drink to honor

tö-bac´cö, n., plant leaves used for smoking

tö-bog´gán, n., long narrow sled

tö-day´, n., this day, present time

tö-do' (dōo), *n.*, excitement, bustle, stir

tōe, *n.*, digit of foot

tö-geth'êr, *adv.*, in a group, at same time, with one another

toil, *v.*, work hard, plod

toi'lĕt, *n.*, lavatory

tō'kĕn, *n.*, symbol, keepsake, evidence, souvenir

tō-ken-ism, *n.*, admission of small number of blacks into schools, business (token effort)

tol'êr-ance, *n.*, sympathy, patience, understanding, **-ant**

tol'êr-āte, *v.*, allow, bear, endure, **-ation**

tōll, *n.*, tax, number, bell ringing

tom'á-hawk, *n.*, light ax used by Indians

tö-mā'tō, *n.*, fruit served as vegetable

tomb (toom), *n.*, grave, gravestone

tomb'stōne, *n.*, memorial marking grave

tōme, *n.*, large book

tö-mor'row, *n.*, day after today, future

tön, *n.*, 2000 pounds, weight measurement, great quantity

tōne, *n.*, musical sound, meaningful attitude, color value, sound

tongs, *n.*, device for lifting

töngue (tung), *n.*, fleshy object in mouth, language, shoe flap

ton'ic, *n.*, stimulating medicine

tö-nīght', *n.*, this evening

ton'sil, *n.*, tissue in back of throat, **-itis**

ton-sō'ri-ál, *a.*, relating to a barber or his work

tōō, *adv.*, also, in addition, overly

tōōl, *n.*, implement of work, dupe

tōōth, *n.*, body structure in mouth, anything resembling tooth

tōōth'sōme, *a.*, tasty, attractive

top, *n.*, upper or highest part, summit, apex

tö'paz, *n.*, gem, yellow quartz

top'cōat, *n.*, light overcoat

top'ic, *n.*, subject for discussion or writing

top'less, *adj.*, female entertainer nude to waist

tö-pog'rá-phy, *n.*, description of geographic features, **-pher**

top'pêr, *n.*, woman's short coat, top hat

top'ple, *v.*, fall over, overturn

Tō'rah, *n.*, Jewish scroll of laws

tôrch, *n.*, light carried by hand, flambeau

tôr'e-á-dôr, *n.*, torero, bullfighter

tôr-ment', *v.*, inflict suffering, annoy, **-or**

tôr-nā'dō, *n.*, violent spiral wind, whirlwind

tôr-pē'dō, *n.*, explosive missile

tôr'pid, *a.*, dull, inactive, **-ity**

tor'rent, *n.*, violent flow, rush

tor'rid, *a.*, extremely hot, ardent, passionate

tôr'sion, *n.*, twisting, rotating, **-que**

tôr'sō, *n.*, trunk of body

tôr'toise (tis), *n.*, turtle, something slow

tôr'tū-ous, *a.*, twisting, painful

tôr'ture, *v.*, inflict extreme pain on someone, cause agony

tôss, *v.*, throw, flip

tō'tál, *n.*, complete, entire, **-ity**

tō-tal-i-târ'i-án, *a.*, dictatorial

tō'-tál-i-zā-tör, *n.*, automatic computer used to figure odds

tōte, *v.*, haul, convey

touch (tutch), *v.*, feel, meet in contact, affect, deal with, reach

touch'dōwn, *n.*, crossing opponent's goal line in football

touch'y, *a.*, sensitive, irascible

tough (tuf), *a.*, difficult to break, strong, crude

toū-pee' (pay), *n.*, wig, hair piece

toūr (toor), *n.*, circuit, journey, trip, **-ist**

toūr'ná-ment, *n.*, series of games

toūr'ni-quet (kit), *n.*, bandage

tow (tō), *v.*, pull with chain or rope, drag

tō·wârd' (tôrd), *prep.*, in direction of, close to, about

tow'el, *n.*, cloth for drying

tow'er, *n.*, *v.*, upper part of church or building, rise above

town, *n.*, small city, hamlet

tox'in, *n.*, poison, **-ic**

toy (toi), *n.*, plaything, pastime

trāce, *n.*, *v.*, indication, copy, follow

trā·chō'må (kō), *n.*, eyelid disease

track, *n.*, *v.*, foot mark, sign, path, follow

trac'tà·ble, *a.*, tame, easy to handle, obedient

trac'tion, *n.*, friction between an object and the surface on which it moves

trac'tor, *n.*, machine for pulling other vehicles

trāde, *n.*, *v.*, business, exchange one thing for another

trāde'-in', *n.*, something exchanged as part of purchase

trāde'märk, *n.*, mark identifying particular product

trādes'màn, *n.*, shopkeeper, craftsman

trà·di'tion, *n.*, unwritten practice passed on through generations, **-al**

traf'fic, *n.*, movement of vehicles or people on streets, roads, etc., business

trag'é·dy (traj), *n.*, drama with unhappy theme, calamity, misfortune

trag'ic, *a.*, unhappy, fatal, lamentable, **-ally**

trāil, *n.*, *v.*, path, track, follow, flow

trāil'ềr, *n.*, unpowered vehicle pulled by powered one, trailing plant

trāin, *n.*, *v.*, attached railroad cars, chain of things which occur, go behind, exercise, achieve skill, instruct, **-er**

trāin'màn, *n.*, employee who works on railroad cars

trāit, *n.*, distinguishing personal mark, habit, peculiarity

trāi'tör, *n.*, unfaithful person, **-ous**

tramp, *n.*, *v.*, bum, hike, walk heavily

tram'ple, *v.*, step on so as to crush, stamp

trance, *n.*, loss of conscious feeling, similar to sleep, daze

tran'quil (kwil), *a.*, peaceful, serene, calm, **-ity**

trans-act', *v.*, carry on business, exchange terms, **-ion**

tran-scend' (send), *v.*, rise over, go beyond, **-ent**

tran-scen-den'tàl, *a.*, outside human experience but not knowledge, **-ism**

tran-scrībe', *v.*, copy, **scription**

trans-dūc'er, *n.*, device to receive then transmit energy to another system

trans'fềr, *v.*, take from one and give to another, copy, change

trans-fig-ū-rā'tion, *n.*, changed appearance

trans-fôrm', *v.*, change appearance of, **-ed**

trans-fū'sion, *n.*, transfer of blood from one person to another

trans-gress', *v.*, sin, violate law, **-ion**

tran'sient (shent), *a.*, passing, temporary, fleeting

tran-sis'tor, *n.*, tiny electronic device

tran'sit, *n.*, passage from one place to another

tran-si'tion (zi), *n.*, change, passing phase

trans-lāte', *v.*, interpret from one language to another, explain, **-lation**

trans-lū'cênt, *a.*, transparent, lucid

trans-mis'sion, *n.*, something sent across or through, device that sends engine power to working wheels

trans-mit', *v.*, send, pass along

trans-mūte', *v.*, change shape or form, convert

tran'söm, *n.*, small window over doorway, lintel

trans-pâr'ent, *a.*, obvious, diaphanous, **-ency**

trans'pôrt, *n.*, *v.*, vehicle

which carries persons, carry, **-ation**

trans-pōse', v., alter, reverse, exchange, **-position**

trans-vêrse', a., across, crosswise

trap, n., snare, device for catching, hazard

trá-pēze', n., swing

trap'pêr, n., fur hunter

trash, n., garbage, undesirable material, refuse

trãu-mat'ic, a., injurious

trav-āil', n., difficult work, slavery, misery

trav'êl, n., v., journey away from home, take trip, **-er**

trav'ê-lõgue, n., illustrated lecture on travel

trav'ês-ty, n., something serious made into joke, parody

trawl, n., fishing net, setline

tray, n., flat carrying board

treach'êr-ous (trech) a., untrustworthy, **y**

tread, (tred), v., n., step, crush, mark

trēa'sön, n., betrayal of a trust, **-able**

treas'üre (trezh), n., rich prize, wealth, something valuable

treas'ûr-êr, n., person responsible for accounts of club, firm, etc.

treas'ûr-y, n., place where valuables are kept, government department in charge of finances

trēat, v., pay another's expense, deal with, act towards, give medication

trēa'tise, n., written document

trēat'ment, n., manner of curing disease, way of handling

trēa'ty, n., agreement between countries

tre'ble, a., threefold, high pitched, shrill

trēe, n., plant with wooden trunk, branches and many leaves

trek, n., hard slow journey

trel'lis, n., framework for holding vines, flowers, etc.

trem'ble, v., shake with fright, **-bling**

trē-men'dous, a.,

extraordinary, unusually large, dreadful

trem'ör, n., shaking, vibration

trench, n., long ditch

trench'ánt, a., clear, sharp, keen, distinct

trend, n., specific tendency or direction

tres'pass, v., intrude on another's privileges, sin

trī'ál, n., hearing of charge in court, attempt, difficulty

trī'an-gle, n., group loosely organized by traditions, etc.

tribe, n., group loosely organized by traditions, etc.

trib-ū-lā'tion, n., a trying experience

trī-bū'nál, n., court of law

trib'üte, n., payment, praise, credit, tax

trick, n., dishonest, playful or clever act, skill, **-ery**

trick'le, v., fall by drops

trī'cy-cle, n., three-wheeled vehicle

trīed, a., proven, subjected to trials

trī-en'ni-ál, a., taking place every three years, lasting for three years

trī'fle, n., something worth little

trig'gêr, n., firing part of gun, stimulus

trig-ö-nom'é-try, n., study of triangles

trill, n., voice quiver, vibrato

tril'lion (yin), n., number with twelve zeros added

trim, a., neat looking, attractive, cut off, remove

trim'ming, n., added decoration

Trin'i-ty, n., Father, Son, and Holy Ghost joined together

trin'ket, n., small ornament

trī'ō (tree), n., group of three

trip, n., v., journey, travel, stumble

trī-pär'tite, a., having three usually equal parts

tri'ple, a., three times

trip'li-cāte, a., three copies of

trī'pod, n., three-legged stand

trī-sect', v., cut into three parts

trīte, a., dull, stale, hackneyed

trī'umph, n., victory, happiness in winning, **-ant**

triv'i-ål, *a.,* not important, commonplace, **-ity**

trog'lŏ-dyte, *n.,* cave dweller

trōll, *v.,* fish by dragging line

trol'lĕy, *n.,* electric streetcar, pole and wheel by which streetcar gets electricity from the wire

trom'bōne, *n.,* brass wind instrument

trōōp, *n., v.,* military unit, march

trō'phy, *n.,* emblem in honor of victory

trop'ic, *n.,* either of two imaginary circles on either side of equator, **-al**

trop'ics, *n.,* hot regions near the equator

trot, *v.,* proceed faster than walking pace

trôth, *n.,* promised fidelity

trot'tĕr, *n.,* horse

trou'ble (trub-il), *n.,* worry, difficulty, disturbance, bother, effort

trou'ble-sŏme, *a.,* difficult, burdensome

trounce, *v.,* beat, defeat

trōūpe, *n.,* group of actors

trou'sĕrs (zėrs), *n.,* male outer pants

trōūs-seau (troo-soh), *n.,* clothing and domestics collected by bride

trout, *n.,* fish

trow'el, *n.,* tool for smoothing plaster, cement, garden tool

trū'ånt, *a.,* absent without permission, **-ancy**

trūce, *n.,* halt in fighting, armistice

truck, *n., v.,* vehicle for carrying heavy loads, carry, **-er**

truc'ū-lėnt, *a.,* cruel, destructive, belligerent, **-lence**

trudge, *v.,* walk wearily

trūe, *a.,* based on fact, genuine, faithful

truf'fle, *n.,* fungus eaten as delicacy

trū'ism, *n.,* accepted fact

trū'ly, *adv.,* sincerely, really

trump, *n.,* card of established suit

trum'pėt, *n.,* brass wind instrument, **-er**

trun'cheŏn, *n.,* staff of authority, club

trun'dle, *v.,* roll, haul

trunk, *n.,* tree bottom, large traveling case, telephone line connection

trust, *n.,* faith, belief, group of businesses, care of another's property, **-worthy**

trust'y, *a.,* trustworthy, dependable

truth, *n.,* that which is real, acceptance of facts, **-ful**

try, *v.,* attempt, put to test

try'ing, *a.,* difficult to undergo

tryst, *n.,* meeting arranged in advance

tub, *n.,* place for taking bath, container

tub'by, *a.,* fat, pudgy

tūbe, *n.,* long, round-shaped pipe of metal, rubber, etc.

tū-bėr-cū-lō'sis, *n.,* disease affecting lungs

tū'bū-lår, *a.,* round shaped

tuck, *v.,* fold under, cover comfortably, put snugly

tuft, *n.,* things gathered together in clumps

tug, *v.,* pull with effort

tug, *n.,* small boat that tows others

tū-i'tion, *n.,* payment for instruction

tū'lip, *n.,* flower

tum'ble, *v.,* fall in rolling manner

tum'blĕr, *n.,* glass for drinking

tū'mid, *a.,* swollen, **-ity**

tū'mŏr, *n.,* diseased swelling, tissue growth

tū'mult, *n.,* disorder, noise, **-uous**

tū'nà, *n.,* fish

tūne, *n.,* melody, agreement, amount, **-less**

tū'nic, *n.,* loose garment

tun'nĕl, *n., v.,* underground pathway, dig pathway

tûr'bàn, *n.,* close-fitting hat, cloth worn wrapped around head

tûr'bid, *a.,* muddy, dense

tûr'bīne, *n.,* wheel turned by force of water, steam

tûr'bū-lent, *a.,* violent, disorderly, stormy

tûrf, *n.,* grass-covered area, sod

tûr'gid, *a.,* swollen beyond normal size, showy as in language and style, **-ity**

tûr'key, *n.,* domesticated fowl, failure

tûr′moil, n., confusion, utter disorder

tûrn, v., n., reverse direction of, make go around, change, part of a rotation

tûr′nip, n., herb, rutabaga

tûrn′ō-vêr, n., change, business cycle, upset, tart

tûrn′pīke, n., expressway, freeway

tûrn′tā-ble, n., rotating platform for phonograph records, lazy susan

tûr′pen-tīne, n., liquid obtained from pine trees

tûr′pi-tūde, n., low morality, depravity

tûr′quoise (kois), n., precious green-blue stone, color

tûr′tle, n., four-footed reptile with hard shell

tusk, n., long protruding tooth

tū′tôr, n., private instructor, **-ial**

tux-ē′dō, n., semiformal evening clothes for men

twang, n., sharp sound, manner of speech, pang

twēak, v., pluck, pinch, twitch

twēez′êrs, n., hand pincers

twelve, n., eleven plus one

twen′ty, n., two times ten

twīce, adv., two times

twig, n., small shoot or branch

twī′līght, n., period from sunset to dark, faint light, period of decline

twin, n., one of a pair

twīne, n., strong cord

twinge (twinj) n., sudden, sharp pain

twin′kle, n., quick gleam of light, **-kling**

twist, v., wind together, interlace

twist′êr, n., tornado, waterspout

twitch, n., sudden jerky movement

twit′têr, n., bird chirping, light chattering

two (too), n., cardinal numeral "2"

two′-fāced′, a., insincere, deceitful

two′-ply, a., having double thickness

ty-cōōn′, n., rich business executive

tym′pa-ni (tim-pĭ-nēe), n., set of kettle drums

tym′pa-num (tim-pi), n., ear drum

type, n., metal figures used in printing, one with special feature with others in group, sort

type′writ-êr, n., machine for printing

ty′phoid, n., disease

ty-phōōn′, n., wild sea storm

ty′phus, n., disease

typ′i-cál, a., representative, like, **-ly**

ty′pist, n., person whose job is typing

ty-pog′ra-phêr, n., typesetter, **-phy**

tyr′an-ny (teer), n., ruthless absolute rule, **-nical**

ty′rant, n., cruel ruler

ty-rō, n., amateur, novice

tzar, n., former Russian emperor, **-ina**

——————————U——————————

ū-biq′ui-tous, a., omnipresent, being everywhere, **-ty**

U-bōat, n., German submarine

ud′dêr, n., mammary gland of cow

ūfol-o-gist, n., devotee of unidentified flying objects

ugh, inter., exclamation of disgust

ug′ly, a., disagreeable to see, offensive

ū-kāse′, n., Russian official order, edict

ū-ku-le′lē (lāy′ley), n., four-string guitar

ul′cêr, n., open sore, **-ous**

ul-tē′ri-ôr, a., beyond present sight, hidden, future

ul′ti-māte, a., primary, eventual, maximum, **-ly**

ul-ti-mā′tum, n., final proposal

ul′trȧ, a., extreme, beyond

ul'trå, *prefix*, meaning *extreme*, or *beyond the usual*. Example:

ul'-trå-crit'i-cål, *v.*, extremely critical

ul-trå-må-rine' (rēen) *n.*, deep blue color

ul-trå-mī-crō, *adj.*, smaller than microscopic

ul-trå-son'ic, *a.*, faster than speed of sound

ul-trå sound, *n.*, sound beyond human hearing

ul-trå-vī'ō-let, *a.*, beyond violet of visible spectrum

uf'ō-låte, *v.*, howl, **-lation**

um-bil'i-cål cōrd, *n.*, cord connecting fetus to placenta

um-bil'i-cus, *n.*, navel, core, heart

um'brå, *n.*, planet shadow

um'bråge, *n.*, resentment, offense, foliage

um-brel'lå, *n.*, covered frame protector against rain

um'pīre, *n.*, judge of game, referee

un-, *prefix*, meaning *not*. *Ex.:* un-ac-cus'tōmed, *a.*, not accustomed, **un-bowed'**, *a.*, not bowed

ū-nå-nim'i-ty, *n.*, full agreement

ū-nan'i-mous, *a.*, in full accord, agreed

un-bend', *v.*, relax, **-ing**

un-bōlt', *v.*, unlock

un-bōs'ōm, *v.*, confess, reveal

un-but'tōn, *v.*, loosen buttons

un-can'ny, *a.*, mysterious, eerie, weird

un'ci-fôrm, *a.*, hooklike

un'cle (kel), *n.*, parent's brother

un-con'scion-å-ble (shun), *a.*, not reasonable, not careful

un-cou'ple (ku-pel), *v.*, disconnect

un-coûth, *a.*, lacking in polish or grace

unc'tion, *n.*, anointment with oil, ointment

unc'tū-ous, *a.*, oily, greasy

un-dáunt'ed, *a.*, fearless, **-ly**

un'dēr, *prep.*, *adv.*, *a.*, beneath, lower than, below, subject to

un'dēr-, *prefix*, meaning *below*, *lower*, *underneath*, or *insufficient* when attached to other words.

Ex.: un'dēr-ärm, *a.*, beneath arm, un'dēr-act, *v.*, act insufficiently

un'dēr-brush, *n.*, shrubs, bushes

un'dēr class'mán, *n.*, student below senior

un'dēr cōv'êr, *a.*, operating secretly

un'dēr cûr-rènt, *n.*, current under the surface

un'dēr-dóg, *n.*, predicted loser

un'dēr-grad'ū-åte, *n.*, a student who has not taken first degree

un'dēr-hand', *a.*, dishonest, sly, **-ed**

un'dēr-ling, *n.*, subordinate person, inferior

un'dēr-ly-ing, *a.*, lying beneath, fundamental, implicit

un'dēr-mīne', *v.*, excavate, secretly weaken, sap

un'dēr-pin', *v.*, support from under, substantiate **-ning**

un'dēr sec'rē-târ-y, *n.*, assistant to the Secretary of State, etc.

un'dēr-sông, *n.*, underlying song

un'dēr-stand', *v.*, comprehend, know meaning of, **-ing**

un'dēr-stud-y, *n.*, substitute actor

un'dēr-tāke', *v.*, attempt, promise

un'dēr-tāk-êr, *n.*, mortician

un'dēr-tāk'ing, *n.*, task to be done, pledge, guarantee

un'dēr-tōne, *n.*, quiet tone, under current

un'dēr-tōw, *n.*, backward pull of current

un'dēr-weâr, *n.*, clothes worn next to the skin and under other clothing

un'dēr-wörld (wêrld), *n.*, Hell, criminal society

un'dēr-wrīte', *v.*, assume liability, **-r**

un-dē-sīr'å-ble, *a.*, unwanted

un-do' (dōo), *v.*, do away with, unloosen, untie

un-doubt'ed, *a.*, without a doubt, **-ly**

un-dress', *v.*, remove clothing

un-dūe', *a.*, improper, not due

un'dū-lánt, *a.*, waving

un-du-late, v., move in waves, -lation

un-du'ly, adv., improperly

un-dy'ing, a., everlasting

un-earth'ly, a., weird, eerie

un-eas'y, a., restless, disturbed, awkward

un-em-ployed', a., out of work, -ployment

un-e'qual, a., not even, inadequate, -ly

un-e-quiv'o-cal, a., absolutely clear, unambiguous

un-err'ing, a., faultless, unfailing

un-e-vent'ful, a., without importance, -ly

un-ex-am'pled (pild), a., without parallel, excellent

un-fail'ing, a., faithful

un-feigned' (fāynd), a., sincere, genuine

un-flinch'ing, a., firm, steadfast

un-fold', v., open out, reveal

un-fore-seen', a., unexpected

un-for'tu-nate, a., not lucky

un-friend'ly, a., hostile, inhospitable

un-frock', v., remove priest from office

un-furl', v., spread out, open to view

un-gain'ly, a., clumsy, coarse

un-god'ly, a., sinful, irreligious

un-gov'ern-a-ble, a., not controllable, unruly

un'guent (gwent), n., ointment, salve

un-hand', v., remove hands from

un-hand'y, a., not skillful, awkward

un-hap'py, a., sad, miserable, unlucky, -piness

un-här'ness, v., remove harness

un-health'y (helth), a., in poor health, unwholesome

un-heard' (hérd), a., not caught by ear, unknown

un-hinge', v., remove from hinges

un-hitch', v., unfasten

un-hur'ried, a., leisurely

un-hy-gi-en'ic, a., not sanitary

ū-ni-cam'ér-al, a., single legislative chamber

ū-ni-cel'lū-lar, a., having one cell

ū'ni-côrn, n., mythical one-horned horse

ū-ni-fi-cā'tion, n., joining together

ū'ni-fôrm, a., n., having same form, alike, official clothing, -ity

ū'ni-fy (ff), v., unite

ū-ni-lat'ér-al, a., one-sided, -ly

un-im-pas'sioned, a., calm, quiet

un-im-pēach'a-ble, a., blameless, irreproachable

ūn'ion (yon), n., being united

ū-nique' (nēk), a., having no equal, unusual

ū'ni-sŏn, n., harmony, oneness

ū'nit, n., single thing, group

ū-nīte', v., join together, -d

ū'ni-ty, n., oneness

ū-ni-vér'sal, a., relating to all, general, -ity

ū'ni-vérse, n., everything, whole world, cosmos

ū-ni-vér'si-ty, n., school of highest learning

un-just', a., not fair, wrongful

un-kempt', a., not neat, disheveled

un-kīnd', a., cruel, harsh

un-knōwn', a., not known, strange

un-läw'ful, a., contrary to law, -ly

un-lêarn' (lèrn), v., purposely forget

un-lêarn'èd, a., ignorant, untaught

un-lēash', v., let loose

un-leav'ened, a., not raised (as bread)

un-less', conj., if not, except

un-let'tered, a., not learned, illiterate

un-līke', a., different from

un-līke'ly, a., not likely, improbable

un-lim'it-èd, a., boundless, undefined

un-lōad', v., remove cargo, get rid of

un-lōōs'en, v., set loose

un-lŏve'ly, a., disagreeable, unpleasant

un-luck'y, a., unfortunate, regrettable

un-māke', v., destroy

un-man'ly, a., cowardly

un-man'nêr-ly, a., poor in

manners, rude

un-mask', v., expose

un-men'tion-a-ble, a., not fit to talk about

un-men'tion-a-bles, n., undergarments

un-mis-tak'a-ble, a., clear, obvious

un-mor'al, a., neither moral nor immoral, amoral

un-moved' (mōovd), a., resolute

un-nat'u-ral, a., not normal, artificial, **-ly**

un-nec'es-sar-y, a., not needed

un-nerve', v., upset

un-oc'cu-pied, a., empty, idle

un-ôr'gan-īzed, a., not working as a group

un-pal'at-a-ble, a., not tasteful

un-par'al-leled, a., unequaled

un-pin', v., remove pins

un-pleas'ant, a., disagreeable, offensive

un-plumbed' (plumd), a., unknown in depth

un-pop'u-lar, a., not popular, disliked, **-ity**

un-prec'e-dent-ed, a., not done till now

un-prej'u-diced, a., fair, impartial

un-prê-ten'tious, a., modest, not showy

un-prin'ci-pled (puld), a., without good principles

un-prö-fes'sion-al, a., not in professional manner or capacity

un-ques'tion-a-ble, a., without any doubt, **-bly**

un-quote', v., end quotation

un-rav'el, v., separate threads, solve

un-rē'al, a., imaginary

un-rēel', v., unwind reel

un-rê-gen'êr-ate, a., wicked, bad

un-rê-lent'ing, a., not forgiving

un-rê-lī'a-ble, a., not dependable, **-bility**

un-rê-mit'ting, a., not slowing up, continuous

un-rê-sêrve', n., direct manner, frankness, **-d**

un-rest', n., turmoil

un-right'eous (rī-chus) a., wrong, wicked

un-rul'y, a., not controllable,

intractable

un-safe', a., risky, dangerous, **-ly**

un-sal'a-ble, a., unable to be sold

un-san'i-târ-y, a., not healthy

un-sa'vör-y, a., tasteless, offensive

un-scâthed', a., wholly unharmed

un-scī-ên-tif'ic, a., not according to science, **-ally**

un-scram'ble, v., resolve, clarify

un-screw', v., loosen screws

un-scrū'pū-lous, a., unlawful, dishonest, **-ly**

un-sēal', v., break seal, open

un-sēa'sön-a-ble, a., untimely, inappropriate

un-sēat', v., remove from office

un-sēem'ly, a., not proper, indecorous, **-liness**

un-self'ish, a., concerned about others, generous

un-set'tled, a., changeable, immature, unpaid

un-shēathe', v., pull out from scabbard, **-d**

un-shod', a., without shoes

un-sight'ly, a., ugly, unattractive

un-skilled', a., lacking technical training

un-snârl', v., bring order, untangle

un-sō'cia-ble, a., not friendly with others

un-sö-phis'ti-cāt-ed, a., not affected, natural

un-sound', a., not perfect, invalid, false, not safe

un-spâr'ing, a., ruthless, liberal

un-spēak'a-ble, a., not to be said, wicked, unalterable

un-stā'ble, a., not fixed, changeable, **-ness**

un-steăd'y, a., shaky, not dependable, **-ily**

un-stick', v., loosen, free

un-strung', a., upset, having strings loosened, nervous

un-stŭd'iĕd, a., natural, simple

un-sŭb-stan'ti-āt-ĕd, a., not proven

un-sūit'ĕd, a., not fit

un-sung', a., not sung or honored

un-tan'gle, v., clear up,

straighten out

un·think'a·ble, *a.*, not to be considered

un·think'ing, *a.*, thoughtless, **-ly**

un·thread' (thred), *v.*, remove thread

un·ti'dy, *a.*, not neat

un·tie', *v.*, make loose, **-d**

un·til', *conj.*, to time when, before

un·time'ly, *a.*, at wrong time, premature

un·told', *a.*, incalculable, kept secret

un·to'ward, (un·tôrd), *a.*, unruly, unfortunate, **-ly**

un·tram'meled, *a.*, not held back

un·true', *a.*, false, disloyal

un·truth', *n.*, lie, **-ful**

un·tu'tôred, *a.*, not informed, naive

un·twist', *v.*, undo something twisted

un·ū'sū·al, *a.*, not ordinary, uncommon, rare, **-ly**

un·veil' (vayl), *v.*, bring into the open, expose

un·war'rant·a·ble, *a.*, not justified, inexcusable

un·war'y, *a.*, not alert, gullible

un·whole'sôme, *a.*, unhealthful, harmful

un·wield'y, *a.*, difficult to handle

un·wise', *a.*, foolish, imprudent

un·wit'ting, *a.*, unaware, inadvertent

un·wônt'éd, *a.*, unaccustomed, rare

un·yōke', *v.*, free, loosen from yoke

up, *adv., prep.*, higher, ascending, toward, advanced, ended

up·brāid', *v.*, scold, criticize, **-ing**

up'bring·ing, *n.*, early training

up'chuck', *v.*, vomit

up·end', *v.*, stand on end

up'grāde, *n.*, upward slope

up·grāde', *v.*, promote, improve

up·hēav'al, *n.*, violent disturbance

up·hōld', *v.*, support

up·hōl'stêr, *v.*, stuff and cover furniture, **-er**

up'kēep, *n.*, maintenance

up·lift', *v.*, raise, exalt spiritually

up'lift, *n.*, good feeling

up·ōn', *prep.*, on

up'pêr, *a.*, higher in rank

up·pêr-class'man, *n.*, junior or senior year student

up'pêr-cut, *n.*, blow at chin

up'pish, *a.*, arrogant

up'right, *a.*, vertical, honorable

up·ris'ing, *n.*, revolt, insurrection

up'rôar, *n.*, loud disturbance, **-ious**

up·rôôt', *v.*, pull up by roots, remove

up·set', *v.*, overturn, **-ing**

up'set, *n.*, unexpected defeat, disturbance

up'shot, *n.*, conclusion, outcome

up'sīde, *n.*, upper side

up·stāirs', *a.*, above first floor

up·stand'ing, *a.*, honest, good character

up'stärt, *n.*, one newly rich or powerful

up'tō·dāte', *a.*, to present time

ū·rā'ni·um, *n.*, metallic element used in atom bomb

ûr'bán, *a.*, relating to cities, **-ize**

ûr·bāne', *a.*, polite, smooth, **-ly**

ûr'chin, *n.*, roguish youngster

û·rē'mi·à, *n.*, disease in blood

ū·rē'thrà, *n.*, duct from bladder

ûrge, *v.*, press, attempt to convince, provoke

ûrg'ên·cy, *n.*, need for attention at once, **-t**

ū'ri·nàl, *n.*, toilet for urinating

ū'rine (in), *n.*, liquid from kidneys

ûrn, *n.*, vase, container

ū·rō·gen'i·tàl, *a.*, relating to sex organs

us, *pro.*, objective case of we

ūs'áble, *a.*, ready for use

ūs'áge, *n.*, custom, way of using, habit

ūse, *v.*, put into action or service, **-able**

ūse (ewes), *n.*, need, power, purpose, **-ful**

ūse'lèss, *a.*, of no worth, ineffectual

ush′êr, n., one who escorts persons to seats

us′tū-lāte, a., blackened by burning

ū′sū-ăl, a., common, ordinary, expected

ū′su-rêr (zhe), n., money lender charging exorbitant interest, **-ry**

ū-sûrp′, v., seize without right, **-ation**

ū-ten′sil, n., useful tool, vessel

ū′têr-us, n., the womb, **-ine**

──────── V ────────

vā′cant, a., empty, expressionless, not occupied, **-cancy**

vā′cāte, v., remove oneself, make empty, annual

vă-cā′tion, n., period of leisure, intermission

vac′ci-nāte (vak), v., inject vaccine, **-nation**

vac′cine (seen), n., bacterial preparation as protection against disease

vac′il-lāte (vas), v., change mind often, fluctuate, **-lation**

vac′ū-ous, a., empty, unintelligent, **-ity**

vac′ū-um, n., space completely empty, void

vag′á-bond, n., idle wanderer, tramp

vă-gâr′y, n., unpredictable action, caprice

vă-gī′nă (jy), n., opening to female reproductive organs, sheath

vā′grant, n., tramp, rover, wanderer, **-grancy**

vāgue, a., not clear, hazy, indefinite, confused

vāin, a., unsuccessful, fruitless, nugatory

vāle (poetic), n., valley

val-ē-dic′tō-ry, a., farewell address, **-rian**

val′en-tīne, n., love message, sweetheart

val′ét, n., personal manservant

val′iant, a., brave, stouthearted

val′id, a., effective, sound, **-ity**

vă-līse′ (lēes), n., small suitcase

ū-til-i-târ′i-ăn, a., useful, practical, **-ism**

ū-til′i-ty, n., usefulness, public service

ū′ti-līze, v., use, **-r**

ut′môst, a., most possible, extreme

ut′têr, a., greatest, most extreme, total

ut′têr, v., say, express, **-ance**

ux-ô′ri-ous (uksôrius), a., excessively submissive to wife

val′lēy, n., area between two hills, depression

val′ör, n., bravery, **-ous**

val′ū-á-ble, a., having worth, rare, important, expensive

val′ūe, v., n., estimate, consider worthy, importance, cost, **-d**

valve, n., device that controls flow of liquid or gas

van, n., large truck

van′dăl, n., one who destroys property, **-ism**

van′guârd, n., group or one in forefront

vă-nil′lă, n., flavoring

van′ish, v., disappear

van′i-ty, n., false pride, conceit, dressing table

van′quish (kw), v., defeat, conquer, **-ment**

vap′id, a., flat, dull, insipid

vā′pōr, n., steam, gas, **-ize**

vā′pōr lock, n., interruption of fuel flow by vapor bubbles

vâr′i-á-ble, a., likely to change, fickle

vâr′i-ánce, n., difference, discord, **-ant**

vâr′i-côse, a., enlarged, abnormally swollen

vâr′ied, a., changed, unlike

vâr′i-e-gāt-ed, a., varied, of different colors

vă-rī′é-ty, n., kind, assortment, change

vâr′i-ous, a., numerous, different

vär′nish, n., liquid coating for wood or metal

vâr′y, v., change, switch

vas-cū-lár, a., relating to body or plant tubes

vāse, n., flower container

vast, a., tremendous, large

väude'ville, n., theatrical entertainment of varied acts

vault, v., n., jump over, safe, arched roof

vaunt, v., brag, show off

vēal, n., calf meat

vēēp, n., vice president

vēer, v., change course, swerve

veg'e-tā-ble (vej-ta), n., edible plant

veg-ē-târ'i-an, n., one who eats no meat

veg'e-tāte, v., grow in the manner of plants, exist

veg-ē-tā'tion, n., plant growth

vē'hē-mēnce, a., ardent emotion, fury, **-ment**

vē'hi-cle (vēe-i-kil), n., conveyance, means of expression

veil (vayl), n., cloth face or head covering

veiled, a., hidden, mysterious, disguised

vein (vayn), n., blood vessel, rib-like streak, tube of leaf, mineral deposit, mood, mineral in rock

vē-loc'i-ty, n., speed, rapidly

vel'vēt, n., smooth, rich, soft cloth

vē'nāl, a., capable of being bribed, mercenary

vend, v., sell, publish

vē-nēer', n., thin covering, false show, gloss

ven'êr-ā-ble, a., worthy of respect, old

ven'er-āte, v., treat with reverence, **-ation**

vē-nē'rē-āl, a., connected with cohabitation

venge'ance, n., punishment in return for harm done

vē'ni-āl, a., excusable, pardonable

ven'i-sŏn, n., deer meat

ven'om, n., snake poison, malignity

vent, n., v., opening, express feelings

ven'ti-lāte, v., circulate air in room, **-lation**

ven-tril'ō-quist, n., one who makes voice appear to come from elsewhere, **-quism**

ven'ture, v., engage in risky activity, take a risk,

-turous

vē-rā'cious, a., truthful, honest, **-city**

vē-ran'dâ, n., porch

vêrb, n., part of speech indicating action

vêr'bāl, a., relating to words, spoken, **-ize**

vêr-bā'tim, adv., word for word, exactly

vêr-bōse', a., using too many words, talkative, **-bosity**

ver-bō'tēn, a., forbidden

vêr'dânt, a., green, immature, unripe

vêr'dict, n., decision of jury, opinion

vêrge, n., edge, brink, threshold

ver'i-fy, v., prove truth of, confirm, **-fication**

vêr-i-si-mil'i-tūde, n., seeming to be true, probability

ver'i-ty, n., truth

vêr-mil'ion (yun), n., brilliant red color

vêr'min, n., troublesome animals, offensive person

vêr-nac'ū-lär, a., native speech or language, dialect

vêr'nāl, a., relating to spring, fresh, young

vêr'sā-tile, a., capable, having various skills

vêrse, n., light poetry, stanza

vêr'sion, n., particular description

vêr'sus, prep., opposed, against

vêr'tē-brā, n., segment of spinal column

vêr'ti-cāl, a., perpendicular, plumb

vêrve, n., energy, vivacity, vitality

ver'y, a., adv., actual, similar, in the extreme, truly

ves'pêr, n., evening prayer

ves'sēl, n., container, ship

vest, n., sleeveless garment

ves'ti-būle, n., hallway entrance

ves'tige (tij), n., trace, evidence

vest'-pock'ět, n., tiny, small

ves'try, n., meeting room in church

vet'êr-ân, n., former member of armed forces, person of long experience

vet- êr-i-nâr'i-ân, n., animal doctor

vē'tō, n., refusal to pass bill approved by lawmaking body

vex-ā'tion, n., irritation, affliction

vi'ā-duct, n., arched bridge

vi'ăl, n., glass container

vi'brănt, a., resounding, lively, energetic

vi'brāte, v., move back and forth, **-bration**

vī-câr'i-ous, a., indirect, experienced through another

vīce, n., wickedness, defect

vīce-, (prefix), assistant

vi'cē-vēr'sä, a., opposite

vi-cin'i-ty, n., neighborhood, proximity

vi'cious, a., savage, malicious

vi-cis'si-tūde, n., natural difficulty, regular change

vic'tim, n., one injured, destroyed or harmed

vic'tō-ry, n., conquest, triumph, **-rious**

vict'uals (vitils), n., food, provisions

vid'ē-ō, n., television

view (vu), n., sight of, vision, something observed, opinion

view'point, n., attitude

vig'il, n., watch, guard, eve of feast

vig'i-lánce, n., watchfulness, **-lant**

vig'ör, n., energy, force, **-ous**

vīle, a., evil, base

vil'i-fy, v., insult, spread evil rumor, **-fication**

vil'lăge, n., little town

vil'lain (lin), n., evil person, scoundrel, **-ous**

vim, n., strength, energy, vitality

win'di-cāte, v., clear name, defend, justify, **-cation**

vīne, n., climbing plant

vin'é-gär, n., acid-type liquid

vine'yärd (vin), n., place where grapes grow

vi'nyl, n., type of plastic

vī-ō-lä, n., stringed musical instrument

vī'ō-lāte, v., act against, break law, **-lation**

vī'ō-lence, n., forceful action, intensity, **-lent**

vī'ō-let, n., flower

vī-ō-lin', n., musical instrument, **-ist**

VIP, n., very important person

vī'pêr, n., snake, scoundrel

vir'gin, n., one who has not had sexual relations, **-ity**

vir'ile, a., manly, energetic, **-ility**

vîr'tū-ăl-ly, adv., almost, in effect

vîr'tūe (chōo), n., morality, valor, potency, **-tuous**

vîr-tū-ō'sō, n., skilled musical artist

vir'ū-lênt, a., poisonous, full of hate, malignant

vi'rus, n., disease causing agent

vi'sá (vee), n., passport endorsement

vis'ăge, n., appearance, face

vīse, n., clamp

vis'i-ble, a., capable of being seen, apparent, evident

vi'sion, n., sight, seeing, something seen

vi'sion-âr-y, a., imaginary, utopian

vis'it, v., go to see or stay with, inflict, **-ation**

vis'tä, n., long-range view, prospect

vis'ū-ăl, a., relating to seeing, visible

vī'tăl, a., relating to life or living, extremely important, essential

vī-tal'i-ty, n., energy, vigor

vī'tă-min, n., energy giving material needed by the body

vī'ti-āte (vi-shi), v., contaminate, debase, invalidate, **-ation**

vit'rē-ous, a., resembling glass

vit-ri-ol'ic, a., biting, sarcastic

vī-tū'pêr-āte, v., insult, berate, scold, **-ation**

vi-vā'cious, a., lively, sprightly, spirited, **-city**

viv'id, a., brilliant, striking, sharp, intense

viv-i-sec'tion, n., operation on live animals to aid research

vō-cab'ū-lâr-y, n., list of words, words used by person

vō'căl, a., of voice, spoken or sung, **-ize**

vō-cā'tion, n., occupation,

calling, career, job, **-al**

vō-cif'er-ous, *a.,* clamorous, boisterous

vōgue, *n.,* style, current fashion, popularity

voice, *n.,* organ of speech and communication, sound, expression

void, *a., v.,* empty space, meaningless, make useless, nullify

vol'ā-tile, *a.,* changeable, fickle, **-tilize**

vol-cā'nō, *n.,* hole in earth from which lava, gas, etc. comes, **-nic**

vō-li'tion, *n.,* will to do

vol'lèy, *n.,* forceful spread of something, gun discharge

vōlt, *n.,* unit of electric force

vol'ū-ble, *a.,* easily rolling or turning, talkative

vol'ume (yoon), *n.,* book, much of something, **-uminous**

vol'un-târ-y, *a.,* done by own

will or choice

vō-lup'tū-ous, *a.,* sensuous, luxurious

vom'it, *v.,* expel from stomach, upchuck

vō-rā'cious, *a.,* greedily hungry, eager, ravenous

vōte, *v., n.,* cast ballot, total ballots cast, **-r**

vouch, *v.,* express faith in one, guarantee, affirm, attest

vouch-sāfe', *v.,* grant, give, bestow, permit

vow, *n.,* solemn promise

vow'els, *n.,* speech sounds: a, e, i, o, u, sometimes y

voy'āge, *n.,* trip, journey, cruise

vul'cán-ize, *v.,* treat rubber

vul'gàr, *a.,* coarse, profane, **-ity**

vul'nêr-á-ble, *a.,* open to attack, **-bility**

vul'ture, *n.,* scavenger bird, predatory person

W

wäd, *n.,* rolled up piece of cotton, large amount of money

wäd'dle, *v.,* walk unevenly

wāde, *v.,* walk through water, study

wā'fêr, *n.,* thin cookie

wäf'fle, *n.,* indented cake

waft, *v.,* float

wag, *v.,* move back and forth

wāge, *n.,* pay, salary

wāge, *v.,* engage in

wā'gêr, *n.,* bet, stake

wag'ôn, *n.,* four-wheeled vehicle, **-er**

waif, *n.,* homeless child

wail, *v.,* lament, complain

waist, *n.,* middle part of body

wait, *v., n.,* remain for, watch, offer food, time spent expecting one, **-ing**

wait'êr, *n.,* one who serves tables

wāive, *v.,* give up rights to, abandon

wāke, *v., n.,* arouse from sleep, night vigil beside dead body

wälk, *v., n.,* move by foot, pathway

walk-a-wāy, *n.,* easy victory

wälk'-up, *n.,* apartment that cannot be reached with elevator

wäll, *n.,* horizontal side of building

wäl'lèt, *n.,* purse, billfold

wäll'flow'er, *n.,* unpopular person

wäl'lŏp, *v.,* hit, beat

wäl'lōw, *v.,* wade in filth

wäl'nut, *n.,* type of nut, wood

wäl'rus, *n.,* sea animal

wältz, *n.,* type of dance, musical time

wän, *a.,* pale

wän'dêr, *v.,* go aimlessly from place to place

wänt, *v.,* desire, need

wän'tŏn, *a.,* inconsiderate, cruel, unrestrained

wär (wôr), *n.,* fight between two sides

wärd, *n.,* person under guardian, section

wärd'ên, *n.,* prison manager, guard

wāre'house, *n.,* building for storing goods, **-man**

wār'i-ly, *adv.,* cautiously

wärm (wôrm), *a.,* slightly hot, friendly, angry, close, **-th**

---

wärn, v., caution against, **-ing**

wärp, v., force out of shape, arrange yarns

wär'ran-ty, n., guarantee

wär'y, a., on guard, cautious

wäsh, v., make clean, flow over, coat, purify, saturate

washed'-up', a., finished, ready to quit

wäsh'êr, n., washing machine, flat ring

wäsh'out, n., failure, place where earth is washed away

wäsp, n., insect

WASP, n., white Anglo-Saxon Protestant

wäste, n., v., garbage, unneeded material, get rid of foolishly, grow thin, **-ful**

wätch, n., v., device for telling time, time division on shipboard, guard, look for, see, **-ful**

wä'têr, n., liquid without color or taste, **-y**

wä'têr-fäll, n., stream falling from high place

wä'têr-mel-ôn, n., large red, round fruit

wä'têr-shed, n., ground source of water supply, crucial dividing line

wätt, n., unit of electricity

wäve, n., v., curling motion, rise of water, move hand up and down

wäv'y, a., curling, undulating

wax, n., hard material made by bees or similar matter, polish

way, n., direction, course, means, road

way-lay', v., lie in wait for

way'out, adj., not conventional

way'wärd, a., unpredictable, disobedient

wē, pro., first person plural of I

wēak, a., lacking strength, ineffective, changeable, breakable, **-en**

wealth (welth) n., affluence, profusion, **-y**

wēan, v., win over, coax away from, estrange

weap'ôn, n., instrument of combat

weâr, v., cover body, become tattered, last long in use, decay through use

wēar'y, a., extremely tired, worn out, **-ily**

weath'êr, n., v., condition in atmosphere, endure

wēave, v., n., manipulate threads into cloth, way cloth is woven

web, n., close network of threads, **-bing**

wed, v., marry

wed'ding, n., marriage ceremony, nuptial

wedge, n., v., tapered piece of wood, press into

wēed, n., undesirable wild plant

wēek, n., seven day period, **-ly**

wēep, v., cry, ooze, **-ing**

wēe'vil, n., food-destroying insect

weigh (way), v., determine heaviness of object, consider

weight'y, a., heavy, **-ily**

wēird, a., mysterious, strange

wel'cöme, v., n., greet, receive with pleasure, cordial greeting

wel'fâre, n., well being of person

well, n., v., adv., opening in ground for getting water, gush, to be physically fit, satisfactorily, enough

welsh, v., fail to pay debt

welt, n., shoe leather piece, raised ridge on skin

welt'êr, n., disorder, confusion, turmoil

wend, v., go, travel

west, n., direction of setting sun, **-ern**

wet, a., containing water, rainy

whack, n., v., blow, beat, chop

whāle, n., large aquatic mammal

what (wut), pro., adv., something which, the thing that

what-ev'êr, pro., regardless of, no matter what, as is desired, anything, any degree

whēat, n., cereal grain

whēel, n., round object which turns on middle axis, (coll.) important person

whēeze, v., breathe with difficulty, wheeze audibly

when, adv., at the time

which, although

whence, *adv.*, from where

where (wâr) *adv.*, at which, in what place

where-as´, *conj.*, since

whet, *v.*, stimulate, excite

wheth´ér, *conj.*, choice of one or another

which, *pro.*, word used as question to distinguish between

whiff, *n.*, smell, breath of, hint

whif´fle, *v., n.*, blow easily, (coll.) short haircut

while, *n., conj., v.*, period of time, during which, pass time

whim, *n.*, thoughtless action

whim´pér, *v.*, cry in broken tone, complain

whim´si-cál, *a.*, imaginative, capricious

whīne, *v.*, utter steady crying sound

whip, *n., v.*, lash at end of stick, beat with lash, -**ping**

whirl, *v.*, spin around

whirl´pōōl, *n.*, water in fast circular motion, maelstrom

whisk´ērs, *n.*, hair on chin

whis´kēy, *n.*, alcoholic beverage

whis´pér, *n., v.*, quiet tone, speak softly

whis´tle, *n.*, high pitched sound, small wind instrument

whīte, *n.*, absence of color

whith´ér, *adv.*, where, to what place

whit´tle, *v.*, chip wood pieces

who (hoo), *pro.*, refers to certain persons

who-dun´it (coll.), *n.*, mystery story

who-ev´ér, *pro.*, whatever person, who

whōle (hohl), *a.*, total, entire, unhurt

whōle´sāle, *n.*, at cost price, in large amounts, indiscriminate

whōle´sŏme, *a.*, healthy, desirable, -**ly**

whŏl´ly, *adv.*, entirely

whom (hoom), *pro.*, objective case of who

whop´pér (wop), *n.*, monstrous lie

whose (hoos), *pro.*, possessive case of who

why (wī), *adv.*, for what

wick, *n.*, lamp, candle part

wick´ėd, *a.*, wrong, evil, sinful

wīde, *a.*, roomy, ample, of great range, -**ly**

wid´ōw, *n.*, woman whose husband has died

wid´ōw-ér, *n.*, husband whose wife has died

width, *n.*, wideness

wiēld, *v.*, use, manipulate

wiē´nér, *n.*, frankfurter

wīfe, *n.*, married woman

wig, *n.*, artificial hair piece

wig´gle, *v.*, shake from side to side

wig´wäm, *n.*, Indian tent

wīld, *a.*, not cultivated, untamed, uncivilized, -**ly**

wil´dér-nèss, *n.*, overgrown forest, confusing place

wīle, *n.*, sly trick

will, *n.*, desire, selection, legal document leaving property after death

will´ful, *a.*, determined, stubborn

wilt, *v.*, become limp, droop

win, *v.*, succeed in contest, obtain

wind, *n.*, moving air

wīnd, *v.*, twist around, coil, turn

wind´bag, *n.*, idly talkative person

wind´ėd, *a.*, tired, short of breath

win´dōw, *n.*, glass used in building, opening

wind´shiēld, *n.*, glass in car front

wind sock, *n.*, fabric cone-shaped indicator of wind direction

wīne, *n.*, alcoholic drink made from fermented fruits

wind´shiēld, *n.*, glass in car front

wind sock, *n.*, fabric cone-shaped indicator of wind direction

wind tunnel, *n.*, tunnel for testing effect of wind pressure

wīne, *n.*, alcoholic drink made from fermented fruits

wing, *n.*, body part of bird that allows flying, part shaped like wing, -**ed**

wing-ding, *n.*, wild or lavish party

wink, v., close and open one eye quickly

win'ning, n., prize, something won

wīno, n., one who is chronically addicted to drinking wine

win'têr, n. season of cold weather, **-try**

wīpe, v., clean off, rub clean, obliterate, **-r**

wīre, n., v., thin metal thread, send telegram

wīre'phō-tō, n., picture sent over wire

wīr'y, a., tall, slender, strong, sinewy

wis'dŏm, n. knowledge, insight

wīse, a., n., smart, using sensible judgment, way

wīse'crack, n., funny retort, jest

wish, v., desire, **-ing**

wisp, n., small bit, fragment

wist'ful, a., longing, yearning

wit, n., intelligence, cleverness, clever one, **-ty**

with, prep., among, in presence of, accompanied by

with-drăw', v., take away from, remove from, retract

with-hōld', v., keep, refrain, retain

with-in', prep, inside of

with-out', prep., outside of, not having in possession

with-stand', v., endure, forbear

wit'lĕss, a., ignorant, foolish

wit'nĕss, n., v., one who observes occurrence, legally sworn observer, observe

wiz'ärd, n., magician, very skillful or clever person

wiz'ĕned, a., dried up, shrunken, withered

wob'ble, v., shake unsteadily, **-bly**

wōe, n., sadness, tragedy, **-ful**

wok, n., Chinese cooking utensil

wolf (woolf), n., wild canine, destructive person

wom'ăn, n., adult female, mistress

womb (woom), n., female organ for holding baby before birth

wŏn'dêr, n., surprise, astonishment, amazement,

-ful

wont, a., accustomed, inclined, apt

wōō, v., court, be in love, seek to gain

wood, n., lumber, **-en**

wool, n., sheep hair, **-en**

wŏrd (wûrd), n., sound that conveys thought, part of language

wôrk (wûrk), n., v., effort put forth to accomplish goal, artistic achievement, labor, do

wôrld (wûrld), n., all of earth, universe, **-ly**

wôrm, n., tiny, crawling animal

wŏr'ry (wûr), n., anxious concern, difficulty

wŏrse (wûrs), a., more undesirable, more incorrect

wŏr'ship (wûr), v., perform religious ritual, **-per**

wôr'stĕd (woos-tid), n., type of woolen cloth

wôrth (wûr), n., merit, riches,

-while

wôr'thy (wûr), a., valuable, estimable

woūnd, n., injury

wran'gle, v., argue, **-r**

wrap, v., enclose in covering,

-ping

wrath, n., anger, **-ful**

wrĕak, v., inflict, do

wrĕath, n., garland

wreck, n., v., destroy, damage, tear down, ruin, destruction, ill person

wrench, v., n., twist, device for turning bolts

wrest, v., remove from by force

wres'tle, v., struggle, engage in body-throwing contest, **-r**

wretch, n., scoundrel, profoundly unhappy person

wretch'ĕd, a., miserable, despicable, inferior

wring, v., twist, contort

wrin'kle, n., tiny ridge, method

wrist, n., joint between hand and arm

wrīte, v., inscribe, compose

wrī'têr, n., author, one who writes, composer

wrīthe, v., twist in pain, wrench

wrŏng, a., improper, incorrect, wicked, immoral

wrought (råwht), *a.*, brought about, created, excited

wry, *a.*, turned to side, wrongheaded, twisted, **-ness**

X

xan'thic (zan-thik), *a.*, yellowish in color

xē'bec (zee), *n.*, three-masted vessel

xē'ni-ål (zee), *a.*, relating to hospitality

xen-ō-phō'bi-å (zen), *n.*, hatred of foreigners, **-c**

Xerox, *n.*, copying machine

Xmas, *n.*, Christmas

X-radiation, *n.*, X-ray exposure

X'-ray, *n.*, short wave ray used to take picture of interior body parts and to treat certain diseases

xy'lem (zy), *n.*, woody tissue of plant

xy'loid (zy), *a.*, relating to wood

xy'lō-phōne (zy), *n.*, percussion instrument

xỹs'tẽr (zis), *n.*, tool used by surgeons to scrape bones

Y

yacht (yot), *n.*, pleasure ship

yam, *n.*, vegetable resembling sweet potato

yank, *v.*, pull with quick vigorous movement

yap, *v.*, bark, chatter

yärd, *n.*, 3 feet, land space near house, court

yärn, *n.*, thread, story

yåwn, *v.*, make wide-mouthed, sleepy sound, gape

yawp, *v.*, squawk, complain

yēan, *v.*, give birth to lamb or goat

yēar, *n.*, twelve months

yēar'ling, *n.*, year old animal

yēarn, *v.*, long for, **-ing**

yēast, *n.*, substance used to raise dough

yel'lōw, *n.*, primary color

yen, *v.*, desire for, longing

yeō'mån, *n.*, clerk in U. S. Navy

yes, *adv.*, expression of positive stand, agreement

yes'tẽr-day, *n.*, day prior to today, times past

yet, *adv.*, till now, still, at present time, however

yew, *n.*, evergreen tree

yiēld, *v.*, give, produce, relinquish, **-ing**

yō'dèl, *v.*, warble in high tones

yōke, *n., v.*, wooden device used to tie oxen together, onus, burden

yōlk (yōhk), *n.*, yellow part of egg

yōre, *adv.*, time long past

yōū, *pro.*, personal pronoun, 2nd person

young (yung), *a.*, being in early years, youthful, immature, **-ster**

yôur, *pro.*, possessive of you

yôur-self', *pro.*, emphasis on you

youth, *n.*, young person, period between childhood and maturity, **-ful**

yuc'câ, *n.*, evergreen plant

Z

zā'ny, *n.*, one who clowns, foolish person, simpleton

zē al, *n.*, eagerness, fervor, passion

zeal'ôt, *n.*, fanatical partisan, **-ry**

zē'brå, *n.*, striped animal

Zen, *n.*, Buddhist sect

zē'nith, *n.*, highest point possible, climax

zeph'ỹr (zef-ír), *n.*, gentle breeze

---

at bāy åkin fâre cär åll end hē dèfy hêr ill īce sîr

zē′rō, *n.*, nothing, nonentity, cipher

zē′rō hour, *n.*, time set to begin military attack, critical point

zē′rō-zē′rō, *adj.*, zero visibility and ceiling

zest, *n.*, enthusiasm, relish, gusto, **-ful**

zig′zag, *a.*, moving sharply from one direction to another, angular

zinc (zink), *n.*, metallic element

zing, *n.*, vitality, vim

zip, *n.*, energy, vim

zip′pêr, *n.*, fastener

zir′con, *n.*, mineral

zith′êr, *n.*, stringed musical instrument

zō′di-ac, *n.*, imaginary broad belt of the heavens covering the lines of 12 constellations (zodiac signs) around which the sun travels

zōne, *n.*, band, district, area

zonked, *adj.*, under influence of drug or alcohol

zōō, *n.*, place where animals are exhibited to public

zō-ol′ŏ-gy, *n.*, science and study of animals, **-gical**

zōōm, *n.*, *v.*, sudden loud, harsh sound, fly upward suddenly

zōōm lens, *n.*, image-varying lens

zy-mō′sis, *n.*, process of fermentation, **-tic**

zy′mûr-gy, *n.*, part of chemistry that deals with fermentation

---

rod ōld wŏn fôr tōō good out oil owl pup ūnit ûrn

PUNCTUATION

Punctuation serves to clarify written language. Although styles may differ, it should be borne in mind that the modern trend is toward less punctuation. Some of the most important rules follow:

Period

The period is used:

- After a declarative or imperative sentence
    It is raining.
    Bring it to me now.
- After abbreviations and initials
    Mon. Tues.   Dr. Mrs.
    J. H. Smith   A.M. P.M.
- To indicate omitted material. Three periods (. . .) in text, four periods (. . . .) at end of text.

Comma

The comma is used:

- Between introductory modifying phrase and subject modified
    As the storm approached, they turned back.
- To separate words or figures that might otherwise be misinterpreted
    In 1946, 18,000 more items were sold.
    To John, Jones is the best.
- To set off parenthetic words, phrases, or nonrestrictive clauses
    The new rule, no matter whom it may affect, will be strictly enforced.
    Mary Smith, who is my secretary, is ill.
    We will not, therefore, attend the meeting.
- To set off words which are in apposition or contrast
    Mr. Jones, the attorney, presented the award.
    Jane, not Susan, won the award.
- Before the conjunction in a compound sentence with an independent clause
    He tried to find her, but she had gone away.
    I am giving a party, and I hope you will come.
- To set off conjunctive adverbs or transitional phrases
    We will not, however, accept the shipment.
- Before a coordinate conjunction between two independent clauses

John will not follow instructions, and he may lose his position.

- To separate declarative clause and interrogative clause

    It's a lovely day, isn't it?

- After interrogative clause followed by direct question

    You understand, do you not?

- To indicate the omission of a word or words

    Once I had everything; now, nothing.

- To set off noun or phrase in direct address

    George, will you please close the door?

The comma is omitted

- Between month and year in dates

    June 1967

- Between two nouns which identify each other

    Thomas Wolfe's novel *You Can't Go Home Again* is my choice.

- Before a dash

- Between a verb and its complement

    Mary said, that she would do the work. (Incorrect)

- Between a subject and its verb or predicate

    Where you go, does not matter. (Incorrect)

- Between a verb and its direct object

    She than played, the *Moonlight Sonata*. (Incorrect)

Semicolon

The semicolon is used:

- To separate independent coordinate clauses connected in meaning where no coordinate conjunction is used

    I did the work for them; they would not accept it.

- Between statements too similar in meaning to be separate sentences, and between contrasting statements

    No; I will not do it.

    Summer is hot; winter is cold.

- Before a coordinate conjunction between independent clauses when one or both contain internal punctuation

    John, who had worked hard, hoped for the

> promotion; but Jim, who had done more research, received it.

NOTE: Avoid the semicolon when a comma will suffice.

Colon

The colon is used:

- Before a final clause that extends or amplifies preceding matter
  > Owning a car is no longer a luxury: it is a necessity.
- Before a list of items or details
  > Please bring the following items: notebooks, pens, rulers.
- As introduction to matter which forms a complete sentence, question, or quotation
  > This question was discussed at the meeting: What policy will we follow in the future?
- To express time
  > 8:45 A.M.
  > 10:15 P.M.
- After salutation of formal or business letter
  > Dear Sir:
  > Gentlemen:
- To express ratio
  > 1:2::3:6

Parentheses

Parentheses are used:

- To set off explanatory or commentary matter which is not part of the main statement or grammatical element, but may be included.
  > The results of the experiment (see Fig. 2) are inconclusive.
  > That day (what a beautiful day it was!) was very happy for me.
- To enclose a number, symbol, or letter used as appositive or confirmation
  > The lease expires in sixty (60) days.
- To enclose enumerations designated by letters or figures in text.
  > In order to survive, man needs (1) food, (2) clothing, and (3) shelter.
- To enclose explanatory word

The Baltimore (Md.) Evening Sun
The Hanover (Pa.) General Hospital

Dash

The dash is used:

- To indicate a break or change of thought in sentence

    Do your remember—of course, you wouldn't—what happened that night?
- To indicate interruption or unfinished sentence

    Wait a moment. What I am trying to say—
- To clarify meaning, instead of commas or parentheses

    We must prepare now—food, clothing, fuel—for the coming winter.
- For rhetorical or elocutionary effect

    He has—at last—made his decision.
- To indicate unfinished word or omitted figure

    Have you seen Mr. B—since that incident?

    Nixon, Richard M. 1913—

Question Mark

The question mark is used:

- After an interrogatory sentence that is a direct query

    Where are you going?
- After each query if more than one query is contained in the same sentence

    Who can solve this problem? can you? can he? can anyone?
- To express doubt or inaccuracy

    She said that she weighs 100(?) pounds.

    Cesare Borgia was born in 1476(?).

Quotation marks

Quotation marks are used:

- To enclose a direct quotation

    When I asked him, he said "No."
- To enclose titles of articles, chapters of books, songs, speeches. (The titles of books, plays, poems, symphonies, operas, and works of art are usually italicized. Italics are denoted by underscoring in typewritten and handwritten material.

- To enclose terms that are misnomers, slang, ironical, coined, or sobriquets

NOTE: Quotation marks are generally placed outside commas and periods and placed inside colons and semicolons.

- Single quotation marks enclose quoted matter occuring within a quotation.

    He told me ''Robert said 'yes.' ''

Exclamation point

The exclamation point is used:
- To express surprise or deep emotion

    I can't believe it is really you!
    What a terrible loss!
- To add emphasis or attract attention

    Hurry! the offer expires next week!
    Look out! You will fall!

Apostrophe

The apostrophe is used:
- To form the possessive case of nouns and some pronouns by adding apostrophe and s. When a noun ends in s, place the apostrophe after the s.

    John's car
    wolves' dens
- To indicate omission of letters or figures

    Couldn't
    I've
    '67 (1967)

Brackets

Brackets are used:
- To enclose parenthetical material within parentheses

    (Follow instructions carefully [see p. 100] for best results).
- To enclose correction, omission, explanation, interpolation, audience reaction

    Ann's birthday is the 7 [8] of July.
    They will go [to New York] next week.
    He learned, to his sorrow, *no es oro todo lo que reluce* [all is not gold that glitters].
    The committee has decided [I do not agree] to increase the membership dues.
    By our united efforts, we shall achieve victory! [Applause.]

THE METRIC SYSTEM

Linear Measure

1 millimeter = 0.03937 inch
1 centimeter = 0.3937 inch
1 decimeter = 3.937 inches
1 meter = 39.37 inches or 3.2808 feet
1 decameter = 393.7 inches
1 hectometer = 328.08 feet
1 kilometer = 0.621 mile or 3,280.8 feet
1 myriameter = 6.21 miles

Square Measure

1 square millimeter = 0.00155 square inch
1 square centimeter = 0.15499 square inch
1 square decimeter = 15.499 square inches
1 square meter = 1,549.9 square inches or 1.196 square yards
1 square decameter = 119.6 square yards
1 square hectometer = 2.471 acres
1 square kilometer = 0.386 square mile or 247.1 acres

Land Measure

1 centiare = 1,549.9 square inches
1 are = 119.6 square yards
1 hectare = 2.471 acres
1 square kilometer = 0.386 square mile or 247.1 acres

Volume Measure

1 cubic centimeter = 0.06102 cubic inch
1 cubic decimeter = 61.023 cubic inches or 0.0353 cubic foot
1 cubic meter = 35.314 cubic feet or 1.308 cubic yards (the unit is called a *stere* in measuring firewood)

Capacity Measure

1 centiliter = 0.338 fluid ounce
1 deciliter = 3.38 fluid ounches or 0.1057 liquid quart
1 liter = 1.0567 liquid quarts or 0.9081 dry quart
1 decaliter = 2.64 gallons or 0.284 bushel

1 hectoliter = 26.418 gallons or 2.838 bushels
1 kiloliter = 264.18 gallons or 35.315 cubic feet

Weights

1 centigram = 0.1543 grain or 0.000353 ounce (avdp.)
1 decigram = 1.5432 grains or 0.035724 ounce (avdp.)
1 decagram = 0.3527 ounce
1 hectogram = 3.5274 ounces
1 kilogram = 2.2046 pounds
1 myriagram = 22.046 pounds
1 quintal = 220.46 pounds
1 metric ton = 2,204.6 pounds

Common Conversions

When You Know	Multiply by	To Find
inches	25.4	millimeters
feet	0.3048	meters
yards	0.9144	meters
miles	1.609 34	kilometers
square yards	0.836 127	square meters
acres	0.404 686	hectares
cubic yards	0.764 555	cubic meters
quarts (lq)	0.946 353	liters
ounces (avdp)	28.349 5	grams
pounds (avdp)	0.453 592	kilograms
Fahrenheit temperature	5/9 (after subtracting 32)	Celsius temperature
millimeters	0.039 370 1	inches
meters	3.280 84	feet
meters	1.093 61	yards
kilometers	0.621 371	miles
square meters	1.195 99	square yards
hectares	2.471 05	acres
cubic meters	1.307 95	cubic yards
liters	1.056 69	quarts (lq)
grams	0.035 274 0	ounces (avdp)
kilograms	2.204 62	pounds (avdp)
Celsius temperature	9/5 (then add 32)	Fahrenheit temperature